HARD STREETS

The Kid, 1919–20.

HARD STREETS

WORKING-CLASS LIVES IN
CHARLIE CHAPLIN'S LONDON

JACQUELINE RIDING

Profile Books

First published in Great Britain in 2026 by
Profile Books Ltd
29 Cloth Fair
London
ECIA 7JQ
www.profilebooks.com

Copyright © Jacqueline Riding, 2026

Photographs and documents from the Chaplin Archives : Copyright © and/
or Property of Roy Export Company Limited. All Rights Reserved.
Charlie Chaplin and the Little Tramp are trademarks and/or service marks
of Bubbles Inc. S.A., used with permission. All Rights Reserved.
Digitisation of the Chaplin Archives by Cineteca di Bologna
Original documents from the Chaplin Archives held at Archives
de Montreux, PP 75, Fonds Charles Chaplin.
Original negatives and photographs from the Chaplin Archives held at Photo Élysée.
Extract from Charles Chaplin's final speech from *The Great Dictator*
Copyright © Roy Export S.A.S. Reproduced with permission.

Extracts from *My Autobiography* by Charles Chaplin, Copyright © 1964
Bubbles Incorporated S.A. Reproduced with permission.

1 3 5 7 9 10 8 6 4 2

Typeset in Garamond by MacGuru Ltd
Printed and bound in Great Britain by
CPI Group (UK) Ltd, Croydon CR0 4YY

The moral right of the author has been asserted.

All rights reserved. Without limiting the rights under copyright reserved
above, no part of this publication may be reproduced, stored or introduced
into a retrieval system, or transmitted, in any form or by any means (electronic,
mechanical, photocopying, recording or otherwise), without the prior written
permission of both the copyright owner and the publisher of this book.

A CIP catalogue record for this book is available from the British Library.

Our product safety representative in the EU is BGC Sustainability & Compliance,
7 avenue du Général Leclerc, Paris, 75014, France https://baldwinglobalconsulting.com

ISBN 978 1 80081 864 4
eISBN 978 1 80081 866 8

To Patricia Betty Robinson Riding (1930–2024)

> ... *because*
> *I love you, Mother, I have woven a wreath*
> *Of rhymes wherewith to crown your honoured name.*
> Christina Rossetti, 'Sonnets are Full of Love' (1881)

ALSO BY JACQUELINE RIDING

Hogarth: Life in Progress
Peterloo: The Story of the Manchester Massacre
Jacobites: A New History of the '45 Rebellion

CONTENTS

Prologue: 'The Dignity of a People'	1
1 Milk Street: 'The Necessaries of Life'	19
2 Victory Place: 'Our Only Crime Being Poverty'	63
3 Hope Street: 'A New World'	103
4 East Street: 'Boiling Water'	143
5 Kennington Cross: 'This Dolorous Period'	195
6 New Cut: 'The Human Relationship'	235
7 Lambeth Walk: 'Girls and their Lovers'	285
Epilogue: 'Pretty Good Metal'	355
Acknowledgements	363
Picture Credits	365
Notes	369
Bibliography	391
Index	405

The cover of a four-page leaflet printed and published by the London Convention Council (an initiative of the Communist Party of Great Britain) in 1941, including a full transcription of Chaplin's speech from *The Great Dictator*.

PROLOGUE

'The Dignity of a People'

In 1943, two years after the Blitz ended, Charlie Chaplin was invited to deliver a BBC radio broadcast from his long-term home in the United States to the land of his birth. He had heard (in error, it turned out) that his childhood haunts in the South London district of Lambeth had been destroyed. Throughout his early life Chaplin had lived in a variety of locations within what were, after 1900, the neighbouring boroughs of Lambeth and Southwark. Yet for him, Lambeth had a particular and visceral pull. And in 1943, his transatlantic listeners would have been familiar with the name, thanks to a catchy song from the hit stage musical (and subsequent film), *Me and My Girl* (1937). As recorded in *The Times* on 18 October 1938, by then the lyrics had been translated into French, Italian and German: 'the Borough of Lambeth, in a few short weeks, became assured of undying fame', inspiring the topical couplet: 'And while dictators rage and statesmen talk, / All Europe dances – to "The Lambeth Walk".'[1]

Five years later, in response to reports of wholesale destruction across England, Charlie Chaplin's message to his fellow 'Lambethians', Londoners and countrymen was unsentimental, but full of encouragement for the present and hope for the future:

> I remember the Lambeth streets, the New Cut and the Lambeth Walk, Vauxhall Road. They were hard streets, and one couldn't say they were paved with gold. Nevertheless the people are made of pretty good metal. And all through your days of trial I was thinking of you, your poverty, your

unbeatable courage and your humour. Although you have suffered, the future will be brighter, for out of the ruins of Lambeth, out of the dust of all your bombed cities, will rise a new England, where poverty should be inexcusable and charity offensive to the dignity of a people who have won the right, by blood and tears, to be profitably employed and to live peaceably.²

On one level, this address was twin to the climactic speech in Chaplin's anti-totalitarian satire *The Great Dictator* (released in 1940), where he breaks the fourth wall to declare: 'You, the people, have the power to make this life free and beautiful, to make this life a wonderful adventure. Then – in the name of democracy – let us use that power – let us unite.'* George Orwell was so impressed by the film's core message and its delivery through comedy that he petitioned the war ministry to subsidise screenings.

In the subsequent radio broadcast, the Hollywood star, one of the most famous human beings on the planet, chose to draw attention to the conditions imposed upon an entire class of Britons, the poorer workers and labourers, which he considered 'inexcusable' and 'offensive': their celebrated humour and courage developed over the generations in the face of perpetual adversity.

As Chaplin infers, poverty is not inevitable, and from the rubble of those hard, indifferent streets, at last something far better could, or should, arise. Given the Beveridge Report, the basis of the post-war reforms that created the National Health Service, had been published the previous November, Chaplin was effectively representing the growing national mood in Britain that would eventually sweep aside Winston Churchill and bring Clement Attlee and the Labour Party to power.† But the passionate empathy

---

*The full speech was reprinted in *The Daily Worker*, 21 December 1940, and in a leaflet printed and published by the London Convention Council of the Communist Party of Great Britain (see p. viii).
†The radical report, entitled 'Social Insurance and Allied Services', by Liberal MP William Beveridge was commissioned by the war-time coalition government led by the Conservative prime minister and Attlee as deputy prime minister, and

of Charlie Chaplin's broadcast was not merely a rhetorical device: for when he spoke of poverty, courage and humour, he knew precisely what he was talking about.

In a public speech in 1901, James Keir Hardie, the illegitimate son of a domestic servant and the Independent Labour Party's first Member of Parliament, defined the majority of 'the poor', who in turn formed the 'great bulk' of the British population, as 'the average man, who had to earn his livelihood by the labour of his hands' and whose existence 'was one perpetual thought of how to obtain the necessaries of life'.[3] In other words, many Britons lived an insecure existence, not knowing where the next meal would be coming from, nor if they would have a roof over their heads. The great irony of Keir Hardie's characterisation is that workers at the turn of the twentieth century were, by definition, employed, but not, to use Chaplin's word, profitably: the value placed on their labour was unconnected to the wealth it generated, whether the coal miners whose graft literally fuelled British industry, or the lone needlewoman in her garret, producing clothing for ready-to-wear boutiques in exchange for a pittance. These are the people with whom Charlie Chaplin identified – and they, in turn, are the focus of this book.

The practice of collective representation and bargaining through trade unions was in train – the Labour Party had emerged in the 1890s as the political arm of this working-class movement – yet, on a fundamental level, Keir Hardie's 'great bulk' of Britons had little or no influence over how they were governed, locally or nationally, nor whether their specific needs would be aired, much less prioritised, in the chambers, committee rooms and bars of the Palace of Westminster. The poor health of working-class volunteers for the British armed forces highlighted the terrible conditions under which these men and their families continued to subsist. Not until 1918, as the guns from the First World War fell silent, was the vote extended to all British men, with women following ten years later.

---

highlighted five 'giants' to be slain in the post-war era: Want, Disease, Ignorance, Squalor and Idleness.

Sir Charles Spencer Chaplin, born in 1889, experienced as a child the impact of this mass disenfranchisement from the key levers of power, alongside a governmental failure (whether Conservative or Liberal) to ensure that national prosperity benefited the whole of society. As a product of poverty, with severely limited opportunities, Chaplin developed a healthy disdain for the impersonal, often callous response of authorities to the plight of the poor. Throughout the nineteenth century and into the twentieth, this was more often than not delivered through forms of 'charity', both privately and publicly funded, to which Chaplin and his immediate family were subjected: as exemplified by the indignities of the workhouse system, the lunatic asylums and the pauper schools, all powerfully exposed in the novels of Charles Dickens, George Gissing and the fiction-as-fact of Thomas Burke.*

Those who were accustomed to holding the reins of power clearly feared the slightest loss, particularly if transferred into the hands of the 'masses'. That these masses, as they argued, did not have the necessary education or 'buy-in' to warrant any say was a self-fulfilling prophecy. Reformers who queried the status quo or showed interest in alternative ways of governing, or simply adapting the current system, were quickly branded extremist: such opposition to change had reached fever pitch after the French Revolution of 1789 and the subsequent wars with Napoleonic France. Britain came close to the brink of insurrection, notably in around 1819 and 1848, but never tipped over. Of course, those at the bottom of society in countries that witnessed revolution still faced similar problems to their counterparts in Britain, and some historians have argued that the slowing down of change, as the British parliamentary system and constitution typically did throughout the nineteenth century, might have protected the emergence of liberal democracy. What is undoubtedly true is that, for the majority locked out of the franchise – including half the

---

*In interviews, Chaplin described roaming the East End at night with Burke, and he declared that his 1918 film *A Dog's Life* was based on Burke's bestselling and evocative (although fictional) descriptions of life in the East London Docks, *Limehouse Nights* (1916).

population because of their sex – the move towards democracy in Great Britain was glacial.

In his late twenties, Charlie Chaplin was intrigued by post-Tsarist Soviet Russia and, as a result, he was accused of being a 'Bolshy', to use Winston Churchill's half-serious description. He lived through the Great Depression, witnessing its effects in Europe and America – including the rise of fascism. His anti-Nazi stance, which would come to full fruition in *The Great Dictator*, was described in the pro-Hitler German press in 1933 as 'the barking of a dog from London's ghetto',[4] and he would be targeted during the 'Red Scare' of McCarthy-era America, eventually to be exiled from his adopted home.

In reality, Chaplin would never align himself to any political ideology – 'I am an artist, not a politician,'[5] he shrugged when quizzed by a journalist in 1921 – but his instinct was to support the social underdog, which made him far more influential than most politicians and, for some, more dangerous. His iconic screen character, the Little Tramp – dented bowler hat, ill-fitting threadbare clothes, unlucky in life but always making the best of it – was first and foremost the spirit of a community, his family, friends and neighbours from the ungilded streets of his youth. But this alter ego also embodied the experience of something essentially and therefore universally human: it was the proliferation of the Little Tramp, via the modern democratic art form of cinema, as Orwell had recognised, wherein lay Charlie Chaplin's power.

Some of the most incisive and accurate contemporary observations concerning Chaplin's politics or social conscience come, unexpectedly, from official UK government documents. *The Great Dictator* was the subject of an inquiry by the Foreign Office from February to June 1939 when the film was still in production. The purpose was to consider whether it should be banned in the United Kingdom, hinting at the sensitivities for Neville Chamberlain's Conservative government and the Nazi sympathisers and appeasers among the British social, political, industrial and media elites. The British Consulate in Los Angeles was asked to discover Chaplin's intentions and the response offers a fair summary of the plot, scenes and *dramatis personae*, observing, of the rival dictators

Adenoid Hynkel and Benzino Napaloni, that the identity of these prototypes 'leaves nothing to the imagination, especially as one of them will wear the famous moustache which is so marked a characteristic of a personage other than Mr. Chaplin'. On a more serious note, the consulate confirmed they had had conversations with the film maker himself 'and find that he is entering into the production of "The Dictator" with fanatical enthusiasm', using his considerable fortune (including a million-dollar production budget) to ensure completion and release in the United States, with or without recourse to his usual distributing organisation. They continue:

> His racial and social sympathies are with those classes and groups which have suffered the most in the dictatorship countries ... his political outlook is not of a quality which is likely to influence him in favour of propitiating the personalities whom he is burlesquing. Indeed, the directness of his attack would seem to be, to him, the picture's only motive and reason. In the circumstances we feel that to suggest modification would be to meet with an immediate and final rebuff, and we are confident that no good result could be achieved.[6]

Rowland Kenney, a senior Foreign Office civil servant, summarised these findings in a letter to Joseph Brooke-Wilkinson, Secretary of the British Board of Film Censors, who, upon further investigation, and in reply to Kenney, quotes from the *Hollywood Reporter* (20 March) regarding Chaplin's irritation at and rebuttal of rumours that he was abandoning the film: 'I am not worried about intimidation, censorship or anything else,' the film maker reportedly declared. Kenney closes the file with a note dated 24 June: 'Open diplomacy with a vengeance! There would seem to be nothing further to be done.'[7]

In the early 1950s, when J. Edgar Hoover was trying to find any hint of sympathy for communism or the USSR, the British Secret Service opened another file on Chaplin: their activities included collating newspaper cuttings, intercepting telegrams, compiling reports on his travels, and instigating a search for his birth certificate, which no one was able to trace. In a typed file note dated 17 November 1952, after assessing the information gathered to date, J. H. Marriott advised, when the agency responded to the American Embassy, 'to confine ourselves to answering the specific questions put by the F.B.I.', concluding: 'If they really want to whip up a case against CHAPLIN, they can read Pravda [the Soviet propaganda newspaper] for themselves.' He considered it 'curious' that no birth certificate could be found, 'but I scarcely think that this is of any security significance'.[8] When Chaplin, who had hung on to his British citizenship, on the strength of the FBI's endeavours was refused re-entry to the United States, another Security Service file note (dated 24 February 1958) by H. P. Goodwyn assessed that 'we are not satisfied that there are reliable grounds for regarding him a security risk. His name has, of course, been exploited in the interests of Communism as one of the victims of "McCarthyism".' Chaplin may, indeed, be a communist sympathiser, Marriott continued, 'but on the information before us he would appear to be no more than a "progressive" or radical'.[9] In dangerous times, compassion is a political act.

In analysing how the film maker drew inspiration from his early years of poverty, some scholars, notably the historian Richard Carr, have considered how these experiences translated into a definably progressive political and social outlook. What remains to be explored is the strong radical tradition that existed in the specific districts of South London in which Chaplin was born and raised. This small geographical area of the twenty-first-century metropolis was the site, for example, of the Great Chartist Meeting in 1848, a mass gathering on Kennington Common in support of the working-class political movement, a milestone on the long march to universal suffrage. Later that century, it was also the location of the stridently progressive Robert Browning Settlement. Keir Hardie had connections with this social mission in Walworth, the area within Southwark where Chaplin was born, at the time when Charlie and his family were living nearby. Whether the young Chaplin realised it or not, social conscience and the will to act for the betterment of your fellow man were in the air he breathed and the dirt beneath his feet.

Information on people from a poor working-class background during the reign of Queen Victoria is limited. Throughout the nineteenth century, the pressure on the average Briton, as Keir Hardie defined them, simply to afford the means of survival was all-embracing, but it is important not to treat the working class, or even the poor working class, as a homogenous group. As we shall see, individuals and families moved up and down the social scale as their personal circumstances changed. Working-class autobiographers who lived in the Victorian age, as David Vincent and Emma Griffin, among others, have revealed, are more prevalent than we might think: the product of rising literacy and, towards the end of the nineteenth century, the labour movement.[10] Of course, those who wrote their life stories had the time, skills and tools to do so, and working-class autobiographers (or autodidacts) were a self-selecting group: almost all were men who had experienced some social mobility and embraced education or undergone self-teaching; they also tended to have done something extraordinary by the conventions of the time – among them the trade unionist and Labour politician Walter McLennan Citrine (1887–1983), born in Liverpool to a ship rigger and a nurse and at his death Baron Citrine of Wembley. And, of course, Charlie Chaplin.

Prior to the 1870 Education Act there were a variety of options for learning, whether at elementary schools run by the church societies, private working-class 'dame schools' or Sunday schools, as well as learning at home. As David Vincent and David Mitch have shown, achievements in literacy in the decades before 1870 were largely driven by working-class demand.[11] What required state intervention, however, was reaching the last section of society, the very poorest. Here there were evident problems with universal education, because the authorities were competing with paid work and the vital contribution of children to family economic survival. There were also deep-rooted cultural legacies, which questioned the value of schooling. But within many working-class families, there was a desire to improve the circumstances for the next generation by grasping whatever opportunities were available. When Mrs Rowlett, the owner of a rag store in a poor area of Lambeth, was interviewed by the photographer John Thomson (for his *Street*

Life in London, 1877) she declared: 'We have nothing to leave our children, but they got a good education', including, for her daughter, private piano lessons, 'so my girl if she needs to work can teach music'.[12]

The provision from 1870 for universal primary education had succeeded, by 1901, in improving basic skills in reading and writing among the working class overall, but children continued to slip through the net: as an adult, Charlie Chaplin admitted that when he was handed his first theatrical script at the age of twelve, he had difficulty reading it. And despite the existence of hundreds of autobiographies spanning the nineteenth century, the lives of the working class, and particularly the poorer sections, were invariably described by those 'above' them in the social order. Any assessment, therefore, no matter how well meaning, was susceptible to class bias and condescension, motivated by reforming zeal and even thoughts of social engineering.

Chaplin recognised the disadvantage of his woeful education and compensated through self-learning. *My Autobiography* (published in 1964) is one of the most famous working-class memoirs ever written: as a global phenomenon, people were rightly interested in the author's stratospheric rise from desperate need to untold wealth and status. (He would be knighted in 1975.) Chaplin's biographer David Robinson described its early section as 'the last great Victorian autobiography, a first-hand account, rich in colour and chiaroscuro, of life in the poor streets of a nineteenth-century London that was still not far from Dickens and Mayhew'.[13] Yet, before the fame and the fortune, Chaplin (by his own admission) was just another talented, working-class variety performer trying to earn a crust: in retrospect, the groundwork for his huge success had been laid, but, at this date, whether the 'dog' from a London ghetto would rise or fall was yet to be determined.

To reiterate – and at the risk of stating the blindingly obvious – Chaplin's early life was far from unusual: what is unusual is that he chose to set it down in his own words. To which end, the experiences of one George Tinworth are not only relevant, but enlightening. George was another of Keir Hardie's 'average men', and by the 1890s had been a neighbour of Charlie Chaplin's

George Tinworth decorating a vase in his studio at Doulton's Pottery, Lambeth, around 1904, with one of his Biblical terracotta reliefs in the background.

maternal relatives in Walworth for some decades. Remarkably, Tinworth would progress from an early life of extreme poverty, via good luck, the support of others and an unquenchable creative urge, towards a solid career, relative financial security and public renown. His life in the same streets, but born into a previous generation to Chaplin, can be pieced together through a draft memoir in his own hand, written in capitals with little punctuation and in vernacular 'Lundun' English. George had no formal education at all and was certainly taught at home by his mother, before, like Chaplin, supplementing this through self-learning in adulthood. His manuscript autobiography would be heavily edited for publication after his death in 1913, but that George Tinworth warranted a published biography at all confirms that his peers considered him worthy of notice and remembrance. And, given the journey his autobiography describes, which raises it above the majority of working-class memoirs of the period, this should come as no surprise to anyone.

Tinworth was born in Walworth in 1843, a few streets away from where Charles Frederick and Mary Ann Hill (Charlie Chaplin's maternal grandparents) would be living in the 1860s and where his mother Hannah (and later he) was born. Rather than music hall, George Tinworth's route beyond a paltry living as a wheelwright was through the rarified world of fine art, and specifically sculpture. With no schooling, George attended evening classes at the innovative Lambeth School of Art, originally established – like the Working Men's College championed by John Ruskin, the art theorist and critic, and the courses delivered by the socialist designer William Morris – for mechanics and labourers to gain experience and skills in the fine arts. He would train at the Royal Academy Schools, then in Trafalgar Square, an immense achievement given that middle-class artists like John Everett Millais and Frederic Leighton were the foremost academicians at the time, before becoming a leading light, back in South London, in the newly established art ceramics studio at Doulton's Lambeth Pottery. Here, in his atelier at the top of Doulton's purpose-built headquarters, a constant stream of illustrious visitors came to meet the celebrated wheelwright-turned-artist. After exhibiting his work at the Royal Academy's annual exhibition, George came to the attention of Ruskin, the champion of another working-class artist, J. M. W. Turner. During Tinworth's lifetime, a street near the Doulton headquarters was renamed by Lambeth Parish Council in his honour.

Few twenty-first-century Britons have heard of George Tinworth: it is debatable whether anyone living in the vicinity of Tinworth Street in Lambeth knows from whence the name comes. But it is fair to say that at the turn of the twentieth century, George Tinworth, and not Charlie Chaplin, was the epitome of a local-boy-made-good.

And for local boys like the young Chaplin, sharing the same poor background as the Doulton sculptor and modeller, it was important that such shining examples existed. The link between Tinworth and Chaplin, other than geography and socio-economics, was the arts. Both men sought beauty and inspiration in the everyday – in this, as we shall see, they were uncommon but not unique among their neighbours – using their creativity to make money while providing joy for their fellows. And both lived in an area where the means for personal development, fulfilment and social advancement had been established, whether an art school for working people, or music hall, the working people's art form.

Both creative forums provided opportunities for working-class employment, of women as well as men, beyond performers and artists, with personnel ranging from bar staff and stage hands – the latter a popular job among moonlighting market porters – to housekeepers and life-class models. But to say George Tinworth was an unusual figure in the nineteenth-century art world is an understatement.

Encouraged by the interest in his personal history shown by the great and the good, in the 1910s George Tinworth decided to write his memoir – titled 'The Life of G Tinworth: A London Boy that become Wheelwright and Sculptor' – and visited the British Museum in Bloomsbury for research. Wandering among the majestic ancient sculptures of Egypt, Greece, Rome and Nineveh, George began to see himself as a living representative of shared artisanal traditions spanning worlds and millennia. As he later wrote, 'the art gift may sleep for a 1000 years and awake with new energy in the decendents of talented people of the ages that are past'.*[14] In his memoir, he recorded that an unnamed 'Old Master ... says in his book, it is a duty incumbent on upright and creditable men, of all ranks, who have performed any thing nobel or praiseworthy, to record in there own writing, the events of their lives'.[15] In response, the stated purpose of Tinworth's memoir was to offer himself as an exemplar for any aspiring youth, particularly one whose route to success was littered with obstacles. Fearing some might dismiss his memoir as picaresque fiction – penned, as it were, by a less learned version of Thomas Hardy's Jude Fawley – or even fantastical, a note on the title page (written by his wife Alice) instructs, 'do not read this as a common place life, but read it as a study of a life'; and then under this, to drive home the point: 'it is not a novel.'[16]

Tinworth and Chaplin are two sides of the same coin. Both produced art that was appreciated for its honesty, anchored in their life experiences, yet at the same time highly valued beyond, as well as within their class, for its originality. Very few individual working-class lives, prior to the mid-twentieth century, have made any impression on the great national narrative, and despite decades of excellent academic social history, the working class even now remain under-represented in the wealth of published popular histories.

No single book can cover every aspect of the working-class experience. *Hard Streets* is framed by the autobiographies of these two men, each written in older age, that effectively span two eras – the Victorian and Edwardian – and seven decades of social and political change and upheaval. It is also worth stating that there is a significant difference in the style, tone and literacy levels between the two autobiographies. Chaplin is whimsical, knowing, urbane, eager to entertain as well as inform. *My Autobiography* is also a fully edited and published work. Tinworth's memoir is

---

*All quotations from George Tinworth's manuscript autobiography faithfully reproduce its unschooled but vividly expressive spelling, though I have occasionally clarified its sense and punctuation within [square brackets].

more direct, artless, less self-conscious perhaps, revealing a greater concern about *what* he is telling his reader: crucially, as an unfinished draft, it remains, to a large degree, the raw data of a life not yet fully digested.

Tinworth and Chaplin, and the life stories they have left to posterity, are the starting point for a biography of people and place, and, between them, there is much to explore. Both experienced childhood trauma living within the stresses and strains of their communities. No one suffers such an environment without deep and lasting impact, and some of the behaviour and attitudes described in the following pages will be challenging to twenty-first-century readers. As Charles Dickens and later George Gissing explored through their fiction – the latter spurred by the premature death of his estranged wife, a sex worker, in a Lambeth slum dwelling – the poor were fair game for criminals and predators, and many were far from safe in their own homes: not all working-class fathers were brutal bullies, but the cliché existed for very good reason, as George Tinworth knew all too well.

Seeking out details of the lives of individual members of the poorer working class, even those as famous and well-documented as Charlie Chaplin, requires detective work. As George Tinworth said, 'We all must have descended from hundreds of ancestors some good and some bad so I do not think we ought to be afraid to face it, people in our day know the pedigrees of their horses and dogs but they do not know the pedigree of their own family's.'[17] The challenge is that the working class over Tinworth's lifetime and Chaplin's early decades left little trace of their existence, beyond birth, marriage, school and death records, the national census (first established in 1801, refined in 1841 and then updated every ten years thereafter) and the occasional working-class autobiography – unless, that is, the individual came to the notice of the authorities. Then further glimpses can be revealed by sifting through institutional records relating to Poor Law Unions and the Old Bailey Proceedings, further supported by police court notices and examples of criminal activity described within local and national newspapers.

Hard Streets is not a study in victimhood: indeed, in recent years there has been a push to consider the 'agency' of marginalised groups, and the extent to which women and the poor working class possessed it and used it. Rather, this is a story of suffering, survival and success against the odds, where, throughout, working-class people came together, as well as in partnership with the more civic-minded middle classes, to address the causes of poverty in the present, to improve the future for every British citizen. A key enterprise – and a core source for this book – was Charles Booth's *Inquiry into Life and Labour in London* (1886–1903). Prior to this detailed data-gathering survey (the work of Henry Mayhew in the 1840s and 1850s notwithstanding), the full extent of poverty in Britain's capital city was suspected, but not proved. In fact, with 35 per cent of London's population judged to be poor,* the reality was far worse than anyone imagined. Crucially, Booth's published survey and accompanying maps – grading the levels of wealth and poverty by colour, street by street, and even within streets – gave textual and visual representation for working-class diversity.†

As intended, social reformers like Booth were now armed with compelling evidence, as well as moral fortitude. Even so, it must be emphasised that Booth's methodology was flawed, shaped as it was by moralistic presumptions, while failing to grasp that people dipped in and out of extreme poverty, as is evident in the experiences of both Chaplin and Tinworth. It was Benjamin Seebohm Rowntree's survey of the city of York, *Poverty: A Study in Town Life* (1901), that introduced the idea of a 'cycle of poverty'.

In preference to the important and oft-used published editions of Booth's survey – the final edition of 1902–3 covering seventeen volumes – the focus, here, is the original investigators' notebooks, where there is a greater wealth of detail, anecdote and opinion, alongside interviews and direct quotation from named and

---

*The poverty line, as defined by Booth, was set at earnings of 18 to 21 shillings a week for a moderate family, with those on less considered to be living in 'abject' poverty.
†The Charles Booth Poverty Map for Charlie Chaplin's London can be consulted or downloaded from The London School of Economics Digital Library: https://digital.library.lse.ac.uk/documents/detail/printed-map-descriptive-of-london-poverty-1898-1899.-sheet-9.-inner-southern-district/54354

unnamed interviewees, whether middle-class vicars and female volunteers, or working-class policemen and housewives.* Those notebooks that centre on the Lambeth and Southwark of Tinworth and Chaplin – written by George Duckworth and Ernest Aves – have been quoted extensively in the following pages. The same is true of papers associated with the late-nineteenth-century settlement movement, specifically those groups established in Lambeth and Southwark – the Women's University Settlement at the LSE, the Robert Browning Settlement at Southwark Archives, and the Lady Margaret Hall Settlement at Lambeth Archives. Like Booth, these reflect, in the main, elite and privileged perspectives, yet also offer vital windows onto the untold lives and experiences of the poor working class across the capital's southern area here called Charlie Chaplin's London.

But before immersing ourselves in a microhistory of Lambeth and Southwark, why focus on *this* area of the metropolis? After all, the streets where Tinworth and then Chaplin lived represent a small part of what is now South London, beginning within Walworth and then panning back to embrace the districts adjacent – Camberwell, Oval, Kennington, Vauxhall, Lambeth, Waterloo, Newington, Elephant and Castle, Southwark, Borough, Stockwell and Brixton. For hundreds of thousands of Londoners, this was their entire world. Even so, it is safe to say that the boroughs of Lambeth and Southwark are not the usual subject for London histories – unlike the 'West End' around Covent Garden; the seat of royalty and government at Westminster; or the 'East End'. But, to take the last named, would the poor streets of Whitechapel hold much interest if Charles Booth had not begun his mighty project in its midst? Or, more important still, if a vicious serial killer had not wreaked havoc within those same dark streets the year before Booth's first volume was published, to be cynically sensationalised by the local and national press, and as the subject of insatiable fixation ever since?

Most Britons do not have illustrious ancestors. We come from modest backgrounds, and many of us – as George Tinworth

---

*These notebooks are now held in the London School of Economics.

observed – would struggle to name our great-grandparents, let alone distant cousins. The lives of our forebears should matter, because the habits formed by them as individuals and communities reach across the centuries to impact their descendants in the here and now. In focusing on the lives of two working-class men, their families and communities, this book dwells on the 'every' man, woman and child that make up the family trees of most Britons: these two lives, and the stories of those close to them, represent a people's history. As amply demonstrated by recent studies of the women murdered by the Whitechapel killer, of the 'Old Nichol' Bethnal Green slum, of the 'vagabond' under-class, of female detectives, and even by biographies of individual street performers, poor working-class lives can be the focus of powerful history.* The popularity of television programmes like *Who Do You Think You Are?* meanwhile reveal that tracing the lost journeys of individuals from humble backgrounds can pack a far greater emotional punch than discovering some loose connection to the rich or famous. The daily existence of everyday people has long been the inspiration for great art and literature, whether by William Hogarth or Thomas Hardy, and within such tales of hardship and woe, there is also humour and fun. To use a well-known quote attributed to Chaplin: 'Life itself is a comedy – a slapstick comedy at that … Whether it is tragedy or comedy depends on how you look at it. There is not a hair's breadth between them.'[18]

Our forebears, in the main, lived unremarkable lives, yet, by exploring the South London experiences of two remarkable men, the names and experiences of long-forgotten Londoners and Britons can be – however briefly – recovered.

---

*By Hallie Rubenhold (2019), Sarah Wise (2009), Oskar Jensen (2022), Sarah Lodge (2024) and Mary Shannon (2024) respectively.

A PHYSICAL FORCE CHARTIST ARMING FOR THE FIGHT.

A John Leech *Punch* cartoon (1848) gently lampooning the Chartist movement. A working-class 'Don Quixote' prepares for battle over his right to vote: a coal scuttle on his head and a meat cover roped to his chest by his visibly anxious wife.

1

MILK STREET

'The Necessaries of Life'

George Tinworth reveals at the beginning of his memoir that he was born on 5 November 1843 at 6 Milk Street, Camberwell Gate, in Walworth Common. From these minimal details, anyone familiar with London's geography and its population boom over the decades since George's birth would glean two key facts: not only was the author from South London, but he was from one of the most densely inhabited and poorest districts in the entire metropolis.

In 1841, when the first full modern census was taken, the population of London was 1,873,676. It was the largest city in Europe and, indeed, the world. It was the centre of government, legislature and monarchy, the focus of major manufacturing, and, by the mid-century, a quarter of Britain's foreign trade was carried on the river that winds through it. By the end of the nineteenth century, London, now with a population of 6,506,889 (including the outer boroughs) had become the capital of a vast empire that encompassed a quarter of the world's population.

Less well known is London's status as the principal centre of production, much of it, over the course of the nineteenth century, based along the south bank of the Thames in Lambeth and Southwark, where now sit such major cultural centres as the Royal Festival Hall, the National Theatre and Tate Modern. When the London-born radical William Blake (1757–1827) wrote of 'those dark Satanic Mills', it is often presumed that he was referring to the industrial topography of England's Midlands and North. As a resident between 1791 and 1800 of Hercules Buildings in Lambeth,

The Lambeth riverfront looking south towards Vauxhall, photographed by William Strudwick around 1867. Among the manufactories are Robert Bains (oar and scull maker) and three potteries: James Stiff & Co, Smith's, and (furthest left) H. Doulton & Co. On the foreshore can be seen pilings for the new Albert Embankment, and within a few years all these ancient wharfs and buildings will have been demolished.

however, Blake was more likely thinking of the towering fire-gutted shell of the former steam-powered 'Albion' Flour Mills, built by the industrialist Matthew Boulton in 1786 near the south side of Blackfriars Bridge in Southwark. Blake lived within hailing distance of the famous potteries lying just to the west, among them the Doulton family business, whose large furnaces belched fire and toxic smoke. The Lambeth riverside, from St Thomas's Hospital opposite the Palace of Westminster, via Lambeth Palace towards Vauxhall Bridge, was crowded with warehouses and wharves, and the Thames itself dense with boats delivering raw materials for the domestic and industrial wares made nearby – from soap to ceramics – which in turn were transported by water, road and (later) rail around the country and beyond.

At the beginning of the nineteenth century, the most significant residential development on this side of the Thames was in the area called Borough, which had sprung up around the southern gate of Old London Bridge. The modern Borough High Street is where Geoffrey Chaucer's pilgrims gathered at the Tabard Inn, a hostelry established in 1307, before setting off for Canterbury.

On early eighteenth-century maps of London, other than dribs and drabs around Lambeth Palace to the west and the Thameside wharves, what would become South London remained sparsely populated – until the mass migration from the Home Counties due to unemployment, which escalated on the arrival of the railways and the development of suburbs and a commuter belt. This caused London to sprawl further into Middlesex, eventually engulfing this county completely; to a lesser extent, the same happened in Surrey. Areas on the north bank of the Thames, such as around the Pool of London, the Docks and the East End, had a long history of dense housing. The most dramatic population shift in the nineteenth century occurred in South London with the greatest impact in the districts closest to the Thames, including around Vauxhall, Lambeth, Southwark and Bermondsey.

Walworth, where Tinworth (and later Chaplin) was born, represents an extreme example of what would happen to the rest of South London. At the beginning of the nineteenth century, it still maintained some village characteristics, surrounded by fields and market gardens, and was home to around 15,000 people. Even in 1845, when a parcel of horticultural land to the west was converted into a cricket ground, called 'The Oval' because of its distinctive egg shape, the area remained semi-urban. By the turn of the twentieth century, within a transformed South London, Walworth was acknowledged as the most densely populated parliamentary division in the capital: just under a mile square but now home to 120,000 people.

George Tinworth lived through this rapid urbanisation, and his life – and that of Charlie Chaplin – would be shaped indelibly by the opportunities and difficulties that such seismic change can bring.

In his early recollections, covering the 1840s and 1850s, George describes a narrow existence for poorer people like his family and

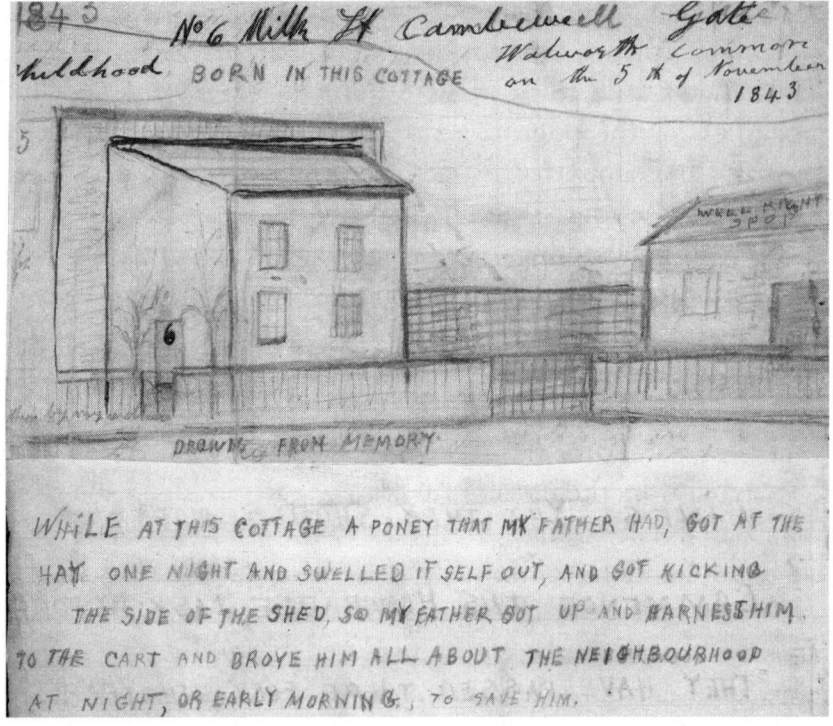

Page 5 of George Tinworth's autobiography written around 1910–13, including Jane Tinworth's pencil sketch of 6 Milk Street and the wheelwright shop. George writes in capitals, while Alice's script can be seen here above the drawing.

their neighbours, with limited scope for work and play. Any political influence, or independence over the direction of their lives and the affordability of such basic necessities as housing and food, was similarly restricted. Yet, as hinted in this section of the memoir, there were small signs that a change might be on the way.

Pasted into the opening pages of George's manuscript is a simple sketch of a cottage.* It is a basic, two-storey dwelling with a slanting roof, four windows on one facade with a central front door and two small trees or shrubs on either side. According to George, the landlord of the property on Milk Street was one of the City-based Guilds, the Fishmongers' Company, and, when

---

*According to a note in George's hand, the sketches of the cottage and workshop were 'drawn from memory', not by the author himself but 'by my mother' (GTA, p. 5).

he was about three years old, he would accompany his mother to St Peter's Alms Houses, the company's establishment at Elephant and Castle, to pay the rent.* These alms houses, charitable lodgings for the poor, were originally built at the company's expense and supported from their revenues. The complex consisted of three courts, with gardens in the rear, a dining hall and chapel, all enclosed by a low parapet wall.[1] George recalled little of the trip to his family's landlord, other than handing over the money to a tall gentleman in a room elaborately decorated with a map of the world on the floor and, of greater significance, that 'these people used to send us a present at Christmas'.[2] (Small recompense, surely, for the income such wealthy trade associations generated from the rents of their poor working-class tenants.) In addition to City Guilds, among the major landowners in the part of South London that included Walworth and the adjoining Kennington were the Archbishop of Canterbury and the Prince of Wales, through the hereditary estate of the Duchy of Cornwall. The latter encompassed land once the site of the medieval royal palace at Kennington, the residence of the Black Prince and his son, Richard II. The traces of this regal history can be found in the street named Prince's Road (later 'Princes', now Black Prince Road) and the Victorian public house, the White Hart (Richard II's cypher), an area recalled in detail by Charlie Chaplin within his travel memoirs and autobiography.

The term 'cottage' – which now conjures up countryside quaintness – related to a type of building which was significantly different from the three- or four-storey 'terraced' houses that dominated town development in the eighteenth century. One striking example of the latter type of housing in South London, still in existence, are the rows of Georgian, Regency and early Victorian terraced houses extending almost the entire length of Kennington Road, a mile-long thoroughfare that had once been the home of middle-class professionals but was generally occupied by multiple families or families with lodgers by the mid-nineteenth century. As

---

*The curious name came from an old coaching inn, and is thought to be a corruption of 'Eleanor of Castile', the name of Edward I's queen consort.

Charlie Chaplin, sometime resident of Kennington Road in the 1890s, recalled: 'By the middle of the nineteenth century most of the homes had deteriorated into rooming houses and apartments. Some, however, remained inviolate and were occupied by doctors, successful merchants and vaudeville stars.'[3] Here Chaplin reveals the limitations to ideas of homogenous working-class neighbourhoods in the Victorian era.

In contrast to the terraced house, the modest, low-level cottage was associated with the rural and urban labouring class, such as fishermen, farmworkers, miners or, in more modern times, railwaymen, as seen in the streets around termini including the main South London station, Waterloo (which opened in 1848). The assumption that the occupants of cottages would have few material possessions of any monetary worth and little cash is inferred by Daniel Defoe's comment from the early eighteenth century (still true over a century later): 'It's a sorry Thief would rob a Cottage.'[4] Some cottages had a small patch of connected land for use as a garden or – as seen in that drawing of 6 Milk Street – a paved yard where pots of flowers, vegetables and herbs could be grown. Observers throughout the nineteenth century noted that Walworth was remarkable for pockets of domestic flower-growing – a legacy of the horticulture that dominated the land south of the Thames into the nineteenth century, and an echo of the former villages of Walworth, Kennington and Camberwell that had been overwhelmed by urbanisation.

Some uncharitable outsiders judged the presence of these flashes of colour in the pots and window boxes gracing poor working-class homes as a sign of vain hope over grinding day-to-day experience, in poignant contrast with the general grime and pollution within the same streets: the squalor can be largely explained by inadequate infrastructure, despite decades of residential development. It is nevertheless true that for many mid-nineteenth-century residents of Walworth and beyond, external areas were purely functional spaces to dry laundry or to dump domestic waste, rather than places where they might nurture a little natural beauty.

On a fine day in March 1857, a reporter from the *Shoreditch*

Observer crossed the Thames at Blackfriars Bridge to view Walworth for himself, beginning in its northern point at the Elephant and Castle road junction. He and his companion strolled, in a southerly direction, through 'several narrow dingy streets'. They then entered 'a whole town of small cottages, fronted by equally small plots of ground, which', he believed, 'the occupiers had originally attempted to convert into gardens'. Such attempts, he notes with barely concealed scorn, were 'in the vain delusive hope of rearing a few flowers and vegetables' – but, he concludes, 'having given up the attempt in despair, they had converted these Lilliputian nurseries into unpaved dirty yards for drying recently washed out garments'.[5]

By the late nineteenth century, the design of cottage would be championed by the social reformer Octavia Hill, a founder of the National Trust in 1895 and an expert witness for the Royal Commission on the Housing of the Working Class, whose report was published the following year. But around the time of George Tinworth's birth, one of the pioneers of working-class social housing was Queen Victoria's consort, Prince Albert. His prototype, two-storey semi-detached cottages, offering accommodation for four families and exhibited at the Great Exhibition in Hyde Park in 1851, was relocated soon after to a plot at the west gate of Kennington Park (near where the Tinworths lived) as comfortable lodgings for the new park's keeper. Each flat had three bedrooms, a living room, scullery (with sink, plate rack and meat safe) and, unusually, an indoor water closet.[6] This, it will become clear, was extremely generous 'ideal' accommodation: very few families in the area around Kennington Park could afford a dwelling half the size. There is a whiff of Marie Antoinette's fake peasant hamlet at Versailles, although Albert was an infinitely more intelligent character, and in earnest about better housing for his wife's poorer subjects as the first president of the Society for Improving the Condition of the Labouring Classes. Even so, enlightened self-interest played a part; since the French Revolution of 1789, the British monarchy had been in a state of high alert against a time when the desperate multitudes might – or would – as the radical poet Percy Bysshe Shelley put it in *The Masque of Anarchy*, 'Rise, like lions after slumber'.⁷ Kennington Park was an interesting choice of location for Albert's worker housing: a prominent and grisly site of public execution in the eighteenth century, it had been common land before enclosure. It was where the hustings for elections were staged and, in recent times, the gathering place for political rallies, where ardent reformers dared to dream of a just future for poorer working people, like the Tinworths, with a vote for every adult male and, thus, a new democratic age when every British family would have representation in the national Parliament.

Within the Milk Street sketch, adjoining the Tinworth family's cottage is a single-storey 'wheelwright shop' with a wide entrance and lone window on the front wall. It is where George's father, Joshua, made his living.

The job of a wheelwright involved physical toil, demanding a high level of fitness and strength. To that end, George recalled, 'My father had a fighting man', a pugilist, 'named Spider to work for him.'⁸ In addition to employing a boxer, George's father hired local children for one-off tasks and regular work. The following anecdote is one of many seemingly random stories that George tells about his father's business, and the family's circumstances more broadly: 'When I was a little boy my father sent a boy that worked for him with a basket to buy some grocery and when coming back with the things, a man stopped him and said here my boy let me give you a piggie back and I will carry your basket for you.' The man then encouraged the boy to go into a sweet shop while he minded the basket. But, 'when the boy come out', sadly, 'the man and basket was gone'.⁹ These anecdotes are just fragments of a childhood, but in the recollection decades later, George Tinworth hoped to impress upon his readership how striking and ultimately devastating these small incidents were for those who teetered on the edge of survival. Such anecdotes, of which there are many examples in George's memoir, also reflect the vulnerability of children who were often left unsupervised. The duplicity of adults, as described here, is the flipside to the tight-knit working-class community, where children were raised 'by the village'. Both, in reality, were true.¹⁰

Within the hierarchy of working-class employment, the

wheelwright would be considered a skilled profession, as defined by the journalist and social reformer Henry Mayhew in articles for the *Morning Chronicle*, which formed the basis of his *London Labour and the London Poor* (published in 1850). Here, in one of the first attempts to survey this sector in the capital, the working-class employed were divided into artisans, labourers and servants. Mayhew observed that artisans were 'not only the most numerous, but the most varied in their occupations' and then subdivides them into mechanics (handicraftsmen) and chemical manufacturers. The former, a dizzying array of carpenters, plumbers, goldsmiths, blacksmiths, masons, potters, bottle-makers, weavers, seamstresses, rope-makers, boot- and shoemakers (the latter the profession of Charlie Chaplin's maternal grandparents). Mayhew then itemises 'the chemical manufacturers', including Lucifer matchmakers, blacking-makers, soap boilers, and 'the mixed arts', notably papermakers, printers and bookbinders. After these came boat and barge builders, wheelwrights, and then occupations connected to provisions such as millers, bakers, butchers, curers, market gardeners, brewers and mustard-makers.[11]

As a wheelwright, Joshua Tinworth made and repaired wheels and wheeled delivery vehicles. With the arrival of sons, he could eventually avoid paying assistants by training his offspring as apprentice wheelwrights. In his memoir, George mentions his father giving him pennies as pocket money, presumably in lieu of wages. In this way, a single man's business becomes a family enterprise, with the potential for a son or son-in-law to eventually take over management. George Tinworth, despite having a physique and constitution unsuited to the trade, worked with his father in the workshop until after Joshua died: these years of malnutrition and hard physical labour eventually took their toll.

Commentators generalised about a peculiarly working-class devil-may-care attitude to what might happen tomorrow. Saving for the future, when income was so tight in the present, was impossible for many; the only option for people like the Tinworths was to work when they could, for as long as they could, then rely on their children to maintain them until death or, failing this, to seek charity from local rate-payers under the Poor Law. Over the course of the century, with significant changes in how poor relief was administered, increasingly the desperate were forced to undergo the shameful trudge to a local workhouse. The threat of this institution was a constant for anyone in the lower social and economic strata, but for those who dipped into extreme poverty and pauperism, like the Tinworths and later the Chaplins, the workhouse might be the only available option.

As a self-employed wheelwright, Joshua Tinworth rented a workshop where he dealt directly with his clients, which distinguishes him from those who were paid a weekly wage, or as piece workers (for a fixed rate per item). In an area full of people moving wares by wagon, cart and barrow, a reliable wheelwright had every expectation of regular employment and a steady income. Joshua's customers included local wholesalers, shopkeepers, carmen – drivers of carts, considered a notch above 'van-men' – and costermongers, the lowliest of all, selling fruit, vegetables, fish and the like from a barrow in the street. Walworth was a popular residence for costermongers, who bought their supplies from the market at Borough, to the north of Elephant and Castle near London Bridge. The costermongers had the most direct connection with poor working-class neighbourhoods, whether hawking their wares door to door, or from pitches in the popular street markets like East Street in Walworth, Lambeth Walk off Kennington Road, or the New Cut and Lower Marsh near Waterloo. And all were dependent on the wheelwright for their livelihood.

But the wheelwright trade was not Joshua Tinworth's choice. He had settled on it after a series of commercial ventures whose failure weighed heavily on his spirit for the remainder of his life. Until his late teens and, following in his father's footsteps, the wheelwright trade would be George's chief occupation, despite his increasing desire to become a sculptor. At least the workshop offered the chance to develop his craftsmanship in his spare time, through carving and fashioning scraps of wood.

When the adult George researched his family history, he recorded that his paternal grandfather, James Tinworth, 'come from Essex about a 100 years ago and settled in Kennington near the Common'. He then says his grandfather had been a landscape gardener in Essex 'to some of the big families there', meaning the landed gentry.[12] James Tinworth's move to South London in the first decade of the nineteenth century is a familiar story across Britain at a time of economic difficulty caused by the ongoing wars with France, a series of bad harvests and rising food prices – exacerbated by vested-interest legislation like the infamous Corn Laws – plus population growth. Rural unemployment forced many to migrate to towns and cities in search of work. People whose families had hardly ventured beyond their village for many generations were now uprooting to decidedly unfamiliar territory. Still, the Kennington–Walworth area, usually described (in parallel with the term 'South London') as in the county of Surrey well into the twentieth century, was a good place for a young gardener to seek employment.

George Tinworth's recollections are supported by the official records, some of which he consulted at the British Museum. If we begin with his father's family, the Tinworths, George's paternal grandmother was Elizabeth Ann née Stansfield (1783–1858). While her husband James Tinworth (1781–1841) worked as a gardener, she ran a laundry, taking in washing for paying clients at the family home near Kennington Common. As Susie Steinbach has observed, 'Very few working families could survive, and almost none could prosper, on a single male wage.'[13] Elizabeth married James on 28 November 1804 at the parish church of St Mary-at-Lambeth.[14] This ancient church adjoins Lambeth Palace near the Thames foreshore (across from the Palace of Westminster) where the great river bends dramatically to flow south to north, before returning to a west-to-east course in parallel to Charing Cross and the Strand.

St Mary-at-Lambeth is where the mother of the English queen Anne Boleyn is buried, alongside the celebrated Tradescant family of seventeenth-century botanists and horticulturists, and (in 1817) Captain William Bligh, infamous for his part in the 1789 mutiny on HMS *Bounty*: perhaps bride and bridegroom surveyed the tombs and grave markers before or after the marriage ceremony. James and Elizabeth Ann's Christian denomination is listed as 'independent' – that is Dissenting or Nonconformist – although they were wed in accordance with the rites and ceremonies of the 'established' Anglican church. The 1753 Marriage Act had rendered any marriage as null and void, if not preceded by reading of the banns or the issue of a licence and if not carried out in an Anglican Church (or Quaker Meeting House) by daylight, so James and Elizabeth had no choice. (In 1837 the law changed with civil registration of marriage: Dissenters – other than Quakers, Catholics and Jews – could have their own places of worship licensed for registration.) In 1804, although both, as stated on the marriage certificate, were 'of this parish' and had been married by the curate, Stephen Swabey, 'by Banns' – an announcement in church on the three Sundays prior to the ceremony – neither James nor Elizabeth Ann were parishioners of St Mary-at-Lambeth.*

The year 1812 saw Luddite riots, Napoleon Bonaparte's disastrous retreat from Moscow and the continuing elevation (since 1811) of the feckless George, Prince of Wales, to the dignity of Prince Regent due to the incapacity of his ailing father, George III. Far away from such events of international significance, James and Elizabeth Ann Tinworth's eldest surviving son – George's father – was born on 10 August and baptised two months later by George Clayton, the pastor at the Nonconformist York Street Chapel, Lock's Fields, in Walworth.[15]

According to the same baptism register for the York Street Chapel, a daughter called Christiana had been born on 11 December 1805 in 'the parish of Lambeth' and baptised on 19 January 1806. Fourteen months later, a son, Jabez, was born – again in the parish of St Mary-at-Lambeth, and baptised a month later at York Street Chapel.[16] They both died in late 1808, their burials in Upminster, Essex separated by just eight days.[17]

Alongside Joshua, in 1812, is recorded the baptism at Lock's Fields of an elder sibling, Keziah (born in 1810), one of three sisters (as referred to in George Tinworth's memoir) who had been named after the daughters of the long-suffering Old Testament figure, Job:

---

*In attendance were two witnesses, as required by law: William Prendered, possibly a friend of the groom, and Mary Stansfield, a relative of the bride.

that is Keziah, Keren-happuch (surely just Keren) and Jemima.*
None of them feature in George Tinworth's manuscript and there
is no official record of a Keren Tinworth.[18]

Keziah, who does appear in official documentation, was two
years old when she was baptised, which hints at some disruption
in the family's circumstances. The entry beneath Joshua's names a
brother, Caleb, and all three siblings (Keziah, Joshua and Caleb)
are recorded as having been born in Upminster, Essex. It may be
that either the family had returned to Essex after the death of Jabez
(which had followed soon after that of Christiana), or, given the
dual baptisms in Walworth and Upminster for Jemima, Keziah,
Joshua and Caleb, that Elizabeth Ann had travelled from South
London to the house of a family member in Essex for the final
weeks before giving birth, perhaps hoping that the country air
would aid her children's survival.[19] This was the practice at London's Foundling Hospital; babies who were admitted to the Lamb's
Conduit Fields site, on the northern edge of London, were soon
after sent into the country to be wet nursed, then fostered there
until the age of four. Generally, the death rates in urban areas were
higher than those in rural populations, a phenomenon dubbed
the 'urban penalty'. (By 1851 over half the population of England
and Wales lived in urban settlements of 2,500 or more, peaking at
around 80 per cent by the 1890s.)[20]

York Street Chapel in Lock's Fields, Walworth, was a 'congregational' church – its origins lay in Calvinist puritanism – built
in 1790. Robert Browning, born on Southampton Street in the
neighbouring parish of St Giles in Camberwell, was baptised at
this chapel in the same year, 1812, as Keziah, Joshua and Caleb Tinworth: the entries for the Tinworth children are listed on the page
opposite the future poet, later famed for his dramatic monologues
and his elopement in 1846 with fellow poet, Elizabeth Barrett.[21]

Where James, Elizabeth Ann and the growing Tinworth

---

*Jemima is listed in the register for baptism as being born in Upminster on 11
January 1809, baptised 10 September 1809, and further documentation confirms
that she survived until the age of sixty-one, under the name 'Jemima Tinworth' (so
unmarried), dying in October 1870.

family were living prior to the 1841 census is not clear. What we do know is that when he was no more than thirteen years old, Joshua Tinworth worked as an assistant to a slater or roof tiler on the new development at St Katharine Docks near the Tower of London. Joshua had told his son stories about this experience that clearly had an impact on father and then son. Some indicate intense rivalry, even intimidation, which reflected how working or labouring men could be tough, even callous, towards their fellows, perhaps when employment was not so easily come by.

In 1824, after years of oppression, trade unions were legalised and associations among skilled factory workers were formed to negotiate pay and conditions. (In 1834, when six unskilled agricultural labourers from Dorset attempted to form a similar union, they were charged under an obscure act relating to sedition and treason, alongside the Mutiny Act of 1797, found guilty and transported to Australia for seven years. They became known as the Tolpuddle Martyrs). George recalled that when his father was part of the workforce building St Katharine Docks, a new labourer showed young Joshua the palms of his hands, which were smeared with blood. The labourer declared, 'the others are trying to run me down but they shant do it, I will stick to it.' Years later, as George recalled in relation to his father's story, a similar situation happened at the Doulton pottery, 'but the man told the manager Bryon and Bryon said, never mind them, go on as youre going, we want men to do a fair days work, and not to work like donkeys'.[22] This recollection hints at why employment at Doulton's Lambeth Pottery was so highly prized in the area: the hope of a fair wage for a fair day's work. But, as Charles Booth discovered later in the century, such attitudes among businessmen and industrialists were far from usual within a climate of rampant, largely unchecked and, frankly, exploitative capitalism.

George's father instilled in his offspring a sense of what constituted honest, useful work and a strong desire to survive by his own wits and abilities. In this sense Joshua's outlook echoed the design for life promoted by Samuel Smiles in his bestselling pamphlet *Self-Help; with Illustrations of Character and Conduct*, first published in London in 1859. (Smiles came from a strict Presbyterian background and supported the Chartists' six-point plan for parliamentary reform.) Yet, on balance, Joshua was a far less encouraging influence than his wife, Jane. As George establishes throughout his memoir, she was party to all the major developments in her eldest son's life, but invariably such things were kept secret from her husband. In his 1883 biographical essay on George, Edmund Gosse observed: 'His early experiences of life were harsh, but salutary. Poverty pinched the household closely, and all through, like a jarring string in an instrument, there went the fear and horror of the head of the house.'[23]

Gosse no doubt based this description on the information provided by his subject. But in his own memoir, George displays greater sympathy towards his father, who was, to all appearances, a decent man at heart, through nature and necessity a hard worker and not without grit, ambition and entrepreneurialism – all of which was inherited by his eldest son. But, as his son goes on to reveal, Joshua was crushed by bad luck and disappointment which resulted in his increasing reliance on alcohol and turned him from a responsible head of household to a tyrant. Money coming into the family via the wheelwright business – needed to feed and clothe the whole family, and pay the rent – would be wasted on brief moments of respite at a local public house, often with disastrous results. Until his children grew up, Joshua was the main breadwinner, and it is hinted by George that his father's despair easily turned to aggression, including physical violence, compounded by further despair, bouts of melancholy and, to dull these feelings, heavy drinking. George observed, with a heart-rending compassion, that 'there are times when you cannot git on try all you know' and 'that['s] the time, men go and git drunk'. Writing in his sixty-eighth year and based on bitter personal experience, he advised that 'every one that goes in for art ought to be a teatot[al]lar for it [i.e. alcohol] takes the strength out of you', both physical and moral.[24]

Later in the century the temperance movement was established, targeted at working men like Joshua whose lives were blighted by excessive drinking – as indeed were the lives of those who relied upon them. As Ellen Ross sets out in her study *Love and Toil*, in such circumstances, 'family survival was the mother's main charge' and 'to mother' 'was to work for and organise household subsistence', no matter how the head of that household behaved.[25]

George returns to his father's ongoing struggles throughout the opening section of his memoir. The young George was conscious of the family's precarious position, which renders the fragments he sets down as cautionary tales all the more powerful. He recalls, as a young man 'my father was said to be the most industrious man about his neighbourhood', achieving some success with a 'small van', a vehicle for deliveries, usually a box on two or four wheels, which he had made himself, pulled by a small team of dogs: 'the leader he named Prin'. On seeing this neat arrangement, George noted, a neighbour was heard to call it, using a local phrase, 'a pretty turn out'. Such acknowledgement was a source of self-esteem and a good start for Joshua's greengrocery business.

In the 1841 census, the unmarried Joshua is listed as living with a single younger brother, James, at Milk Street; Joshua was a 'Fruiterer' and James, aged twenty, a 'J. Smith', a journeyman blacksmith or metalsmith. The term referred to someone qualified at a trade, having undergone an apprenticeship, but not yet a master. Caleb, the brother baptised with Joshua and Keziah in 1812, was in fact Joshua's twin brother; his absence in 1841 suggests that he had died.[26] This is supported by the parish records for St Laurence's Church, Upminster, where Caleb's death at two years old is recorded.[27] The death of his twin – not within days or weeks of birth, but as an infant – would have been a blow to the whole family, but for Joshua as a surviving twin, the sense of absence would have been acute.

Caleb's death may offer one explanation for Joshua's melancholic disposition, or this might be fanciful. Yet such a sense of loss was explored by a contemporary labouring-man-turned poet, whose twin, in this instance a girl called Bessey, had

> left me growing up to sin and shame
> And kept thy innocence untained and free
> To meet the refuge of a heaven above
> Where life's bud opens in eternity.[28]

Bessey Clare died within days of her birth, but the loss was mourned by her brother John for a lifetime. With Caleb's death, of the seven children known to have been born to Elizabeth Ann and James Tinworth senior, three had died in infancy: a tragedy for the family, but typical given urban infant mortality rates.* And this would be replicated in the next generation: George Tinworth recalled a conversation with his mother just before she died, when she told him that 'within the first few years of her married life she could not get her first 3 boys to live'.[29]

In 1841, the Tinworths' neighbours on Milk Street included costermongers, coal porters, carters, a gardener, a shoemaker, a wire worker and a seaman – a mix of skilled and unskilled workers. Several women on Milk Street were, like Elizabeth Ann Tinworth, laundresses: Mary Harris (aged sixty-four) lived with her thirty-two-year-old son James Harris, a labourer, and Elizabeth Wynn, aged fifty. These trades and occupations, from Mayhew's assessment, refer to a few artisans, but were mainly labourers working within 'sweating' trades.

Just a few months after the census was taken, both surviving Tinworth brothers were married on the same day, 2 August 1841, at Holy Trinity Church in Borough, with Joshua's profession now stated as 'wheelwright' and his younger brother's as 'engineer', which might, given James's former occupation as a metalsmith, refer to someone who made or serviced machinery.†[30] However, in the month of their weddings, the brothers seem to have joined forces to build up a wheelwright business; by this date, they must have considered their prospects sufficiently buoyant for each to support a wife and family. The parish records show that their father, James, had died earlier that year and had been buried at St Peter's Church in Walworth (an Anglican rather than Dissenter burial

---

*Ellen Ross summarises London infant mortality (birth to age five) as 75 per cent at the beginning of the eighteenth century, falling to 30 per cent a century later, that is at the time Joshua and Caleb were born, and improving around the 1850s: of course, the rates varied from area to area, from rich to poor families (Ross (1993), pp. 181–2).
†One story concerns Joshua and James trying 'to make a motor but they could not get it to work as they wanted' (GTA, p. 18).

ground). Joshua Tinworth's bride on that August day in 1841, and George's mother, Jane Daniel, is listed on the 1841 census as living at 4 County Terrace Street just to the north of New Kent Road, with her father, George Daniel, a fifty-four-year-old carpenter, her brother George aged twenty-one, a surveyor, and sister Frances, aged seventeen (no profession). George Daniel's wife is not listed: we can presume that she had died, and Frances or Fanny, Jane's younger sister, was managing the Daniel household.

According to his grandson, George Daniel had been a cabin boy on one of 'Green's ships' – built at the Blackwall Yard in Poplar, one of the most significant shipyards in England since the seventeenth century – and had travelled to India with the East India Company at least once. After his time at sea, he was apprenticed to the Walworth builder W. Flack of Lion Street, near Elephant and Castle, where he learned woodworking; he would later find employment at Woolwich Arsenal, on the Thames to the east, as a carpenter.[31] When the Daniel family left Woolwich, they initially returned to the very street where George Daniel had worked his apprenticeship in Walworth, then to County Terrace Street. This constant moving around hints at a change in fortune – such as the death of the wife and mother – impacted by the need to find work, the arrival of children, and strains on time, living space and resources.

The new wife of James, the younger Tinworth brother, was Sarah – née Shepherd – who, according to the marriage register, had been living at 8 Milk Street and was therefore a near neighbour of the Tinworth brothers. Sarah's father George is named in the same document as a 'carman', the driver of a cart delivering goods as diverse as coal and groceries. The 1841 census stated Sarah Shepherd's age as fifteen, very young even then to marry; most people married in their early to mid-twenties when, like the Tinworth brothers, they had enough resources to create a new household. Girls could marry from the age of twelve, but they needed the consent of their parents until they were twenty-one (as did boys). In addition to living near each other, the named trades of the menfolk of these now intermarried families – the Tinworths, Daniels and Shepherds – suggest one way that the newly married couples may have met. The brief survey of the Milk Street neighbourhood reveals these families to be typical of the working-class population of Walworth in the early 1840s: some skilled artisans, but mainly unskilled workers and labourers.

Before her marriage, George Tinworth's mother worked for a pastry cook on Kennington Road, the same street where, some decades later, Charlie Chaplin would live with his mother and – separately – his father. George recalled that Jane served behind the counter for five years. He noted that the shop was still standing in the 1910s, and continued: 'They told her when she first went there that she could eat any pastery she fancied but she soon got sick of that.' Jane told him that now and then the local boys came into the shop to buy a pennyworth of broken biscuits, a small treat for those with very little money to spare. (George stated that 'there was some snobs among the shop keepers at this time' and that the local boys bought broken cake and biscuits because 'they were very poor.')[32] The description of the shop as a pastry cook's rather than a bakery suggests a business making and selling pies and tarts (sweet and savoury) as well as biscuits. To have served behind the counter in such a shop for many years, as well as assisting with the cooking, Jane must have been a well-presented young woman, able to deal pleasantly with customers, and sufficiently trustworthy to handle money. She was certainly literate and, therefore, had benefited from the limited education opportunities available to the working classes in the early nineteenth century.

During those five years, as a valued employee, Jane may have helped with the accounts, ledgers and the ordering of ingredients, although she had said during the winter she was kept in the cold shop, while the owners warmed themselves by the fire in the back parlour. Even so, at a later point in his memoir, George describes his mother as a good cook, who was able to tease out a meal from very little: crucial for family survival among the poor working class.

George's mother also told him that her employer called her the young 'quakeriss',[33] a nickname hinting that Jane, like Joshua, was from a Christian Nonconformist background. George Tinworth is referring to his maternal grandparents, the Daniels, when he writes: 'Before I was born my grandfather and mother use to go to the chaple in the Black Friars Road ... to hear Roland Hill preach.'[34] The Surrey Chapel was an independent Methodist and Congregational church established in 1783 in Blackfriars Road. It later became known as the Ring (due to its round 'temple' shape) and in 1876 the congregation moved to the newly built Christ Church on Westminster Bridge Road. Hannah Chaplin, Charlie's mother, was a regular member of this church in the 1890s.[35]

The religious Nonconformism of both the Daniels and the Tinworths offers another way, aside from their associated trades, that George's mother and father may have become acquainted. As he noted in his autobiography, 'my mother ... become a member of G. Clayton Chaple, w[h]ere the Tinworths attended ... perhaps it was at this place my mother met my father'.[36] George is referring to the York Street Chapel in Walworth, where Joshua and his siblings had been baptised in 1812. The registers for the York Street Chapel confirm that Jane Daniel joined this church on 6 January 1839.[37]

The Reverend Edward White was also a member of the York Street Chapel over the 1830s, when the Tinworths, Jane Daniel – and the Brownings – attended. Writing in 1895, unsurprisingly, the Reverend White particularly recalled his impressions of the young Robert Browning, describing how 'that young gentleman ... was with myself a "dear hearer" of the Reverend George Clayton, in a somewhat distant antiquity'.[38] He further observed that the chapel 'in those days was filled both on floor and galleries, with a prosperous yet devout congregation. There was, indeed then I must confess, far too rigid an arrangement of the "classes" according to the price of the pews.' The pulpit, he continued, stood against the middle of the wall adjoining the old burial ground, and the galleries 'came round the whole circle of the building, and ended on the two sides of the pulpit'. On the right-hand side and upstairs, among the lesser company, 'the Browning family occupied the gallery seat nearest to the great rostrum, and Robert Browning was the last man, and for years sat on the corner seat nearest and quite close to the right hand of our pastor the Revd. George Clayton'. No one within the chapel could have avoided noticing the young poet in such a prominent position. 'His face', the Reverend White concluded, 'was the most wonderful face

Page 13 from George Tinworth's autobiography, illustrating the York Street [George Clayton's] Chapel, Lock's Fields, Walworth. In the 1890s the chapel building was renamed Browning Hall and became the centre of activity for the social mission, the Robert Browning Settlement.

in the whole congregation, – pale somewhat mysterious, – and shaded with black flowing hair, but a face whose expression you remember through a lifetime.'[39] The young Jane Daniel, among the poorer congregation in the gallery, may have noticed this strikingly intense young man – the same age as her future husband – seated across from her. But if she did, she made no mention of Robert Browning to her son.

George's anecdotes concerning his mother's life before her marriage offer a glimpse of early romance – shop work, after all, was an opportunity for respectable young women to catch the eye: 'there was one young man that used to come to the shop she told me that she was fond of.' George concludes his mother's story of young love on a tragic note: 'well the young man died sudden, and she had no more interest in the place, so she ran home to her fathers house.'[40] Joshua Tinworth's proposal of marriage occurred soon after this disappointment. Jane's occupation would have been considered a step above those who were employed doing 'sweating' work, for example the laundress Elizabeth Ann Tinworth, and even her son the wheelwright, and this difference in status may have caused contention between husband and wife, as Joshua's ambitions were thwarted one by one.

There is no suggestion of any passion or love between Joshua and Jane. The details of her registration at the York Street Chapel state she 'withdrew' from the community after her marriage – in so doing, removing herself from a potential source of personal support and comfort.*[41] The bald fact of their marriage seems practical or contractual, rather than emotional. Even the joint ceremony – both brothers marrying on the same day, at the same church – is decidedly work-a-day. Contemporary observers noted the lack of occasion in the nuptials of the working class. One such commentator from the 1870s, the journalist and 'social explorer' James Greenwood (1832–1927), the son of a Lambeth coach trimmer, remarked that when it came to their marriages, working-class couples were as 'cool and businesslike, as though, having paid a deposit on the purchase of a donkey or a handsome barrow, they were just going in with their witnesses to settle the bargain'. Less amusingly, he believed, 'many of them enter on the solemn contract' of marriage 'with no more elevated thought or feeling or consciousness of the tremendous responsibility they are about to undertake, than would accompany a transaction of the kind mentioned'.[42] The social historian Jane Lewis observed: 'Certainly marriage was very much a practical necessity for working class girls, and the chief hope was for a good bargain ... Girls of all classes preferred marriage to being "left on the shelf", but working class girls needed a husband above all for economic support.'[43] Marriage was the only universally accepted context for sexual relations and pregnancy. Even so, illegitimacy was not uncommon, as was the fear of abandonment by a lover before marriage – and then, without financial support, resorting to the workhouse infirmary for help, either pregnant or with a newborn.[44]

Working-class girls understood the toil required to keep a house, while bearing and rearing children: as children themselves, they would have helped their mother within the home. But in return,

---

*Under Jane's name is the note, 'married to Mr Tinworth, 37 Weymouth Street', and then, under 'Remarks', is written 'Withdrawn'.

women expected their husbands, as the main breadwinners, to fulfil their side of the bargain. In exchange for economic support, working-class wives had little choice but to suffer their husband's drinking habits and any verbal or physical abuse that might follow – as Jane Tinworth would discover.[45] The working-class family's financial system, invariably the woman's responsibility to manage, had a variety of elements, beyond the money brought home by the main breadwinner, which were used as and when needed: help from immediate family, extended kin and neighbours; taking possessions to a local pawnbroker's; credit at local shops; part-time work such as taking in washing – as Elizabeth Ann Tinworth had done – or charring; and lodgers. The relentless juggling required, on top of child-rearing and domestic chores, must have been exhausting in itself. And women were always viewed as the 'secondary labourers', even within working-class political movements such as Chartism.[46] But, as historian Susie Steinbach sets out, women had to keep the family 'respectable' rather than 'rough': 'Working-class respectability (which was quite separate from middle- and upper-class standards) emphasised community, political and economic independence for men, and good housekeeping and mothering skills for women.'[47]

The social reformer Anthony Ashley-Cooper (1801–1885), known as Lord Ashley, later Earl of Shaftesbury expressed a belief commonly held among the upper classes that working-class wives were 'much superior to the men in tact, sound judgement, and economy, and yet melancholy to say there were instances every day of the homes of such industrious women being swept away by the rapacity of bad husbands'.[48] Known as the 'Poor Man's Earl', he campaigned for better working conditions, reform of the lunacy laws, education and a limit to child labour – apparently inspired to pursue philanthropy by the care of his family housekeeper, Maria Millis. George Tinworth was a great admirer – he designed and produced a plaque in celebration of Shaftesbury (see p. 282) – and here, within this quotation, his lordship could be describing his admirer's mother. Although such praise may appear flattering, as it was likely intended to be, these opinions put additional strain on women to be the lodestone for their children, their husbands (while managing their resources), their homes and their reputations. And later in the century, as Ellen Ross observes, 'mothers were "discovered" by social thinkers, and the magnitude of their labours was newly appreciated, though legislators soon used this discovery to make mothers the objects of new kinds of government regulation'.[49]

In his summary of working-class employment, Henry Mayhew had separated servants and labourers from artisans like Joshua Tinworth.[50] Another class of worker was the entertainer, who would perform on the streets or in public arenas like taverns: from street 'actors' (including puppeteers, jugglers, dancers and snake-swallowers) to 'the street musicians, and their different classes – as street bands – brass and mixed – street Ethiopians, farm-yard fiddlers, horse organs, Italian organ boys, hurdy-gurdy players, blind and crippled fiddlers, and violoncello and clarionet-players'.[51] The mention of 'street Ethiopians' may be a reference to Londoners from Africa or of African descent, some, like the Regency celebrity Billy Waters, former enslaved people from the West Indies and America.[52] Or this may refer to minstrels in blackface, who he also calls 'Ethiopian serenaders'. Mayhew then quotes from a long interview with a former manservant turned 'Punch and Judy' proprietor – 'a short, dark, pleasant-looking man, dressed in a very greasy and very shiny green shooting-jacket' – who declared: 'The street performers in London lives mostly in little rooms of their own; they has generally wives and one or two children, who are brought up to the business.' The Punch showman highlighted Westminster Road and St George's in the East as areas where these families lived, before adding that a 'great many are in Lock's-fields; they are all the old school that way' (meaning traditional or old-fashioned).[53] That Walworth was notable by the 1840s as a centre for such traditional, working-class entertainment is unsurprising given this part of South London would become a major hub – both domestic and professional – for working-class music-hall performers like the Chaplins, over the second half of the century. 'All our forefathers died in the workhouse', the Punch performer observed of his trade, before concluding, without a hint of self-pity, 'and, in course, I shall do the same.'

Among his earliest dated recollections from these years at Milk Street, when George was aged about three, one concerned a local musician: 'in this neighbourhood lived an old man that used to go about with the base voil [i.e. viol], he used to get drunk at times.' George continues, 'one day he got knocked down when drunk and his base voil got smashed up, after that he got his glue pot and stuck it all together again he said it sounded better than ever after that.'[54] The bass viol is an early style of cello, popular in the eighteenth century and certainly old-fashioned by the 1840s. The aged musician played his instrument on the streets for the entertainment of passers-by. The viol's sound may have improved after the accident, but nothing speaks of resilience coupled with necessity than the sight of this old street musician teasing out a tune on his patched-up instrument. That said, such a touching sight would likely encourage greater generosity in his audiences, hence his sanguine – we might say Chaplinesque – response to misfortune.

George Tinworth described other street entertainment enjoyed by the working people of Walworth. These included English folk traditions connected to the annual May Day, originally an agricultural celebration of May Queens, maypoles and parades to welcome the first signs of summer. (By the late nineteenth century May Day itself would become increasingly associated with 'workers', the trade union and labour movements.) The pagan symbolism included the Jack-in-the-Green parade which, by the nineteenth century, had become synonymous with itinerant chimney sweeps.* The 'Jack' wore a conical wooden frame over his upper body which was covered in dense foliage. He whirled through the streets with other characters, including a 'Fool', dancing around him dressed in extravagant costumes and bedecked in flowers and ribbons, some with coal-blackened faces, banging on drums or playing folk-band instruments, fiddles and horns: the aim was to be as disorderly and as raucous as possible.[55] George recalled that in the Walworth May Day celebrations, an old chimney sweep's daughter would

---

*George Tinworth recalled John Ruskin telling him that he liked the revellers coming to his home in Denmark Hill, Camberwell every May Day, to perform in front of his house (GTA, p. 39).

join the local 'Jack and Green', playing 'the part of the lady with the long brass spoon' alongside a 'tinker', 'a good looking man I remember' who 'was dressed something like Lord Nelson, with cocked hat and knee breeches'. This 'Lady' and 'Lord' spent the whole day dancing together and, as George continues wryly, they remained together all night too.[56] 'As a boy I was often roused up by hearing the sound of the drum,' George declared, and, relishing the memory of chimney sweeps frolicking and performing tricks, 'I should have liked to have been one among them at that time, I could dance and do a bit of conjuring.'[57]

The street was one venue for ad hoc and festive folk entertainment; another was the common ground where regular travelling fairs came to rest. George recalled his mother taking him to Camberwell Green, a short walk from Milk Street, where the district's most popular annual fair was held. Until 1800 Camberwell was, like Walworth, a village surrounded by woods and fields with a main thoroughfare called Denmark Hill,* a village green and the medieval church of St Giles: Charlie Chaplin's family had a connection to this parish, as did Robert Browning. Mineral wells and springs existed at Camberwell until about 1850. One reason why Camberwell remained semi-rural, even into the 1840s, was the relatively late arrival of the railway; Camberwell New Road station opened in 1862. The transformation afterwards, as would be seen in Walworth, was striking. In 1801, the population of Camberwell was 7,059; by 1891 it had ballooned to 235,344.[58]

The main annual fair on Camberwell Green was held over the summer, but by the 1840s, due to campaigning from disgruntled local residents, it had dwindled to just three days in August. On Saturday, 20 August 1842, the *Illustrated London News* noted that this 'old established fair' had opened on the previous Thursday when, from an early hour, 'the road to and from the Elephant and Castle was thronged with "go-carts" and caravans'.[59] The parade, as the paper reported, travelled along Walworth Road from Elephant and Castle, eventually entering Camberwell Road as it neared its destination. Within one such cavalcade, George

---

*Named for the Stuart monarch Queen Anne's Danish husband, Prince George.

Tinworth recalled being struck by the sight of 'human sculptures', men dressed in white to imitate marble and assuming postures: like statues come to life.[60] This, he later judged, caused his first awakening for art.[61]

As the *Illustrated London News* continued, in 1842, the 'fair itself was beyond an average in booths and stalls, though from the opposition of many of the inhabitants, who have long endeavoured to abolish it, the contrary might have been expected'.[62] In fact, due to the local campaign, observed in many press reports over the 1840s, the fair would be abolished completely in 1855 due to 'immoral and riotous behaviour'. George Tinworth recalled, in an anecdote associated with his father's employee 'Spider', that the boxer was walking on a path 'when some students perhaps from Camberwell Fair, come along arm in arm pushing people of[f] the pavement'. They tried to do the same to Spider, who left them with 'black eyes and bleeding noses', adding that 'some of them got locked up'.[63]

The London paper the *Evening Star* described the scene on Camberwell Green that same August as 'the usual paraphernalia of a good old English fair', with a wealth of entertainment and a sensory barrage of the traditional, the uncanny and the exotic:

> The bustle of preparation commenced at an early hour, and by 8 o'clock not an inch of available ground but was covered with peripatetic candidates for public patronage. Here stood Wombwell, with his unrivalled menageries, and his tiger-apparelled band. Here was the immense show lately known as 'Richardson's', now the property of Nelson Lee & Co., with its splendid company of Thespians. Near adjacent was Clark, with his superb stud from Astley's. Here was Saunders with his giants, his fire eaters, his Herculean brothers and set-to's. There also were booths, where the voteries of Terpsichore, despite the weather, tripped it gaily on the light fantastic toe. There were giants; near bye were dwarfs; learned pigs and mischievous apes; and boa constrictors eating up young rabbits. There were conjurors and thimble-riggers; penny shows, penny hops, and three throws a

penny ... There were high-flyers, and merry-go-rounds, and round-abouts.*

Finally, the London *Evening Star* reporter reeled off the food and drink available, such as 'gilded gingerbread and cooked sausage, ham sandwiches, and baked "taturs", brandy balls and penny cigars, porter and ginger-beer, coffee and lemonade, fried liver and bacon', and with the 'scratch backs, tract distributors and all the fun of the fair', the reporter declared the 'day was a lovely one'.[64]

In a report from 1846, when George Tinworth would have been almost three years old, the *Illustrated London News* seemed more interested in the noise, criminality and need for policing:

> CAMBERWELL FAIR.— On Tuesday, at twelve o'clock, the fair on Camberwell Green commenced, in the usual manner, by beating of gongs, firing of cannon, and an extremely large supply of discordant instruments of every variety, which were brought into active service for the occasion ... A large body of police officers of the P division were on duty for the purpose of preserving order, and for the detection of the light-fingered gentry, who generally reap a rich harvest at the metropolitan fairs.[65]

Alongside the circus acts, exotic creatures, fun rides and stalls, the entertainment at Camberwell Fair included theatrical performances, *tableaux vivants* and painted panoramas presenting scenes from recent events and popular history. In 1842, for example, a visitor could witness, without leaving Camberwell, 'the taking of Ghuznee by the British, Jack Shepherd, the War in Affghanistan, the disasters of Caubul, Paul Clifford, Dick Turpin, and his bonny black Bess, all to be seen for one halfpenny'. The references to the capturing of the fort of Ghuznee (or Ghazni) and the 'disasters'

---

*Philip Astley (1742–1814) had been a local celebrity, establishing his home, Hercules Hall, on a road running north from Lambeth Road to the top of Kennington Road – later named Hercules Road as a result. Astley's famous Amphitheatre was located nearby on Westminster Bridge Road.

of Kabul referred to events during the First Anglo-Afghan War (1838–42). For a working-class population, this was one means of gaining some understanding of current affairs, albeit presented with a pungent combination of imperialist jingoism and heart-stirring stories of British military pluck.

Over the course of the nineteenth century, working-class families would be subjected to increasing scrutiny by charities, local authorities and the state, in the form of, for example, health workers, school truancy officers and – in a new development of 1829 – the policing of the capital. The Metropolitan Police Force, mentioned in the *Illustrated London News* article quoted above, was centrally controlled by the Home Secretary and replaced a less professional, parish-led system. The force's Detecting Branch was created in 1842, with Jonathan 'Jack' Whicher (1814–1881) of Providence Row, Wyndham Road, Camberwell, among the first cohort. Charles Dickens did much to promote this new style of policing, through characters like Inspector Bucket in *Bleak House* (1853): unlike the uniformed police constable on the beat, plain-clothed detectives proactively investigated crimes and criminals. Even so, as revealed in Kate Summerscale's *The Suspicions of Mr Whicher*, the business of detection was by its nature covert and intrusive, and these detectives would be subjected to prejudice and derision in the course of their duties. The branch 'employed' some working-class women (often unpaid officers' wives) as well as men like Whicher, and both were unpopular within their communities: an Englishman's home, prince or pauper, was his castle.[66]

From around the 1830s, there was a competitive environment for the reporting of crime – from the single-sheet 'penny dreadfuls' to weekly newspapers – much of it targeted at the lower classes through low pricing, from a halfpenny to sixpence, as well as subject matter. Among the more impressionable readers, such publications might render misbehaviour and lives of crime – past and present – as eminently more exciting than the daily plod of honest toil. Charles Manby Smith reflected middle-class concerns and anxieties when he observed with reference to these 'blood-and-murder, ghost-and-goblin journals' in his *Curiosities of London Life* (1857): 'It would seem that there is a charm in pistols, daggers, bludgeons, and deadly weapons of all sorts, with the assaults and assassinations they suggest, that is irresistible to the population of London.'[67]

The presence of Jack Sheppard and Dick Turpin as subjects for entertainment at Camberwell Fair reveals the ongoing popularity among the working class of rascals and criminals from their own ranks: Jack Sheppard, an inspiration for the scallywags in the works of Henry Fielding and William Hogarth, was the apprentice-turned-thief who escaped from Newgate Prison on numerous occasions, eventually hanged at Tyburn in 1725 at the age of twenty-three; and Dick Turpin was the highwayman who supposedly rode overnight to York from London to evade capture on his horse Black Bess, only to be executed at the York Tyburn in 1739. The re-enactment of Turpin's derring-do was a popular theme in the nineteenth century, although the story of the ride to York was considerably embellished by William Harrison Ainsworth in his novel *Rookwood* (1834).* Indeed, Jack Sheppard's enduring allure was partly down to another Ainsworth novel (1839–40) where the eponymous thief took centre stage. The Reverend John Clay, a prison chaplain, made a study at this time of young offenders and their influences. He found that 'Newgate novels' – the broad term given to such fiction – were a significant feature within material read by, or read to these youths, observing of one inmate (in a report submitted to Parliament in 1846) that he knew little of the Bible, but 'easily comprehended, assisted by coarse but intelligible engravings, the exciting stories of "The Newgate Calendar *Improved*", and of Dick Turpin and his black mare', and in this manner, books, 'fraught with ruin and death, are made level to his capacity and enticing to his imagination'. In 1850 Clay presented a survey of 1,636 males 'under sessions and summary committals': of these, 646 could not name Jesus, 977 were unable to say who the reigning monarch was, but 713 were

> well acquainted with the exciting adventures and villainies of Turpin and Sheppard; – knew that they were famous robbers

---

*A performance of an equivalent pageant of 'Turpin's Ride to York' later featured in Thomas Hardy's novel *Far from the Madding Crowd* (1874).

and prisonbreakers; admired them as friends and favourers of the poor, inasmuch as if they *did* rob – 'they robbed the rich for the poor'; – and were only sufficiently alive to the fact that these heroes were, at last, hung![68]

Decades later, Charlie Chaplin would recall, when a lad, doing a turn as the infamous Dick Turpin, the 'gentleman of the road', in a burlesque for the all-boy troupe *Casey's Circus*.[69]

At the beginning of the nineteenth century, there were hundreds of prisons across the country, all managed by the local authorities. Traditionally, gaols were used to hold those who had been accused of a crime and were awaiting trial, those who had been convicted and were awaiting punishment, those who had defaulted on payment of sureties, and debtors. Houses of Correction, or 'Bridewells', had become places where those convicted of petty offences served short sentences of imprisonment. Over the eighteenth century, prison sentences began to be used more often, and from the 1770s many prisons had been reformed or refurbished, and some were being replaced. Into the nineteenth century the use of sentences of imprisonment increased dramatically, following the rationalisation of England's legal system, nicknamed the 'Bloody Code', where the death penalty covered over two hundred offences, many very minor.[70]

Unlike Sheppard and Turpin, Paul Clifford was not a real individual, but the eponymous highwayman in a work of fiction by Edward Bulwer-Lytton, published in 1830 but set in the late eighteenth century: it was the first to be termed a 'Newgate novel'. On trial for armed robbery, where his life hangs by a thread, Clifford declares to the judge: 'My Lord, it was the turn of a straw which made me what I am. Four years ago, I was sent to the House of Correction for an offence which I did not commit; I went thither, a boy who had never infringed a single law, – I came forth, in a few weeks, a man who was prepared to break all laws!' The author asks whose fault it was, via his highwayman. The Law and those who administer it, is the reply: 'You had first wronged me by a punishment which I did not deserve, – you wronged me yet more deeply, when (even had I been guilty of the first offence,) I was sentenced to herd with hardened offenders, and graduates in vice and vice's methods of support.' In short, 'your legislation made me what I am! and it now *destroys me, as it has destroyed thousands, for being what it made me!*'[71] Arguably among those thousands were Jack Sheppard and Dick Turpin – and potentially many of the young men and women within the crowd on Camberwell Green cheering Sheppard, Turpin and Paul Clifford on. In his own words, the serious lessons Bulwer-Lytton intended should be learned between 'vicious Prison-discipline, and a sanguinary Criminal Code' was the terrible habit of 'corrupting the boy by the very punishment that ought to redeem him, and then hanging the man at the first occasion, as the easiest way of getting rid of our own blunders'.[72]

The stark social criticism at the heart of *Paul Clifford* made it one popular rallying point in the period before and after the Great Reform Act of 1832, the culmination of attempts, over many decades, to regulate parliamentary constituencies across the United Kingdom and to enfranchise the working classes through the expansion of the vote.[73] In the event, concerning universal male suffrage, the legislation fell desperately short. But living in the Walworth area, working men like Joshua Tinworth had opportunities to engage with the broader political issues of the day – and even to witness history in the making.

Those against the reformation of the British Parliament characterised those who supported it as hell-bent on introducing a French-style mob-handed revolution: a period that had ushered in the rise of Napoleon Bonaparte and almost two decades of war across Europe. As ever, international affairs impacted on the lives of the working people, whether through direct taxation – the government of William Pitt the Younger introduced income tax in 1798 to fuel the war effort – or indirect taxation on, for example, basic foodstuffs. There was a genuine and justified fear of revolution and invasion, but this fear was also used to suppress agitation for basic rights and deter demonstrations of valid grievance by poorer working people. The effective status quo was taxation without representation, except for a small proportion of Britain's wealthier citizens – the criteria to elect Members of Parliament related to a man's property value or annual rent of at least £40. Jury eligibility followed a similar restriction, so most of the working class was locked out of active participation in the dispensing of justice too.

As a result, the early nineteenth century had been a time of fraught industrial relations between workers, business owners and the government. The Tory administrations of Pitt, Lord Sidmouth and then Lord Liverpool introduced some of the most repressive laws against any form of social dissent or political opposition ever seen: the Luddites, men whose livelihoods had been destroyed by mechanisation, were rounded up and many were executed under a new anti-machine-breaking law passed in 1812, while, at what became known as the Peterloo Massacre of 16 August 1819, a peaceful mass demonstration at St Peter's Field in Manchester in support of parliamentary reform and 'one man one vote', was brutally suppressed on the orders of local magistrates by local professional and volunteer constables, two yeomanry regiments (these were voluntary cavalries made up for the most part of small businessmen and traders), and British Army regulars. Their actions resulted in the death of eighteen, including a two-year old child, and the wounding and maiming of hundreds. These mass meetings had occurred throughout Great Britain, and if everything had gone to plan, the biggest of all would have been held in London later that August. But with the main speaker, Henry 'Orator' Hunt, and other radicals, including the weaver Samuel Bamford, in prison accused of sedition, the momentum was halted and then killed off through more repressive legislation – the so-called 'Gagging' laws.

In 1830, the radical journalist and publisher Richard Carlile, who had been on the hustings at St Peter's Field in August 1819, took over the management of a building on Blackfriars Road in Southwark that had since 1823 become a centre for radical politics and debate. The reputation of 'the Rotunda' made it of interest to the Home Office, who regularly sent spies to the meetings and lectures held there and eventually closed it down. At the beginning of 1830 the prime minister was the Duke of Wellington, an anti-reform Tory, but by the end of that year he had been replaced by the pro-reform Whig, Lord Grey, who laid the ground for the legislation that would pass in 1832. In addition to creating new constituencies for such industrial northern cities as Manchester and Leeds, the 1832 Reform Act did expand the vote, but based on the traditional criteria of a man's property value or the level of rent paid. This reduction from £40 to £10 enfranchised more of the male middle class, still leaving all women and the working class without a vote. Which left men like Joshua Tinworth, his family and neighbours, politically powerless, save for the extremes of peaceful, lawful displays of might on the one hand, or lawless rioting on the other.

According to George Tinworth, the family remained at the cottage in Milk Street for the first two or three years of his life,[74] from which time George recalled stories of jeopardy that might test the patience of any otherwise lawful citizen. One night, his father and mother were visiting a relation on the opposite side of the street; luckily they decided not to stay for supper, for 'when they got into the cottage they found the rug alight in front of the fire and the place full of smoke'. George was asleep upstairs, but Jane and Joshua put the fire out 'just in time'. In the text beneath his mother's drawing of the Milk Street cottage, George refers to another event when his father's pony ate too much hay, became bloated, and in its agony started kicking the side of the shed. To save the unfortunate creature, Joshua had to get up, harness the pony to a cart and 'drive him all about the neighbourhood at night'.[75] A dead pony was of no use to his business or his family.

Writing his memoir in the 1910s, George may have known the work of popular novelists such as Thomas Hardy, so could have made the connection between scenes taken from real-life events within these novels and his family's own precarious existence. For example, in *Tess of the D'Urbervilles*, first published twenty years before George began writing his memoir, the fatal injury of the Durbeyfields' horse forces the eponymous heroine into the path of her nemesis. But, as George's memoir was emphatically one of real life, he included the Tinworths' pony story, alongside the cottage fire, to show how the family were on constant alert – the descriptions of his childhood a torrent of challenging situations, decisions made in the moment with significant consequences. The Tinworth family rarely had the luxury of leisure. On this occasion, a good night's sleep in preparation for a productive day's work was ruined by the necessity of saving the pony.

It must have crossed Joshua's mind that the intervention of something greater than himself could make his life better, or more secure. George Tinworth recalled that his father had attended at least one political rally on Kennington Common, at which the charismatic public speaker Feargus O'Connor was present. The son of an Irish nationalist, O'Connor had toured England in the early 1830s to rouse interest among people like Joshua in his land reforms. He argued that each working man should be given enough land to grow vegetables and rear animals, in order that he and his family would be less dependent on the meagre wages offered by landowners, factory owners and businessmen. In the spirit of publications like William Cobbett's *Weekly Political Register* (1802–36) and Thomas Jonathan Wooler's *Black Dwarf* (1817–24), between 1837 and 1852, O'Connor was proprietor of the *Northern Star*, a popular radical newspaper among working men that was read out in homes and taverns across the country. It became the voice of a new working-class political movement.

Following the mass meetings and petitions earlier in the century, Chartism developed in London from 1836 – just a few years after the Reform Act had been passed. The Charter, a conscious reference to the medieval Magna Carta, had six demands: that there should be a vote for every man over the age of twenty-one; that ballots should be secret; that there should be no property qualification in order to stand as a Member of Parliament – at a stroke widening the pool from which MPs could be drawn; that MPs should be paid, rather than be reliant on private income or patronage; that parliamentary constituencies should be equal in size (head count rather than land size); and that there should be annual Parliaments (requiring annual elections). These demands echoed those championed at St Peter's Field; the 'Great' Reform Act had been limited, notwithstanding the dissolving of the infamous 'rotten boroughs' and the creation of new constituencies in industrial northern towns.

In 1839 a mass march on Newport in Monmouthshire, led by John Frost, to demand the release of imprisoned fellow Chartists, resulted, as earlier in Manchester, in a confrontation that left around twenty Chartists killed, and their leaders arrested and found guilty of high treason: the sentence (a medieval throwback) was to be drawn, hanged until dead and quartered, but it was later commuted to transportation. Three years after the Newport Rising there was a general strike among factory workers across Britain against the reduction in wages, caused by a downturn in trade. Their grievances expanded the support among workers for Chartism, and mass meetings were held across the country. But when the presentation of a petition to Parliament in support of the Charter was rejected, riots occurred across the country, and the military, as at St Peter's Field and Newport, were called in to restore order.

The historian David Goodway outlined the 'predicament' of the Chartist leadership, who welcomed the 'spontaneous violence of the eighteenth-century riot' as 'an expression of working-class misery (and hence as a means of political pressure)', while moving increasingly towards 'the pacific, disciplined strength' that would characterise the labour movement by the end of the century. Yet, in 'the confrontation with government and police in London' over the 1840s, the prime concern for Feargus O'Connor and his fellows 'was maintaining the rights of public assembly'.[76]

In his memoir, George Tinworth describes how 'Napoleon the Third when he escaped from France come to live in Queens Row, close to Camberwell Gate', which appears to refer to the exile in London between 1836 and 1840 of Louis-Napoleon, the nephew of Napoleon Bonaparte and later Emperor Napoleon III, after the failed coup against the Bourbon monarch Louis Philippe.[77] That Louis-Napoleon lived in Walworth at any time seems unlikely.

George also recalls that his father's grocery business went well 'till the potatoe rot and Great Irish Famine'.[78] This dates the collapse of Joshua's fruit and vegetable business to the mid-1840s and the harvest failure that caused mass starvation in Ireland. Social unrest erupted across Europe, culminating in full-scale revolutions in February 1848, demanding the complete transformation of old entities like the Holy Roman Empire into nation states with greater democratic structures. Barricades were raised in cities through Italy,

Austria and in Paris. The abdication of Louis Philippe ushered in the Second Republic in France. (This, in turn, collapsed after a coup led by Louis-Napoleon Bonaparte in 1851, establishing the 'Second Empire'.) Inevitably, with such turmoil on the European continent, once again there were fears in Britain that the revolutionary zeal might transfer across the Channel; there were plots for uprisings across Great Britain in this year, as well as major riots.

Joshua Tinworth told his son that during a speech on Kennington Common, Feargus O'Connor had asked the assembled people 'why they should be afraid of invasion', given 'you have no land to lose. All the free hold you have is in your flower pots and if the enemy come,' O'Connor suggested humorously, 'you could throw them on their heads.'[79] The threat of an invasion from France, which always accompanied civil unrest on the continent, might hint that Joshua Tinworth was present at the Great Chartist Meeting on that same common in April 1848: on this occasion, too, O'Connor was one of the main speakers.

The English biographer of Louis-Napoleon Bonaparte (Napoleon III), James Augustus St John, writing in the 1850s, was dismissive of the English response to events in France in early 1848: 'When there is a revolution in France, there is generally a subordinate movement in England. The chartists were rendered vivacious by the events of February, and sought in the old jog trot way to promote their own favourite reforms – five or six points or more, by assembling in the open air, hearing bad speeches, and drawing up interminable petitions to Parliament.' What St John fails to recognise is that petitioning the Crown through Parliament was part of the solemn contract between monarch and people, established by the Glorious Revolution of 1688–9 and the English Bill of Rights signed by William III and Mary II: the modern foundation of constitutional monarchy.

By early April, with more ructions in France, as St John continues, 'several timid people of both sexes urged the authorities to take precautions against the poor harmless multitude, which meant nothing in the world beyond exercising its ears and lungs in the fine open air of the southern suburbs'.[80] Again, he underestimates the importance of what Chartism represented: the first popular political movement in Britain, steeped in working-class tradition with, by this time, over three million supporters. No wonder the authorities were uneasy.

In the section of his memoir where he refers to Louis-Napoleon living in Walworth, George Tinworth goes on to state that he 'was made special constable at the time of the riots'.[81] In April 1848 a great number of special constables were indeed sworn in – calculated as up to 85,000 – including, it is believed, the future French emperor during a second period of exile in London. Referring to this surprising development, St John rightly wondered why a Frenchman, exiled once again during unrest in his own country, had any business enlisting into the ranks of English law enforcement against the Chartists.[82] In addition to the police and special constables, the military were kept on alert should the civil powers fail to keep order. The evening before the meeting on Kennington Common, the Duke of Wellington, victor at the Battle of Waterloo, had stationed troops across London.

The government had evidently prepared for a full-blown uprising, but the aim of the Chartist organisers was the opposite: commencing with a parade from central London, then gathering on Kennington Common, and finally another parade to deliver a petition to Parliament, all conducted as a peaceful display of collective resolve and collective strength.

The procession to Kennington Common, in conscious imitation of popular parades, included a four-wheeled cart pulled by four large Shire horses, a fine symbolic breed representing the greatest beneficiaries from longed-for universal male suffrage and parliamentary reform. The square cart had a canopy over it and the attendants held long streamers of fabric in red, green and white, the colours of the Chartist movement. Another cart, twenty feet long, was drawn by six Shire horses 'of superior breed' (noted the reporter from the *Illustrated London News*) 'and in the highest possible condition'. The cart had been adapted for use by the delegation and members of the press. One long side read, 'The Charter. No surrender. Liberty is worth living for and worth dying for', and the other, 'The voice of the people is the voice of God'. Across the back of the cart were the words, 'Who would be a slave that could be free?' and 'Onward, we conquer; backward, we fail'. As had been seen at other political rallies, both carts were decorated with brightly coloured banners, lending the scene a heraldic quality: there were four on each side, including the mottoes 'The Charter', 'No vote, no musket', 'Vote by ballot', 'Annual Parliaments', 'Universal suffrage', 'No property qualification' for either elector or parliamentary candidate, and to that end, 'The payment of members'. These were the demands of the Charter simmered down to pithy slogans that were legible from a distance, by those who could read, to be chanted by the assembled crowds during the triumphal march to Parliament.

Large crowds had formed around the procession from its commencement in London's West End, passing along Goodge Street, Tottenham Court Road, the High Street Bloomsbury, to the National Land Company offices, where five huge bundles containing the petition with millions of signatures were loaded onto the 'Charter' cart. The many journalists present recorded that the windows in the buildings on the route were filled with spectators and, according to the reporter for the *Illustrated London News*, 'amidst much applause, the moving mass took an onward course across Blackfriars-bridge'. On arrival at the old Elephant and Castle coaching inn, yet more people joined, marching eight abreast behind the two carts – 'still everything was peaceable and well-conducted,' observed the *Illustrated London News* journalist – the procession then heading towards Newington Butts and passing the church of St Mary Newington, by which time, continued the same reporter, 'the appearance of the masses was most bewildering'. The two carts and their accompanying crowds continued along the road (later Kennington Park Road) that runs towards Kennington Common, reaching the common itself at half past eleven.[83]

Amazingly, the Chartist mass meeting on Kennington Common was captured in two daguerreotypes, an early form of photography, by William Edward Kilburn that were purchased by Prince Albert.[84] Looking towards industrial buildings and a large house lining one side of the common in the distance, at the centre can be seen one of three hustings from which Feargus O'Connor and William Cuffay, a sixty-year-old London tailor and the son of an enslaved man of African heritage, would speak. Despite the fear of such a large police and military force gathered against them, the crowd on Kennington Common was estimated to be around 150,000 strong: among them may have been Joshua Tinworth, now in his mid-thirties and looking for answers and hope, after the failure of his grocery business.[85] The intention was then to march en masse to Parliament, to present the petition, with its millions of signatures in support of the Charter for parliamentary reform: a measured and peaceful mechanism to bring the voice of the disenfranchised to the attention of Parliament, Queen Victoria and her government, led by the Whig Lord John Russell.

Unfortunately, any mass gathering, no matter how peaceful, attracted troublemakers, and rumours spread of rioting in Camberwell: such disorder played into the authorities' hands. Feargus O'Connor was approached by the inspector of police, who told him that the police commissioner, Sir Richard Mayne, wished to speak to him at the nearby Horns Tavern. O'Connor returned to the hustings soon after and delivered a rousing but unusually short speech. William Cuffay was described in the newspaper reports as furious that O'Connor had covertly agreed to abandon the procession to Parliament, after threats from the police commissioner. In fact the authorities had already closed off all the bridges, including those at Vauxhall, Lambeth and Westminster. The immense crowd was told to disperse: after a prolonged and thrilling build-up, this order was a devastating anticlimax.

The petition was taken to Parliament by the leaders, but – without the persuasive accompaniment of mass physical presence – once again it was rejected by the House of Commons. In an attempt to maintain momentum, Cuffay was part of a gathering of radical Chartists in London the following August. He was arrested for 'conspiring to levy war' against Queen Victoria, on the evidence of a government spy called Thomas Powell. At Bow Street magistrates' court, as reported contemptuously by *The Times* journalist, 'His appearance, viewed in remembrance of the tone and style of his speeches, was perfectly ridiculous. He was scarcely higher than the dock in which he was placed –' Cuffay was 4 foot 11 inches tall, due in part to a spinal deformity – 'although there was no lack

William Cuffay in his Newgate cell, drawn by William Paul Dowling, a chartist and Cuffay's fellow prisoner. Despite the charge of High Treason, which still carried the death penalty, Cuffay appears undaunted, even cheerful.

of impudent assurance in his demeanour before the magistrate. He has a dark, African sort of countenance, and is probably about 40.'[86] At the Old Bailey trial that followed, William Cuffay maintained his innocence to the conspiracy charge. While pleading 'not guilty' he also declared: 'I demand a fair trial by a jury of my peers and equals.' As was the case with voting in elections, jurors had to meet a property qualification, which barred much of the working class from taking part: knowing this, Cuffay was making a point about the unfairness of the justice system – as described in *Paul Clifford* – a system stacked against him and his fellow disenfranchised working men. And so it proved, for William Cuffay was found guilty and sentenced to penal transportation to Australia for twenty-one years.

When he was in his early twenties, George Tinworth, like his father, witnessed his own moment of history. On 16 April 1864, the Italian general, revolutionary and republican Giuseppe Garibaldi arrived in London: just six years later, the cause for which Garibaldi had fought, the unification of Italy, would be a reality. George was standing with the crowds on Westminster Bridge Road, at the junction with Kennington Road: 'All at once we heard a low murmer coming from Kennington Common way, which got louder and louder.' But, to the evident disappointment of the crowd, it was not the Italian freedom fighter, but a chimney sweep riding on his donkey, his face covered in soot 'as if he had just left work'. The sweep mischievously played along, nodding and waving 'like an emperor', until he and his steed were propelled away from the processional route and down Oakley Street. Then, George recalled, 'again there was the low murmer that got lo[u]der and loder and loweder'. Suddenly Garibaldi appeared, 'standing up in the carriage as he come past me, a grand looking man', and, caught up with the excitement, 'I ran some distance with this carriage'. George described the sound coming from the crowds, as Garibaldi was driven in triumph along the road towards Westminster Bridge, as 'a noise almost of worship'.[87]

Reading these scant notes, recorded decades later, it is striking how these events of international importance sit alongside details of personal daily struggle. As an adult, George clearly knew the importance of figures such as Feargus O'Connor, Napoleon III and Garibaldi, but he does not seem to have understood the significance of the political meetings on Kennington Common, as witnessed by his father, nor does he overtly sympathise with the substance of their aims, despite, later in life, benefiting from such campaigns for greater democracy. Chartism, like earlier attempts at radical parliamentary reform, may have stumbled and then died at Kennington Common in April 1848, but the memory and the networks of working-class solidarity lived on, to be galvanised into action half a century later in nearby Walworth.

Out-door Relief.

Out-door Relief by 'Phiz' [Hablot Knight Browne] from James Grant's *Sketches in London* (1840), where the author observes: 'Want of trade, a bad harvest, the high price of provisions, a long continuance of inclement weather, and other causes, compel paupers to seek refuge in the workhouse, who, but for those causes, would have struggled on with the ills of poverty out of doors'.

2

VICTORY PLACE

'Our Only Crime Being Poverty'

George recalled that in a time of prosperity, his father gave him his first sixpence and 'I went out and saw 2 china figures at a pawn shop and went in and asked the price of them, and showed them my sixpence and they let me have them'.[1] Pawning was a way of getting a cash loan, with an item of a certain value left as security. If you repaid the full amount, your item was returned. If you did not, then, as here, the item was available for purchase by someone else. Both George Tinworth and Charlie Chaplin refer to regular visits to the pawn shop throughout their childhood: it was one resource available to poor households.

George also describes how his father, in the days of relative affluence, made his son a child-sized wheelbarrow – a small act of paternal kindness that hints at the universal urge for little sons to mimic their fathers. But the good times did not last, and as a result 'my father took to the drink and so went down and we with him'. The little wheelbarrow was sold to a shopkeeper as a gift for his own son. George concludes this recollection with the statement, 'I never forgot the boy that had my barrow'; in fact, 'I know him now, although it is 60 years ago.'[2] The distress of having belongings taken away and, worse, given to another child is something that remained with George for the rest of his life: the anecdote is relayed with a sense of injustice, and even shame. And surely, for a proud man like George's father, the significance was not lost on Joshua Tinworth. The memory of owning things has a symbolic importance. Some, like the ceramic 'china' figures, were small luxuries that, in George's case, related to a growing fascination for fine art. Others, like the pots of flowers, brought a simple beauty into the life of the beholder. In both circumstances, presence then absence rendered the hardship of life less bearable. It is a source of heartbreak that peppers both George Tinworth's memoir and the early chapters of Charlie Chaplin's autobiography. And finding the comedy within such small tragedies lay at the core of the latter's global appeal.

What is certain is that by the mid- to late 1840s, the period when Chartism held some interest for him, Joshua Tinworth and his family were in much reduced circumstances, which triggered a change in residence: 'When we left Milk St my father took rooms in a house not far away,' George writes. The precise location is not known, but it was somewhere in the Walworth area. The change from an independent cottage to 'rooms' within a shared house indicates the downward slide in status. And while they were at this accommodation, 'the people' – by which George means the owners, or the rent collectors working on their behalf – 'decided to put the brokers man in'.[3]

Charles Dickens, an exact contemporary of Joshua Tinworth, knew something about the terrors of unremitting family debt. In the 1830s he devised a character called 'Mr Bung', a man-for-hire used by landlords to collect outstanding debt, who appears in *Sketches by Boz*. Here, Mr Bung declares, 'a broker's man's is not a life to be envied; and in course you know as well as I do, though you don't say it, that people hate and scout'em because they're the ministers of wretchedness, like, to poor people. But what could I do, sir?' He goes on: 'if putting me in possession of a house would put me in possession of three and sixpence a day, and levying a distress on another man's goods would relieve my distress and that of my family, it can't be expected but what I'd take the job and go through with it.'[4] Consequently, for Mr Bung – whose own circumstances hover perilously between poverty and subsisting – such unpleasant work was a matter of survival: economic necessity forcing a working man to act against another on the landlord's behalf.

In the case of the Tinworths, the broker's man must have been lurking in the street, ready to accost anyone emerging from the

George Cruikshank's illustration *The Broker's Man* from Charles Dickens's *Sketches by Boz* (1836), where a financially comfortable man (seen to the left, laughing) is encouraged by a bailiff, 'Mr. Fixem' (centre), to call in a debt. Fixem's assistant, 'Bung' (right), accepts a fee to visit the debtor and extract payment.

family's address and then force his way onto the premises. George recalled asking his mother to let him go out to play, but she told him 'to wait till the sun went down', explaining that if the door was opened before nightfall 'the brokers man would get in'. It is not clear whether the broker's man was there to take possessions of a certain value to cover a debt, or to evict the Tinworths from the lowly rooms they were renting. Either way, the family's vigilance

– possibly assisted by sympathetic co-lodgers, and neighbours 'scouting' on their behalf – could not hold indefinitely and the broker's man gained access the following day. That night 'me and my father and the brokers man was sitting at the table'. This sentence conjures up a dingy room, with the broker's man, impassive to the circumstances of the debtor sitting before him, holding Joshua's gaze while George, a small child, waits. Unsurprisingly in the circumstances, his father had had 'a drop too much' and, taking up a fork, Joshua 'stuck it in the table before the brokers man'.[5] The threatening vision of the sharp prongs of a fork thrust into the tabletop, a lit candle or fire casting a shadow across the surface, would not have bothered a seasoned broker's man: he had experienced, no doubt, far worse behaviour from desperate people. But, with nothing else left, a drunken Joshua resorts to a futile gesture of aggression and defiance, his dignity in tatters.

This dismal encounter was played out in the full glare of their fellow lodgers and neighbours, adding to the trauma as well as the sense of disgrace for the Tinworths. Whatever the intentions of their unwelcome visitor that night, the family's circumstances soon forced yet another change of address, when 'we moved from there to a little house in Lock's Fields Walworth'. In addition to the little house there was a wheelwright's workshop nearby. At least this new house, echoing the arrangement in Milk Street, allowed Joshua to work within walking distance of home. But, according to George, the residence was barely fit for habitation, a hint that this was all the family could afford.

He recalled that one night there was a heavy thunderstorm 'and I remember my father standing on a chair making holes in the ceiling with a fork to keep the rain from going on the beds'. George speculated whether the landlord had shifted the roof tiles to cause the leaks and force the family to move on.[6]

The new residence may have been on the street called Victory Place, although a 'little house' does not fit the description of the domestic buildings known to have been there, nor other details concerning the Tinworths that can be gleaned from the next national census of March 1851.[7] 8 Victory Place, where the family was registered, is in the area of Walworth called Lock's Fields, where, according to Henry Mayhew's report, street performers and their families congregated. The area's name refers to the medieval Lock Hospital, associated with the care of lepers. By the eighteenth century, 'The Lock' was a term used for hospitals treating those modern 'lepers', sufferers from venereal diseases, some forms of which, like syphilis, had no cure and often led to 'madness' and painful early death.

By the 1830s the 'Lock' parks or, as they were usually referred to, Lock's Fields, had been partially developed by a network of roads including Victory Place, with new residential buildings and businesses laid out to the south of New Kent Road. Victory Place was near to the York Street Chapel, where Joshua Tinworth, his twin brother Caleb and their elder sister Keziah had been baptised in 1812 – and where Jane Tinworth had been a member before her marriage. Other new streets in the area included Trafalgar Place, named, like Victory Place, in honour of Lord Horatio Nelson's greatest sea battle of 1805; the deposed French emperor Napoleon I had died in exile and under British guard in 1821. In 1851, the year of his nephew Louis-Napoleon's coup which led to the birth of the Second Empire in France, Trafalgar, Waterloo and the national bogeyman, popularly nicknamed 'Boney', were firmly within living memory. And in the same year J. M. W. Turner, the working-class artist of international renown, died and was buried in the national pantheon, St Paul's Cathedral, alongside Lord Nelson. The Duke of Wellington, something of a failure as prime minister in peacetime, would die within eighteen months of the 1851 census.

As an indication of the style of accommodation available in these newly established streets, 4 Victory Place (now called 'Elephant House') was built around 1840 to house single working men. It is a building of three storeys and an attic; originally, there were two sets of rooms on each of the three main floors, arranged on either side of a central staircase; that is, six independent chambers in total. This offered accommodation for at least two single men sharing a suite of rooms, perhaps with separate bedrooms and a communal living space, which would mean a minimum of twelve men in total. The kitchens and other facilities, such as for washing clothes, may have been in the basement, although single men would likely outsource such domestic chores to a local laundress like Elizabeth Ann Tinworth. The space as designed might suggest that the expected clientele for 4 Victory Place were office workers, whether those travelling across the river at London Bridge to the City, or via Waterloo Bridge to the West End and Inns of Court.*

However, reflecting the beginnings of the population explosion, with a corresponding increase in pressure on housing stock, the 7 December 1848 issue of the *Morning Herald* reported an accident that had occurred in Victory Place in May of that year, now the subject of a court case for damages. A woman, resident at 4 Victory Place, had left her young child playing in the road one afternoon, presumably to allow her to get on with domestic chores or paid piecework. Within minutes, the mother heard dray horses turn into the street, pulling a heavily laden wagon. She ran to the front door, but no sooner had she glimpsed her child sitting on a small dirt mound on the far side of the street, than the wagon, loaded with manure, blocked her view. The carman driving it said that the child may have wandered out from a garden in front of 4 Victory Place; the first he knew of its presence in the road was on seeing the infant 'in a falling position against the wheel'. The newspaper account included the witness statements of two unnamed neighbours; if the timings are correct, one could easily have been Jane Tinworth; George was aged five, and, in December 1848 she would soon be pregnant with her second surviving son, Thomas.

In her testimony, the injured child's mother said:

> Her first impulse was to look for the driver of the waggon, but there was no driver to be seen, and before she could get up to the child, one wheel of the waggon had passed along the left leg of the child from the knee to the foot. Having picked the

---

*According to a conservation document produced for Southwark Council, Elephant House, the lone remaining example, 'was once one of the many properties fronting on to Victory Place ... It is an early example of this type of social housing ... representing the once numerous 19th-century model dwellings for the lower classes.' As such, it is listed as a building of national importance. (See www.southwark.gov.uk, *Yates Estate and Victory Conservation Area Appraisal*, 2024, p. 14.)

child up, she again looked for the driver, but did not see him near the horses, and her conviction was, that had the driver been with the horses the accident would not have occurred.[8]

By his own admission, the carman, who should have been controlling the horses, had only minutes before been speaking to a Mrs Robinson, and he was distracted as a result.

A surgeon confirmed the infant's injuries were severe, as was the suffering it had caused; in all likelihood, 'the child would be lame for life'. The reporter noted the judge's observation, made in his summing-up, that 'no one could doubt that there had been negligence in allowing the child to walk about the road alone'. This chastisement, aimed at the working-class mother, was easily said by a middle-class man, no doubt accustomed to a wife, servants and the assistance of nannies. Even so, the judge continued, 'if the jury thought that the carman had not taken proper care in driving the cart – that he had an opportunity of avoiding the child, and did not, then his master ... was liable'. The jury took an hour to decide for the child and its family, with damages of £10 awarded.[9] This sum, although sizeable to a poor working-class family and very welcome as a result, would have to stretch to a lifetime of disability if the surgeon's assessment was correct. The National Health Service would not exist for another hundred years. For those whose day-to-day lives exposed them to a constant threat of illness or injury, the separation between being healthy and lame was the work of an instant.

Three years later, in 1851, the Tinworth family members resident at 8 Victory Place are named as Joshua (thirty-seven), Jane (thirty-six), George (eight), Thomas (two) and Charles (two months). Also registered at the same building was John Hubbard, a labourer of seventy years born in Clapham; his wife Elizabeth (sixty-one), a laundress born in the nearby parish of St Saviour's near London Bridge; their son-in-law John Rogers (thirty-six), a plasterer, born in Newington; daughter Ann Rogers (thirty-four, no profession); and their grandchildren, all also born in Newington: Elizabeth (nine), Ellen (seven), John (five) and Annie (two months). This family either had live-in domestic help in the form of a 'servant', Mary Graham, aged eighteen, again from Newington, or else Mary was their lodger. It is notable that most of these individuals had been born within adjoining or nearby parishes. (A separate entry, but part of the same Rogers household, named an 'Eliza Abbott', aged twenty-six.)

Beyond the Tinworth and Hubbard-Rogers families, 8 Victory Place was also home to George White, a married thirty-year-old 'labourer to Iron works' who was not, according to the census, living with his wife or a family. The iron required for London's infrastructure, bridges and items of street furniture was made in privately owned ironworks across London. George White would have worked at one such business within walking distance of his digs in Southwark, some of which were located at Bankside, to the north. Finally, alongside the Tinworths, Hubbards, Rogers and George White, there was a family of four, the Lelants: George, aged thirty-one and a 'lady's shoe maker', his wife Ann, aged twenty-three, a lady's shoe-binder, and their sons George (four) and Henry, who was, like Charles Tinworth and Annie Rogers, just a few months old.[10]

In his memoir, George recalled that at the Lock's Fields house, possibly Victory Place, 'I got to know a poor shoe maker boy' who 'bought ingravings of church windows and coloured them' to sell. This child taught George how to add different colour paint to the black and white prints of the stained glass designs, concluding that this friendship was 'another step towards art'.[11] This enterprising boy cannot be either George Lelant or his younger brother Henry, the sons of shoemakers, both of whom were younger (rather than 'much older') than George Tinworth, but the trade was represented elsewhere within the building and in nearby houses on the same street. It is striking that George placed equal importance on the 'human statues' of Camberwell Fair, the pawn-shop china figures and the hand-coloured engravings by a shoemaker's son as he did on the formal training he received at the prestigious Royal Academy of Arts: knowledge based on observation, gathered informally, not reliant on an expensive education, but rooted in the everyday experiences of the metropolis. This was the modus operandi of other London-born artistes, including Charlie Chaplin.

If 8 Victory Place, like the neighbouring building, was designed as accommodation for single working men, the same accommodation was, within a decade of its creation, the home of eleven adults (a mix of labourers and artisans) and nine children, three of whom were babes-in-arms. Those residents who were craftspeople, such as shoemakers, could take in piecework to carry out from home, while other residents used the yards and gardens for less discreet forms of business, such as animal husbandry. Using common land, like Walworth Common, for grazing would have been run-of-the-mill in this area – Walworth had only recently begun to develop into a recognisable suburb of London – but even so, the nineteenth-century local experience would have included noises and smells now associated with a rural farmyard. George recalled, while the family were living in Milk Street, 'a large pig had wanderd a way from a farm dairy at the other end of the lane when he got up to were I was I jumped on his back'.[12] In the Sherlock Holmes mystery 'The Blue Carbuncle' (first published in the *Strand Magazine* in January 1892), a precious gem is hidden in the crop of a goose reared in a Lambeth backyard.[13] Arthur Conan Doyle was simply using an everyday urban trade to provide a cunning plot device.

What close neighbours might have thought of a yard full of geese, honking night and day, is not explored. But in 1852, the *London Evening Standard* reported on an incident on Victory Place that caused 'GROSS NUISANCE'. Robert Wood, a small tradesman, was charged with keeping pigs 'to the great annoyance and risk of health of his neighbours'. This was a problem across London. Mrs Gaskell, next door, reported that she and her family 'had suffered considerably by the offensive smell caused by the pigs, and during the close and heavy weather she frequently felt so ill from the effects of the unpleasant smell that she felt no appetite for, and could not eat, her breakfast'. Wood declared that the complaint against him had occurred 'merely through feelings of spite, but promised to do away with the cause in a fortnight'. The magistrate permitted the summons to stand for such a time, during which the offending swine would be slaughtered.[14]

With animals and humans living cheek by jowl during a population boom, we might wonder how waste was managed. Animal manure could be repurposed for horticulture and agriculture: the cart that caused the infant injury was carrying a large amount of manure. Sewers were not sanctioned to be constructed in Victory Place, Walworth Road and New Kent Road until 1857.[15] Prior to this date, some solid waste was collected by night soil men going door to door, but the public thoroughfares and waterways would have resembled open sewers and dumps for general waste, and stank accordingly. The Thames was London's main source of drinking water. The impact of poor sanitation on health reached a critical stage in 1831, when cholera arrived in London, adding to the deaths from other water-borne diseases such as typhoid. After nationwide epidemics of influenza and typhoid in 1837 and 1838 there was a government inquiry into sanitation, resulting in the publication of Edwin Chadwick's *Sanitary Conditions of the Labouring Population* in 1842. This would lead to the overhaul of the sewers and the embanking of the Thames.

Despite the opportunities for learning available to the lower classes, George Tinworth does not mention receiving formal education at any point during his handwritten memoir – but this was not the experience of his younger brothers Thomas and Charles, who are both listed as 'scholars' in the 1861 census (they were then aged twelve and ten).[16] In the early nineteenth century there was enough support in Parliament for the establishment of a universal system of elementary schooling, and it was accepted that this schooling should have a moral core. But there was division on who should provide it. The Anglicans? Or, given the range of Christian churches, should it be non-denominational? In 1833, faced again with the 'religious question', and hopeful that voluntary efforts might be enough without major state intervention, the Whig government decided to give money to both the Church of England and the Nonconformists through the grant-in-aid of schoolhouses. The Factory Act in that same year is part of the story, in that social reformers, including Lord Ashley, were keen that young children should be off the streets and attending school – partly to receive basic skills in reading (and some writing) but mainly for moral instruction. The Factory Act excluded children under the age of nine from working and mandated that those children, aged nine to thirteen, who did work should have two hours of schooling per day, although the enforcement mechanisms were weak.

The Committee of the Council on Education was established in 1839 to manage the new policy and inspectorate via 'minutes' presented to and debated in Parliament: grant money for schools became dependent on inspection, and the minutes reshaped the teaching profession, for example in the establishment of teacher training. James Phillips Kay was the chief civil servant appointed to run the committee and its president was Lord Lansdowne. In 1856, the Education Committee became absorbed into a new Education Department.[17]

Despite all this positive activity at state level from the 1840s, when George Tinworth was a student at the Lambeth School of Art two decades later, his modelling master told him he 'should be in a better position' in his education 'then [than] I was[,] so he lent me two grammer books and I tride to make use of them … but I thought more of modeling then I though[t] about nowns and pronowns allthow I thanked him all the same'.[18] Elsewhere, George's biographers state that he learned to read from consulting the Bible, probably under the instruction of his mother, Jane. As this suggests, home learning continued deep into the nineteenth century. David Vincent's study, *Literacy and Popular Culture* (1989) revealed that a child, outside of school, was more likely to learn to read and write if their mother was literate, connected to habitual child-rearing roles, and how teaching might be combined with other domestic tasks. The fathers were more likely to pass on occupational skills, which was certainly the situation within the Tinworth household.

The Elementary Education Act of 1870 introduced compulsory education and allowed schools run by the church societies, as historian Rosalind Crone explains, 'to continue unchanged. However, where there was a deficiency of school accommodation, or where local rate-payers demanded it, a school board could be established with the power to build and run schools and to draw on local rates for funding.'[19] School boards were permitted to use by-laws to compel attendance. (This was the case until the 1880 Education Act, when the state compelled attendance, again through local government mechanisms.) Victory Place Primary School was one of the first 'Board' schools to be built in the metropolis, which highlighted the need for provision in the neighbourhood. In February 1873, the *South London Press* reported the agreement to purchase 'the freehold of a site in Victory-place, Walworth, having fifteen houses upon it, at the price of £1,900'.[20] Perhaps 8 Victory Place was one of the houses pulled down to make way for the new school, which opened in 1875: twenty-five years too late for George Tinworth, but just in time for the next generation, which included Hannah Chaplin (born 1865), and then her children, Syd and Charlie. In fact, according to a former teacher, Victory Place Primary School was one of several institutions attended by Charlie Chaplin in the mid-1890s.[21] But we also know, from his own recollections as well as official documents, that Charlie's schooling was piecemeal at best: his experience reveals the ongoing challenge in enforcing consistent attendance.

The inns and public houses in the immediate vicinity of Victory Place, and therefore Joshua Tinworth's regular haunts while he was living here, included the Victory, built in the mid-nineteenth century on Barlow Street, a road where Charlie Chaplin lived in the 1890s with his mother and brother, and the Gloucester Arms on Mason Street, which opened in 1839. Meanwhile, as Joshua was habitually drinking away his income, Jane was watching the pennies. George recalled that the local baker's shop would advertise the price of a loaf of bread in large letters in the window. When the economy improved, he would watch every day as the prices fell from the top price of fourteen pence a loaf, by one halfpenny at a time, and he would run home to tell his mother.[22] As the social reformer and member of the Fabian Society, Maud Pember Reeves, would later observe: 'To manage a husband and six children in three rooms on round about £1 a week needs, first and foremost, wisdom and loving-kindness, and after that as much cleanliness and order as can be squeezed in.'[23] Irregular income naturally introduced uncertainty, and even chaos. Another well-meaning middle-class observer, Helen Bosanquet, considered this 'the great problem' with the poor working class. The key, she concluded, was 'how to bring them to regard life as anything but a huge chaos. The

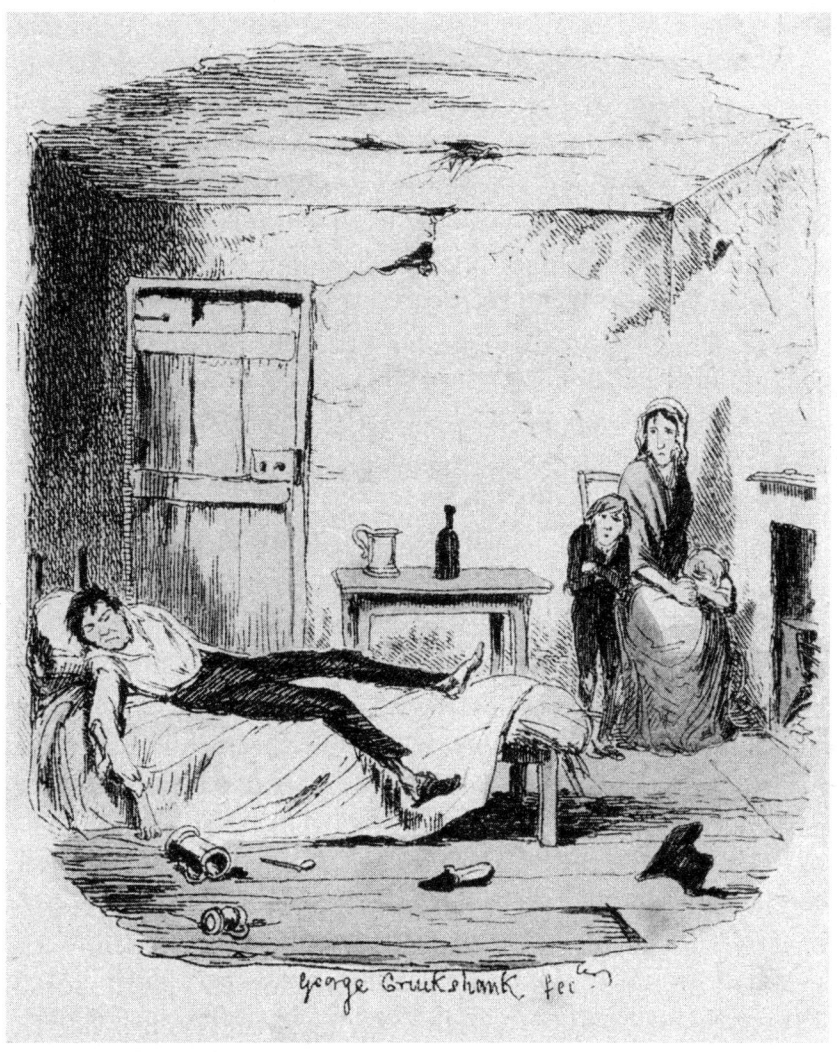

George Cruikshank's *The Drunkard's Home* (published around 1842). Cruikshank had been a heavy drinker, but in the 1840s he became an ardent supporter of the temperance movement. To promote the cause, he produced images such as this, evoking the poverty and despair brought on by alcohol abuse.

confusion which reigns in their minds is reflected in their worlds, and the constant expectation that "something will turn up" is the nearest approach to a law – whether of nature or morality – which they know.'[24]

The suffragist Anna Martin noted that household management was where power rested for working-class women; regarding the provision of school meals, for example, after the 1870 Education Act, she noted that 'the women have a vague dread of being superseded and dethroned. Each of them knows perfectly well that the strength of her position in the homes lies in the physical dependency of her husband and children upon her and she is suspicious of anything that would tend to undermine this.'[25] An unintended consequence of compulsory schooling was the removal of children from the labour market, reducing income for families that replied upon it. Some in authority recognised this conundrum and as a result would act leniently towards the parents of truants.

George Tinworth offers many examples of Jane's role as a steadying influence on the family. One December, he recalled, his father had repaired a pair of wheels for a customer at New Cross in Lewisham but, as Christmas Day arrived, the client still had not paid him. Joshua and George were forced to go to New Cross that morning, to demand the money owed. Returning to Walworth, they persuaded a local grocer to open his shop so they could buy ingredients for a Christmas meal: 'My mother was a good cook and soon made the dinner. She made six small Christmas puddings instead of one big one', for which there was no time to cook. '"Now", my father said to me, "you can tell the boys you have had six Christmas puddings this Christmas".'[26] Both George Tinworth and Charlie Chaplin reveal the importance of meals in working-class culture: food was a necessity for life, but how it was cooked and served was significant too. And the Christmas Day meal, after Sunday dinner, was the most important of all. Perhaps the seasonal present from the Fishmongers' Company, while the family rented in Milk Street, was a much-prized goose for the Christmas table?

Crucially, the Tinworths were clearly living hand-to-mouth at this time; however accomplished Jane was in eking out a Christmas

George Cruikshank's series *The Bottle* of 1847 depicted the effect of excessive alcohol consumption through eight connected scenes, in imitation of William Hogarth's famous engraved 'progresses' on modern moral subjects. The subscript for Plate VI (above) reads 'fearful quarrels and brutal violence are the natural consequences of the frequent use of the bottle.'

meal at the eleventh hour, there must have been an appearance of poverty about the family. The strain on the marriage must have been immense. Joshua's reported interest in the impression he gave, as the breadwinner, through the visible state of his family and the food his income could provide is a subtle hint of the fragility of their lives, the small visible differences that signalled survival or destitution. George does not recount directly what Jane thought of this constant struggle to feed and clothe her children, all while managing her husband's increasing malevolence towards an unforgiving world and everyone in it. That she was kind, caring and protective towards her children comes through powerfully, alongside her resourcefulness and, crucially, her calm resolve to survive, whatever life threw at them.

Despite her efforts, George recounted the following event while the family were living in Lock's Fields:

> One Christmas Eve when I was a small boy I got sliding on the path as it was slippery an old man come along and caught hold of me <he carried a blue bag I remember> and said come to the workhouse[.] I went with him a little way then I got away from him ran home and never come out any more that day and that is the first time I remember any thing about New Kent Road.*27

This recollection is one of only two references by George Tinworth to the institution that all working-class people feared.† If the Tinworths, or any of their relations, had ever entered a workhouse or even received poor relief from the parish, then George does not draw attention to it. Such was the reputation of the workhouse that George stayed at home for the rest of the day, fearing another encounter with the old man.

Why did this stranger want to take a child to the workhouse? Giving him the benefit of the doubt, perhaps George's presence in the street on Christmas Eve, looking hungry and wearing worn, even ragged, clothes, the man believed the only course of action was to bring him under the care of local poor relief, where, at least, a bed and a Christmas Day meal would be available.

Whatever the scenario, this anecdote has a rather Dickensian quality. The writer's second novel, *Oliver Twist; or, The Parish Boy's Progress* was serialised in *Bentley's Miscellany* between 1837 and 1839 and published as a three-volume book in 1838 – just five years before George Tinworth was born, and around ten years prior to this incident. It is generally assumed that Mr Bumble's workhouse, where the orphan Oliver spends his early life, is modelled on a real-life institution, and the St George-the-Martyr workhouse on Mint

---

*Here, and below, all inserted additions to manuscript sources are flagged in my quotations within <angled brackets>.
†The second concerned a tragedy, which occurred when thousands of people gathered to hear a popular Baptist preacher, the Reverend Charles Spurgeon, at the Surrey Gardens Music Hall in 1856. Panic spread through the crowd causing a crush and, according to George, the dead (numbering eight) were taken to the Newington Workhouse in Walworth (GTA, p. 22).

Street near Borough is one prime candidate. As a twelve-year-old in 1824, Dickens had lodged in Lant Street, parallel to Mint Street, while his parents and other family members were living in the Marshalsea Debtors' Prison, located behind a long, tall perimeter wall adjoining the parish church and graveyard of St George-the-Martyr. The Marshalsea would be central to Dickens's novel *Little Dorrit*, first published as a magazine serial between 1855 and 1857.

George Tinworth noted that this encounter with a local workhouse was his first impression of the New Kent Road, a major thoroughfare bordering Lock's Fields at its northern edge. There had been a workhouse on this road, at the junction with Newington Street, from around 1814, but it was destroyed by fire just three years later.[28] The two main institutions in the immediate area were the St George-the-Martyr workhouse on Mint Street, and Christ Church-St Saviour's workhouse on Marlborough Street, to the west of Blackfriars Road and just south of the popular market street called the New Cut. Yet another workhouse was located in south Walworth, originally on Walworth Road and then, after 1858, on Westmoreland Road, Walworth Common. This was variously called the Walworth and then Newington Workhouse, as it was managed by the parish of St Mary Newington. It was in its latter incarnation that Hannah Chaplin and her two young sons would encounter the provision available for local paupers later in the century.

Before 1834, workhouses were managed under the Poor Law of 1601, whereby residents of a parish paid rates used to support the destitute, either in the workhouse itself, or in the form of money and food, so that the individual or family could remain in their home. Under the Old Poor Law, the poor had a right to relief in their parish of settlement. In *An Account of Several Work-houses for Employing and Maintaining the Poor,* published in the early eighteenth century, the case for workhouses was set out in the preface:

> this Method of maintaining the Poor, has met with Approbation and Success throughout the Kingdom. And indeed a better Method can scarce be contrived; for Workhouses, under a prudent and good Management, will answer all the Ends of

Charity *to the* Poor, *in regard to their Souls and Bodies: and yet at the same time prove* effectual Expedients for encreasing our Manufactures, as well as removing a heavy Burden from the Nation.²⁹

The St George-the-Martyr workhouse in Mint Street was here given a glowing account. By October 1731, sixty-eight men, women and children had been admitted. Twenty-five children were provided with basic education, that is learning to read, and taught to say the Protestant catechism.³⁰ It is worth observing that they were receiving a better formal education than the vast majority of their peers beyond the workhouse walls.

Those who followed the rules regarding work – spinning and knitting – were entitled to one penny for every shilling their work earned 'and the rest, who do other necessary Business in the Family, such as dressing the Victuals, Nursing, Washing, cleaning the House, and the like, shall also be allowed such Encouragement Money as their Service shall deserve'. Yet if the money earned was spent on 'Liquors' and the inmates 'disorder themselves', then 'they shall be severely punished'.³¹ The author noted that most of the local parishes in the area south of the Thames had established large workhouses, and 'as fast as there is any Vacancy, Interest is made by the Poor themselves to be admitted'.³² The London section of *An Account of Several Work-houses* concludes with a summary regarding the forty-eight workhouses and the established charity schools within a five-mile radius of central London, most built since the Relief of the Poor Act (1723), during the reign of George I, which collectively maintained and, if able, set to work around four thousand 'Poor, Old and Young'.³³

By the 1820s, the system described a hundred years earlier was criticised for being too lenient. Some thought it was actively encouraging pauperism by undermining the impetus for independent work and, in so doing, was misusing rate-payers' money, as well as impacting negatively on the nation's moral health. In addition, by the early nineteenth century, in some places outdoor relief was being used to supplement low wages (especially of agricultural workers) or to pay seasonal workers when they had no work. This, coupled with the poor's right to relief in their parish of settlement, led to a rapidly rising welfare bill in the changing socio-economic circumstances over the decade and into the early 1830s. And hence demands for reform.

In 1832, the Poor Law Commission (based in central London) undertook a nationwide survey of poor relief, which resulted in the New Poor Law of 1834.* Under this new legislation, outdoor relief was dramatically limited and was now the exception, while residency at the workhouse became the rule: the destitute were directed to the workhouse, which was made as unpleasant a place and experience as possible. Individual parishes formed into 'unions' that were tasked with providing workhouse accommodation for local paupers. These local unions could seek advice and clarity from the Poor Law Commission (and its later iterations) regarding rules, practices and standards.† Just a year later, St George-the-Martyr was constituted as a Poor Law parish and a Board of Governors was elected. The population overseen by this union, as evident from data provided by the 1831 census, was 39,769, with the average annual poor-rate expenditure for 1832 to 1834 calculated as £20,642.[34]

In 1836, the neighbouring parishes to St George-the-Martyr, St Saviour's and Christ Church, joined forces to create the St Saviour's Poor Law Union. (St George-the-Martyr, managing the Mint Street workhouse, joined this union in 1869 and in 1901 this enlarged union was renamed the Southwark Union.) By the 1840s, the workhouse on Marlborough Street was technically under the management of 'St Saviour's' (it is called 'St. Saviour's Workhouse' on Charles Booth's map from later in the nineteenth century),[35] but through local habit it was often known as 'Christ Church' Workhouse due to its proximity to that parish church on Blackfriars Road. To avoid confusion, this workhouse on Marlborough Street will be referred to as Christ Church-St Saviour's.

---

*Also known as the Poor Law Amendment Act
†This correspondence is now housed at The National Archives (MH12), and formed part of a major research project on material relating to Poor Law Unions; see King, Carter, et al. (2022).

The St Saviour's Poor Law Union formally came into being on 11 February 1836, when seventeen 'guardians' were elected to the board representing the two parishes of St Saviour's and Christ Church. Just prior to the passing of the 1834 Poor Law Amendment Act and the subsequent formation of the union, a new workhouse had been built on Marlborough Street, located in the wedge of land bordered by the New Cut to the north and Blackfriars Road to the east. An impressive classical building designed by George Allen, it fronted Marlborough Street, with the dining room and work room on the ground floor, and washrooms, the cook house, nursery, and the male and female wards surrounding a courtyard at the rear. As reported in the *Morning Advertiser* on 22 April 1840, several years after it had opened, a regular vestry meeting was held to elect churchwardens, overseers and other parochial officers. The discussion that followed began with a report from the Guardians of the Infant Poor. These children were housed in a separate building at Norwood to the south. The guardians 'found the boys thoroughly acquainted with history, geography, Scriptures, drawing, and other mental and scientific acquirements, and which they attributed to the introduction of the new poor law'. Again, if this is an honest description of what was happening on the ground, then this is a high level of formal education, a 'positive' result of the 1834 Poor Law, which was not available to the general working-class populace at the time – including Joshua Tinworth and his sons.

That said, education within the workhouses was in competition with the work each inmate was expected to undertake: depending on the workhouse master, time for school each day was limited and could be interrupted. Workhouse schools (like some other schools) aimed to lift the child out of their environment, but also taught the child to despise their parents for 'bringing' them to such a sorry state. And, in any case, the conditions of life in the workhouse could override any benefits of the education the children may have gained. Charlie Chaplin's experience of life in the workhouse and associated pauper schools bears out the pros and cons (mainly the latter) of the system as it had become towards the end of the century: generally considered a more humane system than that of the 1840s to 1860s, but one that still left deep emotional scars.

The same group of guardians had also visited the new workhouse on Marlborough Street, 'which they were sorry to say was insufficient for the accommodation of the poor who were sent there'. One of the officers, Mr Clarke, as well as a Mr Mayhew – possibly the journalist and social reformer Henry Mayhew – spoke in disparaging terms concerning this institution. The latter sarcastically declared that he was satisfied that the institution 'was only fit to place the poor people in, provided it was the wish of the parish that they should die off daily'. Mr Mayhew continued, referring to a recent visit to the cells of Newgate, the infamous prison in the City, that 'he could assure the vestry these cells were preferable to those in the workhouse'. At Newgate, he observed, 'the felon breathed a pure atmosphere, which was not the case at the workhouse'. Here 'cells', where the pauper 'inmates' were kept, had a drain running underneath, causing damp in the rooms. He proceeded to relay the conditions he witnessed, including, even on warm days, how the grounds, where inmates might exercise, were as water-logged 'as if a heavy rain had fallen'. Perhaps worst of all was the use of broken glass bottles along the top of the wall separating the men from the women, 'for the purpose', as Mayhew supposed, 'to prevent an old man and woman from speaking to each other'. 'Shame!' came the cry from his audience.

If Mayhew's description is correct, then a pauper, once within the workhouse, was not only subjected to rank air and sodden floors, but was also separated from family and friends, who had to apply for a 'special order' if they wished to visit, while husbands and wives were kept apart by a high wall and jagged shards of glass. If the intention was to assist those who had fallen on difficult times, then a more depressing and intimidating environment is hard to imagine. No one who had listened to this account seemed astonished that a building less than ten years old was already unfit for purpose. It seems the shift, as a principle, from outdoor to indoor relief was swiftly straining Poor Law accommodation to breaking point.

What did exercise 'to distraction' the gathered officials and guardians was how much this failure of care was costing. For also described in this issue of the *Morning Advertiser* was the Overseers Report, which stated that in the years 1834, 1835 and 1836, the average annual expenditure for the poor was £5,954 11s 7d, which had risen to £7,900 between March 1839 and March 1840. Some of those gathered despaired vociferously that so much money had been wasted. The report observed that 'the new workhouse was deficient in ventilation, that the wards for the men were very confined, and next to the dead-house, the stench from which was extremely offensive, particularly to those who visited their relatives, and that they regretted that so many thousand pounds had been expended on the place'.[36]

The recent change in the provision for the poor and its management was in turn criticised by observers, who considered it cruel as well as a waste of rate-payers' money. Chief among them was George Robert Wythen Baxter, who, like Mayhew, emotively likened the workhouses under the new regime to nothing short of incarceration in a dungeon; in his *The Book of the Bastiles; or, The History of the Working of the New Poor-Law* (1841), the term 'Bastiles' alluded to the notorious prison in Paris, whose storming in July 1789 ignited the French Revolution. The idea that the threat of the workhouse should act as a deterrent to discourage 'misuse' of local charity by the lower classes, and, conversely, as an impetus to find work, was a significant change in attitude towards the poor.

Four years after Baxter's book was published, a letter to the editor appeared in *Lloyd's Weekly Newspaper* concerning the Christ Church-St Saviour's workhouse and the new system of 'Poor Law Union Bastiles' in general. In it, the author declared:

> let us hope that the attempts made to cramp individual generosity and proper feeling towards those whose hearts and hopes have been bowed down by misfortune and misery – those whose tenure of life is but that of a day's purchase, and who are fast floating down the stream of eternity – let us hope, sir, that the 'bruised reed' may not be broken, and that no purse-proud pharasee may be permitted to interfere with

the good Samaritan who binds up the wounds of his fellow men.

This letter was signed, in large capitals for emphasis, by 'A RATE PAYER OF 18 YEARS STANDING'.[37]

Workhouse documentation, including admissions registers, offer brief details regarding the lives of those desperate enough to enter its walls. Even so, these long-forgotten individuals have, due to their difficulties, left some trace of their existence: more than most from the same background.

As an indication of the different people and their reasons for seeking such relief from poverty, the following is analysis from the year 1842 – just a year or so after Mr Mayhew described Christ Church-St Saviour's workhouse as worse than a prison, and the year after Joshua and James Tinworth's weddings at nearby Holy Trinity Church.[38] Among the residents of the Christ Church-St Saviour's workhouse were Ann Burk, a widow born in 1792, and her children Catherine (born in 1829) and Charles (born the following year). The Burks entered the workhouse because they were destitute, with Ann's recent widowhood and the consequent loss of the family's main breadwinner the likely cause. Another new inmate was Charlotte Hone, born in 1821 within the parish of St George-the-Martyr. She was an unmarried servant, listed as able-bodied, but in a state of temporary 'disability' for the reason that she was pregnant. Admission to a workhouse infirmary to receive some medical assistance before, during and after labour was one of very few options for poor, unmarried mothers.* Reform of workhouse nursing occurred from the 1860s, with schemes to train nurses for the workhouse infirmaries established in the 1870s, but 'elderly pauper women still acted as mid wives and childminders'.[39] Although these women often had experience in delivering newborns, there were concerns that older paupers could transfer diseases or be more susceptible to accidents, endangering babies and infants.

---

*By 1907, it has been calculated that 70 per cent of births in workhouses were illegitimate (Lewis (1984), p. 25).

Another new inmate in 1842 was William Palmer, born in 1794 (again in the parish of St George-the-Martyr), a widower seeking relief because he was 'destitute'. The same reason is given for Mary Clough, a widow who had worked throughout her life as a needlewoman. Lawrence Shaw was a married draper, born in the same parish in 1808. Lawrence's religion is listed as Catholic, his wife Elizabeth, born in 1817, also in St George's and able-bodied, is 'E.C.', meaning the Anglican or Established Church. Their sons were Daniel, born 1835, and Lawrence, born 1839, so at their admission around seven and three years of age. The Shaw family had not been claiming relief prior to entering the workhouse, but destitution necessitated this desperate move. It is likely that Lawrence simply could not find work selling textiles (whether as a merchant or shop assistant).

Bell West was born in 1756 – in 1842 she was in her eighties – again in the parish of St George-the-Martyr. She entered the world during the tail end of the reign of George II, was four years old when George III came to the throne, and had lived through the American War of Independence, the French Revolution, the Napoleonic Wars, the Great Reform Act and the accession of Queen Victoria in 1837. These events had likely impacted little on Bell's life, except to increase the burden of taxation on her, alongside every British citizen. One of the ironies of the Great Reform Act is that women were now officially excluded from voting – before that date they could technically vote as long as they were within the property criteria, but in reality very few did. During her adult life Bell had worked as a needlewoman, but she was now a widow, listed 'Old & Infirm' and, as a description of her illness, 'Insane'. Unusually for those admitted to Christ Church-St Saviour's workhouse in 1842, Bell would be discharged into the care of a relative, her niece, on 25 April 1843. Even so, by that time she had been resident in the workhouse for six months.

Also admitted in 1842 was pauper '1558', Joshua Tinworth's elder sister, Keziah.[40] She is listed as born in the parish of Lambeth, that is St Mary-at-Lambeth, where her parents James and Elizabeth Ann had been living at the time of their marriage in 1804. If she was still resident in Lambeth at the time of her admission to the workhouse, it is curious that she was not admitted to the local institution on Prince's Road, managed in the 1840s by a different poor relief union. Keziah's occupation is given as 'servant' and her marital status was single, so she may have been employed as a domestic to a family within the parishes of Christ Church or St Saviour's. Both were very close to where her parents and siblings were now resident.

Under the query as to whether Keziah is able-bodied, the admissions clerk has written 'no', with the further detail that she is considered 'Temp D' – temporarily disabled. To the question of whether she has been receiving poor relief prior to admission, the answer is 'no', but 'illness' is offered as the reason for her seeking relief, without a specific condition given. There is no mention of Keziah's family, who had been living in Milk Street prior to 1841, a mere thirty-minute walk from this workhouse. Her religion is listed as 'E.C.' – despite her being baptised at the nearby Nonconformist York Street Chapel in Lock's Fields – and she was admitted to the workhouse on 21 October 1842, a year before her nephew George was born.

Keziah Tinworth was discharged on 5 December 1842, her time in the workhouse lasting six weeks and four days: the reason for discharge is that she died, aged just thirty-one. She was buried on 9 December 1842.[41] In the workhouse register of deaths the burial ground is given as 'The Lock' and the ceremony was at the expense of 'The Parish', which means that the family, if they knew about her death, could not afford to pay for her funeral.[42] The Lock burial ground was, of course, in the area called Lock's Fields, which is where Keziah's brother Joshua and his family were living by 1851 and where the York Street Chapel was located.

There was no happy ending for Bell West; according to the register, she re-entered the Christ Church-St Saviour's workhouse in 1844, her condition recorded as 'Old & Infirm' and the cause for seeking relief listed as 'distress'. Bell died in the care of the St Saviour's Union aged eighty-eight and was buried at the Lock on 1 April 1846.[43]

In January 1846, while Bell West was still at the workhouse, the *Morning Post* reported a serious incident involving twenty-seven 'able-bodied young men, whose ages varied from sixteen to twenty-five, all of them miserably clad'. They were brought before the magistrate, Mr Traill, 'charged with creating a disturbance and destroying property'. At that time a Mr Bonser, the master, had been awoken in the early hours of the morning by police, who told him that a riot had taken place in the Casual Paupers' Ward, an area offering temporary beds (usually by the night) rather than longer-term residency. As the master approached the workhouse, he heard doors and windows smashing and cries of 'Murder!' The entrance to the ward had been barricaded with wheelbarrows and stones, and when he and the police entered – with a shower of stones thrown at them – 'the scene of destruction was fully displayed before them'. There were broken barrows and pails, blankets strewn about, and several of the defendants were running about naked, attacking their fellows in the ward who refused to join the riot. The workhouse master confirmed that the rioters were not of the parish and therefore had no claim on its relief provision. The distress caused to the occupants who just wanted to live quietly within its walls, or those who were hoping for a safe bed and billet for the night, is evident from the statement of one witness, an old sailor who had been sleeping in the casual ward at the time of the incident. Between three and four o'clock in the morning he was attacked while lying in bed, dragged out and beaten. His waistcoat was taken from under his pillow, emptied of a little money and then thrown at his head, and he was struck hard in the face several times.[44]

The magistrate noted that the accused were all burly and able-bodied, men for whom the shelter offered by a workhouse was never intended. The authorities, he believed, should be given the power to refuse such people entry. He then sentenced eight of the defendants to six weeks' and five more to a month's imprisonment, all at the local House of Correction.[45]

The Globe reported another incident the following year, concerning Mary Green, 'a dirty looking female' who was arrested for being drunk and creating a disturbance. In court, the workhouse porter, Mr Stevens, recalled that the prisoner's husband had died six months before, leaving Mary and their five children destitute.

The court was told that the Board of Guardians had immediately given her assistance, burying her husband at the expense of the parish and providing food and money for those left behind. This suggests that she was in receipt of outdoor relief, which, despite recent changes encouraging in-house provision, was still offered to lone women with children. According to Stevens, no sooner had Mary received the money than she had spent it on alcohol, while the children were abandoned in the street (until they were removed to the workhouse). The reported drunken behaviour and 'riotous conduct' that had brought Mary Green before the magistrate had occurred several times since her husband's death and at various workhouses where she had sought relief.

On the occasion for which she was now in the dock, Mary had arrived 'in a state of intoxication' at Christ Church-St Saviour's workhouse, where she was given two loaves of bread. But because she was not offered money, Mary abused the staff with 'very disgusting and obscene language'. She was taken into custody and searched, at which point ninepence was found about her person.[46] In other words, Mary was seeking relief as if penniless, when she already had the means – albeit very limited – to buy food. One of the Poor Law guardians who was present in court declared that 'every comfort had been afforded to the prisoner, who, if sober and industrious, might be enable to gain a good living for herself and children'. The reality was that Mary was 'a confirmed drunkard, and every penny she got she expended in gin. She had also stripped the children for the same purpose'; the suggestion is that Mary was selling or pawning her children's clothes to feed her addiction. The magistrate remembered her from two previous court appearances – which was unfortunate, as sympathy for her obvious plight was now in very short supply. He considered her to be 'a very depraved character, and deserved to be severely punished'. She was sentenced to ten days in custody, with the guardian present promising 'to take charge of the children and supply them with every necessary during her imprisonment'.[47]

Mr and Mrs Bonser were still the master and matron of Christ Church-St Saviour's workhouse in 1856, when another incident was reported concerning 'A DANGEROUS PAUPER' by the name of

Ellen Petty. Ellen is described as a middle-aged inmate, appearing in court in her workhouse clothes and accused of a violent assault on Mrs Bonser herself. According to Ann Bonser, Ellen had been an inmate for several years and, although at times physically aggressive, 'she received every indulgence that could be afforded her'. One indulgence was that she was allowed to wander about the workhouse without supervision, but on one occasion the matron was walking through the dining hall when Ellen sprang from a hiding place and struck her so violently on the head that Mrs Bonser's hair comb snapped, leaving her injured. Two other inmates prevented Ellen from assaulting Mrs Bonser further, all while she threatened to murder her victim, until Mr Bonser appeared and handed Ellen over to a police constable. The master, who was present in court, could not explain Ellen's behaviour towards his wife; she had a history of committing assaults within the workhouse, but Mrs Bonser had hoped kindness and patience might alter Ellen's manner: 'The prisoner, who was extremely violent during the examination, called all the witnesses liars and other opprobrious names.' The magistrate declared her a dangerous woman who must be put under restraint 'for some time'. The sentence was six weeks in prison with hard labour.[48]

These stories of violent behaviour from workhouse inmates may have given the readership of local newspapers – poor-rate payers among them – the impression that this was typical of the paupers in their area and those whom, at great expense, they were compelled by law to support. No one seems to have queried why Mary Green or Ellen Petty behaved the way they did; there was no hint of understanding that the sudden removal of the main breadwinner and the relentless stress of pauperism might strain the balance of some minds to a dramatic crisis. Regarding workhouse inmates, a quiet, compliant surrender to one's fate was preferred by the authorities.

Joshua Tinworth's drunkenness and violent outbursts, only hinted at by his eldest son, were a direct result of the grind of hand-to-mouth existence with no safety nets, beyond the kindness of neighbours or parish poor relief. The truth is that the vast majority of people did not enter the workhouse through laziness or as a lifestyle choice. Rather, they were unable to support themselves for whatever reason – age, pregnancy, mental health issues – and had nowhere else to go. It was a case of either starvation or survival as an inmate, branded as a pauper, for which the individual surrendered autonomy, dignity and, under such a demoralising regime, a sense of self. There is also a feeling, from the relief providers, that those who had placed themselves in the care of the Board of Guardians and the workhouse master would be subjected to any treatment as a result. Others now controlled all aspects of their lives. The poor were discouraged from seeking assistance, through the associated shame if they did: someone contemplating entering the institution would have to be very desperate indeed. Keziah Tinworth, for example, fell ill and could not afford medical care – and nor, we must assume, could her family – so she, like many others, turned to the provision offered by a workhouse infirmary.

Mr and Mrs Bonser appear to have managed the Christ Church-St Saviour workhouse with kindness and consideration. Everything depended on the quality and compassion of these managers. An advertisement on 8 September 1840 offered a salary of £100 per annum for the position of master, plus £40 for that of the matron – expected to be husband and wife – with the additional benefit of free board and lodging. This would be a considerable financial inducement for anyone to apply, whatever their attitude to inmate care. To deter undesirables, a £300 security on application plus sealed testimonials regarding 'character and capability' were required.[49] Nevertheless, inmates were constantly vulnerable to unscrupulous individuals entering a profession which, by many, was considered a necessary evil: master or not, you were tainted by association and your workplace was your home. There is also a sense that, like a prison, the master and matron ruled over those within their care with little monitoring – or even curiosity – from outside. And the master's responsibility for each inmate extended to the grave, as a scandal that occurred at a workhouse near to Christ Church-St Saviour's illustrates: it was one of the two workhouses with which the Chaplin family would become intimately associated just decades later.

By 1850 the old Newington Workhouse on Walworth Road

was plagued by overcrowding, highlighted by a cholera outbreak which had swept London in 1849: of the twenty registered deaths due to cholera in the Newington area, fifteen were those of inmates.[50] A new orphanage and school on Westmoreland Road, intended to house up to 300 poor children, was adapted and expanded as an infirmary for 70 to 100 poor adults, while accommodating 460 other paupers. The children in residence, like the St Saviour's Infant Paupers, were sent to an institution to the south, at Anerley near Norwood. The bleakly monumental building on Westmoreland Road was designed by Henry Jarvis, perhaps in the spirit of the hardened attitude towards the poor as formalised within the 1834 Act, a law that changed attitudes towards the poor, whose dilemmas were now seen as self-inflicted. The term 'inmate', in common usage for those housed within the workhouse, added to the sense that such institutions were prisons by another name.

In late March 1857, the destination of the reporter from the *Shoreditch Observer* was Newington Workhouse, by reason of the 'strict system laid down by the Poor Law Board having been frequently stigmatised in my presence as one of cruelty and oppression, whilst waste and extravagance which I had often vainly expostulated against were honoured by the titles of kindness and liberality to the poor'. He and his companion, after walking through the 'several narrow dingy streets' of poor working-class Walworth,[51] eventually arrived at the workhouse on Westmoreland Road. They presented their names to the porter for entry in the visitors' book, and then 'ascended to a stone causeway, white and clean as a gentleman's terrace, and arrived at the master's office'. The reporter and his friend were then taken on a tour of the workhouse by the master himself. He noted the master's centrally positioned residence, which separated the male and female wards. They then entered the chapel, which doubled as a dining room: a 'capacious and lofty room, where our attention was attracted to the grained beams and roofing and were informed that the whole of the painting and graining in the establishment was done by the pauper inmates under proper supervision'. They walked past supply rooms, where bread, butter and cheese were prepared, and the kitchens with coppers for cooking meat. They then inspected the dormitories, which they found to be clean and airy, with iron bedsteads, flock mattresses and bolsters, two sheets, two blankets and a rug, the materials and condition of which 'gave evidence of cleanliness and comfort, and sufficient to afford warmth to the most aged'. There was one inmate to every bed; they retired to bed around seven or eight o'clock at night and arose at seven in the morning. After breakfast, those who were able proceeded to their daily labour in the yard: stone-breaking and wood-chopping, which the reporter describes as having 'no appearance of being an amusement'. Of course, the workhouse was not intended as a permanent place for the able-bodied, who, according to the rules, should be seeking work beyond its walls. Next to the work yard were two large paved courtyards for the inmates to exercise, 'weather permitting'.

The elderly were employed in picking oakum, a loose fibre produced by untwisting or 'picking' old rope, 'not as a test of labour' or in lieu of the cost of their 'relief', but, as described by the reporter, 'to prevent the evils arising from the "having nothing to do"'. Idle people are, the reporter observed, the most likely to grumble, and besides, 'oakum having been previously beaten yielded more readily to the fingers, and ... the persons working at it fancied they were doing something useful – certainly they evinced no appearance of being dissatisfied' – hardly surprising, given the reporter was accompanied throughout the visit by the workhouse master.

The lunch bell rang, signalling midday, on the sound of which the inmates gathered in the hall, males on one side, females on the other; the master with two assistant officers served each the allotted portions – five ounces of cooked meat and twelve ounces of boiled potatoes. The meat, the reporter declared, 'was extremely good, and the joints were cut up in an expeditious and artistic style'. A signal was given for all inmates to rise for 'grace', after which the meal commenced and the master with his assistants then dispensed the food for the infirm, sick and infant inmates. The reporter was shown the accounts, from which he noted that 5 ounces of meat was allowed three times a week, on two days 1½ pints of soup with 5 ounces of bread, and on the final two days, 14 ounces of

A Workhouse Dinner by Phiz [Hablot Knight Browne] from James Grant's *Sketches in London* (1840). The author describes a woman aged sixty, who had lived in comfort, but now reduced to entering the workhouse: 'she felt as if she were an outcast from the world: the heart-harrowing conviction took possession of her mind, that she must never again expect to hear the whisper of sympathy, nor see the hand of friendship extended to administer to her wants'.

suet pudding. After an hour, the inmates returned to their various occupations. The reporter noted that provision for supper was the same as for breakfast – 7 ounces of bread and one pint of gruel, and, for the older, more infirm inmates, tea with bread and butter. The reporter then observed that this system of 'comfort with care' and 'method with economy' was so successful that the number of inmates had dropped from 800 to 550, the inference being that offering a healthy, temporary environment assisted in reducing the pressure on the workhouse facility, with the effect of reducing the parish rates. The reporter and his companion 'retired well pleased with all we had seen', only regretting that such a regimen was not universally followed.

Much of the reporting about the inmates and conditions within the workhouses – indeed the working-class experience as a whole – is filtered through the attitudes of the associated middle-class professionals, such as the workhouse-masters, surgeons, reporters and lawyers, and the social reformers. Some descriptions have the air of a scientific inspection involving a completely different species, or caged animals in a zoo. There are examples of undercover investigations, most famously, on the subject of dire workhouse conditions, by James Greenwood, the social commentator and journalist. Dressed as a vagrant, he spent the night in the casual ward of the Lambeth workhouse on Prince's Road and then published his findings as a series of sensational reports in the *Pall Mall Gazette* in January 1866. Such reporting needs to be approached with caution, for men like Greenwood were prone to emphasise the horrors in order to satisfy their audience's desire for vicarious immersion in all things 'dreadful', and to make the case for reforms that were shaped by middle-class ideas and values.[52]

In recent decades, historians have sought to uncover the voices – and 'agency' – of workhouse inmates and paupers through material within institutional archives. The existence of inmate letters is another indication of the availability of learning among the poor working-class population prior to compulsory education.[53] Much of what James Greenwood described in 1866 had been set out in a letter, published in the *Weekly Dispatch* four years earlier, purported to have been written by a workhouse inmate (we can suppose it is genuine, given the material recently uncovered at The National Archives). The institution concerned was the Newington Workhouse. The editor prefaced the transcription of this letter with the statement that if any of the descriptions within were proven to be incorrect, then he would happily publish a retraction: 'But,' he continued, 'the very poor have so few opportunities of making their grievances known, that they naturally appeal to the Press; and we at least assure them a fair hearing.' The letter's author, in addition to revealing the distress for inmates who were made to carry corpses to the 'dead-house', detailed below, sets out the various humiliations to which they were subjected. Firstly, on arrival, they were led to the receiving ward and inspected by the medical officer. Then, before dressing in the workhouse uniform, they had to bathe – 'but, Sir, you will be surprised when we tell you that by order of the master, no matter how many are in the receiving ward, they are all bathed in the same water, one after the another, dirty or clean'. This, he observed, was disgusting to a person usually clean in his habits. If you were unfortunate enough to arrive with an infection, you would be put in a ward where the beds were dirty and the blankets so slicked with ointment that they were 'thick and matted together'. During the winter that had just passed, the accommodation had been so inadequate 'that two men in a state of nudity have been placed in the same bed together' and only three bath towels were provided per week for use by about 150 men: 'therefore it is not to be wondered at that we can pick vermin off them, which we often do'. In fact, 'no clean person washes himself in the wash-house but on a Sunday morning, when he can use his dirty shirt in the place of the towels to dry himself'.

The worst accommodation was provided for the sick, both inmates and the outdoor poor; there were only about forty beds, 'and at the present time we have men lying about in damp day halls because there is no room for them in the sick wards'. Many of the men were suffering from a variety of conditions – rheumatism, bad legs, bronchitis – and they were currently confined in a damp shed used for chopping firewood. The workhouse was built at the edge of a ditch, which caused damp. 'So fearfully cold is it in the winter that the men are cramped and almost perish; and in the summer, what with the smell from the ditch outside and the privy in, it is a wonder that some infection has not broken out.' Concerning their only pleasure, smoking a pipe, 'in order that we may be made to feel where we are', the master had threatened with punishment anyone found smoking within the building, 'and it is too cold this weather for old men to smoke in the yard, this being the only comfort we poor creatures have here'. The author concluded: 'we little thought in our days of prosperity, when we paid rates, that we should ever be subject to such treatment in our old days, our only crime being poverty; and there is no wonder that many prefer a prison to such a place as this.'[54]

The core complaint concerned the debasing of human beings, treated worse than animals and made to feel their 'place'. The observation from the author that many inmates once paid the local rates that funded such an institution is a cautionary reminder of the adage, 'There but for the Grace of God go I.' So much for 'comfort with care' and 'method with economy'.

In fact, within months of the glowing review of the Newington Workhouse in the *Shoreditch Chronicle* – no doubt intended to silence critics of the system, while reassuring advocates – and prior to the published inmate letter, a scandal broke regarding the disposal of 'unclaimed' bodies from this workhouse's infirmary, particularly those sold for dissection to Guy's Hospital Anatomy School, located near London Bridge. This was where, earlier in the century, John Keats had trained as a surgeon-apothecary. The treasurer of Guy's Hospital, Mr Mark Shaddock, confirmed that he had on occasion paid the former Newington Workhouse master, Alfred Feist, who had already been sacked by the guardians, for bodies. In 1856 this had come to a total of £19 10s, and in 1857 the sum of £27, which equated to around 10 shillings per cadaver. According to Shaddock, the money was given to Feist as a gratuity 'for the trouble he had in obtaining the necessary certificates relating to the bodies that were sent to the hospital for dissection.'[55]

The inmate's letter published in the *Weekly Dispatch* included a distressing description of how the dead were carried to the morgue of the Newington Workhouse: 'Sir, upon the death of every person four young men are selected to bring down the corpse, and to their disgust they have to put the body in the coffin almost in a state of nudity, except a bit of calico about four feet long and twelve or thirteen inches wide, which is put over the front of the body, which often gets displaced in shifting it from the bed to the coffin, so that the whole person of the corpse, male or female, is exposed to view, no matter of what disease they die.'[56]

The *Morning Post* (7 January 1858) relayed the story that bodies had been supplied to Guy's Hospital by Feist, in collaboration with an undertaker, Robert Hogg of St George's Road, Southwark, who had been employed officially by the St Mary Newington Union for five or six years to bury the local paupers. The whole sorry affair revealed the level of disdain in which poor residents were held by those charged with their care: they were not people but bodies, whether alive or dead. This alone was troubling, but there was further embarrassment for the Board of Guardians: the substitution of bodies. This racket had been uncovered due to the vigilance of family members, and revealed double accounting between Guy's Hospital and the workhouse providing them with bodies. It was discovered that coffins were sometimes filled with stones, or that the bodies of loved ones were swapped with those of other inmates.

The solicitor for Feist cross-examined Hogg in terms that transformed impersonal data into real individuals, in this instance concerning the body of Mary Whitehead, who had died on 30 January 1857 and whose daughter, Louisa Mixer, was present in court. It appeared that Feist's defence, in this case, was that the undertaker had told him that no one would be accompanying the body to the grave. This was backed up by one William Bull, formerly clerk to Feist, who said that Hogg had access to the morgue key: 'He used to bring the bodies of outdoor paupers to the deadhouse at the workhouse, and also the remains of the dissected bodies from the hospital.' It was in the latter fact that the double accounting was discovered – the hospital had paid for the bodies, and then in sending them back to the workhouse to be buried, the undertaker would claim another fee. In some cases, he was being paid twice for the 'disposal' of the same body.

Feist's lawyer, as reported in the newspaper, observed that 'from the extremely lax, he might say scandalous, manner in which the bodies of paupers were treated in the parish, his client was not free from blame, yet he very much doubted, indeed – particularly as the sale of the body for profit must form a particular ingredient in the case – that any indictment could be framed with any success of a conviction'. He considered Hogg the undertaker to be the true villain; he had, after all, admitted to a motive and interest in disposing of the bodies in the manner described. Any further debate was interrupted by the magistrate, Mr Elliott, who considered the situation sufficiently serious to require the attention of a higher court – not least because 'at common law no power is delegated to dispose of a body for dissection'. Not even a gaoler holding a person already sentenced to death could do so, unless the sentence passed by the judge had included dissection.

The 1832 Anatomy Act had established a protocol for providing bodies, invariably of poor people, for dissection in the name of science. This became necessary after a spate of graveyard 'body-snatching' incidents and murders committed 'on demand', including by the infamous Burke and Hare, and their female accomplices, in Edinburgh. But under this act no master of a workhouse had any authority to dispose of bodies in this way, let alone profit from this macabre business venture. The extent of Feist's authority, as workhouse master, appeared to be the disposal of *unclaimed* bodies. Yet, in the case of Mary Whitehead, he had known full well that the deceased had friends, and the magistrate was convinced this was the case. As a result, Feist, the former workhouse master, was found guilty of a fraud 'of a most revolting description, that is, of substituting the body of one for another, and making the friends believe they were following to the grave the body of their own relative'. The magistrate also considered the Board of Guardians culpable, by allowing unclaimed bodies to be brought back from the hospital to the workhouse for burial. This last observation drew applause from those present in court. Evidence for another case was heard, that of Phoebe Clark who had died in the workhouse on 19 February. Her corpse had been sent to Guy's for dissection and another was substituted for the funeral. The presence in court of Phoebe's sisters, who had accompanied a stranger's coffin to Victoria Park cemetery, believing it was their sibling, and watched it lowered into the ground, were living confirmation that Phoebe could not be described as 'unclaimed'.

Emma Greenland, whose husband Charles had entered the workhouse on 5 May 1857, was also in court. She had applied to see her husband before his death on 20 May but was refused permission. When she and her brother-in-law, John Greenland, went to the workhouse the next morning, they were shown the body and Feist asked whether she wished to bury her husband herself. Emma could not afford to do so. She asked if she could have the clothes he had been wearing when he arrived at the workhouse, but was told that 'if she had the clothes she must have the body also, as the clothes would be the property of [the] parish if they buried him'. The funeral had been arranged for the following Saturday, but Emma was taken ill and could not attend. John Greenland followed what he thought was his brother's coffin – with the name 'Charles Greenland' chalked on the lid – to the graveyard, but again, it was actually that of a stranger. A third body, that of Mary Thompson's husband who had died on 10 March 1857, had been treated in a similar manner. The case for the prosecution concluded that it could be proved that the bodies of Charles Greenland, Mary Thompson's husband and Phoebe Clark, which their relatives believed they had followed 'to their last resting place', in fact had been sent to Guy's Hospital 'and subsequently dissected'.[57] Feist's solicitor continued to repeat his argument that any misadventure was more likely to be by the undertaker Hogg, rather than the former workhouse master, given it was Hogg who had a clear financial incentive and the opportunity to swap one body for another – receiving by his own admission £3 10s for the burial of all bodies taken to the hospital, compared to 5s 6d 'for the ordinary parish funeral'. In the event Alfred Feist was found guilty, but his sentence delayed, and the guilty verdict quashed on appeal.[58] The key result was a greater fear and loathing for Poor Law institutions among the poor working class, in tandem with the Act of Parliament that had codified a two-tier system towards the dead.

A tragic report in the *South London Times and Lambeth Observer* of 22 May 1858 hinted that anything was better than throwing yourself on the mercy of the workhouse. It stated that a coroner's inquest had been held in the boardroom of Newington Workhouse to consider the discovery of the body of Martha Harris, aged seventy-five: 'It appeared from the evidence that the deceased was found dead in a kind of van, situated near Walworth Common, which she had occupied for some years. Mr Cooke, the officer, stated that ... the body was in a most filthy condition, being completely covered with vermin', so much so that he had to burn most of her clothes before the body could be conveyed to the workhouse morgue. 'The jury returned a verdict of "Natural Death".' This woman in her seventies had been living in a 'van' – perhaps a form of caravan – just a few streets away from where the Tinworths had resided in Milk Street, and within yards of the entrance to the Newington Workhouse. She preferred to die as she did than to enter the walls of that institution: riddled with lice, but independent.

For other Walworth residents, including by the 1860s Charles Frederick and Mary Ann Hill, Charlie Chaplin's grandparents, such reports would have confirmed what they already knew: the workhouse was the very last resort. The way workhouses were managed did change, arguably for the better, towards the end of the century. But the fact that Mary Ann would find herself an inmate of Newington Workhouse, followed by her daughter and grandsons, reveals how desperate the family would become and how poverty blighted generation after generation.

George Tinworth's terracotta relief *Study from Life* (1870).

3

HOPE STREET

'A New World'

The death of a family member in the workhouse with her burial 'by the parish', and a visit from the broker's man, are just two indications that the Tinworths were living on the edge of survival. When the 1861 census was taken, the family had moved again, and they were now closer to their first home in Milk Street: 'Then we moved to 5 Hope St Walworth,' recalled George, 'and had a wheel wright shop' in Clandon Street.[1] This section of the census covered a total of 194 dwellings, with the houses and cottages on Hope Street numbered 1 to 25.[2] George Duckworth, one of Charles Booth's leading investigators, visited the area in the 1890s and noted that Hope Street was a 'flagged' stone 'passage' connecting Thornton Street to Wooler Street. Duckworth observed that the old buildings on the north side of the passage were of two storeys, on the south side one storey, and that the residents included Italians, alongside 'casual street hawkers'. Clandon Street is the next road to Hope Street in Duckworth's notebook and at that point occupied by 'costers' and 'jam & ginger beer workers'.[3]

In 1861 George was aged seventeen and his recorded profession was wheelwright. The street's name must have seemed sardonic and prophetic in equal measure to the young Tinworth, already daring to dream of a career in fine art. But the 'jarring string' that was Joshua Tinworth remained.

George recalled an event at Hope Street, which he thought revealed 'what sort of man my father was' when he was 'hard up'.[4] Joshua and Jane had been invited to a relation's house for lunch. It is not clear who the relative was, but Joshua's younger brother

James was among the company. George's uncle and aunt had moved to the parish of St Luke in Finsbury, north of the Thames and located between Shoreditch, the City, Holborn and Islington. In 1851, the family had been resident at 52 Rahere Street and were listed as James (thirty-four), a wheelwright smith; Sarah (thirty); Elizabeth, their daughter, born in 1844 at St Anne's Westminster, a parish located in Soho; Martha, aged four, born in the parish of St John the Evangelist in Westminster – and sons James (aged three) and Thomas (aged one), both, like Martha, born in the parish of St John, Westminster. This simple list of ages and birthplaces tells a bigger story: that James and Sarah had ventured across the river, from Walworth to Soho, within a few years of their marriage; while starting a family they had moved at least once within Westminster and then relocated north-east, to Finsbury. Ten years later, they had moved again, but within the same area of north London – to Leinster Terrace in Islington. James is still a wheelwright smith, Sarah keeping the home and family together, Elizabeth (seventeen) is now a dressmaker, Martha (fifteen) has no occupation, James (thirteen) is a printer's boy, and Thomas is eleven. In the years since the previous census, the family had almost doubled in number to include four more daughters: Sarah (nine), Caroline (seven), Mary (four) and Emma, just two months old. So it is likely that the fifteen-year-old Martha was fully occupied helping her mother.[5]

This change of residence every few years – packing up belongings, gathering the children, and then building relationships and threads of mutual support from scratch within a new neighbourhood – is typical for London's working-class couples with a growing family seeking employment. It may explain why observers believed that Londoners lived isolated existences relative to other communities. In the north of England, collective working – such as in large textile factories – was echoed in domestic arrangements; workers lived together within purpose-built or designated workers' housing and therefore developed a sense of worker, trade or class identity.

The debate among historians of London's poor over the nineteenth century concerns the extent to which communities were stable and supportive on the one hand, or in flux and plagued by anomie on the other. The truth, as ever, is somewhere in between: there was a lot of movement, but the ability to build strong community networks existed nonetheless, with neighbourhoods able and willing to embrace newcomers. But as the social historian Andrew August observes, regarding the working-class neighbourhood throughout Britain: 'The dense web of interdependence and intimacy developed out of crowded conditions. Poverty and insecurity encouraged mutual aid, without which many women would have found making ends meet impossible.'[6]

Life cannot have been easy for James and Sarah. By 1861 they were providing for a family of eight children aged between two months and seventeen years, albeit with two offspring who were earning. The number of children, all mouths to feed, suggests no contraception was practised by James and Sarah. 'Protection' was encouraged to combat venereal diseases, but there had been advocates, like Jeremy Bentham, and Richard Carlile in his *Every Woman's Book; or, What is Love?* (1826), for the encouragement of birth control and smaller families, partly to reduce the impact on family finances, alongside the Malthusian fear that population would outstrip food supply.* Later in the century, birth control would be championed by Annie Besant, who in 1877, with Charles Bradlaugh, would be tried in court for indecency after republishing the 1832 pamphlet *Fruits of Philosophy: An Essay on the Population Question* by the American campaigner Charles Knowlton. The book considered methods to tackle infertility and impotence, alongside contraception involving a vaginal douche of diluted chemicals, and the controversy created a bestseller. Besant followed up with her pamphlet *The Law of Population: Its Consequences, and Its Bearing upon Human Conduct and Morals* (1878).

Despite the size of their family, James Tinworth's circumstances and prospects seem, on the face of it, at least steady if not quite buoyant – in sharp contrast to his elder brother. Returning

---

*The English cleric, economist and demographer Thomas Robert Malthus (1766–1834) argued that with unchecked population growth, poverty was inevitable, that those who had no seat at 'nature's table' would die, and that a strict limit to human reproduction was the only hope for 'civilisation'.

to the fateful lunch (called 'dinner' by the working class) at Hope Street, George continues, 'when they were sitting down to dinner my Uncle was silley enough to say I will give poor Josh[u]a dinner, then my Father jumps up and said D[AM]N your dinner', upon which 'father and mother left the house'.[7] This must have been the incident that caused the estrangement of the two brothers; James Tinworth is not mentioned again by his nephew until much later in the narrative. Despite knowing his brother and his volatile moods, James's thoughtless comment, which came dangerously close to gloating over his elder sibling, meant that Jane and her children were separated from close family members who might have made their collective lives less stressful through practical assistance, or more tolerable through moral and emotional support. The anecdote emphasises once again the cultural importance of food and meals to working-class families: any hint that Joshua was not providing for his family was a slur on his status as the main breadwinner. His angry response was an indication of what was actually occurring behind the front door of 5 Hope Street.

George occasionally offered some context regarding his father's behaviour. Possessions were important, as was a certain level of domestic comfort – not just for the day-to-day ease of the family, but to keep up appearances for the benefit of relatives and, perhaps more importantly, neighbours. Possessions, like food, signalled small degrees of success when times were good, but the loss of them signified when times were hard. As we have already seen, possessions were also a means of getting short-term cash loans through pawning. In his memoir, George continues to record random events and impressions that stayed with him over the intervening decades, many of which relate to 'things'. As one example, he described a circumstance concerning the Tinworths' neighbour: 'The wife of a neighbour in Hope St died and after the funeral the relations come home to tea and began to have words about his wifes things.' This could be a scene from the pages of a Dickens novel: the relatives picking over material remains, with the deceased barely cold in her grave. But then again, handing on possessions, which, in this instance, could include those items of the woman's clothing that were still serviceable, whether to wear or sell on, would be important to those who cannot afford to buy new.* Why pay for second-hand items when your relative has no further use for hers? George recalled that his neighbour, the widower, in response to badgering and bickering from his in-laws, 'told them if there was much bother about her things, he would put them up in a heap and burn the lot'.[8]

A thief may be desperate enough to steal from a poor man's cottage, but a wheelwright's workshop was a different matter – it was how an entire family survived and, if stolen, equipment was a significant financial burden to replace:

> At Clanden St Wheel[w]right shop we used to lock up the shop at night with a padlock and father used to say that thieves would not break in because there was a lamp opposite, but one morning some one come and told us the shop had been broken open, and the tools had been taken. So we had to go round to the pawn shops and buy one here and one there, we never found out who had taken them, there are some fiends in this world.[9]

The loss of Joshua's work tools – to him invaluable – must have been shattering, with the expense of replacement an additional strain, reinforcing his view that no one, whether family or neighbour, could be trusted.

Joshua was particularly irritated by criticism while he was on a job. In one instance, when George was older, father and son were working on a cart for a local shop owner. The man and his wife came to see how they were getting on and, according to George, the woman kept interrupting her husband, which 'got my father out of temper'. After telling George that they would do no further work for this shop owner, Joshua's parting words, hurled at the man, were that he should 'take of[f] his trouse[r]s and give them

---

*When the wife of the pauper Charles Greenland, an inmate of Newington Workhouse, could not afford to bury her husband, his personal clothing was considered the property of the parish, in lieu, either to sell or repurpose for another pauper.

to his wife ... she was the one to wear them'.[10] This comment hints at Joshua's attitude towards women in general – that they should know their place – and the dynamic at home in particular: in this he was very far from unusual.[11] Hostility and stress seemed to follow him around like a dark cloud. And there is a sense that the merest slight – real or imagined – would trigger a disproportionately extreme reaction. On another occasion, Joshua told George to go to a local shop to ask the owners for two loaves 'on trust for a day or two'; if they refused, when he got another job and some money, 'he would go to that shop, and say good morning I want 2 loaves 1 pound of butter half a pound of tea 2 pounds of sugar 1 pound of candles', and when these items were weighed and wrapped and lying on the counter, 'he would say let me see, I have made a mistake I have come into the wrong shop, you would not let my boy have 2 loaves the other day, I cannot buy any thing of you,' and, turning on his heel, 'he would walk out'.[12]

Joshua's response is understandable. There was little point in being accommodating when all was going well; it was in times of hardship that some understanding was needed, to allow a family to eat, or to light their dwelling and place of work. Of course, the shopkeeper needed to live, too. There is a deep-rooted idea of a man's dignity, that a father should not feel a failure towards, and in the eyes of, his dependants, and that you should do to others as you would have done to you. Even so, George recalled little such accommodation being shown to his father; rather he is continually beset (as Joshua would see it) by patronising comments and crowing. Joshua was a man whose ambitions had been thwarted: something his son, despite his many successes, would come to understand.

Yet the boot could be on the other foot. Every man – even the shopkeeper – needed to be paid in a timely way for the work he did or the provisions he supplied. George recalled a time when 'my father owed something to a master sweep, and this sweep said that he would worrey him as long as he lived'. True to his word, the chimney sweep haunted his debtor. Sometimes, when George and Joshua were at work, he 'would suddenly come and stand before us', his face black with soot 'which always gave me a turn'.[13]

This recollection leads George to recall a conversation with an old sweep, of about seventy, who spoke of how he was mistreated by his master when a child: 'he said when he got to be a man his old master said to him dont you remember me wacking you if you would not go up the chimney'. The sweep, beaten as a child worker (or 'climbing boy') to 'encourage' him to crawl up narrow, filthy chimneys, retorted that he did indeed recall the beatings. Whereupon the old sweep continued: 'I put up my fists and said to him you cannot do it now.'[14] This anecdote reveals how prevalent casual violence was among the working class, how it was experienced from an early age, and how it passed through the generations.

Another anecdote regarding George's father raises the stakes of his hostility still further, revealing how volatile Joshua's behaviour could be and how he behaved while drinking in local hostelries, likely under fraying sufferance from the landlord. George recalled: 'About this time <when about 14>' – so a date of around 1857–8 – 'I carved a pistol out of wood, that I copied from some where.' Why George decided to fashion such an object in wood is not explained. 'I did the steel work over with black lead,' he adds, and 'bored the hole of the barrel.' This fake pistol was accurate enough to convince a bystander that it was a real weapon. Joshua Tinworth certainly thought so, and 'my father took it to a publick house and went into the tap room and pointed at one man he [k]new and said to him, I said I would do it for you, and now I will.' Even as a joke – and a sick one at that – this suggests that, when drunk, George's father would threaten people with injury or even death. Unsurprisingly, 'it frightened the man', who cried, 'dont be a fool no no dont be a fool Josh.' Local newspapers offered numerous examples of deaths occurring after drunken arguments in public houses, so this man sitting in the taproom had every reason to be fearful.[15]

A contrast is made by George when relaying episodes – vanishingly rare – when his father was not drinking, which complicates the idea that Joshua was the embodiment of the clichéd working-class father as largely absent from the 'family' unit and brutal when he occasionally reappeared. In one instance, George recalled a time when Joshua had been sober. Why this occurred is not revealed – perhaps through lack of money, or the influence of the temperance movement encouraging a renewed sense of personal accountability: 'About this time we got the order to make a dog cart for a pawnbroker and this gentleman let my father have 5 pound on acount' – an enormous sum for those living weekly on shillings. Joshua had not touched alcohol for a year and George recalled that 'he was a grand man when sober'. This last comment is the tragedy at the heart of the Tinworth family. It explains why Jane – an even-tempered, practical, loving and religious woman – had considered Joshua Tinworth a safe enough bet as a life partner and father of her longed-for children.

Unfortunately, now with money in his pocket, Joshua, after surviving a year without liquor, got drunk and then, during an argument with the pawnbroker, threw what remained of the advance money back at him. His unpredictable, self-destructive behaviour when drunk drove friends and family to despair, severely trying the patience of those who knew him to be a man with domestic responsibilities, and a hard and skilful worker when sober. George comments that this 'set us all a crying for we knew what a life we should have',[16] which is exactly the scenario that the temperance movement encouraged working men and women to avoid: as George himself declared, drink 'takes the strength out of you'. Alcoholism did not just affect Joshua, but also his hard-pressed, exhausted wife, and his three young, vulnerable sons.

This unremittingly insecure life meant, as already stated, that there was little or no time for schooling, or even home learning, and during his childhood and young adulthood George details a great variety of casual work he had to take on, as well as modest money-making ventures. He had a group of friends that he used to play with in the street, or venture further afield to swim in the Surrey Canal at the edge of Walworth Common. These boys were taken on at a fireworks manufacturer in Peckham. Understandably, given how dangerous this business was, 'my father did not want me to go'. The master of the factory sent George with a large parcel of 'squibs' – ready-made fireworks – to a shop in Hackney, which involved crossing the Thames, either at Blackfriars or London Bridge. On the return he was to bring back 14 pounds of gunpowder in brown paper bags, which he carried in a basket on a horse-drawn omnibus: 'when I got back to the house at Peckham,' George continued, 'we found one of the bags had broke open and the powder had been running into the basket.' If someone had been smoking on the bus and a spark from the cigar or pipe had fallen into the basket, the entire vehicle could have been blown sky high – 'and I should have got the worst of it'. George contemplated his luck that day, for if he had been seriously injured or died, as happened to so many working children, 'I should not have designed and modeled terra cotta panels, or done any thing in Doulton ware.'[17]

The level of risk here was extreme, even for Joshua who, as George states, did not want his son to get involved, no matter how hard up they were. But the poorer working class was exposed constantly to danger. Even rough play among friends could result in an injury that removed a young and fit lad from the labour force, depriving a family of an income generator. Whether that loss was temporary or longer-term was largely dependent on what medical care the family had access to or could afford.

On that subject, George recalled an incident when he was wrestling with some boys: 'I fell and broke my arm and was taken by a stranger to a surgeon, to have it set.' The medic knew how to set the bone, but he 'could see I was a poor boy', and so unable to pay for the treatment, and therefore refused to do anything, 'but said I must go to the hospital'.[18] Over the nineteenth century, medical provision continued to be a hodgepodge of parallel systems supplied by workhouses, hospitals and private practitioners. Guy's and St Thomas's hospitals offered basic medical care to the poor of Southwark and Lambeth, respectively. With the spread of such diseases as typhoid and cholera, in 1855 (after the Public Health Act of 1848) London had been split into forty-six Metropolitan Districts, all requiring a Medical Officer, and in that year the first Chief Medical Officer to the government was appointed.

George walked home to Hope Street in agony, 'with a little crowd fo[llo]wing me, and my father took me to Guys and I was taken in and my father brought my clothes home'. Jane, on seeing the clothes without George 'began to cry', thinking her son was dead. Then the medic who should have dealt with George at the hospital had an accident himself during a game of football, but no one came to help the lad in his stead. George's arm swelled up, could not be reset, and ice bags were used to reduce the inflammation over six days and nights. 'I was in great pain all this time,' George indignantly recalled, because of the hospital staff 'not doing there duty.' Joshua, meanwhile, was afraid that the arm would need to be amputated – a simple resetting procedure escalating into a week of agony and the threat of life-long disability, when the loss of an arm would be devastating for a craftsman – all this due to a local Walworth doctor who would not treat a poor child without payment, followed by the carelessness of the hospital staff or (more likely perhaps) the pressures of acute need among the local poor on an overstretched hospital. However, the arm was eventually set and 'I was in there about 3 weeks'.[19]

Again, it is striking how vulnerable to difficulty poor people were. The boys, without money or opportunities, entertain themselves by wrestling or fighting, which throws them in the way of injury. But because they are poor and unable to pay for treatment, their access to care is unpredictable or the treatment unaffordable, leaving them dependent on the caprice of medical men – who chose to treat or not as their inclination (and personal circumstances) dictated. The result is that a perfectly capable boy, able to work and with ambition, could easily become lame or impaired, or even die, through want of basic care – as witness the actions of the family at 4 Victory Place, taking the carman and his master to court to get compensation for the severe, likely life-changing injury to their child. Would this have happened to a middle-class family? Danger existed for everyone, but access to care, prior to the establishment of a national health service, was greater and immediate for the middle classes, their day-to day lives cushioned from harm because of the neighbourhoods in which they lived and the professional support they could afford.

The fourteen-year-old George was also hired for three weeks by 'hot pressers' at Watling Street in the heart of the City of London, which could either refer to the preparation of paper for printing presses or the steam-pressing of linen (both trades existed in Watling Street at this time). George describes walking to and from

Watling Street each day – 'I had to git there by 7 in the morning and stop there t[i]ll 9 at night' – for which he earned four shillings a week. The walk would have taken about an hour, through Elephant and Castle, passing the church of St George-the-Martyr on Borough High Street and then over London Bridge into the City. George left home in the morning with some slices of bread and butter for his lunch, and a penny in his pocket. Sometimes, as part of his work, 'I was sent about the city with a truck at night', likely delivering pressed paper to businesses such as book and newspaper publishers, or crisply laundered linen to hotels or restaurants.[20]

When such temporary work was not available, the desperate need for money remained. At such times George would do errands for neighbours as well as strangers: 'When living in Hope St the next door neighbour kept a laundry, she was an old Welsh woman and she sent me one after noon to Fernavels Inn Holborn, with a basket of washing which I carried on my head.'[21] Furnival's Inn, the name connected to an old Inn of Chancery on High Holborn, was, by the early nineteenth century an apartment building for single gentlemen of means. Charles Dickens rented rooms here between 1834 and 1837 and the accommodation is described in *Martin Chuzzlewit* (originally published in 1844): 'a shady, quiet place, echoing to the footsteps of the stragglers who have business there; and rather monotonous and gloomy on summer evenings'; 'There are snug chambers in those Inns where the bachelors live, and, for the desolate fellows they pretend to be, it is quite surprising how well they get on.'[22] Bachelors were good business for a laundress, although it is curious that the client of the Tinworths' neighbour could not find a 'necessary woman' closer to his Holborn lodgings. But perhaps the quality of service coming from Hope Street was prized by him and, in any case, the additional effort in picking up dirty linen and then the returning of it washed and ironed, was taken on by the laundress: the three-mile walk would have taken George about an hour each way, again via Blackfriars Bridge.

The 1861 census provides information about laundry women in Hope Street, from which we might identify George's casual employer.[23] At No. 4, on one side of the Tinworths, lived Ebenezer Dimmock, a shoemaker, and his wife Sarah, a laundress, both in their thirties. Other nearby families included the bootmaker Charles Fox and his family at No. 1; William Pearce, a window blind maker and his family at No. 2; William Corby, another shoemaker, and his family at No. 3; Edward Wolfe, yet another a shoemaker, and family at No. 7; the carpenter Mark Gills and his wife Ann, a charwoman, who were seventy-two and sixty-one respectively. Nos 1–4 Hope Cottages were the residence of fishmonger Edward Walett and his wife Elizabeth, both in their early twenties; the costermonger Augustus N. Cole and his family; the cab driver Daniel Brewer, his wife and children; and William Hugman, a 'general dealer', his wife Maria, a 'Hawker' (both in their late thirties), and family.

But living on the other side of the paved passage to the Tinworths, at No. 6, was 'Ann Davies', the unmarried – not widowed – head of the household. Born in 1786, Ann was listed as being from the county of Kent although her surname is of Welsh origin. Crucial to George's anecdote, she was still working as a laundress into her seventies, so she would have seemed 'old' to her fourteen-year-old neighbour. Ann's household included an unmarried lodger, Mary Berry, aged forty-eight and also a laundress, and Mary's daughter Mary Ann Berry, likewise unmarried, aged twenty-four and working as a domestic servant. The three women seem to have been running a laundry business from their home, with customers potentially including single, middle-class gentlemen as far afield as the City of London.

George recalled how he once delivered the basket of clean and pressed laundry, as usual, only for his curiosity to get the better of him as he returned over Blackfriars Bridge: 'I stopped to look at the pictures outside the Rotunder, I thought I would like to see inside. So I paid my 2 pence and went in, it was the first time I had been [to] the place or any theatre.' After its reputation as a focus for radical politics under Richard Carlile, from 1838, under the management of John Blewitt, the building still called 'the Rotunda' operated as an early form of 'music hall' (it was one of the first to use this term) and, according to the historian Harold Scott, 'for many years carried on an intermittent existence, gathering a kind of fame in the locality, and often harbouring artists of note; one of the last being the infant Dan Leno'.[24] (It closed, under the name of the Britannia Music Hall, in 1886.)[25]

As this suggests, the variety or 'music hall' entertainment that George Tinworth was paying to experience had its roots earlier in the century, in the money-making ventures of the enterprising landlords of taverns and public houses.[26] Eventually pub games like bar billiards were introduced, to entice punters in and to keep them there, while impromptu amateur musical gatherings were encouraged, around an upright piano, or itinerant musicians brought in to entertain the clientele. This developed, sometimes in purpose-built rooms or, eventually, halls attached to the bars; one surviving London establishment, which grew from the 1850s in this way, from backstreet drinking den to full-blown theatre with drinking area attached, is Wilton's Music Hall near the Tower of London. By the mid-1850s, such 'music halls' existed around London and across Britain; in the 1890s, the Chaplin family of music-hall entertainers would spend as much time touring around the kingdom as they would within its capital. Even so, one music hall in particular gained the reputation as the model both as a building and a business: the Canterbury on Westminster Bridge Road in Lambeth, which developed from an old tavern, the Canterbury Arms, reopening as the largest venue for variety and music in 1854.* In addition to its scale and glamour, the Canterbury's proprietor, Charles Morton, made a point of promoting the venue as a place that was suitable for women and children – in one stroke diversifying and expanding his audience.

George Tinworth recollected that the first performance at the theatre on Blackfriars Road, which he calls the 'Rotunder', was from seven to nine o'clock in the evening. At this time, there were two 'houses' a night; those waiting for the second performance gathered in a large waiting room: 'I remember there was a lot of river men playing at leap frog, so I set down on my clothes basket, till the doors opened.'[27] George conjures up a charming scene, with the audience waiting for an evening performance to begin: the casual laundry lad sitting on the upturned basket, while watermen

---

*Charles Chaplin senior, Charlie's father, later performed there.

or lightermen – who for centuries had transported people and goods across and along the Thames – leapfrog over each other to while away the time.

George then describes the evening's entertainment. The first act was a male singer, followed by Spanish dancing. Then there was a humorous sketch where one actor played several parts, the last character being a villain. The climax involved a stuffed dog 'seizing' the villain by the throat, which unleashed some knockabout physical comedy. After this, moving from the ridiculous to the sublime, there was a 'balley' (i.e. ballet), 'which ended up with red and blue fire', upon which the evening's spectacle was over. George observed that 'there was also a circus at this place' and concluded by stating some local lore: 'I should say this was the spot w[h]ere Shakespare performed.'[28] Unfortunately for George, a 'man come to me and told me I ought not to be there', presumably because as a young lone boy some of the performances were considered a little risqué. However, more trouble was in store for George when he arrived home, somewhat late: 'my father was in a terrible way, thought some one had stole the washing, one of the laundry women was sent to know wether I had been to Fernavels Inn.'[29]

By the time George was fourteen years old, Joshua would have been in his late forties. George's recollections include incidents – general and specific – which mark his father's mental state, his reliance on alcohol, his frayed temper. Desperate situations seemed to trigger a collapse into drunkenness. As George noted in the section titled '5 Hope St Walworth', 'While at this house we would all go to bed some times not knowing w[h]ere a breakfast was comeing from.'[30] Joshua would leave the house early in the morning, but no one knew whether he was going to the wheelwright shop or, as likely, a local pub: 'In the morning my father would get up and go out, so I had to go and look after him in the diferant publick houses and beer shops, I would look into the diferent places, and push open taproom door.'[31] In the 1861 census, the public houses listed in the immediate area around Hope Street included the Sun Beer House – registered under the name 'Robert Mann' – and the Cooper's Arms, both on Portland Street. On 18 July 1848 the *Morning Advertiser* had included notice of 'secured

Rentals, arising out of the Sun Beer house, Brewery, Dwelling houses, and Shops, with valuable Reversion'. The rental at that point was £47 16s per annum, guaranteed for sixteen years.[32]

The census also notes the presence of a beer house called the 'Anchor & Hope' on Clandon Street, where Joshua's wheelwright shop was located, with the keeper named as George Chisley. In 1861 Chisley, a Shropshire man, was aged fifty-two; his wife Eliza was forty-six and listed as his 'helper' in the business. Ellen S. Chisley, their daughter, had been born in 1851 in Newington – the couple had been resident in the Walworth area for at least a decade – and attended a local school: there was no necessity for her to earn money, for beer houses in the area could clearly do very good trade. On 18 May 1847 the *Morning Advertiser* was promoting a free ale and beer house to let at £24 per annum 'in a very populous neighbourhood in Walworth, doing a fair business, fitted-up with every convenience, and in good repair ... Apply to Mr. Rose, 2, Trafalgar-street, Walworth';[33] fifteen years later, in 1863, the *Sainsbury's Weekly Register and Advertising Journal* announced a free beer house was available to rent for only £25 per year, situated in a 'thorough beer-drinking neighbourhood' in Walworth, doing a monthly trade of fourteen to fifteen barrels. The premises comprised a 'neatly fitted-up bar, bar-parlour, large club-room, two good bed-rooms, capital cellarage, yard, with back entrance into a large neighbourhood'. The advertisement concluded that this free house 'in the hands of some men, a trade of 30 barrels monthly might be done'.[34] On the one hand, these beer houses were community hubs, offering light relief, entertainment and camaraderie for those in desperate need – but it was also a temptation to drown sorrows. And, knowing the suffering of the Tinworth family as a result of alcohol abuse, the notice that 'in the hands of some men' this beer house could double its current trade in 'a thorough beer-drinking neighbourhood' has a very ominous ring. Every penny spent on drink was money not available for food for the family table. The greatest impact of this would not have been felt by Joshua – culturally his higher status as main 'breadwinner' would have guaranteed him the best of what little they had – but by his wife and children. This was a family that went to bed not knowing where breakfast would come from. At times of extreme hardship, Jane may well have skipped meals in order to provide something for her sons, particularly when they became regular workers themselves: think of young George, the hot presser's boy, with his packed lunch of bread and butter.[35]

To address what was seen as an epidemic, the British Association for the Promotion of Temperance had been formed in 1833, with the Band of Hope, which specifically targeted children, founded in 1847. The movement created 'drink maps' to draw attention to the scale and concentration of public outlets for alcohol consumption.[36] Standard street plans were adapted, marking the location of individual taverns and beer houses from Glasgow to Norwich and Aberdeen to Southampton. The purpose was to convince magistrates not to renew or grant new licences in areas that were already densely populated with such outlets. The temperance movement initially advocated moderation rather than outright abstinence and was mainly focused on the working and labouring classes; middle- or upper-class alcohol abuse was kept hidden behind the closed doors of homes, private gentlemen's clubs and country estates. Some perceived different attitudes to drunken behaviour depending on social status, and this was reflected in the justice system. Thomas Burke, a favourite author of Charlie Chaplin, declared in his semi-fictional 'autobiography' *The Wind and the Rain*: 'If a poor man got drunk on a Bank Holiday, it was "Father Has his Fling". If a titled youth got drunk on Boat Race Night, and kicked over old men's baked-potato cans and knocked women down, it was "Lord Henry Slummocks' Daring Escapade".'[37]

But regarding the working poor, there was justifiable concern that easy access to alcohol fuelled their poverty, encouraging domestic violence and criminality, while having a devastating impact on their mental and physical health, plus (as middle-class campaigners would argue) their moral and spiritual well-being. Here mention should be made of the moral statistics movement of the 1830s to 1850s, which attempted to establish a direct link between the lack of Christianity practised within the working class and immorality – illegitimacy, pre-marital sexual relations, drink and crime. Opposition to bills for new parliamentary laws intended to curb the thriving drinks industry came, inevitably, from vested interests in positions of social and political power, such as brewery-owning Members of Parliament. There is a direct connection between these 'beer map' examples of civic-minded propaganda and Charles Booth's famous colour-coded 'poverty maps' later in the century.

The Clandon Street wheelwright's workshop would be of profound importance to George Tinworth. As his memoir established, it was here, as a child and then as a youth, that he was also carving and sculpting in secret. The need for concealment is explained by Edmund Gosse in his biographical sketch of the sculptor and his career: 'For in the eyes of the elder Mr. Tinworth such trifling as this was mere wicked waste of time that ought to be better spent in tinkering up a costermonger's broken cart.'[38] George's manuscript includes a small photograph of one of his clay bas-reliefs depicting 'The Wheelwright Shop in Clandon St Walworth' (overleaf).[39] There are at least two versions of this scene by George. The first, dated to the 1870s includes a shop sign, 'JOSHUA TINWORTH WHEELWRIGHT', along the back wall. Beneath hang various tools, such as saws and hammers, and leaning up against the wall is a large cartwheel. Along the bottom of the image, 'G. T. IN HIS FATHER'S WORKSHOP' is incised into the clay, with George shown working on a wooden figure held in a vice, further chisels and a plane resting to one side. A little boy sitting on a stool appears to be keeping watch. In the central doorway stands a woman, the young artist's mother Jane, intrigued by what her eldest son is crafting while 'watching over' him as his guardian angel. (The second version, the one George uses to illustrate the memoir, has George as an older man. The two versions represent different stages of his life.)

George explained the story behind this image in the section of his memoir entitled 'What caused me to go to Doultons'. He says: 'I carved a small figure ... of the infant Samuel in wood,'[40] a reference to Samuel in the Old Testament. This biblical figure had great significance for George's mother. In the section of his memoir that includes Jane's recollection that her first three sons had died as babies, George goes on to say that Jane made 'the same

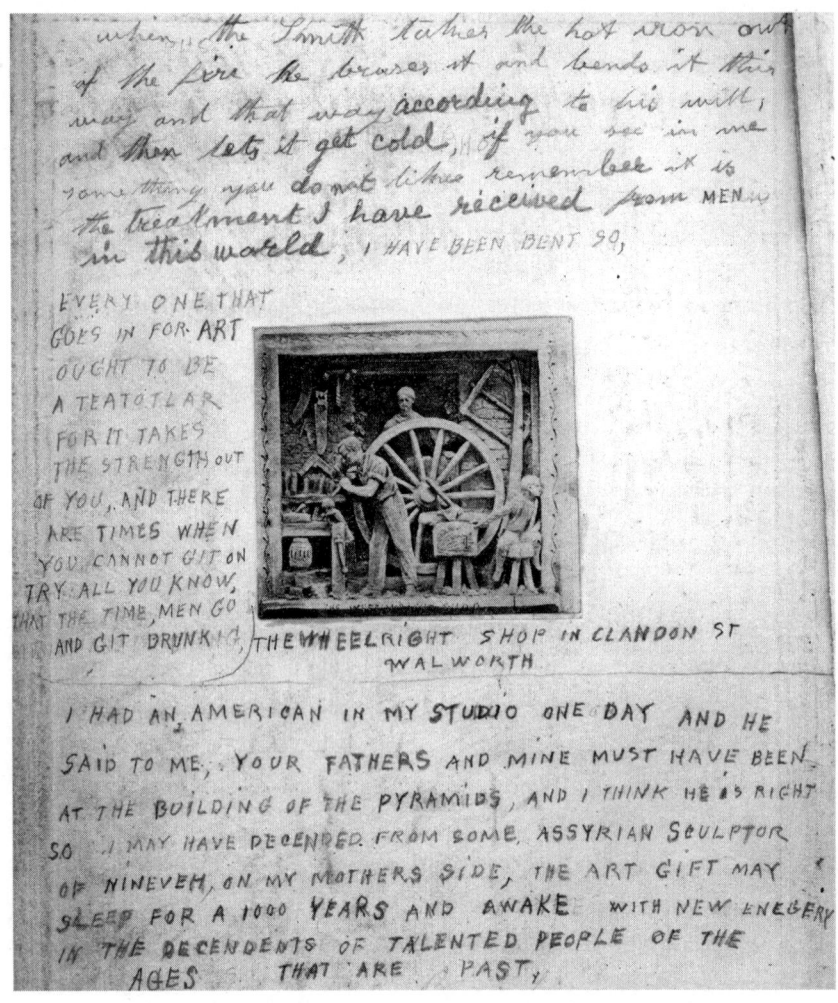

Page 1 from George Tinworth's autobiography, illustrating his terracotta relief *The Wheelwright Shop* (made around 1880).

vow that Samuels mother made', that is, 'to lend me to the Lord when I was born if I should live'.[41] This is a reference to the First Book of Samuel, where Hannah prays to God to give her a son, and in exchange, 'I will give him unto the LORD all the days of his life' and as a sign of this pact 'there shall no razor come upon his head'(1 Samuel 1:11). George concludes this anecdote by observing, 'no razor as ever come upon my head'; Jane's vow, too, had been fulfilled. Images of George Tinworth as an adult confirm that he wore a full beard. Among them is a Doulton pottery drinking vessel, decorated with a moulded self-portrait in profile, entitled, with a self-deprecating humour, 'G.T., his mug'.[42]

George would reject organised religion – 'I hope I belong to the church of God, but not to bricks and mortor church'[43] – but he remained a man of deep Christian faith throughout his life. The Bible would be a core inspiration for his art, with scenes from the Old and New Testament as subject matter for his distinctive terracotta reliefs. But Samuel was a talisman for mother and son. George continues his story by describing how on finishing the figure, his mother showed it to a master plasterer living nearby, who declared that the young wheelwright displayed such promise that he ought to go to an art school: Samuel might prove lucky once more.[44]

Encouraged by this response, George used every available moment to do wood carving 'when me father was out'.[45] While George was at work on a figure, a boy acted as lookout for his father's return and when he had the signal, George would remove the figure from the vice and throw it to the other end of the shed. Yet he still desired the good opinion of his father, for 'some times I would show him what I had done'. He recalled one such carving, a wooden serpent; on seeing it, Joshua cried, 'Ah my boy you may thanks me for that,' adding, 'and you have got enough wood in your head to make another one.'[46] Little wonder that George kept his ambitions secret from his father. This is the type of comment, sharp but ultimately belittling, that will either challenge the child to prove the parent wrong or crush whatever ambition might exist: Joshua's personal disappointments tainted the next generation in more ways than one.

But George, as steady as he was stubborn, continued in the desire to change his destiny from wheelwright to artist. As he recounted: 'I was told there was an art school at Vauxhall Lambeth, so I went up Kennington Lane to Vauxhall Bridge but could not find it.' However, 'one morning I had anither try'; he wandered around the streets between Kennington and Vauxhall until, finally, he found what he was looking for.[47]

Lambeth School of Art (now City & Guilds of London Art

School on Kennington Park Road) was established in 1854 by Canon Robert Gregory, vicar at the Anglican parish of St Mary-the-Less, in the buildings of a day-school opposite his church on Prince's Road: George recalled that Canon Gregory 'was a nice man'.[48] Gregory's parish was one of two – the other was St Mary-at-Lambeth to the north, where George Tinworth's grandparents had been married – within which the Doulton pottery works and river wharves were located, and therefore where many of their workers lived. According to John Sparkes, a Royal Academy-trained sculptor and teacher born in Brixton around 1833, Canon Gregory originally intended 'giving his parishioners a means of gratifying their taste for drawing', with the hope 'that the potters of Lambeth would take advantage of their opportunities'.[49] Two years later, Sparkes joined the school as a teacher, becoming principal in 1858 (until 1900). He proved a visionary advocate for the institution beyond his role as art master, and early on developed a relationship with Henry Doulton.[50] By now Doulton's company had been closely associated with the overhaul of the city's sewage system, which had occurred as a result of the 1846–60 cholera epidemic* and concurrently the Thames's 'Great Stink' of 1858, when the health crisis was literally under the noses of parliamentarians at Westminster. Doulton's provided the ceramic pipes, tiles and associated sanitary appliances for this major civil engineering project led by Joseph Bazalgette. Despite John Sparkes's passionate advocacy, Henry Doulton could not see why the art school on his doorstep should be of any interest to him.

Cohabiting with a primary school was convenient enough in the first few years, but the rooms used by the evening art classes needed to be cleared each night, ready for the children's arrival in the morning. As the art school gained popularity, the decision was made to move out of Prince's Road to purpose-built facilities in Millers Lane, on land once occupied by Vauxhall's pleasure gardens – a venue historically associated with the fine as well as performing arts, including the celebrated William Hogarth and

---

*The source of an outbreak on Broad Street in Soho was traced to the water supply, which had been contaminated by sewage.

George Frideric Handel. Edward VII, when he was Prince of Wales, laid the foundation stone of the new art school in 1860 in the presence of the Archbishop of Canterbury, John Bird Sumner, and Sparkes's mentor Henry Cole, then the director of the South Kensington Museum (which would later become the Victoria & Albert Museum), a position he would hold until 1873. It was the future king's first public engagement, and attracted huge interest and publicity for Lambeth School of Art as a result.

Even so, Henry Doulton remained unconvinced that he should be producing anything other than useful ceramics – whether industrial or domestic. Edmund Gosse noted, in his biography of Sir Henry, that on meeting John Sparkes, Doulton was 'polite but indifferent' and clear 'what they had to do at Lambeth was to provide a utilitarian class of goods for the general public, and to see that they were the best of their kind for practical purposes'.[51] But by 1863, he had been persuaded to become a committee member of the art school's governing body – and then, when Doulton was extending his premises nearby, Sparkes convinced him to commission terracotta decoration for the exterior, designed by Sparkes and modelled by his students.

The art school was, therefore, of very recent foundation, and its relationship with Doulton's still tenuous, when the young George Tinworth was scouring the Lambeth streets in search of it in around 1861. Even so, through the leadership of John Sparkes, it was fast establishing itself both locally and nationally.

George described how he loafed around outside the new building on Millers Lane, uncertain what to do next. The facade was a little foreboding: a plain double-height brick wall, with two small doors at street level and no ground-floor windows. Then, he recalled, 'I saw an old lady going into the school and she invited me in.'[52] This was Mrs Butt, the school's caretaker.[53] What happened next would transform his life; the small door on a normal Lambeth street opened into a sequence of spaces containing all the paraphernalia associated with the fine arts: casts of classical Greek and Roman statues for students to copy, with pencil on paper, or to model in clay; sketches in watercolour of life models pinned up on boards; the smell of fresh paint and plaster lingering in the air.

'I felt in a new world,' the young wheelwright confessed. He turned to Mrs Butt and declared, with the confidence of youth, 'if I had the stone I could carve the statues before us,' not then understanding 'the grandour of the antique ... as I do now'.[54]

When George speaks of the 'grandeur of the antique', he is describing the veneration for specific examples of ancient sculpture reproduced as casts for students to copy. It was the basis, with the 'life class', of traditional art training. As a young man from Walworth, with no knowledge of this 'new world', George simply and instinctively saw the statues in front of him – perhaps recalling the 'human sculptures' of Camberwell Fair – as things he could replicate in wood, clay or stone. The older George hints that had he known what he was looking at, he would have shown a little more humility and respect. In any case, he asked Mrs Butt 'if I could come and be taught art'.[55] Years later, in recollecting this event, he would declare to his wife: 'I was thinking what happy moments I had the first morning I found out the Lambeth School.'[56]

With Mrs Butt's encouragement, George decided to come back the next night with a friend, who lifted him up so he could look through the high window into one of the main school rooms, his nose pressed against the glass. He decided to return the following evening, this time with a bust of the composer Handel that he had carved in Portland stone.[57] Standing at the door with his sample carving, George asked a man who was passing 'if I could come and be taught modeling, and he said come in and see what we are doing, and introduced me to Mr Bale': the man passing by was John Sparkes, and Edwin Bale was the modelling master. Sparkes, after seeing the skilfully crafted Handel bust, proclaimed, 'hears [i.e. here's] a new student for you Mr Bale.' George would keep this bust, a treasured thing, for the rest of his life.[58]

The establishment of the school and its focus on developing local craftsmen chimes with the innovations of the Christian socialist F. D. Maurice and the founding of the Working Men's College in Camden, which offered artisans a liberal education through evening classes. Maurice was supported by John Ruskin and the

AND ASKED HIM IF I COULD COME AND BE TAUGHT 47
MODELING, AND HE SAID COME IN AND SEE WHAT WE
ARE DOING, AND INTRODUCED ME TO MR BALE THE
MODELING MASTER SAYING HEARS A NEW STUDENT
FOR YOU MR BALE, SO THAT WAS ALL RIGHT, BUT
HOW WAS I TO GET THE 4 SHILLINGS TO PAY THE
[...] MY MOTHER GOT IT FROM SOME
[...] TELL MY FATHER ANY THING
[...] TIME AFTERWARDS, THEN I
[...] HE SAID I GIVE YOU MONEY BUT
[...] ANY, AFTER I HAD BEEN THERE
[...] FOR THE 2 POUND PRIZE
[...] NEL, OF THE SAVIOUR BEING
[...] SOLDIERS, I COULD NOT AFORD
[...] ME I GOT MY BROTHER TOM
[...] ME TIMES I STOOD MYSELF
I CARTED IT ABOUT FROM HOPE ST TO LAMBETH SCHOOL
AND FROM SCHOOL TO WALWORTH MY BROTHER
CHARLEY BROUGHT THE PANEL IN CLAY ONE
NIGHT WHEN THERE WAS A MODEL SITTING YOU
HAD TO GO TO THE OTHER DOOR THOSE NIGTHS
BUT LARKEY STUDENTS FROM THE OTHER SCHOOL
TOLD MY BROTHER TO KICK HARD

Page 47 from George Tinworth's autobiography, with a photograph of his teacher, mentor and friend John Sparkes. In 1868 Sparkes married the painter and illustrator Catherine Adeline Edwards, who had been his student at Lambeth. When she died in 1891 he founded scholarships for women at the Royal Academy in her memory.

economist John Stuart Mill. But, although it was aimed at local men like George, the Lambeth art school was not free to attend. A weekly fee of four shillings was required, which either Jane found or George would save from the money his father paid him. For a while, nothing was said to Joshua about his son's attendance at the school. To keep the secret, sometimes George had to pawn his 'Sunday' or best coat to raise the school fee.[59] Eventually George was forced to confess all to his father, 'for he said I give you money but you have never got any'.[60] An arrangement was made between them, with George working at the wheelwright's shop during the day and attending art school in the evening.

The weekly fee was one issue for someone with George Tinworth's limited means; the other was the expense of materials, including graphite pencils, paper and clay. To reduce the significant outlay, George recycled the unfired clay sketches he had been moulding in the evening classes: once they had been seen and his progress judged by his tutors, they were broken up for the next project. Destroying every figure must have been heartbreaking at first, but George learned quickly to be unsentimental.

In addition, the school offered various cash prizes for the best work; if he was successful, George could use them to pay his weekly fees, and buy a regular supply of clay, rather than scrimping and pawning every week. After he had been attending the art school for some time, he entered a 'relief' he had designed and modelled in clay for a school prize: the subject was Jesus being mocked by the Roman soldiers before his crucifixion. George says he could not afford to hire a male model from which to copy any of the figures, so his brother sat for him; when Tom was not available 'some times I stood myself', using his own reflection in a mirror. George moved this work in progress in a cart between the art school and Hope Street (roughly a forty-minute walk). One evening, on George's behalf, his youngest brother Charley brought the panel to Millers Lane, while George was modelling in the life class. Unbeknown to Charley, who was wearing clogs, the standard footwear for workers, the usual entrance was locked but, as a joke, some 'larkey' students told him the door was just stuck and he should kick it, and hard. George was in the main room when the deafening sound of clog on locked door could be heard thundering down the corridor: 'the attendent run out and so did I' – only to find a red-faced Charley standing on the street. But George had the last laugh: this panel won the £2 prize.[61]

Robert W. Bowers, a local board school scholar, was a fellow student at Millers Lane. He recalled that George and an unnamed friend 'near examination time ... often worked at the school through the night, wrapping themselves in the school curtains to sleep an hour or two before dawn'.[62] While attending the evening art classes, George made friends with like-minded young men from similar backgrounds, including Robert Wallace Martin (1843–1923), who may have been the student mentioned by Bowers, grabbing some rest wrapped in a classroom curtain.

In 1851 the Martin family had lived in Shoreditch, Hoxton, in the East End of London; ten years later they had moved south of the river to 5 Johns Terrace in Walworth. By this point, occupying the whole property, the family members were the father Robert Thomas Martin, aged fifty-four and a wholesale stationers assistant, his wife Margaret, aged thirty-eight and in the census return defined, unusually, perhaps by her own insistence, as a '<u>Good</u> Housewife' ('goodwife' being an archaic term by the mid-nineteenth century), eldest son Robert Wallace, aged seventeen and a 'sculptor', William (sixteen, a solicitor's clerk), James (eleven, a 'Sunday School Scholar'), daughter Frances (also a scholar aged eight) – so a working-class family that used the opportunities then available for formal education – then Walter aged three, and one-year-old Edwin.[63] (By 1871 the Martin family had moved again, to 398 Kennington Road).[64]

As a teenager and prior to attending drawing classes at Lambeth School of Art, Robert Wallace Martin had worked for the architectural sculptor John Birnie Philip of Vauxhall Bridge Road in Pimlico while his company was supplying carvings for the Palace of Westminster to the north. The new home of the Houses of Parliament, designed in the Gothic Revival style by Charles Barry and A. W. N. Pugin, had been steadily rising from its Thameside location since the 1840s, encouraging the opening of government art and design schools to provide the craftsmen needed. Martin was already a student at the new Lambeth School of Art when George Tinworth was admitted in around 1861.* Decades later, Martin, in recounting his first impressions of Tinworth, described how, during one modelling evening class, 'a rough looking youth timidely presented himself'. Martin then pauses in his recollection: 'perhaps I ought not to say rough, for there was nothing low about him though poor & hard worked' – a comment that reflects the 'levels' within the working class, while indicating that George had a bearing that belied his poverty. Martin, as a working-class man himself, may also have checked and then corrected himself in the use of the term 'rough', for as the acknowledged negative of 'respectable' within this social class, he would have been judging George's mother unfairly, as well as George, whom he considered 'evidently a young genius'. 'We became great friends,' Martin continued, '& walked home together as we both lived in Walworth & he had to pass my parents door, which soon, often opened to let him in, he became a welcome guest & must stop to supper sometimes.'[65]

George, in turn, recalled that Robert Wallace Martin 'lived my way' in Walworth, so they would walk home together at night after art classes.[66] George lived the furthest away, but despite the invitation to meet Martin's parents he at first refused, saying he 'did not care to go into peoples houses'.[67] This hints that George, under the weight of his father's domineering character, had grown to be a rather taciturn, self-contained, even 'timid' young man. It may be that he feared, in accepting an invitation from Martin, that he would be forced to reciprocate. But eventually George crossed the threshold of 5 Johns Terrace and was introduced to Mr and Mrs Martin, along with 'the rest of the happy family' – a description that inevitably stands in contrast to the Tinworths. The father, Robert Thomas Martin, a working man of a similar age to Joshua Tinworth, presented an alternative model for the working-class patriarch: friendly and generous, rather than bitter and belligerent. George Tinworth declared that 'Martins father and mother I liked very much for they were allways kind to me', offering a

---

*Robert Wallace is said to have seen a bill poster with the headline: 'DRAWING USEFUL TO ALL' (Blacker (1922), p. 211).

An Associate of the Royal Academy Inspecting the Lambeth School of Art from *The Graphic* (1884), depicting the life room in Millers Lane, top lit by a single central lamp, with various casts after antique sculpture including, left, the *Borghese Gladiator*. The ARA's studied nonchalance contrasts with the assembled men and women who await his judgement.

philosophical thought: 'I think some times that the great creator prepar[e]s people who are to be our friends at stated times in our lives, and ... creates for us our frendships, and then thay are to be a help to us in our jurney of life.'[68] Perhaps it was the boisterous, kindly Martin family who teased the shy George Tinworth from his shell.

What is certain is that with the encouragement of his peers and tutors, George thrived at the art school in Millers Lane; with Robert Wallace Martin, he was admitted to the Royal Academy Schools as a probationer on 22 December 1864 (his presentation piece was a figure of Hercules). His life journey was now firmly on a very different path. But he had to tell his father, because he was required to be at the academy for classes every day, between ten in the morning and one o'clock in the afternoon. To his surprise, Joshua 'said I might go', and 'when I got home at dinner time my mother was crying with pleasure which made me feel like doing the same.'[69]

Every morning, George left home early to get to the wheelwright shop to do some work. He then walked home again for breakfast, before heading on foot to the academy at Trafalgar Square, where he remained until one o'clock in the afternoon, then walking back to Walworth and Clandon Street to continue working with his father. If there was an evening lecture or class at the academy, this journey had to be done twice in one day – and with no money to catch an omnibus. 'I did this for a long time,' George recalled. Regarding materials, he continued in the habit he had developed at the Lambert School of Art of reusing his clay 'sketches': 'I used to do the same with my life studys <at the RA> in the life school after I had finished them, because I wanted the clay. I had got what I wanted out of them, and I could not afford to buy more clay.'[70] In this, George would have stood out from his wealthier classmates.

George recalled that the sculptor Henry Weekes (1807–1877) was the tutor who encouraged him most. One evening while both were in the life school, Weekes turned to George and said: 'You will do it because you stick to it.'[71] George not only won a silver medal for his work in the life school, but (as his memoir records) the president – whether Sir Charles Eastlake, concurrently the director of the National Gallery, who died in December 1865, or his successor Sir Francis Grant – 'said my life study was the best life study they had seen for years'.[72]

George Tinworth's attendance at the academy schools was very unusual for someone from his background and education. But the Royal Academy, alongside art schools and the art world in general, offered employment opportunities for working people beyond art training. These included porters, housekeepers, cleaners and models. The official documentation at the Royal Academy relating to students during the 1860s is scanty, but one cashbook, covering George Tinworth's first three months at the Royal Academy Schools (January to March 1865, called the Ladyday Quarter), provides details about who was teaching, the names of the life models and how much they were being paid. On 4 February the 'visitor' or tutor was John Everett Millais, a founding member of the Pre-Raphaelite Brotherhood and famed painter of *Ophelia* (1851–2).* The male model that day was called 'Westhall', who was hired for six sittings in the life school and paid £1 10s.[73] George Tinworth mentions this model in his memoir and the conversations they had as the art student modelled Westhall's figure in clay. Westhall had been a soldier in the Foot Guards when an artist discovered him. There would have been something about his appearance and physique that made him, in George's words, 'a splendid model' and so Westhall began earning half a crown an hour posing for artists. But in order to attend life classes at the Royal Academy the guardsman had gone absent without leave from his regiment and when another model, George recalled, 'split on him', Westhall was sent to prison. John Sparkes told George that the artists clubbed together 'and bought him out of the gards'.[†74] Two weeks later, Millais was again teaching, and this time the model was a 'Miss Watkins', hired for six sittings, again in the life school, and paid a higher fee of £3 3s.[75] (The appropriate fee appears to have depended on whether the model was male or female, and perhaps also whether 'draped' or 'nude'.) The identities of and payment to these individuals is relevant here, for academy life models, and artist models more generally, were invariably from the lower classes, whether beggars (literally enticed off the street for food or money) or guardsmen, or, like George Tinworth, manual workers and artisans. According to legend, the model for Millais's *Ophelia*, Elizabeth Siddal, a cutler's daughter, had been working in a shop, like George's mother Jane, before her 'discovery'.[76] Physique, bearing and a beautiful or interesting face, rather than 'breeding' or education, were the

---

*Alongside Millais, George refers in his memoir to the academicians Baron Carlo Marochetti, Charles Landseer, Henry Weekes, George Jones (the intimate friend of J. M. W. Turner, 'drest like Wellington'), and John Henry Foley, with a page dedicated to the Albert Memorial and Foley's sculpture of the prince (GTA, p. 108).
†Among the unnamed models mentioned by George are 'an arab girl' and a Frenchman. While the latter was posing in the life school, he 'caught site of something crawling about the floor' and startled the students by crying out, 'THERE A MOUSE!' This prompted the academy to buy a cat: 'I said we ought to put RA on its tail' (GTA, p. 55, insert).

criteria: besides which, it was not considered appropriate for middle-class women to be scrutinised by young men, even in the name of art.

In one anecdote from his early life, George recalled swimming in the Grand Surrey Canal near where he lived – used by locals partly for exercise, partly for recreation, and partly to wash themselves: 'I remember a poor looking young man coming down the bank and taking of[f] his ragged clothes to have a swim ... I could not help seeing the great contrast for he was a fine figure'.[77] George Tinworth, with the naturally appreciative eye of a sculptor, reveals the terrible irony of a fine-toned 'heroic' physique, the naked body of a classical god, emerging from a pauper's rags.

The sums paid by the academy – if compared to what George and Joshua were earning as wheelwrights – were substantial, revealing why the poor and poorer working men and women were attracted to such employment. But attitudes towards lower-class artists' models were usually ambivalent, and often derogatory. William Powell Frith, a teacher while George was at the Royal Academy Schools, famed for his multi-figure race-day painting *The Derby Day* (1856–8), hired many people for his private studio, among them an orange seller whom Frith described as 'of a rare type of rustic beauty', a 'Miss B—' who also modelled nude at the Royal Academy Schools, to keep her father from debtors' prison, and a young crossing-sweeper, again in Frith's words, a 'low, dull, Irish boy ... one degree removed from a pig'.[78]

George Tinworth had succeeded against the odds to gain admission to the Royal Academy Schools, but the environment was competitive, rife with class snobbery and, as Frith's comments suggest, bigotry. Buoyed up by his success in the life school, George decided to go for the gold medal, used all his savings to pay for models to pose for him, supplemented by £10 from his mentor John Sparkes. But this time he did not succeed, later recalling:

> I do not know what I think of this medel business it is not worth any think to an artist you cannot wear the medals if you gain them if you were a boot maker you might show them in your window. They do no good to the student if he

An engraving by Charles William Sharpe after William Powell Frith's painting *The Crossing Sweeper* (1864). Crossing sweepers, like the tragic character Jo in Dickens's *Bleak House* (1852–3), were a common sight in London working a regular patch in an upmarket area, where they brushed the dirt out of the path of the well-heeled or assisted them to cross a busy street in the hope of a tip. Here the young, bare-foot sweep touches his forelock in deference to the elegant young woman whose attention is fixed on the traffic.

gits one, but the disipointment if he dose not git one, I think shortens his life ... I think insted of giving medels give them a 5 pound note to put in the Post office savings bank.

In this section of his memoir, George admits to pawning the silver medal he had won at the Royal Academy for 15 shillings.[79]

Even so, George was taught by academicians, and such training, he hoped, would bring him into contact with prospective patrons, contemporary art collectors and commissioners. With that in mind, in 1866 he submitted a single work to the Royal Academy Summer Exhibition, a group display of hundreds of works by academicians, associates and students, as well as professional and amateur artists. This was the forum since 1769 – when Thomas Gainsborough and Sir Joshua Reynolds were founding academicians, the latter its first president – where a career could be launched. The academicians in 1866 included Sir Edwin Landseer, John Frederick Lewis, Millais, Frith and, among the associates, Frederic Leighton, the future president of the Royal Academy.

George's work was displayed in the sculpture room – alongside portrait busts of worthies, classical and biblical subjects – under the catalogue entry: '979 Peace and Wrath in low life ... *G. Tinworth*'.[80] The use of the phrase 'in low life' places the subject firmly within his own lived experience. It also aligned the wheelwright-student with what were traditionally – and disparagingly – considered everyday events, such as tavern scenes and the labouring class at work and play, in contrast with 'elevated' subjects from ancient history, classical literature or the Bible. George would have understood, in using the term 'low life', the connection with William Hogarth's *A Harlot's Progress* and *Industry and Idleness*, as well as those lampooning so-called 'high life' – most famously *Marriage A-la-Mode*, a source of inspiration to generations of artists and graphic satirists. The six painted canvases from this latter series had been on public display in the National Gallery at Trafalgar Square since the 1830s. Until it moved to Piccadilly in 1868, the Royal Academy shared a building with the National Gallery; George Tinworth's modest 'low life' clay panel was, therefore, not only on display within the same building as Hogarth's paintings, but in the same

Royal Academy rooms where the academician J. M. W. Turner had exhibited acknowledged masterpieces of European art, including *The Fighting Temeraire* (1839). Turner had died just fifteen years before George Tinworth submitted his panel to the selecting committee, and many of the celebrated landscape painter's friends and associates were still actively involved in the academy.

Some years later, when surveying George's career to date, Edward Salmon described *Peace and Wrath in Low Life* as depicting 'a scene common enough in slum life. Two streets arabs were engaged in a stiff fight; two little girls were interfering, and a dog barked in huge delight at the battle.'[81] The phrase 'street arab' was standard in the nineteenth century to describe poor children, making a direct comparison between those on the streets of London with those in lands around the Eastern Mediterranean. The art critic Marion Harry Spielmann commented that in George Tinworth's work 'there is ample justification for the public favour. Not for their art's sake, but for the vivid drama and intense passion with which the subjects are presented'; then adding, damning with faint praise, that 'they go straight to the heart of the devout or the unsophisticated spectator'.[82] Edmund Gosse offers a further description of George's first exhibit at the Royal Academy:

> He sent a work which had no sort of connection with his academic studies, but was the first expression of his peculiar realism. It was a group of four or five small figures in plaster, and he named it 'Peace and Wrath in Low Life'. The scene was taken from his own doors; it was a page from the gutter-life at Hope Street, Walworth. Two little boys were fighting, two little girls were trying to separate them or egging them on, as the case might be. A dog in the foreground was barking with lively interest in the whole affair.[83]

George Tinworth had maintained his distinctively quirky style throughout his years of formal art training. But this perception, pompous and patronising, that his sculptures were realistic, powerful and skilful (to a point), but too crude or unacademic for 'true' connoisseurs of fine art – appealing ultimately to the religious or the unrefined observer – would have a deadening effect on his ambitions and his sources of patronage. (It would become a cause of profound distress and despair for the artist.)

Within months of his son's first exhibit at the Royal Academy, Joshua Tinworth was dead, his death certificate stating the cause as 'Pleuro Pneumonia', after decades of heavy drinking, the strain of work and perpetual worry; he was fifty-four years old.[84] As George recalled, 'When my father was dying I asked him if I should read to him for he had said if a minister had come to him when he was dying, he would push him down the stairs.' Bullish to the end, Joshua nonetheless agreed, and George chose texts from the scriptures to read to his ailing parent. Joshua would say to his son, 'George I often say God be mercyfull to me a sinner'; it was, George recalled, 'the first time I had heard him say these words', for prior to this Joshua had been too proud. But encouraged by his father's contrition, with little time left, 'I said to him would you like to see your brother'; Joshua consented 'as the two had not spoken to one another for many years'. According to his nephew, James came to 5 Hope Street, and George left his father and uncle alone together. He heard the two brothers embracing and kissing one another, and then 'my father died soon after'. Despite everything that had happened, George adds, 'I was sorry to lose him for I was fond of my father.'[85]

Unfortunately, as with Joshua's elder sister Keziah twenty-four years earlier, there was no money to pay for a dignified funeral, and we 'did not know w[h]ere to borrow any, so we had to bury him by the parish'. George kept watch over his father's body, which lay in a simple wooden coffin, while he awaited the undertakers. It was usual for the coffin to be left open, so that family, friends and neighbours could pay their respects. The undertaker would replace the lid and seal the coffin with nails, before transporting it to the cemetery, with the family walking behind. Jane Tinworth would be buried at West Norwood Cemetery in 1881, one of the large municipal graveyards replacing parish church internments in London, and George was placed in the same plot in 1913. But although Joshua's burial was 'by the parish', it is not clear where his remains are located. The undertakers were so late in arriving at Hope Street that, after kissing his father's forehead for the last time, a tender gesture of love, understanding and forgiveness, George closed and nailed down the coffin lid himself.[86] At the time of Joshua's death, there was no money for a headstone, either. Writing fifty years later, George stated: 'In recent years I have tried to find his grave to place a memorial stone over it – but I have not been able to find it'.[87] Perhaps the 1899 terracotta relief of the Clandon Street Wheelwright Shop was intended as the marker for his father's last resting place.

Through necessity George continued working at the wheelwright business in Clandon Street but, as Edmund Gosse observed, it was clear that 'he had neither health nor aptitude' for such physical work and he 'could scarcely earn enough to support his aged mother and himself'.[88] In fact, in addition to Jane, the household still included George's younger brothers, Thomas and Charley. Robert Wallace Martin, just like his friend George, was unable to survive as an independent sculptor despite achieving success at the Royal Academy Schools; he took work as an assistant to leading sculptors, while designing in his own time.

During the prize-giving ceremony at Millers Lane in the December after the 1866 Royal Academy summer exhibition, when Robert Wallace Martin was one of the recipients, Canon Gregory 'gave great commendation to Mr. Henry Doulton, who had employed the students to make the models for his new building in the neighbourhood – a display of good taste and feeling on the part of a Lambeth manufacturer towards a Lambeth school which did him the highest credit'.[89]

The ambitious John Sparkes, later head of the Government Schools in South Kensington,* had, finally, persuaded Doulton to develop a range of art pottery – items skilfully fashioned and decorated, rather than solely functional, some purely decorative – in partnership with the new Lambeth School of Art. It was the idea of expanding into high quality ceramics, with a distinctly 'Lambeth' style, that brought George Tinworth into Henry Doulton's employ.

---

*Now the Royal College of Art.

George Tinworth's terracotta bust, possibly of John Sparkes (made around 1890). George was an accomplished sculptor of portraits, among them of Sir Henry (see p. 141) and Henry Lewis Doulton, Edwin Chadwick and, in full length, the Liberal MPs Charles Bradlaugh, family-planning advocate, and Henry Fawcett, husband of suffragist Millicent, the latter unveiled in Vauxhall Park in 1893.

At the annual prize-giving in 1866, Tom Taylor, an author and the art critic for *The Times* and later *The Graphic*, delivered a speech to the assembled Lambeth School of Art students, alumni and faculty. The address was always presented by a worthy from the broader art world and the substance was invariably on an art-related subject. But this year, as the *London Evening Standard* observed, Mr Taylor offered 'an interesting address to the students, selecting for his subject the importance of cultivating, among the classes of the people, a sense of beauty and a love of art'. His speech clearly resonated with one former student, for George Tinworth would echo many of Taylor's sentiments when writing his memoir over four decades later. Taylor's remarks, as reported in the *London Evening Standard*, are worth repeating in full:

> In these times, more than in the days of old, the lower classes were almost wholly deprived of every opportunity of art education, except such as were specially put in their way. The growth of London was so rapid that, if it were not for excursion trains and the parks, the artisans of this huge city might pass their whole lives without ever seeing the green grass or smelling the sweet breath of the country. The ugliness of our modern suburbs, the sordidness of so many of the phases of nineteenth-century life, the universal haste to be rich at any cost of mental cultivation – these and other influences of the same description exercised a deteriorating effect upon the national life. Proof of this might be found, if proof were needed, in the general ignorance of art which was manifested in the workmen's exhibitions that had recently been held throughout the country. To remedy this was an object of special importance in these times, when politicians were agitating a reform question, and everywhere there was the feeling that education was the fittest preparation for the exercise of political power.[90]

It had been suggested, during the course of the evening, that some student specimens, including George Tinworth's *Peace and Wrath in Low Life*, should be sent to an international art exhibition in

Paris the following year: a wonderful opportunity to promote the school and its alumni.* At this time, however, George's mentor John Sparkes was as much concerned for his protégé's mental and physical health, now he was back at the wheelwright's shop, than his artistic reputation; Sparkes, Gosse recalled, felt his 'heart ache to see such a man digging out mortices in a nave of a wheel, or breaking his back over rickety barrows and broken-down cabs'.[91] The Tinworth wheelwright business made barely thirty shillings a week, as Edward Salmon observed, 'and modest as were his requirements it would have been strange if more congenial employment could not be found to yield him as much'.[92] George himself stated: 'One day I was by myself in the wheelwright shop ... and a strong wish come over me that I might get into some place were I could do nothing but modeling, the wish was like a prayer.'[93] The indomitable John Sparkes was the answer to that prayer. He approached Henry Doulton, asking whether it was possible to find some modelling work for George Tinworth. It was through this deep sense of responsibility towards the welfare of his students, as well as their development as artists and artisans, that Sparkes would 'for many years' be described as 'the most prominent art teacher in the Country'.[94] After all, training working men and women in painting and sculpting can only make sense if they can gain profitable employment using these skills as a result – and the most obvious outlet was in the applied arts: furniture, glass and ceramics. Doulton agreed to meet George, initially offering him the thirty shillings a week to cover the loss of the wheelwright business. 'I went to see Mr H Doulton at the pottery,' George recalled, 'and it was seteled I should come to work for them.' George was one of the first of many Lambeth-trained artists and craftsmen employed directly by Doulton's pottery. Not only was he a trained artist, but he was now earning a regular wage doing something he loved. And his aspiration and drive, supported by his mother, brothers and even his father, meant the family might, at last, find security and, in turn,

---

*But according to Gosse, George's terracotta 'attracted no attention in the Royal Academy, and after going to Paris in 1867, was broken up before it occurred to anybody that it might be worth preserving' (Gosse (1883), p. 13).

Page 69 from George Tinworth's autobiography, with photographs of his portrait bust of Sir Henry Doulton and (beneath) the new Doulton Manufactory (the great chimney to the right) on the Albert Embankment. The headquarters, with offices and artist studios, was located nearby on the corner of Broad Street and Lambeth High Street.

progress beyond their current circumstances. George concluded this part of his memoir by recalling that 'when I got home and told mother, we danced round the table with pleasure'.[95]

Hannah Chaplin began her career in music hall at the age of sixteen and in late 1884 she was performing at the Castle in Camberwell Road. By 1886 she had an agent, Frank Albert and began placing advertisements in *The Era* as 'That Charming little Chanter. LILLIE HARLEY'. She appeared in a benefit concert at the South London Palace of Varieties in May of that year. Topping the bill was the male impersonator Vesta Tilley, and at the bottom, beneath Hannah, a young Marie Lloyd.

4

EAST STREET

'Boiling Water'

Charlie Chaplin's maternal grandfather, Charles Frederick Hill, was a journeyman bootmaker, born on 16 April 1839, a few years before George Tinworth. His wife Mary Ann (née Terry) assisted him in his trade. They had married on 16 August 1861 at St Mary-at-Lambeth, and both had been married before. The identity of Charles Frederick's first wife (he is described as a 'widower' on the 1861 marriage certificate) is unknown; Mary Ann's first husband was Henry Lamphee Hodges, a sign-writer and grainer who had died in a road accident, and by whom she had a son, Henry, who was five years old when his mother remarried. In August 1861, both Charles Frederick and Mary Ann are listed as resident in Lambeth Walk, the popular market street that ran to the west of Kennington Road, in parallel to Broad Street and Prince's Road.[1] It is possible, as mature individuals with experience of life and sex, that the two had been living together before the wedding; marriage was the norm but cohabitation was both a pragmatic and culturally acceptable option for many working-class couples.[2]

Four years later, the Hills had moved to Walworth, and on 6 August 1865 Hannah Harriet – Charlie Chaplin's mother – was born at 11 Camden Street, a road that connects York Street to the north and East Street to the south. East Street – or East Lane, as locals were inclined to call it – is one of the thoroughfares emerging from Walworth Road. To the immediate south-east is Walworth Common and Camberwell, and to the west is the Oval, now the home of Surrey County Cricket Club.

In his autobiography, Charlie Chaplin described his mother's family as follows:

> Mother was the elder of two daughters. Her father, Charles Hill, an Irish cobbler, came from County Cork, Ireland. He had rosy apple cheeks, a shock of white hair and a beard like Carlyle in Whistler's portrait. He was doubled over with rheumatic gout due, he said, to sleeping in damp fields hiding from the police during the nationalist uprisings. He eventually settled in London, establishing himself in a boot-repairing business in East Lane, Walworth.[3]

Charlie's grandfather may have left Ireland for political reasons, but it is more likely that he was part of the mass migration to England after the potato blight and famine that had ruined Joshua Tinworth's nascent grocery business. However, in the various census records, Charles Frederick Hill's history is far less romantic than his grandson believed, his place of birth named as a little closer to Walworth than County Cork. Charlie was not the only storyteller in the family.

The Hills were living at 39 Bronti Place in Walworth when Hannah's sister Kate was born on 18 January 1870; by the time of the census a year later, they had moved to 77 Beckway Street in the same area. In 1871, Charles Frederick Hill was recorded as a thirty-two-year-old boot riveter, Mary Ann as a boot-binder (also thirty-two), and Henry as a fifteen-year-old bootmaker (so joining the Hill family cobbling trade), while Hannah is five and Kate aged one.[4] This constant moving around, from street to street and house to house, echoed the experience of Joshua and Jane Tinworth; a combination of a growing family and irregular income causing difficulty in paying the rent may be the explanation here too.

Mary Ann Hill is thought to have had unusual ancestry, although as with her husband's Irish origins, there is some confusion. In his autobiography, in the section describing his mother's parents, Charlie Chaplin observes of her that 'Grandma was half gypsy. This fact was the skeleton in my family cupboard.'[5] He then says that this grandmother's maiden name was Smith, a common

John Thomson's photograph of 'London Nomads' from *Street Life in London* (1877). Thomson met this group on vacant land in Battersea, gathered around the caravan of William Hampton. The accompanying text states: 'London gipsies proper, are a distinct class, to which, however, many of the Nomads I am now describing, are in some way allied. The traces of kinship may be noted in their appearance as well as their mode of life, although some of them are as careful to disclaim what they deem a discreditable relationship as are the gipsies to boast of their purity of descent from the old Romany stock.'

British Romani family name. Neither Mary Ann's maiden name nor her name from her first marriage was Smith. According to Chaplin's biographer David Robinson, Smith was the maiden name of Charlie's *paternal* grandmother, Ellen Elizabeth Smith, a Romani from Ipswich in Suffolk. She married Spencer Chaplin, Charlie's grandfather, on 30 October 1854.

Further confusion concerning Charlie Chaplin's Romani heritage has occurred since the discovery, following the death of his wife Oona in 1991, of a letter from an eighty-year-old man from Tamworth in Staffordshire, signing himself Jack Hill, which informed Charlie Chaplin that he was born 'in a caravan [that] Belonged to the gipsy Queen who was my auntie you were Born on the Black Patch in Smethwick near B[irming]ham'.[6] It is possible, as observed by Romani historian Ian Hancock, that Charlie Chaplin had Roma ancestry on both sides of his family.[7] Certainly, there was a strong Romani tradition and ongoing presence in Walworth, particularly in the Lock's Fields area, where Charles Frederick Hill and Mary Ann were living in the 1860s and 1870s.

Writing in the early 1910s, George Tinworth recalled seeing a 'gipseys incampment' near Dulwich Wood, south of Walworth, '58 years ago', that is in the mid-nineteenth century. In fact, Dulwich and Norwood have been called the 'epicentre of Romani life' in the south-east of England;[8] the neighbourhood known as Gipsy Hill was named after settlements that had existed in this part of South London since the early seventeenth century. The diarist Samuel Pepys, for example, recorded in 1668 a visit his wife had made 'to see the gypsies at Lambeth' for the purpose of consulting the Romani fortune tellers.[9]

Jack Hill's letter refers to 'the Gipsy Queen, who was my auntie'. The most famous 'Queen of the Norwood Gipsies' was Margaret Finch who, legend states, was born in 1632 in Sutton (then in Kent) and died at the venerable age of 108. According to a portrait dated 1739, Margaret travelled the kingdom for many years 'as Queen of ye Gypsie Tribe'. Generally with a pipe in her mouth, and attended by her faithful dog, 'her place of residence was at Norwood about eleven years before her decease; & by her constant Custom of Sitting on ye Ground with her Chin resting on her Knees ... her

Sinews became so Contracted that she could not extend herself or change her Position'.[10] Her habitual crouching posture, which she maintained until her death, required the fashioning of a cube-shaped coffin. Margaret's 'Gipsy-house' was maintained by the publican of the inn on Gipsy Road, which displayed a sign bearing her portrait. Daniel Lysons, in his *Environs of London*, published in the late eighteenth century, described the Finch house as situated on a small green in a valley and surrounded by woods. 'On this green,' he observed, 'a few families of Gipsies have pitched their tents, for a great number of years, during the summer season. In the winter, they either procure lodgings in London, or take up their abode in barns in some of the more distant counties.'[11]

The common and wood at Norwood were enclosed by an Act of Parliament in 1808, at which point most of what had been 'common' land was parcelled off into allotments. What was left of the wood was owned by the Archbishop of Canterbury, a major landlord and landowner in Lambeth and beyond. Benjamin Pitts Capper, in his 1808 *Topographical Dictionary of the United Kingdom*, declared that Norwood was 'once noted as the haunt of a numerous horde of gypsies'.[12] Allan Galer, in 1890, believed that Norwood had been abandoned completely by them due to the enclosure earlier in the century, but nonetheless they could still be found in adjoining Dulwich Wood, as George Tinworth would confirm.[13]

The significant presence of Romani families over the centuries in South London may explain Mary Ann Hill's suggested parentage. If her ancestry was kept from her descendants, it certainly did not trouble Mary Ann; as Charlie Chaplin recalled, despite her wandering spirit, 'Grandma bragged that her family always paid the ground-rent'.[14]

The Hill family's restless roving, as seen with their Walworth neighbours the Tinworths, was less to do with Roma culture and more to do with the experience of trying to eke out a living in London. By the 1881 census, Charles Frederick Hill, now aged forty-one and still listed as a 'bootmaker', had moved to 132 Southwark Bridge Road along with Mary Ann, who is recorded as having been born in Newington. This suggests that if she had any Roma ancestry, it was from a family that had connections to Walworth. And, rather than Ireland, Charles Frederick's birthplace is named in this census as St Giles in Surrey – the parish in Camberwell just south of where the Hills had been living for decades. It may be that it was Charles Frederick Hill's father, rather than Charles himself, who had migrated from Ireland. Perhaps the famous Camberwell Fair had brought the Hills to South London? Even so, the evidence states that both of Charlie Chaplin's maternal grandparents were born and still lived within this small area of South London.

Mr and Mrs Hill were just a few years older than George Tinworth, who, like them, had been born and raised within this small grid of streets: George's recollections of life around Walworth are part of their – and therefore their grandson's – history, and they would have been near neighbours during the 1860s, so George's life stories once again reflect the Hill family's environment, too. By 1871, though, George Tinworth had moved away from Walworth and was living with his mother and brothers at 40 Thomas Street in the parish of St Mary-at-Lambeth (in the district of Vauxhall), within easier walking distance of his studio at Doulton's on the corner of Broad Street and Lambeth High Street. The widowed Jane is listed in the census as the head of household, aged fifty-five and of 'no occupation'; George was now twenty-seven and a full-time 'modeler'; Thomas, by now twenty-one, was a 'letter presser', and Charles ('Charley'), aged nineteen, was a wheelwright – according to George, at another business.[15] Combined, the Tinworths now had regular incomes from three very different trades and a greater degree of financial security as a result: after decades of struggle and dread, Jane could now expect some stability and comfort.

Since joining Doulton's in 1866, George was gaining in confidence and reputation. In 1869, a fountain designed by John Sparkes and modelled by George had been presented to the people of Lambeth and set up in Kennington Park: when Charlie Chaplin recalled spending time in this park as a child with his mother, this modest monument would have been a prominent feature.[16] Two years later, the International Exhibition at South Kensington became an additional spur for the embryonic art pottery studio at Doulton's. George Tinworth, with the assistance of two fellow

Lambeth School of Art students, decorated pieces of Doulton Lambeth pottery for display among the venerable names of Wedgwood, Minton and Worcester: as he recalled, for the 'exhibition at Kensington ... I put my shoulder to the wheel and we made all manner of things', including a display case 'full of art pottery which took the fancy of the publick, afterwards called Doulton ware'. In the wake of this artistic and commercial success, Henry Doulton began employing in earnest students from Lambeth School of Art in his new art pottery studio. Alongside the leading modeller and sculptor George Tinworth was the twenty-year old Hannah Barlow, Walter and Edwin Martin (Robert Wallace's brothers) and Frank A. Butler, an artisan who was profoundly deaf and mute. Hannah Barlow, who specialised in painted and scored decoration on items like vases, was joined at the company by her sister Frances a few years later. George Tinworth writes that Hannah 'told me she had a sister that was cleverer then she was, I told her to bring her':[17] it is clear that these former Lambeth students were learning their craft in ceramics under George's gentle direction and with his quiet encouragement. The collaboration between the art school and the pottery had created exceptional opportunities for single middle-class women to work as professional artisans and to live independently, and provided at least one working-class man with the wherewithal to make the move from lowly craftsman to esteemed artist. By 1874, former companions of George Tinworth had moved on from Lambeth completely. The Martin brothers – Robert Wallace, Walter and Edwin – established their own pottery in Fulham with a shop in Holborn, crafting distinctive art ceramics that were the antithesis of academic refinement.*

A year later George Tinworth had moved back to Walworth; he appears on the electoral register at 122 Hill Street in the parish of St Mary Newington from 1875 to 1881.[18] In fact George had been listed as a voter in the years 1872 and 1873, too, while living at 40 Thomas Street.[19] He therefore fulfilled the property qualification to vote in local and general elections, following the 1867

---

*They later moved to Southall. Their gloriously grotesque 'Wally Bird' tobacco jars are extremely sought after by modern ceramic collectors.

George Tinworth, possibly wearing the medal he was awarded on becoming an officer of the French Academy in 1878. The writing beneath appears to be in Alice's hand.

Representation of the People Act (also known as the Second Reform Act), which expanded the vote to urban working men (householders and lodgers) who paid annual rents of £10 or more.* This still meant that most adult men – and all adult women – could not vote, but there is an overarching story of change and improvement for sections of the working classes – as represented by George Tinworth – from the 'hungry forties', through the 1860s and 1870s, and then (as we shall see) from the 1890s onwards.

George's fame was increasing with his social status. John Ruskin drew attention to George's work in his much-anticipated review of the Royal Academy annual exhibition of 1875. Regarding three terracotta reliefs, one depicting the New Testament story of 'The Release of Barabbas', Ruskin observed that the style was 'Full of fire and zealous faculty, breaking its way through all conventionalism to such truth as it can conceive; able also to conceive far more than can be rightly expressed on this scale'.[20] He sensed that Tinworth, with his unconventional outlook and training, coupled with a very particular approach to storytelling, was tapping into a raw energy that set him apart from – and potentially in conflict with – conventional taste. At the same time George's studio, at the uppermost part of the Doulton's new building, became a visiting place for royalty, worthies and celebrities. Among the bishops and aristocrats, George recalled one very special visitor: 'She had rather a plain face but you forgot all about her face when you had been in her company 3 minutes.'[21] This was Mary Ann Evans – the novelist George Eliot (1819–1880).†

When the 1881 census was taken, George Tinworth was still in Hill Street, Walworth, named as the head of household and an 'artist sculptor' aged thirty-seven.[22] He is also listed at this address in the Southwark Rate Books ('General, Sewer & Met. Con.') and the Poor Rate Books for St Mary Newington (supporting local paupers, including those housed at Newington Workhouse) for the year 1880; the property's rateable value was then £15, with the

---

*An Act of 1872 had introduced secret ballots for elections.
†George recalled Sir Henry Doulton describing her as the Shakespeare among women (GTA, n.p.); see overleaf.

THE YORK MINSTER PANEL

1. OUR SAVIOUR ON THE CROSS
2. GIVING STUPEFING STUFF TO ONE OF THE THIVES
3. PETER BEHIND THE TREE
4. THE MOTHER
5. JOHN
6. MARY MAGDELEN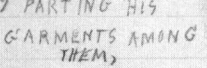
7. CASTING LOTS FOR THE COAT
8. THE COAT
9. PARTING HIS GARMENTS AMONG THEM

THESE VISITORS COME INTO MY ROOM WHEN MODELING THIS PANEL GEORGE ELLIOT AND AND MR G. LEWIS AND SIR H COLE OF SOUTH KENSINGTON WITH SIR H DOULTON H COLE SET DOWN IN FRONT OF THIS PANEL AND SAID. IT IS NOT VERY ORIGHNAL, NOT AN ORIGHNAL SUBJECT, THEN G. ELLIOT COME AND SPOKE TO ME, SHE HAD RATHER A PLAIN FACE BUT YOU FORGOT ALL ABOUT HER FACE WHEN YOU HAD BEEN IN HER COMPANY 5 MINUTES SHE WANTED TO SEE HOW I HAD TREATED THE RELEASE OF BARRABUS BUT I COULD NOT FIND THE SKETCH. SHE TOLD ME NOT TO VEX MY SELF AT THE MOMENT, MR G. LEWIS WAS LOOKING AT A SKETCH OF MINE RAISING OF LAZARUS AND HE SAID I HAD GIVEN POWER TO ONE OF THE FIGURE, WHICH I COULD NOT GET FROM A MODEL, SIR HENRY SAID THAT GEORGE ELLIOT WAS THE SHAKESPERE AMONG WOMAN.

Unnumbered page from George Tinworth's autobiography, with a photograph of *The Crucifixion*. Beneath, George recalls meeting the novelist George Eliot and her partner George Henry Lewes, which dates this event to before his death in 1878. Eliot was ostracised for this loving but 'clandestine' relationship, something that clearly did not concern Tinworth or Sir Henry Doulton.

owner of George's home (and the six properties either side) named as one 'H. Jordan of 39 Finchley Road'.²³ George's mother Jane, now sixty-five, was still living with him. In addition to joining the minority of working men who could vote, this census offers details of another dramatic change in his circumstances: he was married. Alice Digweed (born in Ham, a village on the border of Berkshire and Wiltshire) was twelve years younger than George on their wedding day (8 February 1881) at St Philip's Church on Kennington Road.²⁴ She was the daughter of William, a labourer, and she met her future husband while working as the upper housemaid in Sir Henry Doulton's household in Tooting: by the time of the 1891 census, around 1,649,000 people were working as domestic servants in England, the majority of whom were women.²⁵ It can be inferred, from a diary she kept during 1888 – along with notations she made to her husband's memoir manuscript twenty years later – that Alice had benefited from greater access to education than her husband. The twelve-year age gap between George and Alice means that she would have been of primary school age in the 1860s, when attendance was still voluntary. But over this decade society was settling down and improvements had occurred for sections of the working classes, all of which would have given Alice – the daughter of a labourer – a greater chance of regular school attendance and learning, beyond basic reading and writing skills.

In her diary for 1888, Alice reveals that George had been commanding prices worthy of an established fine artist when she notes the sale eight years earlier of one of George's panels for the enormous sum of 500 guineas (a guinea was twenty-one shillings, with twenty shillings to the pound). This boost in income around the year 1880 may have encouraged him to consider a future independent of Doulton's company.²⁶ It certainly encouraged his marriage and the establishment of a new household. When the census was taken in April 1881, the last-named occupant of the newly-weds' home was Amelia Goodhugh, single, aged fifty-five and a 'lady help', meaning perhaps a domestic servant to assist Alice in the housekeeping. Nothing signalled upward mobility more than the hiring of domestic servants, just as the loss of them is an indication of a decline in status. As a further hint of relative affluence, it may be that Amelia was hired to 'help' both Tinworth ladies – Alice and her mother-in-law. This might have included assistance with dressing in more expensive fashions (daywear, evening wear, accessories) for women who did not work, along with the more ornate 'dressed' hair styles with appropriate headwear that accompanied them – though it is difficult to imagine Jane acquiring expensive tastes in anything. The help from Amelia may have included some form of nursing. George recalled that, long before his own wedding, both his brothers had married, leaving just Jane and himself alone at their house. An unnamed 'old friend come to be with her', he writes – possibly her 'lady help' Amelia – after which Jane fell ill: a situation that continued for many years until her death soon after the 1881 census was taken. '[W]hy should some people suffer so[?]' George asks in his memoir, before recording that he 'had retten on her grave stone, thes words ... such was her faith'. The inscription he made was from the Book of Job (13:15): *Though He Slay Me, Yet Will I Trust in Him*. He concludes, citing another passage from the same Old Testament book: 'It is retten man is born to truble as the sparks fly upwards, some of us know what it is for them to fly downwards again and burn us prety deep.'*27 As will become clear, there are also darker hints that Alice's constitution was not strong.

In addition to the great loss of his beloved mother, it seems that George's success and sense of achievement over the 1880s was further moderated by the vagaries of selling his art beyond the specific work he was given by Doulton's. In short, his style of modelling large terracotta friezes was becoming less fashionable. He suffered a particular blow in 1882, when his large panel depicting the Crucifixion was rejected by the Royal Academy for display in the summer exhibition that year.† This was one venue, and an

---

*Compare: 'Yet man is born unto trouble, as the sparks fly upward' (Job 5:7).
†Of this large-scale relief, George later recalled: 'When my panel was in Kensington Museum I took my wife there one night for her to see it. When we got near the panel, ther was a half a dosen people looking at it, so I would not go near as I know what a silly thing that is for an artist to do, so I went into another room, but my wife went among them, and heard one man say, if you was to see this man that modelled this panel, you would not think that he could say boo to a goose' (GTA, p. 87).

important one, where artists could promote themselves and the sale of their work. George wrote a letter to Edmund Gosse, his supporter, future biographer and a prominent figure at the Royal Academy, full of bitter disappointment and incredulity at the academy's decision – allegedly due to size – bemoaning, 'I must say that I reckon the academy no better than a private house,' and, returning to the rejected art work, 'I consider it the best work I have done.' He goes on to ask Gosse whether he considered the behaviour of the Royal Academy 'fair play'.[28] In his later memoir, George confused this Crucifixion with another biblical panel, *The Return of the Prodigal Son*, but his anger is still evident thirty years on when he notes: 'This panel was rejected by the fiends of the R.A.'[29] (Another panel, *The Meeting of Jacob and Joseph* was, however, accepted the following summer.)[30]

In 1883, in the light of such disappointing treatment by the Royal Academy, Henry Doulton put on an exhibition of George Tinworth's work at a showroom in Conduit Street, off Regent Street in the West End, and Edmund Gosse contributed to a handsome publication entitled *A Critical Essay on the Life and Works of George Tinworth*, with thirty illustrations (produced by The Fine Art Society Limited, Bond Street, London). The exhibition was opened by the future Edward VII, as he had the new Lambeth School of Art, and the Princess of Wales, the future Queen Alexandra. An invitation was extended to Sir Henry and George for them to meet the prime minister, William Gladstone, and his wife Catherine, and have 'tea on the lawn' of a house in Whitehall. In his memoir, after noting this meeting, George states that 'the longer I live the more re[a]lity becomes like a dream to me'.[31] But he came down to earth with a thud after Sir Henry gave him £20 from the ticket sales of the exhibition. As George later complained, 'the income tax people took £17 out of it … It is a hard nut to crack that a man gets up from the greatest poverty and by his talent and industry enriches his country and then the Government steps in and takes from him part of that which he has honestly earned.'[32] How George Tinworth – among the newly enfranchised – voted in general elections is not known, but his conflicted feelings in regard to income tax is more than evident.

Alice Tinworth's diary from 1888 charts her husband's struggles five years later, including bouts of depression and visits to the seaside town of Brighton to restore his physical and mental health. The clear script and phrasing Alice uses throughout the diary confirms not only that she had benefited from a better education than her husband, but also, supported by other evidence, that she acted as his secretary, writing letters (including the one to Edmund Gosse quoted above) that were then sent out under George's name. She was certainly involved with the preparation of his memoir, possibly writing the second handwritten manuscript that irons out George's more idiosyncratic stories, phrases and spellings. 'George often feels dreadfully discouraged,' she wrote in February 1888, 'his panels not selling directly he finished them[;] he often says what a difference with him & painters: when a noted man paints a picture it is sold directly'; and then, in a section redacted with black ink, can be made out the following: 'George says after 20 years of hard struggle and hard work he does not meet with the encouragement from the rich which he has the right to expect',[33] echoing elements of Tom Taylor's speech at the Lambeth School of Art prize-giving in 1866.* On Tuesday, 6 March 1888, Alice recorded that Sir Henry Doulton and John Sparkes had visited George in his studio. He had told them he was unwell and intended to go to Brighton for the weekend. In response to his proposed sojourn, Alice writes: 'I hope it will do him good for I feel quite distressed.' On the following day: 'Poor George hasnt known how to work lately, when he has any thing particular to do he goes at it like a race horse but he does not get the reward he hoped for.' She then notes, 'but as he says perhaps he was a little too ambitious through the unexpected success of [a] large panel which was sold for 500 Guineas in 1880.' A few days later, on Saturday, 10 March, Alice writes: 'My dear husband has gone to Brighton this morning to stay till Monday. I do hope the change will do him good for he seems so exhausted and worn out with dissapointments.' She acknowledges that George had mixed feelings 'leaving me at home as I have always been his companion now turned seven years'. Her final entry that

---

*George mentions Tom Taylor in his memoir (GTA, p. 87).

day records: 'I have felt very distressed about him lately. May god bless him and protect him.'[34]

While the Tinworths' fortunes were evidently on the rise (by small but significant incremental degrees), even if George's artistic frustrations were rising in tandem, those resident in 1881 at the Hills' address in Southwark Bridge Road were still living hand to mouth. They included a fifty-one-year-old lodger called Edmund Donnelly, and Charles and Mary Ann's second daughter Kate (aged ten and a 'scholar').[35] The couple's eldest daughter Hannah, aged fifteen, is listed as a 'Mantle Machinist'. This refers to a type of loose cape-like garment worn by women over their day clothes, whether indoors or, as became fashionable in the 1870s and 1880s, outdoors: exactly the type of garment that Alice Tinworth could now afford. It also means that Hannah had evidently joined the family 'business' of making clothing in the capacity of journeyman – working for others rather than themselves. In 1881, Hannah would have been using a model of mass-produced 'Singer' sewing machine to make the mantles. The 'No. 1' (1851) was set up on the box it came in, while the 'Turtle-Back' (1856) was the first to rest on an iron stand. Newer models including the 'New Family' (1865) and the 'Medium Machine' (1870) were also available, and more technological developments occurred throughout the 1870s. Hannah's circumstance was common across London's poorer districts: workers were crafting garments, for pennies or shillings, that were sold to customers by West End retail outlets at inflated prices. To survive in such economic circumstances, the lodgings of the Hill family boot- and mantle-makers in Southwark Bridge Road must have tapped and clattered with the sounds of relentless industry.

After the 1881 census, however, as Charlie Chaplin observed in his memoir, the 'two pretty cobbler's daughters quickly left home and gravitated to the stage'.[36] Hannah Hill took the stage name Lily Harley. Her expectations as a singer in the music halls were promising and through this change in career she met the handsome Charles Spencer Chaplin (born in Marylebone, London, on 18 March 1863), whom she married on 22 June 1885 at the church of St John the Evangelist in Walworth. Hannah's age in the marriage register is given as nineteen, and her husband's as twenty-two, with Charles listed as a 'Professional Singer'. Both provided 57 Brandon Street as their address, with the groom's father, Spencer Chaplin – the husband of Ellen Elizabeth Smith – recorded as a 'butcher' and Charles Frederick Hill listed as a 'boot maker'. The witnesses were George Bailey, perhaps a friend of the groom, and Mary Ann Hill. Hannah and Charles were married 'according to the Rites and Ceremonies of the Established Church', 'after banns', and the ceremony was conducted by G. T. Cotham, the vicar of St John's.[37] In fact, by the time of her wedding in Walworth, Hannah already had a three-month-old child (born on 16 March 1885). The identity of Sydney John's father has never been settled, but, despite a strong similarity in appearance as an adult, it was always presumed by family members that he was not Charles Chaplin.

It is also generally agreed, despite what Jack Hill wrote in his letter, that on 16 April 1889 Charles Spencer Chaplin junior, always known as Charlie, was born in his cobbler-grandfather's lodgings somewhere on East Street, where, it is assumed, Hannah was also living.[38] Charlie Chaplin's film *Easy Street* (1917) is thought to have been inspired by this long, thin road in Walworth which, throughout the nineteenth century, was the venue for a lively street market. The area, as evident from the census records since 1841, was a resort for costermongers, who plied their noisy trade the length and breadth of East Street: the showmanship required to grab people's attention in such a crowded field has been cited as one inspiration for the young Charlie Chaplin.

Ten years after Charlie's birth, Charles Booth's investigation had reached this area of Walworth, in the patrician form of George Herbert Duckworth (1868–1934), a high-ranking civil servant, Eton College and Cambridge University educated, and the half-brother of Vanessa and Virginia Stephen (later Bell and Woolf respectively). Duckworth acted as an unpaid secretary, as well as investigator, to Booth between 1892 and 1902. This was vital data gathering, for which he and his fellow investigators deserve praise. But given what George Duckworth witnessed over that decade, and the personal commentary and attitudes he expressed in his notebooks, it is pertinent to remark that both Vanessa and

Virginia accused him, and his brother, of sexual abuse: Virginia stated that it began around the year 1895 when she was thirteen years old, while her half-brother was investigating the experiences of the poor working class, including sexual relations and prostitution, in areas where the Tinworth, Hill and Chaplin families lived.

The buildings on East Street are described by Duckworth as consisting of two and three storeys, and the road cobble-paved, with '3rd rate shops on either side'. The market was 'not so busy as it used to be', but even so, it was 'busiest on Sunday mornings when all shops are open & the place is filled with hawkers, quack doctors & all sorts'. Duckworth's companion on this inspection, Sergeant E. Wyatt, observed that on Sundays 'you could walk on the heads of the people there is such a crowd'.[39] Francis Herbert Stead, a resident of Walworth in the 1890s recalled that a 'moving spectacle ... is found at the Sunday morning market in East Street. Besides the indefinite variety of commodities and purchasers, East Street is a true agora' – the term for 'marketplace' in Ancient Greek. 'It is', Stead continues, 'the open-air market for a profuse diversity of mental wares. Most social and political panaceas are hawked with vigour.'[40] Charlie Chaplin's first months would have been accompanied by this cacophonous mix of preachers and costermongers. Herbert Stead, as we will see, had a great interest in the social, political and religious life of the people of Walworth. Within years of Charlie's birth, he had founded an institution that would tap into the radicalism of the area – the *genius loci* or spirit of the place – notably the Chartists' unfulfilled demand for universal male suffrage, in tandem with the rise of socialism and a political party that would, finally, represent the labouring man in Parliament.

At the western end of East Street, in the section called 'Manchester Buildings' near Walworth Road, George Duckworth noted sixteen two-storey houses, with 'careful fronts' and flowers, which were occupied by old tenants. One was a woman of about fifty, who told Booth's investigator that she had been resident in her house for forty-two years and her mother had died there. This resident would have been a close neighbour of Charles Frederick Hill in the late 1880s, as well as his daughter Hannah and her two young sons. The woman informed Duckworth that 'I've buried my husband these 10 years'; the investigator noted that 'she still lives on there with her children' paying eight shillings a week for four rooms and a wash house – perhaps she was earning money as a laundress. But as a long-term sitting tenant, this was a far cheaper rent than was paid by other residents in the immediate area; properties of the same size were being let for ten shillings and sixpence, and fourteen shillings a week for a larger residence.[41] If, as a wheelwright, George Tinworth was making just thirty shillings a week, it could be calculated that between a third and a half of the income of these poorer working-class households was likely spent on rent alone. This also means, as a resident of East Street for forty-two years, that the woman Duckworth interviewed had been in this part of Walworth since the 1850s and had therefore been a neighbour of Joshua Tinworth and his family at nearby Hope Street.

Charlie Chaplin states that soon after his birth in 1889, he, his brother Syd and Hannah had left East Street and moved to 32 West Square, between Kennington Road and St George's Road, with the ominous presence of the Bethlem Lunatic Asylum nearby. 'According to Mother,' Charlie recalled, 'my world was a happy one. Our circumstances were moderately comfortable; we lived in three tastefully furnished rooms. One of my early recollections was that each night before Mother went to the theatre Sydney and I were lovingly tucked up in a comfortable bed and left in the care of the housemaid.'[42] Three rooms and a domestic servant suggest comfort. Echoing George Tinworth's childhood recollections, Charlie also describes the 'things' furnishing their lodgings, in his case including a painting of Nell Gwyn (the mistress of Charles II), long-necked decanters, and a music box, 'with its enamelled surface depicting angels on clouds, which both pleased and baffled me'. 'But,' he continues, 'my sixpenny top chair bought from the gypsies I loved because it gave me an inordinate sense of possession.'[43]

Duckworth would shortly afterwards record houses on West Square that had three and four full storeys, with garrets above, and on the east side of the square were households that kept servants. Under 'General Remarks', Duckworth's companion, here the local policeman Inspector Green, observed that the area had changed over the previous decade. The bad streets 'are not quite so bad as they were', whereas 'the good streets are not nearly so good'.⁴⁴ Inspector Green had spent many years in North London and he had noted, since moving south of the river, that the people seem 'to live in the street more than they do North of the Thames: courts swarm with children & the main streets with working men & women going to & from their work: more loafers here at the street corners: top hats rarely seen' – an indication of an area's affluence; Duckworth, the upper-middle class gent, would have been wearing a top hat. But around West Square and beyond, 'bowlers soft felt hats & caps [are] the usual head gear'.⁴⁵ Even so, West Square was a definite improvement on East Street, the haunt of street sellers and costermongers.

Charlie's recollection that the first years of his life were spent in some ease signals the calm before the storm. Only 'a year after my birth my parents separated. Mother did not seek alimony ... Only when ill-fortune befell her did she seek relief.'⁴⁶ So Charles and Hannah's marriage had effectively ended around April 1890. It is likely that Hannah's husband may not have lived, at any point, with his wife and her children – certainly Charlie's impressions of this early period of his life do not include his father. This is not completely surprising, given that by 1890 Charles had achieved success as a music-hall performer. In fact, that year he was touring the United States as a singer of comic airs reflecting everyday working-class life and relationships with troublesome wives, girl-friends and mothers-in-law. His best-known songs included the franglais ditty 'Oui! Tray Bong!' and, his own composition, 'The Girl was Young and Pretty'.*

By the next census, taken a year after the demise of her short-lived marriage, Hannah, Syd and Charlie were living at 94 Barlow Street in Walworth, near to Victory Place in Lock's Fields (the Tinworths' former residence) and the school of the same name at which, according to a teacher, Charlie would be a scholar. George

---

*Herbert Stead (1912) noted the popularity of music-hall ditties: 'The Londoner tries to doctor himself with the tripping catchy jingle of the music hall. The vogue of this cheap song is something wonderful. But as it is shouted and whistled everywhere, it is sometimes an aggravation rather than an alleviation of the misery of noise' (p. 80).

Sheet music cover (published 1900) where Charles Chaplin senior appears in the character of a 'swell', a wealthy, fashionable man who enjoys a lavish champagne lifestyle. The cover of an earlier hit 'Eh! Boys?' (published around 1890), included images of nagging wives and their long-suffering husbands.

Duckworth observed that the street was a place where 'the Walworth Coster is to the fore: though not poor if his earnings are considered it is he that is responsible for the band of light blue & dark blue streets & courts lying between East Street & the Rodney Road'. The colour coding that Duckworth referred to indicates poverty in the context of the Booth 'poverty maps', but not of the most extreme kind (black). 'Only a small proportion of his money', Duckworth continues, regarding the Walworth costermonger, 'is spent on his home. His numbers increase yearly [as the area] becomes more densely populated: house rooms become precious & rents rise. There is a great demand for school accommodation.' The large school on nearby East Street, he concludes, 'takes in the poorest & roughest of the children'.[47] From this description, the Barlow Street area was decidedly less affluent than West Square and similar to East Street: the infant Charlie, only just two years old, had come full circle.

The building next door to Hannah, 96 Barlow Street, was being rebuilt, so there were no occupants listed there on census night. Their neighbours on the other side, at No. 92, occupied three rooms – like Hannah and her boys. They were fifty-five-year-old John Hawkins, a 'cooper' (a barrel or cask maker); his wife Emma (also aged fifty-five, no occupation); their son Fred (twenty-five), a 'Wood dealer'; daughter Emma (single, aged twenty-one), a machinist; daughter Carrie (nineteen, also single), who was a 'Packer, Tea Grocer'; and son Albert (fifteen) a 'Wood chopper's boy'. This family of six was occupying a similar space to Hannah Chaplin and her sons, but the Hawkins children were all older than either Syd or Charlie, and at least one of them, Emma, as well as living at Barlow Street, may have been operating as a pieceworker from within these three rooms. In addition, other family members could have been using a yard at the back of the building to store work-related items – for example Fred the wood dealer, whose younger brother Albert chopped wood.

Hannah Chaplin is named as the 'Head' of her household and married; her age is given as twenty-four, Syd's as six, while Charlie had just celebrated his second birthday. Hannah's profession is recorded as 'Professional singer Music'. Also living at the address was Hannah's mother, but Mary Ann Hill is listed separately to her daughter and grandsons – for the purposes of the census, hers is viewed as a distinct household, on a different floor within the same building. Mary Ann was described as aged fifty, married and a wardrobe dealer. On census night she was joined in her two rooms by two unnamed women, aged thirty and thirty-five, who, according to the census documentation, 'were admitted Saturday night & turned out Monday without information being obtained'.[48] Was Mary Ann bringing in extra money by subletting a room at No. 94 to single women, perhaps in this instance (given the scant details offered and their unceremonious exit from the premises) sex workers?

At the time Mary Ann and Hannah were living on Barlow Street, the perpetrator of the Whitechapel Murders was still unknown and, as far as anyone knew, still at large. The way the women victims had been described in increasingly sensational and visually graphic newspaper reports has only recently been the subject of in-depth analysis and, as a result, challenge: the reality is that sex work, in itself a difficult term to define, was undertaken by women in a variety of different situations, none of which would warrant branding the women as anything other than victims of economic circumstances that had placed them in the way of danger. As Judith Walkowitz has observed: 'most women's entry into prostitution appears to have been circumstantial rather than premeditated' and, belying the cliché of the swaggering, leering harlot, 'less frequently a result of deliberate migration to specific centers of "gay life" than a response to local conditions of the urban job market': not a lifestyle choice, where other options were available, but a 'rational choice, given the limited alternatives open to them'.[49] Indeed, some women might consider the 'bargain' of physical protection and financial security, through marriage or cohabitation with a male 'breadwinner', in exchange for housekeeping and the 'right' to sexual relations, as a form of sex work: some cohabiting women were described (or described themselves) as prostitutes. It is also important to state, as Charles Booth himself concluded, that many women, some in appearance 'nicely and neatly dressed', did not see or feel any shame in prostitution:

'The plain and simple truth is, that for the most part, they have no desire at all to be rescued. Perhaps the most painful part of the whole work lies in the fact that so many of these women do not, and will not, regard prostitution as a sin.'[50]

Elizabeth Grimwood, called Eliza, may have been one such young woman. In 1838 she was lodging at 12 Wellington Terrace, Waterloo Road, Lambeth, with William Hubbard, a married man who was estranged from his wife, and at least one other couple. Eliza, it was reported 'independently of that circumstance', was 'in the habit of frequenting the theatres, and taking home gentlemen'. On such occasions, Hubbard would retire to another room in the same house, leaving Eliza to take her friends into the downstairs back parlour, which was furnished as a bedroom. Hubbard stated in court that 'he had objected to the girl's prostituting herself at first' but got used to it: in reality, as reported, 'both received a benefit by her prostitution'. One Friday night in late May, Eliza took a gentleman to this back room. The following morning she was discovered lying on the floor, her head almost severed, with defence cuts to her hands and multiple stab wounds over her body. She was clothed, excepting her gown and, so the newspapers reported, the attack must have occurred after sex: 'there having been impressions on the pillows in the bed, as if two persons had been lying down'. The case was a sensation – amplified through morbidly detailed press reporting – although Eliza, 'the poor deceased', was allowed to be a sober, well-behaved young woman, who 'was altogether a better conducted and more respectable person than girls of her class usually are'. Eliza's murderer was never caught. The police, prior to the creation of the detective force, was mainly concerned with crime prevention and failed to make links between the manner of her death and that of other women, which, in retrospect, strongly suggested a serial killer. Four years later the London-wide detecting force was created. But the fact that Eliza could have been murdered in a house where several people were living – including, that same night, her partner and a housemaid – revealed how vulnerable women were who earned their income from sex.[51]

The Criminal Law Amendment Act of August 1885 was an

attempt to protect women and girls from exploitation. Investigations by William T. Stead, brother of Francis Herbert and editor of the *Pall Mall Gazette*, exposed, in lurid detail, the evils of child prostitution – in part, the 1885 Act responded to the ensuing outcry, including a 250,000-strong demonstration in Hyde Park – while epitomising, as Judith Walkowitz observes, a 'new preoccupation with childhood sexuality' alongside a broader 'cultural paranoia' in Britain 'as its industrial pre-eminence was seriously challenged by the United States and other new industrial nations, its military position and imperial holdings by Germany, and its domestic peace and class structure by the spread of labour unrest and the growth of socialism'.[52] The Act should be seen in the context of what historians like Walkowitz have termed the social and sexual 'purity' movement: raising the age of consent to deal with the perceived sexual precociousness of working-class girls; clauses on prostitution to disrupt the trade, including the provision for summary proceedings against brothels, which the police, now, in Walkowitz's words, with 'far greater summary jurisdiction over poor workingwomen and children', enacted with rigour; and an amendment, brought by Henry Labouchere, MP, criminalising all male homosexual acts as 'gross indecency'.* So, in many ways and for many people, the Act made life far worse. Street prostitution was now more likely, with the closing of brothels, and therefore a context far more dangerous for the women.[53] When the reports of the serial murderer known as Jack the Ripper began to circulate in late 1888, South Londoners were reminded of the infamous unsolved 'Lambeth Murder' from fifty years before.

Just a few months prior to the vicious killing spree in Whitechapel, George Gissing, a journalist and later a novelist, was informed of the death of his estranged wife Marianne Helen in a Lambeth lodging house, 16 Lucretia Street, near Waterloo: the area where Eliza Grimwood had lived, worked and died. The immediate cause of Marianne's death was acute laryngitis. She had been in such dire financial straits that she had left a pawn ticket in a nearby public house as security for a debt of 1s 9d, which in

---

*This is the amendment by which Oscar Wilde was convicted in 1895.

turn related to an item she had exchanged for cash at a pawn shop: her wedding ring. In the company of the landlady, Mrs Sherlock, Gissing entered the room where Marianne had died, describing it in the diary entry for Thursday, 1 March 1888:

> It was the first floor back; so small that the bed left little room to move. She took it unfurnished, for 2/9 a week; the furniture she brought was: the bed, one chair, a chest of drawers, and a broken deal table. On some shelves were a few plates, cups, etc. Over the mantelpiece hung several pictures, which she had preserved from old days. There were three engravings: a landscape, a piece by Landseer, and a Madonna of Raphael. There was a portrait of Byron, and one of Tennyson. There was a photograph of myself, taken 12 years ago, – to which, the landlady tells me, she attached special value, strangely enough. Then there were several cards with Biblical texts, and three cards such as are signed by those who 'take the pledge', – all bearing [a] date during the last six months. On the door hung a poor miserable dress and a worn out ulster: under the bed was a pair of boots. Linen she had none; the very covering of the bed had gone save one sheet and one blanket. I found a number of pawn tickets, showing that she had pledged these things during last summer, – when it was warm, poor creature! All the money she received went in drink; she used to spend my weekly 15/– the first day or two that she had it. Her associates were women of so low a kind that even Mrs. Sherlock did not consider them respectable enough to visit her house. I drew out the drawers. In one I found a little bit of butter and a crust of bread, – most pitiful sight my eyes ever looked upon. There was no other food anywhere.

He then describes his wife's body, lying on the bed with a single sheet as a covering:

> It is more than three years, I think, since I saw her, and she had changed horribly. Her teeth all remained, white and perfect as formerly. I took away very few things, just a little

parcel: my letters, my portrait, her rent-book, a certificate of life-assurance which had lapsed, a copy of my Father's 'Margaret'* which she had preserved, and a little workbox, the only thing that contained traces of womanly occupation.

'I felt that my life henceforth had a firmer purpose,' Gissing concludes. 'Henceforth I never cease to bear testimony against the accursed social order that brings about things of this kind. I feel that she will help me more in her death than she balked me during her life. Poor, poor thing!'[54]

The various police officers interviewed by Charles Booth's researchers in Lambeth and Southwark in the 1890s often comment on the presence of brothels within the area, usually hiding in plain sight on a street of terraced houses; most of them had been closed (officially, at least, as the 1885 law had required) and, according to the officers, the occupants had moved on. In an effort to shut down the remaining 'bawdy houses', one police officer in the Barlow Street area told George Duckworth that he 'has had men out dressed as females to convict the brothels'; the undercover ploy never succeeded, Sergeant Sales observed wearily, for the brothel keepers 'always know'.[55] By its nature, providing numbers for women involved in the sex trade – whether 'casual' or 'professional' – is extremely difficult to calculate. By the 1890s, the official data suggested around 8,000 – though some modern historians believe another zero should be added to cover all forms of activity. But it is safe to say that for most of his early years, Charlie Chaplin lived in streets where women offered sex for money, sometimes touting in the streets, sometimes taking clients to their lodgings, and sometimes within brothels.

The one person who is not named as resident in either household at 94 Barlow Street is Charles Frederick Hill, which supports the information provided by Charlie many decades later that his grandparents had separated. The reason, Charlie recalled, 'neither grandparent would tell',[56] though according to family lore, Mary

---

*Thomas Waller Gissing, *Margaret and Other Poems* (London: Simpkin, Marshall & Co., 1855).

Ann was caught in a compromising position with a lover. One possible scenario, far from unusual in the circumstances, is that Mary Ann was herself an occasional sex worker. When times were desperate, women might resort to selling the one commodity they had left: their bodies. We know that mother and daughter were effectively living together because they were each now estranged from their husbands. Aged fifty, deemed advanced in the 1890s for a labouring-class woman, Mary Ann Hill had lost one husband before separating from her second. Her daughter, at just twenty-four, was separated from her spouse – with one child born outside of this marriage and another within. 'To gauge the morals of our family by commonplace standards,' Charlie Chaplin observed in his final autobiography, 'would be as erroneous as putting a thermometer in boiling water.'[57] Mother and daughter were living at the same address in the capacity of the 'heads of household'; both, too, had lost the supporting income of their husbands: neither appeared to be receiving any maintenance. The pressure on them to bring in enough money to feed themselves and the children would have been immense; continual financial need is a strain on even the most entrenched moral scruples.

According to Chaplin's biographer David Robinson, after her second marriage collapsed, Mary Ann Hill had turned increasingly to drink, while earning a meagre income from selling old clothes in the street, likely from a wheelbarrow or cart – and at the same time was becoming increasingly eccentric in her manner.[58] The 1891 census described her as a 'wardrobe dealer', which refers to the buying and selling of clothing. But whether from her rooms at Barlow Street, in the street, or by carting her wares from door to door is not so clear.

She cannot have been generating much income trading in used clothes – nor indeed subletting a room – for by February 1893 her situation had come to a head in a dramatic and distressing way. Mary Ann, whether she was compelled to do so or did so voluntarily is unknown, entered the Newington Workhouse on Westmoreland Road, the institution which in the late 1850s had been embroiled in the 'body snatching' scandal. It is also the place that Martha Harris had avoided for the last years of her life, preferring to live in a van in the street, until her dead body was discovered crawling with lice.

Even so, the workhouse was not a static institution, nor was provision identical across the English regions. As Anne Digby first explored in *Pauper Palaces* (1971), through the prism of how the Poor Law was administered in Norfolk, the institution that Mary Ann and later Hannah and her children experienced was different from the workhouses of the 1840s to early 1860s, with a perceptible softening of the workhouse regime, that now placed less emphasis on deterrence and more on health and education – this shift surely driven by the election of women and working-class men as Poor Law guardians from the 1890s. This more enlightened attitude was evident also in the building of new facilities, and in the improvement of existing ones. There had been further expansion of the inmate accommodation at the Newington Workhouse throughout the 1860s and 1870s, due to increasing numbers of poor, sick and homeless. A second storey had been added to house a female 'vagrant' ward and, after 1869, a new female laundry and bakery were built on Thurlow Street. In 1877, the workhouse was converted into an infirmary due to the large numbers of sick within the St Saviour's Union – fuelled by recent outbreaks of smallpox: an issue for local residents, as well as the one thousand inmates. In response, a new infirmary was built on Champion Hill in Dulwich. By the mid-1890s, when Mary Ann entered the workhouse gates, there were 1,300 inmates.[59]

Until the mid-1840s, when new legislation required separate provision for 'idiots' ('natural fools from birth') and 'lunatics' ('sometimes of good and sound memory and understanding and sometimes not'), those judged to belong to these groups were housed in workhouses or local prisons (also called 'houses of correction'): we might recall the case of Ellen Petty, defined as a 'dangerous pauper' at Christ Church-St Saviour's Workhouse. Wealthier families could send patients to private asylums. The poet John Clare was resident at High Beach Asylum in Epping Forest between 1837 and 1841; Wilkie Collins tapped into the fear of false incarceration within such institutions in his bestseller, *The Woman in White* (published in 1860, but set ten years earlier). The

1845 Lunacy Act, which continued until it was revised in 1890, had encouraged a different attitude towards mental health; it compelled authorities to open purpose-built county asylums, funded by local rates but now pooling finances and mental health expertise and subject to regular monitoring.[60]

The St Saviour's Union Lunatic Report Book notes that Mary Ann had been transferred as 'a Mental Case' from the workhouse infirmary on 17 February 1893, to be remanded in the main workhouse for fourteen days (likely in a separate 'lunatic' ward).[61] Her habits were described as intemperate, and the supposed cause of her attack related to alcohol. In the same documentation, Charles Frederick Hill's address was recorded as 97 East Street. Under the section covering 'earliest symptoms and mode of development' is the following: 'She is incoherent, she says that she sees Beetles, rats mice and other things about the place'; 'she states that the doctors at the inf[irmar]y tried to poison her, she makes a lot of rambling statements and frequently contradicts herself.' Over the following days, the medical officer noted that although Mary Ann continued in this same condition, on 21 February she became 'much worse noisy and troublesome', then, over subsequent days, 'no better', 'ditto' and, finally, 'still the same'.[62]

Study of the entries adjacent to the case notes for Mary Ann Hill reveals other individual tragedies. Entry 193 concerns Annie Maud Isaacs of 39 Henshaw Street, admitted on 13 February aged just nineteen, perhaps of 'irreg[ular]' habits, the supposed cause of her attack (again) 'alcohol?' Annie Maud's occupation was given as 'taker-off', an attendant whose job was to remove each printed sheet from a press. Her mother was recorded as saying that her daughter had made several attempts to jump out of the window of their home, that 'she thinks she is the Queen of England, that she has seen the heavens open & that she saw God, that she says she is a witch & that she knows what is going to take place in the future'. Later notes reveal she had been diagnosed with acute mania as a result of her 'raving, shouting ... swearing'. As there was no alteration in her condition, on 16 February she was discharged to Cane Hill Lunatic Asylum, one of the various such institutions available to the St Saviour's Union.[63]

Sarah Ann King, admitted to Newington Workhouse the day after Annie Maud, was a twenty-eight-year-old unmarried dressmaker of temperate habits, living with her family at 19 Nursery Row. Her next of kin were named as her father, John, and her sister, Elizabeth Kate. The supposed cause of the attack was her 'Mother's death', which presumably occurred a few weeks before admission. Elizabeth Kate said that Sarah Ann had accused her and their father of trying to poison her, that 'she sees letters of blood' and believed that people had been following her and watching her every move. Another note from the medical officer stated: 'She is strange in her manner talks in a rambling way about people watching her and talking about her. She says they go in front of her and write crosses & broad arrows on the pavement.' Over subsequent days her condition remained the same; on 17 February, like Annie Maud Isaacs, she was sent to the lunatic asylum at Cane Hill.[64]

Mary Ann Hill's condition was assessed, as were those of both Annie and Sarah, under the terms of the 1890 Lunacy Act, whereby an individual would receive psychiatric help if they were first certified as insane and then admitted to an asylum. On 23 February 1893, she was assessed by the district's head medical officer and resident doctor at the Newington Workhouse, Dr John Frederick Williams. He concluded that Mary Ann was 'a person of unsound mind'. Under the section of the form requiring details 'indicating insanity observed by myself at the time of examination', Dr Williams wrote, repeating earlier assessments, that 'she is very strange' and 'sees rats and mice running about the place and that there are beetles in her bed'. Furthermore, Mary Ann 'states that the doctors at the Infirmary tried to poison her, and that she is some-times very incoherent, and makes many rambling statements'.[65]

Other details are supplied by James Whitham, relieving officer of the St Saviour's Union. Mary Ann was fifty-two years old, married and a 'hawker', with her religion as 'Church of England'. The incident that resulted in her admission to the infirmary is described as her first attack, the duration of which has been getting 'gradually worse for several months'. Mary Ann was not suffering from epilepsy, nor was she suicidal, and the officials considered it 'doubtful' whether she was a danger to others. It was not known whether another family member was afflicted by 'insanity'. The supposed cause of her attack is put down to 'Drink and worry'. Satisfied of the veracity of Dr Williams's assessment, that Mary Ann was of unsound mind and, therefore, 'a proper person to be taken charge of and detained under care and treatment' in the St Saviour's Union 'asylum', Justice of the Peace, George Leonard Turney, issued an 'ORDER FOR RECEPTION OF A PAUPER LUNATIC'.[66] Charles Frederick Hill, still officially Mary Ann's husband, was ordered to pay four shillings a week to offset her care while at the asylum; his address was given as 87 St George's Road (having, apparently, recently moved from East Street). There is little further evidence of Charles Frederick Hill, in official documentation or his grandson's memoir, until he too enters a workhouse infirmary a few years later.

Mary Ann Hill's situation, and the analysis provided by Dr Williams and James Whitham, recall the reports, four decades earlier, concerning events at Christ Church-St Saviour's workhouse and the disruptive behaviour of Mary Green and Ellen Petty. In this instance, Petty had imagined killing the workhouse officials; both women may have turned to excessive drinking to dull the reality of their unbearable circumstances and then, helplessly addicted to strong liquors, were unable to stop. And, again, given the precarity of such lives, it is little wonder that the mental as well as physical strain took its toll. Charlie Chaplin remembered his Grandmother Hill as 'a bright little old lady who always greeted me effusively with baby talk' and who died 'before I was six', which would suggest a date around April 1895.[67] He does not mention Mary Ann's mental health issues – though the description of her 'baby talk' may be a hint, or else simply reflect the affection and love shown to young children – nor her admission to Newington Workhouse and eventual commitment to an asylum, which is curious: this sequence of events will become a recognisable pattern within his immediate family, albeit one echoed among their neighbours. But at the time Charlie was perhaps too young to realise what had happened; his mother kept the situation from her children to protect them, and the details had become obscure by the time he was writing his autobiography.

The asylum to which Mary Ann Hill had been committed was the London County Asylum at Banstead.[68] Known simply as 'Banstead Asylum', it was located in the village of Belmont near Sutton in the county of Surrey, twelve or so miles south of Walworth – no easy distance for a concerned relative to travel on visiting days (if allowed). It was an immense building, designed by Frederick Hyde Pownall in the ecclesiastical Gothic Revival style, which had opened in 1877. With its signature lofty towers and pointed arches, multicoloured brickwork and stone mullions, Gothic Revival architecture was by now a standard design for imposing civic buildings – and businesses, like Doulton's new headquarters in Lambeth. When used for an asylum or hospital, it self-consciously harked back to an ancient, almost monastic concept of pastoral care, while keeping the inmates at a good arm's-length from the rest of society: an inmate might expect to be cared for, but not cherished. When it was built, Banstead Asylum was intended to provide accommodation for 1,700 inmates. But two subsequent expansions – in 1881 and then 1893, the year Mary Ann entered its walls – speak of the growth in the population of South London as a whole, the correlating pressures on the mental health of these populations, and how the authorities chose to respond: not by addressing effectively the root causes – low-wage employment, poor accommodation, limited healthcare – but by 'dealing' with their effects. A few years before Mary Ann was admitted, Banstead Asylum had come under the management of the newly incorporated London County Council (created in 1889), which had London-wide power over certain aspects of local government, notably education and 'lunatic asylums' (these Surrey County asylums were transferred into LCC control because of the pressure on institutions within the council's territory).

Mary Ann was formally admitted to Banstead Asylum on 1 March 1893, the only admission that day. Her initial assessment reads: 'Has delusions of suspicion thinking that she has been poisoned', while 'unclean in habits' and refusing food. The supposed cause of her bout of insanity was (again) 'Drink and worry'. According to the asylum records, Mary Ann was reassessed a year later, on 10 February 1894, and again on 2 February 1895. By this date, Mary Ann was considered 'recovered' – and she was therefore discharged on 15 March. Even so, she had been an inmate at the asylum for two years continuously.[69] Sadly, according to the St Saviour's Union Records, Mary Ann was readmitted to Newington Workhouse in early 1896, and discharged to Banstead Asylum on 13 April.[70] What happened to her after this is currently unknown; the Banstead Asylum registers, covering the years 1896 to 1900, offer no clue.[71] Charlie Chaplin believed his grandmother died 'before I was six', but, until more information comes to light, we can only suggest it happened when he was between the ages of seven and eight.

The fact that Mary Ann Hill disappears from the record in her mid-fifties is standard for working-class people: Joshua Tinworth's last resting place is not recorded, and it is a detail his son omits to mention. But it only feels strange in the case of Mary Ann Hill because she was a close relative of a celebrity. We do know, however, that three years after she was first admitted to Newington Workhouse in February 1893, her eldest daughter would likewise find the worry of her own stressful and unpredictable life too much to bear.

Following her separation from Charles Chaplin, Hannah had begun a relationship with another music-hall performer, Leo Dryden. David Robinson cites Wheeler Dryden, who said that Hannah and his father Leo lived together as man and wife for one or two years. Hannah gave no recorded theatrical performances over the early 1890s, so, Robinson concludes, given she was able to afford three rooms (possibly in West Square, or her next residence in Barlow Street), 'it can only be supposed that Leo Dryden was providing this temporary prosperity'.[72] However, this cohabiting relationship – and the financial respite it seems to have offered – ended almost as soon as it had begun, following the birth of another illegitimate child on 31 August 1892 – the third child by three different fathers. But Leo Dryden, unlike Charles Chaplin and Syd's unnamed father, returned in the spring of 1893 to remove his son from Hannah's care, when the infant was less than a year old: a distressing episode that would have intensified Hannah's already fragile state. At the time, Charlie was three and half years old and Syd was seven or eight.[73] Neither boy would know anything about their half-brother, Wheeler Dryden, until decades later, when all three were living and working in California. The Hill-Chaplins, like the Tinworths – with family members dying in workhouses or suffering from alcoholism – and countless other working-class families, lived with trauma and secrets.

Hannah Chaplin's life, like that of her mother, seemed to exemplify working-class 'uncertainty' and 'chaos', as observed by the middle-class social reformer Helen Bosanquet. In Charlie Chaplin's account, his mother's theatre career was effectively ended by a physical collapse during a performance at Aldershot; the event has become legendary as the moment when little Charlie Chaplin first stepped in front of a live audience. She 'never regained her voice', Charlie tells us, and as 'autumn turns to winter, so our circumstances turned from bad to worse'. The money Hannah had saved was soon spent, along with her jewellery and other possessions, which she pawned, 'hoping all the while that her voice would return. Meanwhile from three comfortable rooms' – which, as already seen, may refer to West Square, but possibly to their later accommodation at 94 Barlow Street – 'we moved into two, then into one, our belongings dwindling and the neighbourhoods into which we moved growing progressively drabber'.[74] This is the same sort of constant domestic disruption that the Tinworths had experienced in the 1840s and 1850s.

To bring some structure and spiritual comfort into her life, at around this time Hannah joined the congregation at Christ Church, at the junction of Kennington Road, Hercules Buildings and Westminster Bridge Road. This was the independent Nonconformist community that had moved in 1876 from the Surrey Chapel on Blackfriars Road (where George Tinworth's maternal family had been members). The Reverend F. B. Meyer was well known for preaching against prostitution and drunkenness, but one of his parishioners, Charlie Chaplin, described the interminable Sunday services, sitting through organ music by J. S. Bach followed by Meyer's thundering sermons, his voice 'echoing down the nave like shuffling feet'. The only highlight, Charlie recalled, was the partaking of communion wine, with Hannah restraining her son from unseemly over-indulgence.⁷⁵

George Duckworth joined a Sunday service at Christ Church a few years after Hannah and Charlie Chaplin became regular attendees. Looking around at the congregation, he noted: 'Everyone was well dressed, very quietly dressed. They looked as though they were the families of retired Walworthians now living in Brixton' – the latter located to the south and deemed a step up from Walworth. The sermon, Duckworth thought, was 'rather too long but earnestly delivered'; the key messages related to 'reverence' and 'self respect'. 'He is certainly a very good preacher,' Duckworth concluded, although 'it seemed to me that his audience w[oul]d have preferred something a little more sensational than what he gave them.'⁷⁶

From anecdotal evidence gleaned by Charles Booth's project, Hannah's immersion into active church attendance may have been unusual among the poor working class in the vicinity of Kennington Road. George Duckworth's colleague covering the Southwark–Lambeth districts was his fellow Cambridge University graduate, Ernest Harry Aves (1857–1917).*⁷⁷ When Aves asked the Reverend George Bromfield about attendance at his church in the 1890s – St Mary-the-Less on Prince's Road, the church connected to Lambeth School of Art – Bromfield exclaimed, 'Oh! no; as a rule, I should say that nobody goes to church. It has always been so ... You can work up a connexion, with comparative ease, but attendance at church is not the natural sequel, it is not the natural thing.' The cleric spoke of a man who had arrived in the parish from Durham in England's north-east. There, he had not only been a regular parishioner but a churchwarden. Once he arrived in Reverend Bromfield's South London parish, however, the man never once set foot inside his church; by the same token, he knew people whom he rarely saw in his church, but having moved out of London and into the countryside, would immediately commence regular church attendance: a description, albeit anecdotal, which suggests that developing a sense of community was more difficult among a constantly shifting urban population.⁷⁸

---

*From 1889 to 1907 he was the secretary to the Universities' Settlements' Association.

'It is not a dislike, and not an unbelief,' the Reverend Bromfield continued; 'all the mothers bring their children to be christened and I myself feel like a grandfather in the parish.'[79] Ultimately, he put down the cause of absence at church to the difficulty of their lives and a desire to use what little rest time they had in other ways: 'No one is stirring here on Sunday morning until eleven or so, and I think that, although a good many get right away' – to visit relatives, perhaps, or to the seaside – 'the great majority are actually in their homes.' He offered another example by way of explanation. A woman who was employed as a cleaner at St Anselm's (the parish's nearby mission church at Kennington Cross) had a son aged about fifteen, 'a good boy who helped his mother in a good many ways':

> But the children gave the cleaner trouble on Sunday, and so she asked her son to come to church, and try and keep them in order, and prevent them from making things in a mess. This was the boy's reply: 'Mother, I'll clean for you, work for you, do almost any-thing for you; but, if you talk to me of going to church – I'll enlist!'

For this young lad, joining the British Army and fighting, for example, in South Africa during the Boer Wars (1880–1 and 1899–1902) was preferable to going to church. In conclusion, the Reverend Bromfield believed that there were two classes of young people who were attracted to – and retained by – the church: 'the cleverer, and the very stupid'.[80]

Another vicar, the Reverend Allen Edwards of All Saints in south Lambeth, told George Duckworth that despite every effort to attract people into his church, 'they remain utterly stubborn', declaring that 'we have piped to them and they have not danced'. The reason for their non-attendance at church, Edwards believed, was 'the same reason that I don't go to race meetings: it does not interest them, they know nothing about it. I have had the Bishop of Rochester here to preach but it does not attract them: they know no more of the Bishop of Rochester that I know of Dan Leno.'[81] In other words, this is an example of the working class exerting what little agency they had: being entertained by one of their own, considered the greatest music-hall performer of the day, rather than being harangued and preached at by some toff in a mitre.

In contrast, the cleric from the adjoining parish of St Mary-at-Lambeth, the Reverend Reeve, told Ernest Aves that attendance at his church was around 400 on a Sunday morning, 600 on a Sunday evening, with the congregations in the winter season the largest: perhaps because, huddled together, the church was warmer than many poor working-class homes. (This is the church where George Tinworth and Charlie Chaplin both had family associations, via the marriages of their grandparents.) Easter communicants numbered about 400 and, overall, 'Those who come are poor.'[82] The vicar then explained that the 'majority of the people are of the unskilled class; occupations are very mixed. Many of the women work, and the men are often brutes "that is, often live on the labour of their wives".'[83] 'In one respect', noted Aves, 'the parish is unique, for it contains' – here quoting the Reverend Reeve – '11,000 poor and the Archbishop of Canterbury, and nobody in between.' Reeve was the chaplain to the Archbishop, Frederick Temple, who had been in post since 9 November 1896.* According to Reeve, Temple attended services at St Mary's as a parishioner: 'I thus have the care of his soul. He often attends the Church, but always as an ordinary worshipper, coming in and taking his seat like any miserable layman.'[84]

There is another reason why working-class Londoners might have distrusted organised religion, and the Church of England in particular, despite the presence of such affable clerics as Temple and Reeve. As the State Church, it was essentially conservative and, constitutionally, part of the hierarchical system maintaining a status quo that continued to exclude many workers from having influence over most aspects of their lives. Put simply, the Established Church looked after 'the Establishment'.

In his autobiography, Charlie Chaplin offered a poignant description of the impact that religion had on Hannah and her children, as a way of accommodating their troubles within a

---

*He would serve until 22 December 1902, and officiated at the coronation of Edward VII that year.

broader world of collective suffering: such hardship would have been evident in the streets around them, as well as within their own family. By the mid-1890s, Hannah, Syd and Charlie had reached the point where they were sharing a single room in a property on Oakley Street (now Baylis Road). This street, near where George Tinworth witnessed Garibaldi's triumphal parade in 1864, connects the junction of Kennington Road, Hercules Buildings and Westminster Bridge Road, with Waterloo Station, Lower Marsh and the New Cut. At the east end of the latter was the Christ Church-St Saviour's workhouse, and at the west end, at the junction with Oakley Street, was the theatre that by 1880 was formally called the Royal Victoria Coffee and Music Hall but was already known by the affectionate nickname the 'Old Vic' – one of the many establishments that offered entertainment while encouraging temperance among the working class.

Charlie later recalled 'an evening in our one room in the basement at Oakley Street'. He was 'in bed recovering from a fever', and his mother

> sat with her back to the window reading, acting and explaining in her inimitable way the New Testament and Christ's love and pity for the poor and for little children. Perhaps her emotion was due to my illness, but she gave the most luminous and appealing interpretation of Christ that I have ever heard or seen. She spoke of his tolerant understanding; of the woman who had sinned and was to be stoned by the mob, and of his words to them: 'He that is without sin among you, let him first cast a stone at her.'[85]

Hannah's references connect precisely with her own personal circumstances; whether an exact recollection or a scene invented by an empathetic son, it has the effect of an appeal not to judge, nor to forsake her, but to look upon her with kindness, to help a suffering woman. In his film *The Kid* (1921), Charlie was clearly thinking of Hannah when he created the character of the unmarried woman 'whose only sin was motherhood', driven to abandon her infant. The Oakley Street anecdote also emphasises the idea of Jesus as

Sunday Morning in the New Cut, Lambeth from the *Illustrated London News* (1872). On Sundays, trading was allowed at the New Cut market before church services. The reporter notes: 'many working-class families in Lambeth cannot get their needful purchases for Sunday made on Saturday night, because they work late on Saturday and do not receive their wages till the evening.'

the champion of the poor and downtrodden. 'In that dark room in the basement at Oakley Street,' Charlie concluded, 'Mother illuminated to me the kindliest light this world has ever known, which has endowed literature and the theatre with their greatest and richest themes: love, pity and humanity.'[86]

Hannah Chaplin may have gained comfort as a member of the Christ Church congregation, but as described by Charlie, their situation was wretched. Since Hannah had joined the church, she had lost touch with her theatre friends – 'That world evaporated' – and was increasingly dependent on the church for paid work, as well as moral and spiritual support: 'jobs were hard to find and Mother, untutored in everything but the stage, was further handicapped. She was small, dainty and sensitive, fighting against terrific odds in a Victorian era in which wealth and poverty were extreme, and poorer-class women had little choice but to do menial work or to be drudges of sweatshops.' The 1881 census had recorded that

Hannah had trained as a sewing machinist in her mid-teens, before moving into a music-hall career. It was, at least, a skill that offered the opportunity of earning money while working from home. As Charlie wrote, 'she was expert with her needle and able to earn a few shillings dressmaking for members of the church. But it was barely enough to support the three of us.'[87]

Financial and personal distress – 'drink and worry' – had been offered as the cause for Mary Ann Hill's collapse and admission to the workhouse, her hallucinations and paranoia testament to her anxiety. Now her daughter was battling 'terrific odds' in an age when, as Charlie would later observe, the separation between the wealthy and the poor was extreme, and when the means to survive were limited, particularly for women. The Reverend Meyer might use his pulpit to harangue against the wages of sin, of selling sex and self-anaesthetising with alcohol, but elsewhere a practical form of Christianity was offering a different course – and one where the working class had taken matters into their own hands.

Just as Mary Ann Hill was spending her first months at Banstead Asylum, James Keir Hardie was preparing to make a speech at the Labour Church on Walworth Road. This was a new religious movement, in tandem with the formation of the Independent Labour Party, which combined the teachings of Jesus with socialism. The illegitimate son of Mary Keir, a domestic servant from Newhouse in Lanarkshire, Keir Hardie had been raised by his mother and stepfather, David Hardie, a ship's carpenter. He was working by the age of seven and at ten he was employed in the coal mines. Of a strong Christian faith, discovered through the temperance movement, as a young man he had been a member of the Evangelical Union Church in Hamilton, where the future missionary and explorer David Livingstone had been an associate. Keir Hardie believed that the 'rich and comfortable classes have annexed Jesus and perverted His Gospel. And yet he belongs to us ... Make no mistake about this. The only way we can serve God is by serving mankind. There is no other way.'[88] He saw no contradiction between Christianity and socialism, which he expressed through this simple phrase: 'Believe, says the preacher. Believe and Act, says the socialist.'[89]

James Keir Hardie, taken around the time he won the West Ham South parliamentary seat in 1892. He was attacked in the press for wearing a tweed suit, red tie and deerstalker (as seen here) in the House of Commons, rather than the usual parliamentarian 'uniform': morning suit, including a black frock coat and cravat or tie, and silk top hat.

Prior to the 1892 general election, it was presumed that any hope of expanding the vote of working men and their representation in Parliament would be dependent on support from the Liberal Party – the descendants of the Whigs who had instigated the Glorious Revolution and the supremacy of Parliament over monarch. But in that year, Keir Hardie had been elected an independent Member of Parliament for the constituency of West Ham South, along with John Burns in Battersea and Havelock Wilson in Middlesbrough. A conference in 1893 at the Bradford Labour Institute, operated by the Labour Church with the support of the Trades Union Congress, became the foundation event of the small Independent Labour Party, with Keir Hardie as its chairman. The playwright George Bernard Shaw was in the audience.* The object of this new party was 'to secure the collective and communal ownership of the means of production, distribution and exchange', with a progressive programme of social reform, including of housing, welfare for orphans, widows, the elderly, the sick and disabled, the abolition of child labour, a minimum wage, and an eight-hour working day.

Keir Hardie was also a follower of the temperance movement; he had been a total abstainer his entire life, partly as a stand (echoing George Tinworth) against the drunken abuse meted out by his adoptive father to his mother and himself. In his 1893 speech, before a crowd of Walworth locals, and as summarised in the *South London Mail*, Keir Hardie began by considering the dependency on alcohol among the working class: a dependency, he believed, encouraged by vested interests such as wealthy distillers and brewers, who, as part of the moneyed classes, made profit from workers. The advertisements promoting the sale of beer houses in Walworth's 'thoroughly beer-drinking neighbourhoods' – and the opposition in Parliament to any attempt to rein in the licensing of such establishments – proved his point. And, as Keir Hardie,

---

*Shaw was a founding member of the Fabian Society, established in 1884, alongside Emmeline Pankhurst, Beatrice Webb and H. G. Wells. The Fabians established the London School of Economics in 1895 and helped bring the various elements of the labour movement together as the British Labour Party in 1906.

George Tinworth and Mary Ann Hill knew all too well, excessive drinking could have a devastating impact on the family as well as the individual. Keir Hardie believed temperance among his fellow workers would solve their fundamental difficulty; as he argued, a sober people would not tolerate 'what men put up with who [had] lost their senses in liquor'. He then observed that the issue of the day was how those who produced the wealth of the country, the workers, 'might be allowed to spend it'. And he meant *every* worker – be they a wheelwright or a mantle-machinist.

The biblical references that followed in Keir Hardie's speech on Walworth Road were delivered in a tone more caustic than that used by Hannah Chaplin. Albeit delivered in the wry humour of a class used to making the best of a bad situation, his message was just as serious. Using the analogy of lilies growing in the countryside (in direct allusion to the Sermon on the Mount),* all with equal access to sunshine and rain, he then invited his audience to imagine some monstrous lily claiming nine-tenths of the dew, the rain and the sunshine. How, he asked, would other lilies thrive? 'That', he declared, 'was the state of things in the industrial world,' and given this, 'how could they expect people to live under such conditions?' He raised the issue of housing as a particular iniquity, whereby landlords – locally notable among them the Prince of Wales's lucrative Duchy of Cornwall estate, the Church of England, and City companies – fed off their poor tenants, leaving everything beneath in the deadening shade of what he termed the 'overshadowing fungi of landlordism'.

Some advocates of raw capitalism had argued that Darwinian 'survival of the fittest' was as natural to human beings as animals. Addressing this head-on, Keir Hardie recalled seeing, during a visit to the British Museum,† the enormous remains of an extinct species of animal: 'Nature found that these huge animals were too

---

*'Consider the lilies of the field, how they grow: they toil not, neither do they spin' (Matthew 6:28).
†Keir Hardie must be referring to a visit some years before because, prior to the opening of the Natural History Museum in South Kensington (1881), such collections were displayed at the British Museum in Bloomsbury.

expensive to keep, and so they were allowed to die out, and smaller ones were created which cost less.' He hoped that one day, on a visit to the museum, he and his audience would be able to view a specimen of a landlord, stuffed and displayed in a glass case with the following description attached: 'These monsters used to roam this earth and devour the living of the people, but it costs too much to keep them and so they were allowed to die out.' This comment generated laughter of recognition from the working men gathered.[90]

For Hannah Chaplin, however, and her fellow 'poorer-class women' in the mid-1890s, there was little to laugh about. Charlie Chaplin recalled how, in 'the depth of this dolorous period', his mother began suffering from severe headaches, which forced her to give up needlework. She would lie for days in a darkened room.[91] 'Picasso had a blue period,' he continued. 'We had a grey one, in which we lived on parochial charity, soup tickets and relief parcels.'[92] (Chaplin's autobiography is littered with such references to 'high' culture, reflective of Charlie's self-education – matching that of George Tinworth's – as well as the access provided by his wealth and his increased social standing.) Unsurprisingly, Hannah and her sons were now surviving on 'outdoor' poor relief – food and money – rather than 'indoor' relief at a local workhouse. A stroke of good luck one day brought a purse full of cash, found by Syd, who was now selling newspapers in the street and on omnibuses, and Hannah immediately took her sons on a trip to the seaside at Southend with the proceeds. It was an understandable desire to have some temporary liberation from the grind of poverty, as well as the first time that her sons had seen countryside – and, more powerful still, the sea. Charlie adds to the poignancy of this episode, for the respite from their struggle was all too brief: 'Like sand in an hour-glass our finances ran out, and hard times again pursued us. Mother sought other employment, but there was little to be found. Problems began mounting. Instalment payments were behind; consequently Mother's sewing machine was taken away.'[93]

If Charles Chaplin senior was earning any money as a performer, he was certainly not providing for his estranged wife and her children. He was also, by this point, an alcoholic and, in addition to lingering in the theatre bars between and after performances (to raise alcohol sales from punters), a regular at the public houses around Kennington Road. 'Because of Father's drinking,' Charlie wrote, 'his theatrical engagements became irregular, as did his payments of ten shillings a week. Mother had now sold most of her belongings. The last thing to go was her trunk of theatrical costumes.'[94] And by the time Hannah had lost her sewing machine, and therefore any obvious means of earning money, 'Father's payments of ten shillings a week had completely stopped.'[95]

Presumably due to her headaches and inability to work, Hannah Chaplin was admitted to the Lambeth Infirmary, adjoining the workhouse on Renfrew Road, on 27 July 1895. The workhouse had been built by the Lambeth Board of Guardians in 1871 – the foundation stone laid by John Doulton, Chairman of the Board of Guardians and the founder of the celebrated Lambeth pottery nearby – with an enormous water tower that loomed over the area like a beacon of dread. The infirmary opened in 1877.[96] This, as Hallie Rubenhold has revealed, was the recently established institution at which Mary Ann or 'Polly' Nichols arrived in 1880, after leaving her adulterous husband: admission to a workhouse, by claiming desertion, was one of the few ways a working-class woman could secure an unofficial separation at this time.[97] Polly would return to this same workhouse in 1882, 1886 and 1887; the final time was in mid-1888, after which, in the August, she walked north, crossing the Thames, and found herself homeless in the East End area of Whitechapel, only to be later murdered there by its infamous serial killer.[98]

Seven years later, in July 1895, Hannah's mother, Mary Ann Hill, was still resident at Banstead Asylum, so Hannah had been without maternal support for several years. At the same time as Hannah's admission to the infirmary, Syd entered the Renfrew Road workhouse, and was then transferred to the infant paupers' school at Norwood, where he would remain for over two months.

The infirmary register, regarding the 'Examination of Mother by Relieving Officer', noted the admission of 'Annie Lilian Chaplin', a jumbling of Hannah's real and stage names, which seemed to reflect her state of mind at the time. Hannah is recorded as being twenty-five years old (she was actually four years older), married, and admitted from an address on York Road (number 164), where she had been resident for nearly two years. The officer's notation then takes the form of reported speech: 'left my Husband Charles a Professional now at Canterbury Music Hall, he is now residing at 9 or 10 Penton Place, Newington Butts'. That Hannah knew where her husband was lodging, just a few minutes' walk from the workhouse infirmary where she and Syd were then sitting, may be connected to the payments she had been receiving from him. If Charles Chaplin was performing regularly at the famous Canterbury Music Hall on Westminster Bridge Road – in his autobiography, Charlie says he saw his father perform there – then he would have been able to offer some support, practical as well as financial, to this small, desperate family. Indeed, as Charles Chaplin would discover, Poor Law guardians considered an able-bodied husband responsible for the upkeep of his wife and children and, accordingly, would pursue him for reimbursement, via the magistrates' court if necessary. The entry continued: 'Married at St. John's, Walworth 10 years ago M/N [maiden name] Hill I cannot give date.' Again, being unable to recollect the date of her wedding may hint at Hannah's confusion. The name 'Sidney', with the number 10 (her son's age), is written in the margin under 'Annie Lilian Chaplin' and alongside her assigned infirmary ward.[99]

The notes taken by the social investigator George Duckworth give a sense of where Hannah and her two boys had been living for the past two years. They record York Road, running to the west of the railway line into Waterloo Station, as full of 'variety agents; warehouses: hotels: prostitutes', with 'many hotels' that are 'little else than brothels'. (Major railway stations, like Waterloo, were a magnet for sex workers and their clients.) Sergeant Saltmarshe, his police companion at the time, observed of York Road, that 'girls live there & bring men home'. Duckworth also noted that there were 'some servants'. The adjoining College Street he described as 'mixed: two houses on the W[est] side given up to prostitutes'. Sergeant Saltmarshe described these houses as prostitutes' 'homes', explaining that only some houses would allow sex workers to lodge with them, and those that did 'were called "homes" by the police'. Duckworth quoted the police officer's empathetic declaration that these women must live *somewhere*; in their defence, he concluded, they did not bring men back to their lodgings; 'those who work the same road like to live together'.[100]

The entry preceding that for Hannah and Syd in the infirmary register concerns Rosina Wright of 33 Harriet Street, aged twenty-two and admitted on the same day as the Chaplins (27 July 1895).[101] By the time George Duckworth was exploring the area a few years later, Harriet Street had been renamed Grindal Street. It was located near Lower Marsh, running parallel to Oakley Street, where there was 'a very busy shopping street, barrows all along the N[orth] side'. Duckworth described Grindal Street as 'rough, low class Irish ... all doors open ... street full of women & children', and concluded that 'though this is a poor district all the children are remarkable for their clean faces'.[102] Rosina had arrived at the infirmary with her baby son Samuel, aged just five weeks – but as noted by the relieving officer, the child had since died. Oakley Street, where Hannah and her sons had been living prior to York Road, is described in Duckworth's notebook on the same page as Harriet Street, with York Road located just to the west. So Hannah, Syd, Rosina and her newborn Samuel had been resident in adjoining streets on the day they had all made the walk to Renfrew Road.

According to the official documentation, Rosina had been living on Harriet Street for just two weeks; prior to that, she had lived for two months at 10 Crossbow Road in Bermondsey.* According to Rosina, she had married Charles Wright at Lambeth Church (i.e. St Mary-at-Lambeth) on 8 July 1891. But less than four years after their wedding, and just a few months before Rosina had entered the infirmary, her husband had committed suicide by jumping from Westminster Bridge. As a resident – now pauper – of the Lambeth area, she was already able to claim assistance from the Board of Guardians; she now offered the relieving officer the additional information that her husband 'was bred and born in Lambeth', details she may have felt the need to offer if she herself

---

*Before that, for about ten months, Rosina was at 36 Neale Street, Camberwell, and before that, again for just a few months, at 68 Willow Street, Walworth.

had been born elsewhere.[103] The few details contained within the official record offer a further tragedy: that Rosina was probably pregnant when her husband took his own life; she had given birth, and then struggled to survive alone with a tiny, desperately sick baby. That Samuel had died so soon after he and his mother had entered the Renfrew Road infirmary is a double tragedy.

However, a report concerning her husband's death in the *South London Press* – suicides were inevitably newsworthy – suggests an even more complicated domestic situation. Under the headline 'BERMONDSEY MAN'S TRAGIC SUICIDE', the report stated:

> Charles Thomas's second romance ended sadly. He was aged 33, and a slater in Goswell-street, Bermondsey. He dropped off Westminster Bridge into the river about 1 o'clock on the morning of April 2. Evidence was given by his relatives to the Westminster coroner, and by Rosina Wright, a young woman who passed as his wife, to the effect that poverty, through lack of employment, had unhinged the man's mind. He was a widower. An hour or two before turning to the river, Thomas, who had sold up his home, got Mrs. Wright admitted to the Bermondsey Infirmary to be confined with her second child, and his brother said he believed that having to do this broke his heart. Mrs. Wright was now in court with her infant, and seemed very weak and ill. Her superior appearance led the coroner to enquire who were her friends, and it was stated that her father was a station master in North London, and that he disowned her, so that she would have to go back to the workhouse. The jury found a verdict of suicide while of unsound mind, and with the coroner subscribed a small sum for the woman.[104]

What happened to Rosina's first child is not known, although it is possible he or she was adopted by Charles Thomas's blood relatives or, like Samuel, had died. But the report confirmed that she was not Charles's wife (his surname was Thomas, while she is described as 'Mrs. Wright' who 'passed as his wife'), that the couple had been living together (no doubt the reason for her father disowning her), and that Charles's inability to maintain his family had driven him to a desperate course of action.

Rosina's story can be traced through official documentation. After she and Samuel were admitted to the Renfrew Road workhouse infirmary in July, at the same time as Hannah Chaplin, Rosina entered the Lambeth Workhouse on Prince's Road, alone, on 23 August 1895. Her occupation was then listed as 'servant' and her year of birth as 1873. She was discharged at her own request two weeks later. She was then readmitted to the same workhouse, and then discharged to the adjoining infirmary on 5 October. A 'Rosina Wright' entered the Newington Workhouse on Westmoreland Road on 16 May 1897, aged twenty-six; her year of birth was recorded as 1871, her religion was given as Roman Catholic, and she was then resident in the parish of St George-the-Martyr. If this is indeed the same Rosina Wright, her Roman Catholicism may explain why she and Charles Thomas had not married: 'Mrs. Wright' might perhaps have been already the wife of someone else. This Rosina Wright's occupation was simply given as 'needle' – a seamstress, like Hannah Chaplin. Finally, on 3 June 1897 Rosina Wright was discharged to Claybury Asylum, yet another London County Council lunatic asylum to the north-east of London.[105] In 1896 this institution had the capacity for 2,500 inmates.

Charlie Chaplin did not enter the Renfrew Road infirmary or workhouse with his mother and brother in early July 1895, but remained at 164 York Road – where, according to the surviving paperwork, Hannah and Syd had been living prior to admission – in the care of John George Hodges, a relative of his maternal grandmother's first husband. Hannah left the Lambeth Infirmary on 30 July, while Charlie was admitted on 2 September 1895 to a local school on Addington Street. In the documentation, Charles Chaplin is named as Charlie's parent. It confirms that the six-year-old was resident in York Road – as noted, near to the one-room abode on Oakley Street – and under the column 'Last School (if any) Attended', the answer is 'none'.[106] So, despite compulsory state education for working-class children, Charlie had been denied any schooling at all for around a year. The constant moving from lodging to lodging was one explanation, although we cannot ignore the fact that the adult in charge was responsible for registering the child: something Hannah had, apparently, failed consistently to do. Here we have a good example of the continued problems in getting the poorest children to school, related, as seen here, to the precariousness and difficulties of their lives: the situation was not always static; it was constantly volatile.

Syd remained at the Norwood Schools until mid-September, when he returned to the Renfrew Road workhouse and was discharged. However, this was just the first encounter for Hannah Chaplin and her sons with Poor Law Unions. According to David Robinson, Hannah, as 'Lily Chaplin', had performed at the Hatcham Liberal Club on 8 February 1896.[107] But at around the same time she had been trying to extract money from her estranged husband; in her youngest son's words, in 'desperation she sought a new solicitor, who, seeing little remuneration in the case, advised her to throw herself and her children on the support of the ... authorities in order to make Father pay for our support'. This was not forthcoming. So, in poor health, with two children, and all other options exhausted, Hannah 'decided that the three of us should enter the Lambeth workhouse'.[108] It should be reiterated that no one did this on a whim. With her husband untraceable, her mother in an asylum and her father paying for his estranged wife's care, presumably there was no one left (including her sister Kate) upon whom Hannah could rely.[109]

Decades later, the adult Charlie Chaplin would blur and conflate the various events experienced by his family in the mid-1890s at two separate workhouses and their associated infirmaries and pauper schools. When Chaplin talks of the 'Lambeth Workhouse', there were two such institutions: one on Prince's Road near where the Lambeth School of Art had been established, and the more modern building on Renfrew Road, the location known to Hannah, Syd and Polly Nichols. And then there was the Newington Workhouse on Westmoreland Road in Walworth, the institution to which Mary Ann Hill had been sent prior to her removal to Banstead Asylum. The Renfrew Road and Westmoreland Road institutions were within a mile of each other, but were located within distinct parishes, under the management of different Poor Law Unions and administrative areas. It is confusing enough for a modern researcher, but the records show that within a year of Hannah and Syd entering the Lambeth Infirmary and Workhouse on Renfrew Road, they, and now Charlie, were admitted to the Newington Workhouse in Walworth.

A Lambeth pauper boy called 'Tommy' and a local police sergeant, photographed for the article 'A Day in the Life of a Workhouse Child' in the *Leisure Hour* (July 1902). See also p. 214.

5

KENNINGTON CROSS

'This Dolorous Period'

In the last decades of the nineteenth century, mothers were 'discovered' by social thinkers; as Ellen Ross describes it, 'The sense in which mothers are responsible to the state and are under its scrutiny, expected to turn out a child schooled in specific ways and cared for as prescribed by medical and associated professionals, was a distinct product of this era.' At the same time, from the 1880s or 1890s, as Ross continues, 'official and voluntary bodies were also at work trying to create a new kind of father: sober, a steady worker, and responsible for his children'.[1] The admission of Hannah, Charlie and Syd to the workhouse triggered, not for the first – or last – time, an attempt by the St Saviour's Board of Guardians to trace the elusive Charles Chaplin senior for maintenance payments.[2] At their meeting on 9 June 1896, the Board of Guardians agreed 'that the Collector be instructed to collect the sum of 15s. per week from Charles Chaplin of 15 Gunters Grove, Fulham, in respect of the maintenance of his two children, Sydney aged 12 and Charles aged 7', both of whom were then in the workhouse proper – though they were 'about to be sent to Hanwell School', meaning the London Central Schools for Pauper Children, to the west of the city and ten miles from Newington Workhouse.[3] They were transferred on 18 June, and Hannah was admitted to Champion Hill Infirmary on East Dulwich Grove in Dulwich soon after that.[4]

The move from an address in Newington Butts to accommodation in West London suggests that Hannah's husband was performing at a nearby theatre and was therefore capable of supporting his wife and her children financially. (Charles had composed another successful song, 'She Must be Witty', which was published in 1896.) On the same page of the St Saviour's Board of Guardian's minute book, the committee had also recommended that a warrant be applied for against one George Pudney 'for deserting & neglecting to maintain his four children and that a reward of £1 be offered for information leading to his arrest'.[5]

Charles Chaplin's ability to support himself and his family was dependent on how much he was able to earn as a music-hall performer – his pay for each performance, as well as their regularity. In late January 1896, just a few months before the meeting of the St Saviour's Board of Governors, where the Chaplin and Pudney cases were discussed, George Duckworth was sitting in the office of Frank Hall, secretary of the Music Hall Benevolent Fund at 58 York Road, one of the many streets in the area where Hannah and her sons had lived over the previous years. As ever, these extended interviews on behalf of the Charles Booth project offered a snapshot of the situation at a particular moment in time; Hall's summary referred directly to Charles Chaplin senior's experience of the music-hall circuit and his potential for employment. The secretary of an industry-focused charitable organisation – the existence of which revealed how precarious the business could be for performers and other associated workers – was well placed to comment on the day-to-day lives of his membership, as well as the provision available for those who fell on hard times.

Hall observed that what he inelegantly called 'Death money' to the sum of £5 5s, 'is always granted to prevent any member of the profession ever being buried as a pauper'.[6] No matter how difficult the circumstances in life, performers and theatre workers wanted to avoid the indignities of a pauper's burial, which could expose the deceased and their families to callous disregard and exploitation, as seen at Newington Workhouse. Concerning where performers and their agents tended to congregate, Duckworth noted that 'Lambeth & Brixton are the centres in London for Music Hall artistes tho' of course not exclusively'; he quoted Hall directly as saying that 'They certainly abound in Lambeth'. The prime location for variety agents was the network of streets around Waterloo Station; Waterloo Road, York Road and Stamford Street were lined on both sides with their offices. That said, in recent years, there had been 'a tendency now for the agents to migrate over the water & set up in Wellington St. etc ... Covent Garden'.[7] Hall confirmed that engagements were made chiefly through these agents, of which (by this date) there were about sixty. Among 'the best known' was 'R. Warner' – Bohemia-born Richard 'Dick' Warner (1856–1914) – who helped launch the Musical Hall Benevolent Fund.[8] For those without professional representation, the situation at this date was generally pretty desperate. Frank Hall described, briefly, the process of seeking casual work, which he called 'out-at-elbows corner' but was also known as 'Poverty Corner': 'On Monday morning the corner of the road ie York Rd & Waterloo Rd is crowded with needy artists seeking engagements.'[9]

On the subject of agent fees as they related to their clients' earnings, Frank Hall stated that agents usually charged between 5 and 10 per cent.[10] Perhaps unsurprisingly, agents, Hall further observed, 'are always willing to take on persons whose names are known', and 'also profess to bring out unknown names but they dont really often do so'.[11] This explains the difficulty for artistes with modest talents like Hannah Chaplin. But for successful performers, Hall continued, where salaries were large and engagements easily found, the agents were paid a fixed yearly figure of around £50. Hall then named two of the most successful music-hall acts of the 1890s. The first was Albert Chevalier (1861–1923), who specialised in cockney-related humour, based on a costermonger character for which he gained the nickname the 'Costers' Laureate'. Among his hit songs was 'Wot Cher!, or, Knocked 'em in the Old Kent Road'. The second was Dan Leno (1860–1904), perhaps the most famous comic performer of the late Victorian era. A vicar in South Lambeth had compared his own deep admiration of the Bishop of Rochester to that of his working-class parishioners for Leno, who is credited with raising the pantomime dame to a lead part – Mother Goose and Widow Twankey (in *Aladdin*) were his favourite roles – and, in the process, transforming the traditional Christmas-season entertainment. By the mid-1890s Leno (born George Wild Galvin in St Pancras, North London), like many of his fellow music-hall performers, lived in the South London district of North Brixton: a prime location for the aspirational working class at the turn of the twentieth century, as Duckworth had noted while attending a service at Hannah Chaplin's church. Both these superstar music-hall performers paid their agents a fixed amount, because the usual 10 per cent on their weekly earnings, as Hall continued, 'which are probably over £80 would be too large a sum'.[12] When we consider the income of these top performers, the appeal of music hall as a means of earning money becomes crystal clear – it was one industry where talent, persistence and luck was within the grasp of poorer working-class people, with public adulation and unimaginable wealth the ultimate prize. Put another way, being working-class or even poor was not a barrier: in fact it could be a benefit.

Thomas Burke observed in *The Wind and the Rain*, while describing the lead character's difficulty gaining employment in the City of London, 'I didn't believe that anybody who got on had ever been really poor. No matter how clever you were, you had to look respectable, and how could you get a decent suit out of ten shillings a week?'[13] In his memoir George Tinworth recalled: 'I was told by a tradesman of Lambeth Walk that went just as he was to a large shop at Charing Cross to buy some salmon and he asked one of the men in the shop the price of the salmon.' This man looked at the tradesman, up and down, and responded, 'You do not want any salmon.' At this rebuff, the tradesman went home, 'washed himself and put on his best things', returned to the shop and asked the same man the same question. The shop man now responded with the price of the salmon and called the Lambeth-Walk tradesman 'sir'. Who are you calling sir? asked the tradesman. You, replied the shop man. No you are not, retorted the tradesman, 'you are sirin [i.e. addressing as 'sir'] my clothes.'[14]

As Charlie Chaplin would discover, variety theatre and music hall had other priorities than a smart suit. Of course, a performer of Dan Leno's calibre and celebrity was rare, the exception that proved the rule – the latter exemplified by the modest career of the panto-megastar's exact contemporary, Charles Chaplin senior – but Leno was nonetheless a glittering role model for any aspiring performer. As Charlie Chaplin recalled:

A postcard of Dan Leno in the role of 'Sister Anne' from the pantomime *Blue Beard*, c.1901. *Blue Beard* opened at the Drury Lane Theatre in December 1901 and Sister Anne became a popular 'dame' role for Leno, alongside Widow Twankey (*Aladdin*), Dame Durden (*Jack and the Beanstalk*) and the eponymous Mother Goose.

> On Sunday morning, along the Kennington Road one could see a smart pony and trap outside a house, ready to take a vaudevillian for a ten-mile drive as far as Norwood or Merton, stopping on the way back at the various pubs, the White Horse, the Horns and the Tankard in the Kennington Road. As a boy of twelve, I often stood outside the Tankard watching these illustrious gentlemen alight from their equestrian outfits to enter the lounge bar, where the elite of vaudeville met, as was their custom on a Sunday to take a final 'one' before going home to the midday meal. How glamorous they were, dressed in chequered suits and grey bowlers, flashing their diamond rings and tie-pins! At two o'clock on Sunday afternoon, the pub closed and its occupants filed outside and dallied awhile before bidding each other adieu; and I would gaze fascinated and amused, for some of them swaggered with a ridiculous air. When the last had gone his way, it was as though the sun had gone under a cloud.[15]

Charlie, cleverly, would use the signs of poverty and failure, as defined by Thomas Burke – the threadbare, mismatching coat and trousers, the outsized worn shoes, the battered bowler – as a symbol of resilience and resistance. Regardless of their condition, the Little Tramp wears a full complement of clothing – hat, jacket, waistcoat, collar, tie, trousers and shoes. If knocked down, he picks himself up, neatens his tie, dusts his hat before placing it carefully on his head. For Charlie Chaplin understood better than most the reality behind the glamour. Leno's declining health led to his confinement in a privately run lunatic asylum, Peckham House in Camberwell, after a severe mental health crisis in 1903. He remained there for several months and died the following year aged just forty-three: a sobering reminder of the heavy toll paid by some for a dazzling career 'in the halls'.[16]

Since its origins in semi-amateur tavern entertainment in the 1840s, music hall – and popular culture more generally – had by the century's last decade been totally transformed through commercialisation and mass-marketing: what historian Peter Bailey, from a Marxist perspective, considers culture made *for* the people, but not *by* the people. The larger halls in particular had become highly complex, multifaceted businesses, where proprietors, called 'caterers', stage-managed everything: from decor, via food and drink, to performers' contracts. These larger-than-life characters, more often than not, would be present at their theatres in the role of 'mine host' to hundreds, or thousands of customers, dressed to the nines as a sign – along with the quality of environment, victuals and entertainnment – of their financial and social success. William Holland of the Canterbury (from 1867 to 1876) and Charles Crowder of the Paragon on the Mile End Road, Bailey notes amusingly, 'modelled themselves explicitly on Napoleon III', the nephew of the French emperor defeated at Waterloo, 'in dress, manner and moustache'.[17] Beyond pure entertainment and escapism, a key strand of popular music-hall songs focused on life's hardships, with working-class performers, known for drawing on their own raw experiences, giving heartfelt voice to their audiences' own lives: which in itself, as an expression of agency, challenges the idea that this was culture not made by, or from, the working class.

However, Frank Hall's description of the frenetic nature of the life of a music-hall performer – at the raw end of the money-making drive – may offer some explanation for the burn-out some experienced. Music-hall artists were engaged for a specific number of turns, a 'turn' being one appearance including any encores.* The worst turn was the first of the evening, so beginners would be selected for this, while the best came between half past nine and eleven o'clock. Frank Hall continued to explain, as noted down by George Duckworth, that a popular artist would do four turns in a night, in four different places; dashing between venues may have been thrilling, or another source of anxiety. At music halls, the number of turns offered to the public each night ranged between

---

*A 'turn', meaning a short performance among many others, each given by different artistes, was a term in use by the early eighteenth century; Charles Morton, for example, operated a 'turn' system between the Canterbury Music Hall, Westminster Bridge Road, and his other theatre, the Oxford, in the West End, during the 1860s, the performers travelling between the two locations by brougham (see Morton and Newton (1905), p. 68).

ten and thirty – an increase in recent years, Hall observed – with performances usually lasting from 7.45 to 11.30 p.m.[18] In regard to pay, Hall stated that working men's clubs (where beginners might start their careers) offered five shillings a turn, while a small music hall paid twenty shillings per week for the worst turns, and from £3 to £7 per week to the 'star' in the best. A theatre in the West End paid £4 per week for the 'padding' (or first turns), while for the later turns 'they give as much as £25 & upwards'. He continued: 'One <good> man could do 2 early turns say at £9 each, 2 good turns at £25 & one late turn at £10 = £80 per week. This is not uncommon.'[19] Under the section entitled 'The road to the top', Duckworth noted that 'men are nearly always past their best at 50 & the numbers who drop out of the profession must be enormous'.[20]

With reference to the style of performances that were popular in the mid-1890s, Frank Hall observed that musical and comedic sketches had come to the fore in recent years, and that these sketches (short performances, focused on a character or situation) had become more like those at a regular theatre. There had been traditionally a clear separation between theatre and music hall, the former regulated by the Lord Chamberlain (a senior member of the royal household, who issued theatrical licences and therefore had extensive powers to censor).* But now, even in music hall and variety sketches, acting ability was needed; as Hall concluded, 'the tie bet[ween] the M[usic] H[all] & the Dramatic stage has thereby been drawn closer'.[21] Duckworth summarised what Hall had told him about the earnings of the various levels of music-hall performer: 'The yearly earnings on the Music Hall stage he put at £150 to £400 for 3rd rate men'; '£400 to £700 for 2nd rate men'; '£1000 to £2 or £3000 for 1st rate men.'[22] It would seem that Charles Chaplin senior, if finding regular employment – albeit as a second- if not third-rate performer – could have earned between £150 and £700 a year: enough to keep his family out of the workhouse.

As Charlie Chaplin later recalled: 'Although we were aware of the shame of going to the workhouse, when Mother told us about

---

*The office of the Lord Chamberlain (which succeeded that of the Elizabethan Master of Revels) was formalised in 1737, and not abolished until 1968.

it both Sydney and I thought it adventurous and a change from living in one stuffy room.' The three of them would have joined the queue of weary and dejected people lined up outside the gate on Westmoreland Road – young and old, male and female, an entire family or alone – all desperate enough to throw themselves on the mercy of local poor-rate payers, the workhouse master and his staff. As his idea of an adventure (unlike Syd, this was the younger brother's first time) transformed into an awful reality, Charlie recalled that 'on that doleful day I didn't realise what was happening until we actually entered the workhouse gate. Then the forlorn bewilderment struck me.'[23] They were separated, Hannah to the female ward, her sons to the ward for children. Charlie describes 'the poignant sadness' of the first visiting day, the shock of seeing Hannah enter the room 'garbed in workhouse clothes' her expression 'forlorn and embarrassed'. The clothing provided by the workhouse was partly a practical measure to prevent, for example, the spread of lice. The items were marked, which discouraged theft and any attempt to escape. But such a practical provision could also be dehumanising – these were uniforms by any other name. In one week, Charlie recalled, his mother 'had aged and grown thin ... She smiled at our cropped heads and stroked them consolingly, telling us that we would soon all be together again.'[24]

This passage in his autobiography offers a personal recollection of working-class attitudes toward the workhouse and how it felt to enter such an institution. Only those who have done so can possibly understand the sensations new inmates experienced. Charlie offered a child's perspective – as far as that can be the case, given it was written by that child now an adult. Even if the details are incorrect or blurred, or heightened for effect (he was, after all, a consummate storyteller) the feelings as described are still relevant and valid. Charlie's recollections – elegantly phrased, filtered through the intervening decades, embellished perhaps – have at their core a truth: the terrible impact of childhood trauma.

By the 1960s, at a time when a working-class background was no longer deemed a hindrance – think of Terence Stamp from Stepney and his early friend Michael Caine, born in Rotherhithe and raised in the Elephant and Castle – Chaplin was prepared to describe his childhood pauperism in some depth. In previous travel memoirs and press interviews he had intimated that his empathy with the poor and downtrodden came from painful personal experience, but not in detail. George Tinworth had recounted his family's hardship in part as an explanation for his father's decline into alcoholism, followed by redemption as a 'poor sinner'. George's attitude is stoical, perhaps reflecting his strong religious upbringing, while underpinned by a toughness and indeed a measure of pride. But there was no mention of his aunt's death in a workhouse, nor any hint that the family might have resorted to poor relief at any time. Both George Tinworth and Charlie Chaplin judged their personal success, achieved after great suffering, worthy of recollection, but the older Charlie Chaplin, now in his seventies, clearly wanted to reveal that his rags-to-riches story was no mere myth – in fact, it was more extreme than anyone had realised.

During their brief stay at the Newington Workhouse, prior to being transferred to the pauper schools at Hanwell, Charlie recalled that the midday meal, served at a long table with the other children, was one bright spot in 'an overcast sadness': 'It was presided over by an inmate of the workhouse, an old gentleman of about seventy-five, with a dignified countenance, a thin beard and sad eyes.'[25] One anecdote explains why Charlie Chaplin hated having his hair cut and felt his dark, naturally curly locks were a crucial element of his identity and charm. The old gentleman, he relates, 'elected me to sit next to him because I was the youngest and, until they cropped my head, had the curliest hair'.[26] Twenty years later, Charlie Chaplin, now on the cusp of global fame, joked that, in preparation for the press interview, 'I even went and got my hair cut, which is my pet aversion. In fact, I never get it cut until the boys along the street yell at me.'[27]

By the 1890s five 'District Schools' were providing education for paupers from fifteen London Poor Law Unions. Hanwell covered the unions in the City of London, East London and St Saviour's in South London. It was an immense, austere building, on 190 acres of countryside on the outskirts of West London, housing 1,200 children, with a working farm – the Cuckoo Farm – after which the school was nicknamed. The school had a strict,

Infant pupils from the Hanwell Schools photographed in 1897. Charlie is identified as the child with short dark hair located centre right, three rows from the front.

military-style regime, with corporal punishment in routine use. Through connections to the armed forces and merchant navy, the school (along with other London Poor Law institutions) sent boys from the age of about twelve to train in seamanship on HMS *Exmouth*; originally a ship of the line, it had seen service in the Crimea in the 1850s and was now moored on the Thames near Grays in Essex, on loan to the Metropolitan Asylums Board (established in 1867). According to Charlie Chaplin, the author Thomas Burke, born in Clapham Junction in 1886, also attended this school. ('Do you know,' Chaplin is quoted as saying in a press interview in 1925, with reference to *The Wind and the Rain*, 'Burke and I went to school together? It was at Hanwell in the Parish of Lambeth. Burke writes about himself in this book and remembers how hard were those beginnings. I haven't forgotten, either, those early squalid surroundings in which I struggled. You will find something of me in *The Gold Rush*.')[28] However, Anne Witchard confirms that Burke attended the East London Orphan Asylum in Watford from 1897 and that it is this institution, not Hanwell, that he covers in his semi-fictional 'autobiography'; the school was founded 'for Fatherless Children who are Respectably Descended But Without Adequate Means to Their Support', so represents a different social context to that of Charlie Chaplin.[29]

Chaplin recalled the journey to Hanwell in a horse-drawn bakery van as 'rather a happy one under the circumstances, for the country surrounding Hanwell was beautiful in those days, with lanes of horse-chestnut trees, ripening wheat-fields and heavy-laden orchards'. He noted that, ever since, 'the rich, aromatic smell after rain in the country has always reminded me of Hanwell'.[30] On arrival at the school, as Charlie recalled in adulthood, he and Syd were placed in the 'approbation ward' (for medical inspection), and then separated: Syd to the ward for 'big boys', Charlie to the infants:

> We slept in different ward blocks, so we seldom saw each other. I was a little over six years old and alone, which made me feel abject; especially on a summer's evening at bed-time during prayers, when, kneeling with twenty other little boys in the centre of the ward in our night-shirts, I would look out of the oblong windows at the deepening sunset and the undulating hills, and feel alien to it all as we sang in throaty off-key voices: Abide with me; fast falls the eventide; The darkness deepens: Lord, with me abide ...[31]

'It was then', he continued, 'that I felt utterly dejected.'[32]

Hannah arranged for her sons to be released temporarily, but they were soon returned to the Newington Workhouse and then back to Hanwell, this time for almost a year, 'a most formative year, in which I started schooling and was taught to write my name "Chaplin".'[33] So, even with greater opportunities for some form of schooling since the 1870 Act, Charlie only experienced a sustained period of education when he entered a designated pauper school. On Saturday afternoons, the bath house was reserved for infants, who were washed and bathed by older girls. Charlie Chaplin, still not seven years old, recalled that 'a squeamish modesty attended these occasions; having to submit to the ignominy of a young girl of fourteen manipulating a facecloth all over my person was my first conscious embarrassment.'[34]

Having passed the age of seven, Charlie was moved to the section for boys aged up to fourteen. Although, in retrospect, he and Syd were well looked after at the school, being regularly fed, clothed and schooled – in Syd's case spending over a year aboard the training ship *Exmouth*, where he learned to play the cornet and bugle in the ship's band – it was still, in Charlie's words, 'a forlorn existence'.[35] He recalled walking with the other pauper school children, two abreast, through the country lanes around Hanwell: 'How I disliked those walks, and the villages through which we passed, the locals staring at us!' Charlie added: 'We were known as the inmates of the "booby hatch", a slang term for workhouse.'[36] There was one boy, Charlie recalled, 'a desperate character' according to the others, who attempted to escape.[37] He failed, but any such attempt would require punishment from 'Captain Hindrum' (or Hindom), a retired Navy man, according to Charlie, 'weighing about two hundred pounds'. With one hand behind his back, the other 'holding a cane as thick as a man's thumb and about four feet long', he stood poised, 'measuring it across the boy's buttocks'. Then slowly he raised the cane and 'with a swish' brought it down on the boy's backside: 'The spectacle was terrifying, and invariably a boy would fall out of rank in a faint.'[38] Charlie then described receiving three strokes of the cane for something he did not do. The pain, he recalled, 'was so excruciating that it took away my breath; but I did not cry out, and, although paralysed with pain and carried to the mattress to recover, I felt valiantly triumphant.'[39]

Charlie also described an epidemic of ringworm (a fungal infection) at the school, and how the infected were taken to the isolation ward on an upper floor and had their heads shaved, before their pates were painted brown with iodine: 'They were a hideous sight and we would look up at them with loathing.' One day, he relates, a nurse paused as she walked behind him, inspected his head and cried out, 'Ringworm!':

I was thrown into paroxysms of weeping. The treatment took weeks and seemed like an eternity. My head was shaved and iodined and I wore a handkerchief tied around it like a cotton-picker. But one thing I would not do was to look out of the window at the boys below, for I knew in what contempt they held us.[40]

It is important to see beyond Charlie Chaplin's lightness of touch in describing his childhood experiences. His eldest son (also Charles) recalled in his own memoir, *My Father, Charlie Chaplin*, that after many months under the Hanwell regime, the young Charlie 'came out a quiet, well-mannered boy',

> or at least that is how Cyril Holden describes him to me. Mr Holden, who is the son of Fred Holden, former manager of the Canterbury Theatre, and who is exactly my father's age, used to see my father often when they were eight, because Grandfather Chaplin was at the time playing theatre. My father learned well the manners that poverty teaches. It was only when Mr Holden looked into his ice-blue eyes that he could see something there that was unbroken, something single-minded, intense, much bigger than his small, wiry body. Call it my father's colossal ego if you wish. It kept him going when there was nothing else.[41]

Over the year that the Chaplin brothers had been in the care of the Hanwell paupers' school and TS *Exmouth*, the St Saviour's Board of Guardians had been continuing their dogged efforts to track down Charles Chaplin senior, whose peripatetic lifestyle kept him one step ahead of the authorities. To that end, the guardians wrote to Charles's brother, Spencer William Tunstill Chaplin, the proprietor of the Queen's Head public house on Broad Street in Lambeth. The letter, dated 16 November 1897, read: 'I shall esteem it a favor if you will kindly inform your brother Charles Chaplin that the Guardians desire him to relieve them of the future maintenance of his two children Sydney and Charles within 14 days from this date: – I am compelled to write to you not knowing his address.'[42]

On 1 January 1898, the *Croydon Express* offered its readers a review of the entertainments at the Empire in Croydon on Boxing Day evening: 'This house was filled to overflowing with an audience bent on enjoying the admirable programme arranged for them. Each item was received with abundant applause, and it was remarkable how appreciative and yet quiet the vast concourse was.' The main event was 'Juleen's Wonder of the World', an extravaganza of sound and visual effects: 'Every instrument you can think of is played by electricity, and these are placed in different parts of the house as well as on the stage. Realistic storms, illuminated balloon ascents, and dozens of other attractive items are included in the "wonder of the world". But' – the reporter continued – 'the variety business is equally good.' The performers included Walter Howard junior, in blackface (described at the time as 'an interpreter of negro minstrelsy');[43] the Sisters Grace; Professor Wragg and Sharp 'and their marvellous military exploits'; Charles Chaplin and Fred Percy (who, the reporter declared, were 'more popular than ever'); Professor Horace, 'with his intelligent dogs and cats'; and Major Mite, promoted as 'the smallest man on earth' and, along with Juleen's 'whizz-bang' spectacular, 'another wonder of the world'. Altogether, the programme on offer was 'prodigious'.[44] Further details of this season's entertainment were given in the *Croydon Times* on 5 January, and notable among the 'assembly of performers' was Charles Chaplin, the 'Comic and Descriptive Vocalist'.[45] Yet another local newspaper, the *Croydon Chronicle and East Surrey Advertiser*, observed that the Empire had been crammed full 'from floor to ceiling' every night, with some 3,000 people in the audience on the Monday night alone. Major Mite topped the bill and was 'a very pronounced favourite', while Charles Chaplin was praised as 'a very clever artiste, and gave some excellent patriotic songs, which were well received'.[46] Patriotic songs were gaining popularity in the latter part of the decade, thanks to Queen Victoria's Diamond Jubilee in 1897 and with full-scale war in South Africa looming.

Charles Chaplin travelled around the country in early January 1898, and all the performances were promoted in the local press, as well as national trade newspapers. At the New Empire Palace of Varieties in Leicester, for example, the comic singer was listed alongside such other 'newcomers' as 'Mr Fred Darby, legmania comedian', 'Miss Daisy Vernon, burlesque actress', 'Miss Jessie Reed, serio [i.e. serio-comic performer] and dancer' and 'the Ross Combination, in an amusing sketch entitled *Maloney's Troubles*'.[47] Charles Chaplin's music-hall career, unlike that of his estranged wife, appeared to be on a sure footing; a situation which would no doubt have come to the attention of the St Saviour's Board of Guardians.

Just days after the eye-catching report on his performance in Leicester, the *South London Chronicle* was describing a very local public appearance for Charles Chaplin, which was altogether different from the thrills of the Empire Theatre of Varieties. On 15 January 1898, under the headline 'A COMEDIAN IN COURT', the journalist reported:

> Charles Chaplin, 33, described as a comedian, of no fixed abode, was charged before Mr. Denman on a warrant with neglecting to maintain his son, Charles Chaplin, aged 7 years [in fact he was eight], and his wife's child, Sydney Hill, aged 11 years [in fact twelve], whereby they had become chargeable to the Guardians of the St. Saviour's Union. – Mr. E. S. Oldman, general relieving officer to the Guardians, said the children in question had been chargeable to the Union since June last. The prisoner was a music-hall performer and was well able to maintain the children. Before Christmas [the] witness wrote to him requiring him to remove the chargeability of the children, but he received no answer to that communication. He understood, however, that the prisoner was prepared to come to terms with the Guardians and he asked that the case might be adjourned to enable that to be done. – Mr. Denman adjourned the case accordingly, but released the prisoner on his brother's bail.[48]

The pointed reference to 'Sydney Hill' as 'his wife's child', rather than Charles Chaplin's own son, could be a statement of fact, but considering the context it is more likely an attempt by the errant father to remove any personal responsibility for this child. Even so, given that he had married Hannah Hill, the St Saviour's Board of Guardians would have seen no difference in status between Syd and Charlie. (Syd was baptised 'Sidney John Hill' on 1 April 1885, with just Hannah Hill named as a parent, but on 3 March 1890, almost a year after Charlie's birth, 'Sidney Chaplin', then almost five, was registered at the King and Queen Street Infant School by his parent-guardian 'Charles Chaplin' of 68 Camden Street, Walworth.)[49]

The following week, the *South London Press* offered an update on 'A COMEDIAN AND HIS FAMILY': Charles Chaplin had surrendered to bail, 'to further answer the charge of neglecting to maintain his son, Charles Chaplin ... and his wife's child, Sidney Hill ... whereby they had become chargeable to the guardians of the St Saviour's Union.' The same general relieving officer to the guardians 'now stated that during the adjournment the prisoner had reimbursed the guardians the expenditure incurred by them in connection with the maintenance of the children, and they were now no longer chargeable to the parish. He, therefore, proposed to withdraw from the prosecution. The prisoner was accordingly released.'[50]

In an otherwise identical report, the *South London Chronicle* offered the additional humiliating detail that Charles Chaplin 'had been apprehended at Leicester on a warrant by P. C. Barnes, one of the warrant officers of the Court'.[51] The *South London Mail* included the same story under their 'LOCAL POLICE SUMMARY', where Charles Chaplin's appearances were placed among a variety of other cases from the same court session. These included that of Richard Bills of Maydwell Street in Camberwell, for attempting to sell three turkeys at his stall on Westmoreland Road. The sanitary inspector for Newington Vestry, as well as the magistrate, both of whom had seen the birds soon after their seizure, considered them 'in a state absolutely unfit for human food'. Bills was ordered to pay a penalty of £3 plus costs. Meanwhile Harry Kemp, described as a painter, was charged with disorderly conduct and assaulting one William Rosenbaum. Kemp was seen outside the Black Horse public house on Brixton Road, 'holding the barman down on the ground and shaking him like a rat'; when Rosenbaum intervened, Kemp set upon him too, fists flying. No explanation worthy of the name was given and Kemp was ordered to pay a fine of five shillings, plus ten shillings costs to Rosenbaum, or face seven days in prison.[52]

Then there was the labourer James Bush and his wife Esther, both in their forties, who had been charged with 'placing themselves in a public place for the purpose of inducing the giving of alms' – effectively begging, which was illegal under the Vagrancy Act of 1824. The couple were also charged with 'causing their children: James, aged 8 years; Mary, aged 6 years; and Florence, aged 16 months, to be in a public place' for the same purpose. A police constable said he saw the prisoners and their children in Heiron Street in Walworth on Sunday afternoon – a street in the parish of St Agnes, Kennington Park, but within minutes' walk of St Paul's, Lorrimore Square, and All Souls, Grosvenor Park. James was carrying the baby, and he and his wife were singing the plaintive hymn 'It Is Well with My Soul', written in 1873 by Horatio Spafford, in response to extreme personal suffering. The magistrate, unmoved, 'bound them over in their own recognisances in the sum of £5 to be of good behaviour', meaning that they had to pledge to pay that sum, promising not to beg again, or else forfeit it. This was an enormous amount of money for anyone from the working class to find, but for the Bush family, poor enough to be begging, more so than most.

How desperate might you have to be, to stand in the street with your infants about you, singing soulful hymns in the hope of kindness and charity from passers-by, many of whom were from the surrounding streets of Walworth and far from wealthy themselves? Still, people at all levels of society could be generous and charitable. This real-life report is echoed in a vignette from the streets of Lambeth in George Gissing's locally set novel *Thyrza: A Tale* (1887):

> Next came a sound of distressful voices, whining the discords of a mendicant psalm. A man, a woman, and two small children crawled along the street; their eyes surveyed the upper

windows. All were ragged and filthy; the elders bore the unmistakable brand of the gin-shop, and the children were visaged like debased monkeys. Occasionally a copper fell to them, in return for which the choragus exclaimed 'Gord bless yer!'[53]

One can only guess whether or not Charles Chaplin felt any shame: firstly for being dragged up in front of a court in this manner, and then secondly, as reported through the South London newspapers, as a man who abandoned his child to the Poor Law Union, the equal to a seller of food unfit for human consumption, a pub-drunk guilty of common assault, or a father begging in the street with his family. He was probably more annoyed than ashamed at being run to ground by the authorities after months of evasion. And if Hannah had been attempting to cover Syd's illegitimacy by marrying him back in 1885, then imagine her distress when the fact of her son's debated parentage was splashed across the local press for all and sundry to gossip about. That said, illegitimacy was relatively common within parts of the working class, so it could be argued that shame was only felt by those with pretensions of 'respectability'. At the very least, though, this must have placed an additional strain upon Hannah's already fragile mental health.

Following Charles Chaplin's reimbursement of costs to the St Saviour's Board of Governors, however, Charlie and Syd were able to return from Hanwell to the Kennington Park area. Charlie recalls that his mother found accommodation, a room in a cottage at 10 Farmers Road, 'and for a while she was able to support us.'[54] Unfortunately, though,

> it was not long before we were back in the workhouse again. The circumstances of our return were something to do with Mother's difficulty in finding employment and Father's slump in his theatrical engagements. In that brief interlude we kept moving from one back-room to another; it was like a game of draughts – the last move was back to the workhouse.[55]

CAUGHT IN TIME

'Tommy' is described in the 1902 article 'A Day in the Life of a Workhouse Child' as the 'ragamuffin' son of 'homeless wanderers' who 'do almost anything they like with their children – drag them from workhouse to workhouse, half starve them, let them shiver with cold'. Here (left, see also p. 194) Tommy is shown before his admittance to Lambeth workhouse on Renfrew Road and (right) after his transfer to the Norwood Schools.

On 21 July 1898, all three were admitted to the Lambeth Workhouse on Renfrew Road, apparently discharged on 12 August (at their 'own request'), and then readmitted on the following day. Three days after that the two boys were sent to the Norwood Schools, Syd for the second time.[56] Norwood, Charlie later recalled, 'was more sombre than Hanwell; leaves darker and trees taller. Perhaps the countryside had more grandeur, but the atmosphere was joyless.'[57]

However, things were about to get far worse for Hannah. While Charlie and Syd were resident at the Norwood Schools, they were told that their mother had been transferred (on 6 September) from the Renfrew Road workhouse to the infirmary, and then, after further assessment, to Cane Hill Asylum near Coulsdon on 15 September: the same institution to which the nineteen-year-old

Annie Maud Isaacs had been sent five years before, after declaring she was the 'Queen of England', along with Sarah Ann King, who had suffered a collapse on the death of her mother.[58]

Cane Hill was a vast site that, at its peak, housed 2,400 inmates from South London's vulnerable poor and beyond. The asylum records, quoted by David Robinson, described Hannah's behaviour as ranging from 'very strange in manner ... abusive & noisy' to 'using endearing terms' to 'shouting, singing and talking incoherently': a similar assessment to that of her mother five years before. At one point she was confined to a padded room on account of 'sudden violence' towards another patient, as well as being 'depressed' and 'crying'. She asked staff 'if she was dying', said she 'was sent here on a mission by the Lord' and, perhaps most distressingly, that 'she wants to get out of the world'.*[59] The abbreviation 'Syp.', used by the medical officer while examining Hannah, has caused speculation as to whether she was suffering from syphilis, which in its later stage can affect the brain. (The biographer Barry Anthony, based on the death certificate description 'general paralysis of the insane', believed that Dan Leno, too, may have suffered from neurosyphilis.)[60] Her son feared 'madness' as much as poverty, and reportedly used extraordinary methods to protect himself from sexually transmitted diseases.[61] Hannah's potential syphilis diagnosis has also raised the spectre that, in addition to sexual activity outside of her marriage, she had, at some time in her early life, resorted to casual sex work (usually framed in Victorian Britain as both a public health as well as moral issue), but no evidence has come to light to support this hypothesis. Hannah told her young sons that she had lived briefly in Cape Town with a wealthy gentleman (believed to be a bookmaker called Sidney Hawkes) by whom she became pregnant with Syd.[62] In his biography *Chaplin: A Life*

---

*Searches of the Lambeth Board of Guardians and Cane Hill Hospital (Asylum) records for 1898 have as yet failed to uncover Hannah Chaplin's case notes. In one such volume (TLA, LABG/140/045: 'Examination to Settlement'), Hannah's full-page entry is listed in the index as p. 210, but according to a pencilled note by 'A. W. Rowe Asst Archivist' on p. 212 (dated 17 June 1965), this particular leaf was 'found to be missing'.

(with an introduction by Geraldine, Charlie's daughter), the psychoanalyst Stephen Weissman conjectures that Hannah, having been encouraged to travel abroad by Hawkes, 'ended up with an out-of-wedlock pregnancy and, quite likely, a case of syphilis, which she probably contracted as the result of a brief encounter with prostitution in the South African gold rush of 1884.'[63] In the 2001 revised edition of his Chaplin biography, David Robinson believed any trip to South Africa could not be verified either way, while Syd Chaplin's biographer, Lisa Stein, referring to Hannah's story concerning her eldest son's conception, notes: 'Evidence cannot completely support stories such as this one.'[64]

For a brief time – a matter of months – while Hannah was in Cane Hill Asylum, Charles Chaplin senior was compelled by a second Poor Law Union, run by the Lambeth Board of Guardians (the administrators of the Norwood Schools), to provide accommodation and financial support to his biological son and, whether he liked it or not, his 'wife's child' Syd. In this union's settlement officer case book, under the section 'Names and Addresses of persons who may be applied to for information', a note reads: 'Husband Charles, a comedian 289 Kennington Rd neglects to maintain.'*[65] This house was towards the southern end of that main thoroughfare, at the junction with Kennington Lane, Sancroft Road and Cleaver Street called 'Kennington Cross', and a short walk from both the popular Horn's Tavern and Theatre (where Feargus O'Connor had had his ill-fated meeting with the police commissioner in April 1848) and Kennington Park (where the Chartism movement died). Charlie recalled that he and his brother were told about this surprising development at the same time as the sad news of their mother's confinement in the asylum. The 'prospect of living with Father was exciting. I had seen him only twice in my life ... And now we were going to live with him. Whatever happened, Kennington Road was familiar and not strange and sombre like Norwood.'[66]

To an extent – and unlike his in-laws – Charles Chaplin senior came from a family who seemed to have been regularly employed,

---

*Charlie Chaplin gave the number as 287 (*MA*, p. 33).

or were the owners of small but prosperous businesses that kept the family members in comfort and security. Charles's father (Charlie's grandfather) Spencer, at one time a butcher, was now landlord of various public houses in London, while in the 1890s his elder brother, also called Spencer, was running the Queen's Head on Broad Street in the Lambeth parish of St Mary-the-Less, and the payment to the St Saviour's Board of Guardians, which had allowed Charles to walk free from court just a few months before, had been made by his publican brother. Public houses in this area were considered valuable properties, in large part due to their takings. While interviewing the Reverend Reeve of St Mary-at-Lambeth, Charles Booth's investigator Ernest Aves had noted an incident concerning the sale of a public house on Kennington Road, which a brewery had offered to buy for £3,000; Reeve, who was tasked with selling it on behalf of a parish trust, decided it should be put on the open market, only for it to sell at auction for £20,150 to the very brewery that had offered £3,000 just weeks before. 'The house is not a large one,' Aves noted, but the clergyman mentioned the sale in passing, 'partly as illustrating the great value of public house property'.[67]

George Gissing described the pubs around the Lambeth Walk market on a Saturday evening in his novel *Thyrza*: 'Through the gaping doors you saw a tightly packed crowd of men, women and children, drinking at the bar or waiting to have their jugs filled, tobacco smoke wreathing above their heads. With few exceptions the frequenters of the Walk turned into the public-house as a natural incident of the evening's business.'[68] The Queen's Head on Broad Street, along with the Windmill on Lambeth High Street, was a local hostelry for the workers at Doulton's Pottery; by 1897 the company employed over 4,000 people, from furnace stokers to artists, many of whom lived within walking distance of their workplace, on streets like Lambeth Walk, Vauxhall Walk and Lambeth High Street. In these streets, the presence of Doulton's was everywhere to be seen. George Duckworth, while wandering the area, noted that Pearson's Place was 'very respectable', and among the old residents were Doulton's 'Moulders', the same people George Tinworth had been working alongside for thirty years. Duckworth also observed a piece of Doulton ceramic over a doorway, 'an elaborate Virgin & Child after Della Robbia' with a blue background, a wreath of coloured leaves and fruits surrounding it. Underneath was the inscription, 'He died that we might be forgiven. He died to make us good'.[69]

Along Lambeth High Street, the residents were a mix of Doulton's foremen and 'many poor'. Ferry Street's residents were nearly all Doulton employees, and in Bunyan's Place, Duckworth saw 'stacks of earthenware drain pipes being laden on to carts', with the furnaces on the south side. In Norfolk Place, he noted the 'houses belong to Doulton's & inhabited by their men', but they were 'very poor': five shillings a week for two rooms, a 'copper & small back yard'.[70] Broad Street itself was poor, with old houses and small shops.[71] He noted some old red-tiled, well-kept houses in the area, with one woman who had been living in the same house for thirty-three years, and another for forty years, respectively paying six and seven shillings for five rooms. One of Duckworth's interviewees told him that her husband's family 'had lived in the same house for well over 100 years' (which is possible, given that the date 1769 is carved into some of their facades). As he wandered west along Broad Street, he came to 'Gunner's Cottages' (located behind Doulton's pottery) and entered through a wooden swing door to find four two-storey cottages, which, he noted 'used to be tenanted by notorious dog stealer, on his death 50 dogs were found concealed in the yard'.[72]

By the 1890s, when Spencer Chaplin was managing the Queen's Head, Gloucester Street (one of the streets to the south of Broad Street) had been renamed 'Tinworth Street' in honour of Doulton's leading modeller. Soon afterwards, a delighted George met a member of the parish board and asked him whom he should thank for this accolade: 'He said thank yourself you brought it about by your work.'[73] By this date George no longer lived in Lambeth or Walworth – he and Alice were now resident in more affluent Kew, near the Royal Botanical Gardens – but he continued to work at Doulton's, commuting by train every weekday, developing their sought-after line in Lambeth-made Art Pottery.

Locals were also very proud of this fact, as the renaming of the street affirms. When an American dentist called Charles Horatio Shepherd, whom Charles Chaplin senior had befriended while in New York, visited London in early 1897, he was hosted by Charles, his brother Spencer and their father. As a parting gift in memory of his visit to Lambeth, they bought Dr Shepherd several pieces of Doulton pottery. In a letter to Charlie Chaplin, sent from New York on 10 July 1915, Shepherd enquired whether he was writing to the son of the music-hall performer and, if he was, 'then I am very glad to know that my old friend Charlie Chaplin's son has far exceeded his father in the present line of work'. He goes on to recall that on meeting 'your father and your grandfather Spencer Chaplin, and also your Uncle Spencer Chaplin who at that time kept the Queens Head at Lambeth ... they gave me a very very Royal time during my stay which lasted about three months and when I returned they gave me several pieces of Doltin Ware, which I still have.'[74] It would be a wonderful synergy if these examples of 'Doltin Ware' had been designed by the celebrated George Tinworth, or decorated by one of the next generation of ceramic artists, such as Hannah Barlow. At the very least, the existence and popularity of Doulton's Art Pottery was a direct result of Tinworth's talent, alongside his patient teaching of these younger craftsmen and women. Such products were a focus of local pride in internationally renowned and beautiful items of quality produced in the neighbourhood; Reverend Reeve of St Mary-at-Lambeth observed in 1899 that 'there is a good deal of local feeling, especially among the lighter folk, and to be a "Lambethian" means something in the district'.[75]

Charlie Chaplin's later descriptions of the characters, circumstances and events during the months he spent in his father's care at 289 Kennington Road are vividly observed. He recalled that he had seen his father only twice before: once during a performance at the Canterbury Music Hall; and then standing outside this very house with a woman Charlie did not recognise. On arrival at No. 289, in the company of the Lambeth official, Charlie described how the door was opened by the same woman: 'She was dissipated and morose-looking, yet attractive, tall and shapely, with full lips and sad, doe-like eyes ; her age could have been thirty. Her name was Louise.' After the formalities of signing release papers, the official left the two boys with Louise, who led them upstairs to the first-floor landing and into the front sitting room.[76]

The first floor of a Georgian terraced house, such as this one, usually boasted a greater size, ceiling height and expanse. On entering the front room, Charlie saw 'a most beautiful child of four with large dark eyes and rich brown curly hair: it was Louise's son – my half-brother.'[77] If this child was four years old in late September 1898, then Charles Chaplin senior had been cohabiting with Louise for most of the time he and Hannah had been estranged.* This would certainly explain Charles Chaplin's reticence to support Hannah from around 1893. Louise, like Rosina Wright with her partner Charles Thomas, would have considered Charles Chaplin her husband in all but name – which would be fair enough, given the length of their relationship and now with a child, even if he was still married to Charlie and Syd's mother. Charlie Chaplin's three (known) half-siblings signal the often-chaotic private as well as professional lives of music-hall artists – and, despite the pioneering efforts of Annie Besant, the fact that birth control remained a largely hit-and-miss affair. Whatever the truth, such a chaotic life had certainly caught up with Charles Chaplin, who now had one son, Charlie, within marriage; another, Syd, his wife's child, whom he had effectively adopted; and another son, by his 'common law wife' Louise – all now living uncomfortably together under the same roof.

'The family lived in two rooms,' Charlie Chaplin's description continues, 'and, although the front room had large windows' – this would be the main room, with three tall windows overlooking Kennington Road – 'the light filtered in as if from under water': a hint of the smoggy atmosphere from domestic and industrial coal fires. Everything in these rooms, Charlie recalled, looked as miserable as Louise; the wallpaper, the chairs upholstered with horse hair; 'the stuffed pike in a glass case that swallowed another pike as large as itself – the head sticking out of its mouth – looked gruesomely sad'. Louise had put a bed for the brothers to share in the back room, but it was too small. Then Syd suggested he

---

*Sad to say, Louise's surname is not mentioned, nor the name of her son.

sleep on the sofa in the main room.[78] This did not endear him to Louise: they were there under sufferance and these two rooms were already home to two adults and a young child. 'Our reception was not an enthusiastic one and no wonder,' Charlie observed. 'We sat mutely watching her preparing the table for something to eat. "Here," she said to Sydney, "you can make yourself useful and fill the coal-scuttle. And you," she said turning to me, "go to the cook-shop next to the White Hart and get a shilling's worth of corned beef."'[79]

While they were resident at 289 Kennington Road, Charlie noted that Louise drank a lot and that there was 'something frighteningly irresponsible about her'. He recalled how she would smile 'with amusement at her little boy with his beautiful angelic face, who would swear at her and use vile language'. Sometimes Louise sat in the main room drinking and brooding, anxious about their stretched resources with two extra mouths to feed, but also, perhaps, fearful that the presence of these children might stir up a long-buried fondness in Charles for his wife. Or, perhaps more likely, she was worried that her partner might abandon her, as he had Hannah – Louise being more vulnerable, given their unmarried status and unenviable living conditions. Whatever fears were passing through Louise's mind, however, Charlie found her resentment frightening. Syd, on the other hand, four years older, more independent and resourceful after his time on the *Exmouth*, 'paid little attention to her; he seldom came home until late at night. I was made to come home directly after school and run errands and do odd jobs.'[80] At least Charlie, since leaving Norwood, was continuing with some formal education.

Charlie never looked forward to Saturdays, officially a half-day holiday from school, because rather than relaxing in Kennington Park or playing football, it invariably meant scurrying around the flat doing chores, with Louise looking on.

> She would sit with a lady friend, drinking and growing bitterly morose, complaining quite audibly to her friend of having to look after Sydney and me and of the injustice imposed upon her. I remember her saying: 'That one's all right' (indicating

me), 'but the other's a little swine and should be sent to a reformatory – what's more, he's not even Charlie's son.'[81]

Such verbal attacks on his brother, Charlie records, 'frightened and depressed me and I would go unhappily to bed and lie fretfully awake. I was not yet eight years old, but those days were the longest and saddest of my life.'[82] The following year, 1899, the Reverend Reeve, rector of St Mary-at-Lambeth, noted that alcohol consumption in his parish, for both sexes, was rife: 'Drinking is, he thinks,' Ernest Aves recorded, 'about as bad as may be. Some of the public houses he described as being of the nature of clubs, and very decent, while others are "hells".'[83]

Charlie described how Louise was often infuriated when Syd came home late and raided the larder for scraps. On one occasion, when she had been drinking, she challenged him, demanding that he get out of the lodgings. But Syd was ready for her:

> He reached under his pillow and whipped out a stiletto, a long button-hook which he had sharpened to a point. 'Come near me, he said, 'and I'll stick this in you!' She reared back, startled. 'Why, the bloody young sod! – he's going to murder me!' 'Yes,' said Sydney, dramatically, 'I'll murder you!'[84]

To which Louise cried: 'You wait til Mr Chaplin comes home!' 'But,' as Charlie ruefully concluded, 'Mr Chaplin seldom came home.' This laid bare the tension under which everyone at No. 289 was living. It is obvious how violence could so easily occur when alcohol was involved – whether outside the Black Horse on Brixton Road, or threatened by Joshua Tinworth, brandishing a fake gun as if he were in a Wild West saloon.

In his memoir, Charlie also recalled another scene, ripe for transfer to the cinema screen. Charles Chaplin senior was 'in an ugly mood' after he had been drinking, sitting with Louise, Charlie, their landlady and her husband in the latter's front-room parlour on the ground floor of 289 Kennington Road. The landlady may have mentioned that the main breadwinner among her family of lodgers owed her rent, which resulted in Charles Chaplin, with 'menacing eyes', suddenly pulling a handful of coins from his pocket and throwing them across the floor: 'Under the candescent light Father looked ghastly pale, and ... was mumbling to himself.'[85] This is a curiously similar scenario to George Tinworth's description of his father and the debt collector, 'the broker's man'. Both fathers had been caught owing money and, in response, were stirred to a rage fuelled by injured pride and liquor.

One Saturday afternoon, when Charlie arrived back at the house, only the landlady was present. There was no food in the larder and Syd was playing football, 'so in desolation I went out, spending the afternoon visiting nearby market places':[86] what George Gissing described as 'the sole out-of-door amusement regularly at hand for London working people.'[87] Charlie wandered through Lambeth Walk, Lower Marsh and the New Cut, 'looking hungrily into cook-shop windows at the tantalising steaming roast joints of beef and pork, and the golden-brown potatoes soaked in gravy'. For hours he gazed at the hawkers and quacks touting their wares. 'The distraction soothed me,' Charlie recalled, 'and for a while I forgot my plight and hunger.'[88]

George Duckworth also visited New Cut and Lower Marsh on market day, which his companion, Sergeant Waters, described as 'the common meeting place & market street'; the area was always busy, he noted, but especially on Friday and Saturday nights and Sunday mornings. Duckworth took notes concerning the wares on offer at the various food stalls, recording prices for basic and more exotic foodstuffs: fourpence for a four-pound loaf of bread; meat scraps from $2d$ to $3\frac{1}{2}d$ a pound; pork chops, '(first rate)', at $6\frac{1}{2}d$ each; cooked half-chickens were available for eight- or ninepence, although, to Duckworth's eye, 'not appetising'; uncooked sheep heads were fivepence each; 'best' eggs were being sold at three for $2\frac{1}{2}d$; a whole skinned rabbit for $6\frac{1}{2}d$; and lemons for three a penny. He saw cucumbers sold from barrows, and then noticed that the biggest crowd was congregating around a fishmonger selling cod, plaice, whiting and pollock. The buyers were all women and engaged in a 'no excitement' Dutch-auction, with each fish cut in half and held up, the seller fixing the price and gradually lowering it until the fish was bought. In the local shops, either side of the

R. Johnson greengrocer, 118 Lambeth Walk, c.1897–8. In 1899 the proprietor was Mrs Emily Jones, 'fruiterer' (*The Post Office London Directory*, p. 519). The arch and Robinson's Brewery sign to the right (at No. 116) belong to the Plume of Feathers public house (a reference to the local landowner, the Prince of Wales) located at the corner with Paradise Street. Another photograph taken earlier the same day (LA 11401) shows a horse-drawn delivery wagon en route to this shop laden with wares from London's main fruit and vegetable market at Covent Garden. The three delivery men and a lad are here seen standing with two smiling women, one of whom may be Emily Jones.

market stalls and barrows, the 'good' rump steaks sold for between nine- and elevenpence, and the mutton chops for between eight- and ninepence. Alongside the stalls and barrows laden with fish and fruit, there were carts filled with brightly coloured flowers 'fuschias, geraniums, & small bedding plants in wooden boxes', more barrows loaded with old keys and iron work, others with haberdashery. New Cut and Lower Marsh were, Sergeant Waters informed him, 'quiet' and 'shy' during the day, 'but the glory of the Lower Marsh is by night'.[89]

Lambeth Walk, where Charles Frederick Hill and Mary Ann had lived prior to their marriage, was just to the north of Broad Street and Prince's Road. The popular market on this long street was also visited by a lonely and hungry Charlie Chaplin, just as the late afternoon light dipped into evening. It is this moment, when the market was in its 'glory', that George Gissing described in his Lambeth-based novel:

> The hot air reeked with odours. From stalls where whelks were sold rose the pungency of vinegar; decaying vegetables trodden under foot blended their putridness with the musty smell of second-hand garments; the grocers' shops were aromatic; above all was distinguishable the acrid exhalation from the shops where fried fish and potatoes hissed in boiling grease. There Lambeth's supper was preparing, to be eaten on the spot, or taken away wrapped in newspaper. Stewed eels and baked meat pies were discoverable through the steam of other windows, but the fried fish and potatoes appealed irresistibly to the palate through the nostrils, and stood first in popularity.[90]

Describing 'the great proletarian order', Gissing continues:

> Children of the gutter and sexless haunters of the street corner elbowed comfortable artisans and their wives; there were bare-headed hoidens from the obscurest courts, and work-girls whose self-respect was proof against all the squalor and vileness hourly surrounding them. Of the women, whatsoever

their appearance, the great majority carried babies; wives themselves scarcely past childhood balanced shawl-enveloped bantlings against heavy market baskets. Little girls of nine or ten were going from stall to stall, making purchases with the confidence and acumen of old housekeepers; slight fear that they would fail to get their money's worth. Children, too, had the business of sale upon their hands: ragged urchins went about with blocks of salt, importuning the marketers, and dishevelled girls carried bundles of assorted vegetables, crying, 'A penny all the lot! A penny the 'ole lot!'[91]

Having wandered around the area, milling among the crowds and market traders but unable to buy any food himself, even for pennies, Charlie Chaplin walked the short distance back to the Kennington Road lodgings in the hope that someone would have returned. But still no one was there. Kennington Cross itself was deserted, but for a few evening loiterers: 'All the lights of the shops began going out except those of the chemist and the public houses, then I felt wretched.'[92]

At these times, Charlie found music, as well as local street life, a respite from his depressing situation.[93] One episode, recalled by Charlie at various times, followed on from his day wandering aimlessly around the local markets. The public house, the White Hart, was located to the rear of No. 289, with the cook shop next door selling corned beef. This pub is still to be found on the east side of Kennington Lane, towards the square then called Prince's Square (now Cleaver Square) and adjoining Methley Street (the site of another Chaplin family lodging). While Charlie was sitting dejectedly on the pavement kerb at Kennington Cross, as the street gaslights were being extinguished, leaving just the two local pubs, the White Hart and the Roebuck glowing in the darkness, he heard the sound of a harmonium and clarinet drifting out from the former. 'I forgot my despair and crossed the road to where the musicians were. The harmonium-player was blind, with scarred sockets where his eyes had been; and a besotted, embittered face played the clarinet. It was all over too soon and their exit left the night even sadder.'[94] Kennington Cross, Charlie later declared,

Kennington Cross, around 1903. A new electric tram travels south along Kennington Road, while men (including an aproned pot man) loiter outside the Roebuck Public House on the corner of Kennington Lane. To the right, just out of shot, is the White Hart, in the distance (centre left) the spire of St Philip's Church, where George and Alice Tinworth had been married, and two doors to the left of the Roebuck is 289 Kennington Road.

was where 'I first discovered music, or where I first learned its rare beauty, a beauty that has gladdened and haunted me from that moment'.[95]

Another childhood episode concerned the Roebuck (now the Dog House), on the corner of Kennington Road and Kennington Lane – again at the 'Cross', just a few doors along from where Charlie was now living. 'Sometimes on a Saturday night, feeling deeply despondent,' he recalled,

> I would hear the lively music of a concertina passing by the back bedroom window, playing a highland march, accompanied by rowdy youths and giggling coster girls. The vigour and vitality of it seemed ruthlessly indifferent to my unhappiness, yet as the music grew fainter into the distance, I would regret it leaving. Sometimes a street-crier would pass: one in particular came by every night who seemed to be shouting

'Rule Britannia', terminating it with a grunt, but he was actually selling oysters. From the pub, three doors away, I could hear the customers at closing time, singing drunks, bawling out a maudlin, dreary song that was popular in those days.[96]

The song Charlie remembered, 'For Old Times' Sake', was written by Charles Osborne in 1898 and made famous that year by the young music-hall singer, Millie Lindon:

> For old times' sake don't let our enmity live,
> For old times' sake say you'll forget and forgive.
> Life's too short to quarrel,
> Hearts are too precious to break.
> Shake hands and let us be friends
> For old times' sake.[97]

'I never appreciated the sentiment,' Charlie observed of this song, 'but it seemed an appropriate accompaniment to my unhappy circumstances, and lulled me to sleep.'[98]

During his interview with Margaret Sewell, a 'settlement' social worker from nearby Nelson Square, George Duckworth noted various comments she made concerning children and their attraction to public houses, as part of a general conversation on levels of drunkenness in the area in which she lived and worked. She observed that children, carrying large jugs and pitchers, were often sent by their parents to the beer houses, to fill these vessels as 'take-aways' for the adults to consume at home. She queried whether children drank beer themselves, for she had seen a drunk child only once during her time working in the area. Rather, she believed, the 'attractiveness of the public house to the child is not in the inside but in the outside. The lights are bright, the pavement is carefully mended & smoother for marbles & other games', while street performers, including organ players, 'come to play & sing there'.[99]

In other words, as Charlie Chaplin himself recalled, the public house, as well as a potential snare, could also be a beacon of light and orderliness, a gathering place for the music and entertainment of working people, situated within streets and alleys that at night were deadly dark. And, from the children's perspective, the entertainment did not stop at games played on the pavement, or the street performers. For, as Sewell goes on to describe, 'at night there is the sight of the drunken men being chucked out or trying to get home, some times ... hauled off by the policeman'. She had watched children re-enact the whole scene, one playing the drunken man, another the landlord or barman, (the 'chucker out') and a third the policeman.[100]

Sewell's account is of interest for many reasons, not least because she had witnessed poor children mimicking adult behaviour – or, to be more accurate in the case of the tavern drunks, misbehaviour. The observed movements, gestures and expressions of drunks as they were propelled by a burly cellarman through a crowded bar and then tossed onto the street, or as they tumbled through the tavern door at closing time, to be led home by the local bobby, would be distilled and then re-presented by Charlie Chaplin just a few years later, in his breakthrough role as the 'inebriated swell' for Fred Karno's variety sketch, *Mumming Birds*.* The 'swell', a classic music-hall type by the 1860s, as Peter Bailey observes, suggested 'in a single word both an ideal and its debasement': in the words of George Leybourne's song 'Champagne Charlie' (1866),

> What matters if to bed I go
> Dull head and muddled thick?
> A bottle in the morning
> Sets me right then very quick.[101]

Charlie Chaplin's writings contain many evocative descriptions of local Lambeth characters, which he had stored up for some future use in his performances. In his 1922 travel memoir *My Wonderful Visit*, he recalled wandering around the Kennington Road area during his triumphal return to London in 1921:

---

*Renamed *A Night at an English Music Hall* for the tour in America, the sketch would inspire Chaplin's 1915 film, *A Night in the Show*.

Who is that old derelict there against the cart? Another landmark. I look at him closely ... Well do I remember him, the old tomato man. I was about twelve when I first saw him, and he is still here in the same old spot, plying the same old trade, while I—

I can picture him as he first appeared to me standing beside his round cart heaped with tomatoes, his greasy clothes shiny in their unkemptness, the rather glassy single eye that had looked from one side of his face staring at nothing in particular, but giving you the feeling that it was seeing all, the bottled nose with the network of veins spelling dissipation.

I remember how I used to stand around and wait for him to shout his wares. His method never varied. There was a sudden twitching convulsion, and he leaned to one side, trying to straighten out the other as he did so, and then, taking into his one good lung all the air it would stand, he would let forth a clattering, gargling, asthmatic, high-pitched wheeze, a series of sounds which defied interpretation.

Somewhere in the explosion there could be detected 'ripe tomatoes'. Any other part of his message was lost.[102]

Two decades later, the same man 'just stood there inert in his ageing'.[103]

The most famous local character referred to by Charlie Chaplin in various media interviews was Rummy Binks, 'one of those old habitual drunks', who minded the horses stabled at his uncle's pub in Broad Street.[104] Rummy's bandy gait was mimicked by the young Charlie, to the delight of his friends, and later recycled for his popular Little Tramp character. This mimicry of a gait likely brought on by a medical condition such as rheumatism, rickets, or just old age reflects an aspect of physical comedy and, to an extent, the more unsentimental features of working-class humour, which can tip from playful teasing into pitiless mockery. The photographer John Thomson captured the image of one Jack Smith in 1877, who, Thomson recalled, in addition to mudlarking along the Thames foreshore between Westminster and Vauxhall Bridges, was well known in the Lambeth–Kennington neighbourhoods

Sufferers from the Floods photographed by John Thomson for *Street Life in London* (1877). Mrs Rowlett (see also pp. 8-9) stands in the doorway of her Lambeth rag store talking to a woman carrying her infant. Both were victims of recent floods that impacted the Vauxhall and Broad Street areas. As Mrs Rowlett wryly observes, 'The water don't come into the drawing-rooms of fine folks. We would hear more of it if it did.' Jack Smith, the local mudlarker and comedian, stands to the right smiling.

as a local comedian, 'whose tricks, contortions, and grimaces are the delight of many a pot-house audience. "Yes," said an admirer of Jack, "he's a rum'un, he is ; he can do the 'born cripple', or the man starved to death, or anything a'most."' Another speciality was mimicking a jury's individual reactions, as they sat through a coroner's inquest into the discovery of human remains.[105]

'Whether it is tragedy or comedy,' as Charlie himself observed, 'depends on how you look at it,' largely whether you were the mocker or the mocked. Charlie Chaplin's observational skills and comic antennae were clearly well tuned, although Margaret Sewell's comments indicate that he was not alone among the youngsters of South London. The fundamental difference between Charlie and most of the kids roaming the same streets in the 1890s is that he transformed an ability to observe and imitate into a career in variety theatre – and then, through a new medium for mass entertainment, in cinema, using the details and concerns of working-class life to create poignant comedy that would chime across the globe.

Charlie would have found the inspiration for a habitual drunk, the tics and mannerisms, closer to home. As an older man, he made constant observations about his father's drinking and his behaviour when drunk. It is clear from his son's recollections that Charles Chaplin senior ate very little to sustain himself through long, exhausting nights doing turns at the various music halls. In preparation, at about eight o'clock, he would swallow six raw eggs mixed in port before leaving for the theatre – that was his only sustenance. 'He seldom came home, and, if he did, it was to sleep off his drinking.' No wonder Louise felt neglected, left with her own child and the two sons of her partner; and, with his absent wife in a lunatic asylum with no prospect of imminent release, the future must have seemed grim.

But there were also times when Charles brought fun and laughter to the little family on Kennington Road: 'On a Sunday morning, when he had not been drinking, he would breakfast with us and tell Louise about the vaudeville acts that were working with him, and have us all enthralled. I would watch him like a hawk, absorbing every action.' On one occasion, in a light-hearted mood,

Charles senior 'wrapped a towel round his head and chased his little son around the table, saying: "I'm King Turkey Rhubarb."'[106] This recollection, a respite from the tensions caused by circumstances and worsened by drunkenness, was the tragedy of Kennington Road – as it had also been for the Tinworths of Hope Street.

However, for Charlie and Syd, neglect, rather than nurture, was the watchword. Within weeks of their arrival, Louise received a visit from the Society for the Prevention of Cruelty to Children 'and she was most indignant about it': presumably, Louise considered she was already going beyond what should be reasonably expected of her. The SPCC officers called at 289 Kennington Road 'because the police had reported finding Sydney and me asleep at three o'clock in the morning by a watchman's fire. It was a night that Louise had shut us both out, and the police had made her open the door and let us in.'[107] The London branch of the society had been established in 1884, with the social reformer Lord Ashley (the Earl of Shaftesbury) – George Tinworth's hero – its first president. The police patrolling the district were not just looking out for criminals and unsocial behaviour around public houses at tipping-out time, but also the welfare of children found on the street at an unusual hour. Three o'clock in the morning was certainly remarkable, even for an area where kids worked and played well beyond daylight hours. This new situation signalled another potential change: the authorities were involved, again, but another agency was now querying Charles's custodianship of the boys, and the behaviour of the woman he had left in charge of them.

However, Charlie recalled soon afterwards, 'while Father was playing in the provinces, Louise received a letter announcing that Mother had left the asylum'.[108] Hannah was discharged from Cane Hill, because she had 'recovered', on 12 November 1898.[109] And a 'day or two later the landlady came up and announced that there was a lady at the front door to call for Sydney and Charlie: "There's your mother," said Louise.' The reunion, Charlie recalled, was joyful. 'There was no umbrage or ill-feeling on either side – in fact, Louise's manner was most agreeable', even towards Syd 'when she bade him good-bye'.[110]

Dorothy Tennant's drawing of a poor girl, *Playing Mother*, is one of several preparatory sketches for the publication *London Street Arabs* (1890). When her husband, Henry Morton Stanley, stood for North Lambeth in 1892, the year Keir Hardie entered the House of Commons, Dorothy accompanied him on the hustings and the *Illustrated London News* reported that she 'is known as a kind lover of the poor London "street Arabs"' and for capturing 'their childish grace, their droll gestures, their wayward frolics, with a touch of womanly pity and charity'.

6

NEW CUT

'The Human Relationship'

Difficulty was ever present for Hannah, her estranged husband and their dependents, as had been the case for previous and current generations of the Hill, Chaplin and Tinworth families. Yet, on the face of it, the Chaplins and Tinworths were not, as Keir Hardie had defined it, from the most desperate in society: the slum poor. Rather, to continue his definition, they were from the vast bulk of the working class who spent their waking hours worrying about where the money for the basics of life was coming from. However, through following closely the experiences of George Tinworth, Charlie Chaplin, their families, friends and neighbours, we see that the boundaries between getting by, struggling, and destitution were porous: families and individuals became more comfortable and more desperate according to circumstances, fate and fortune. It was at those times, when life was a matter of survival from day to day, that difficulty turned to crisis.

At what point, and in what manner, the authorities intervened (if at all) was crucial. The collective attitude from officialdom, as experienced by these working-class families, begs several questions: who, beyond the individual workers, their families and their communities, cared about the quality of life experienced by millions of Britons? Rather than just responding when individuals and families were at their lowest ebb, who in society wanted to do something about the root cause of this precarious, pan-generational struggle; to help lift legions of their fellow citizens out of the poverty trap? And who, as a result, would be willing to step out of their own comfortable lives, to witness at first hand how others existed and use their privilege to drive forward lasting positive change?

The Reverend Samuel Barnett (1844–1913), rector of the East London parish of St Jude's in Whitechapel, had called for university-educated men and women to 'settle' in areas of privation, to better understand the circumstances of the poor and to break down the separation of classes into geographical silos. Barnett's pioneering work alongside his wife Henrietta (1851–1936) at Toynbee Hall on Commercial Street, with a team of all-male Oxbridge alumni as social workers, including Ernest Aves, was copied by other like-minded reformers in deprived areas across London and the nation. It was an inspiration for Charles Booth's data-gathering project, with the 1881 national census the starting point for an inquiry into conditions around London's East End, before spreading to encompass the whole of the metropolis.* Each settlement adapted to the specific needs of the population within its immediate vicinity, but the first to be established in the areas of South London known intimately to the Tinworths, Hills and Chaplins over the late 1880s and into the 1890s introduced further innovations, most strikingly the inclusion of women among the workforce and even women-only personnel. At the same time, women were becoming a presence in local government. From around 1870 they were able to stand in elections to committees such as sanitary boards, local school boards, and local councils. And the regulation of communities – whether through boards or settlements – dovetailed with the philanthropic work in which middle-class women had already been engaged.

After an inspirational lecture by Henrietta Barnett, the new women's colleges at Oxford and Cambridge Universities† formed a joint committee to found a settlement to 'promote the welfare of the people of the poorer districts of London, and especially of the women and children, by devising and promoting schemes which tend to elevate them physically, intellectually, or morally, and by giving them additional opportunities for education

---

*Booth's right-hand man, Jesse Argyle, was, unusually among the project's personnel, the son of a travelling salesman from the Mile End Road.
†They were soon joined by alumnae from the University of London, founded in 1836 to promote greater and broader access to higher education.

and recreation'.[1] In 1887, the first women-only settlement was established in a Georgian terraced house on Nelson Square in Southwark, just to the east of Blackfriars Road at the junction with New Cut. This modest abode, over subsequent years extending into adjoining buildings, was the base and home for the unmarried women social workers. As espoused by the Reverend and Mrs Barnett, the purpose of living among the poor was considered vital, as a means of immersing in the everyday difficulties and needs of the individuals and their families. Only by knowing the poor could the women assist them in the short term, while, over time, impressing upon those they visited the 'elevated' behaviours and morals required to improve their lot. Such an attitude jars in the twenty-first century – Ellen Ross connects the 'social explorers' of London's poor districts with the colonial impulse and terminology of bestsellers like Henry Morton Stanley's *In Darkest Africa* (1890)[2] – and even at the time these middle-class individuals were nicknamed 'squires in the slums' and accused of being 'slum travellers'. But given the levels of precarity and suffering – what Beatrice Webb described as the 'skeleton at the feast of capitalist civilisation'[3] – those who displayed a genuine and fundamental desire to be a good neighbour or 'Good Samaritan' were responding to a terrible situation with practical help and compassion: a situation that had persisted despite, or because of, the limited relief offered under various iterations of the Poor Law.

Throughout British society, middle-class women felt entitled to influence the domestic environment of poorer women. Even so, the idea that the working classes were pliant recipients of whatever largesse was on offer, or perfectly content to allow unsolicited intrusion into their lives, was far from the truth. George Duckworth, strolling through these crowded, dirty streets sporting a distinctive top hat among the many cloth caps and bowlers, might expect docility (if not deference) from the women standing on pavements and in the open doorways of their crumbling lodgings, bare-headed, aproned and with sleeves rolled up. Even so, the number of people willing to speak to him – let alone invite him into their homes – was relatively few: a distrust and reticence that settlement workers would recognise. Duckworth was left hovering on thresholds or peering through smog-tinged windows trying to assess the quality of domicile, furnishings and cleanliness. No matter how desperate, individuals could – and did – take exception. Indeed many, unlike their 'saviours', may not have seen their situation as desperate; it was simply how life was. The knack was making the best of it. And note should be made of the development in the 1880s of what became known as 'eugenics' – the term invented by Francis Galton and first promoted in his 1883 book *Inquiries into Human Faculty and Its Development* – which inevitably hovers over the attitudes of those who would consider themselves socially superior, genetically superior even, to their 'inferiors': 'Whenever a low race is preserved under conditions of life that exact a high level of efficiency,' Galton opines, 'it must be subjected to rigorous selection. The few best specimens of that race can alone be allowed to become parents, and not many of their descendants can be allowed to live.'[4] This coincided with new ideas about criminality: a shift from seeing crime as a choice, to viewing criminals either as a product of their biology or of their environment (or of both).[5] Charles Booth and his survey was not immune from some of these ideas; there was a strong moral disapproval of people defined as 'Class A' (occasional workers, loafers and semi-criminals), and he thought people in 'Class B' (casual labourers and those living hand to mouth) could be sent to 'industrial or labour colonies'.[6]

Charlie Chaplin's attitude towards middle-class social workers may have echoed that of his contemporary, Thomas Burke, as set out in the fiction-real-life hybrid *The Wind and the Rain*, a book Chaplin considered 'so full of bitter pathos'.[7] Here Burke described 'those old women and earnest young men from the Universities' as interferers, who did not have 'the grace or the intelligence to perceive the impertinence of their intrusion in offering us spiritual enlightenment and social example'. He acknowledged the conditions under which some people lived were 'disgusting', but 'they carried some blessed armour that lifted them above their conditions. The more foul the environment, the more people will fight, the more they will laugh, and the greater is their capacity for joy in little things.' Chaplin would echo this sentiment in his broadcast of 1943 and later in *My Autobiography*. Burke concludes his passionate and somewhat romantic declamation with a statement that resonates with those by George Tinworth as well as Chaplin: 'We fought for beauty,' he cries, 'for a kipper for tea, for a new pair of boots, for education, for a better job; our self appointed teachers knew nothing of these battles.'[8] Burke has a point: 'squalor', as with beauty, can be in the eye of the beholder. The agenda of social reformers meant that they did not simply misunderstand what they saw, but needed to emphasise the squalor in order to justify calls for reform, and to rally support for their cause. And, lest we forget, there are occasions when the best things in life can be free. Yet in some cases, the local populations were not only happy to join forces with these middle-class social workers, but were determined to take control of their own destinies.

One purpose of settling in an area – rather than simply visiting for a few hours, as Duckworth did – was to break down these barriers between the middle and lower classes, with the laudable objective of raising the quality, appearance and security of neighbourhoods that could otherwise succumb to uncleanliness, crime and despair. In this sense, the settlement movement offered a challenge to Thomas Burke's critique of the 'cold-water homilies' of patrician writers (like John Ruskin in his critical economic essay *Unto This Last*): 'I felt that people who wrote polished sentences about the spiritual dignity of poverty should try it for a month – in Bermondsey.'[9] To their credit, this was exactly what the settlement social workers did. Would Mary Ann Hill or Hannah Chaplin have rejected help, respectfully offered, which literally came knocking at their doors, if it might have alleviated the relentless 'worry', the humiliation of the workhouse, as many in their situation viewed it, and the stigma of the lunatic asylum?

The working-class poor were not the only potential beneficiaries. There was a strong camaraderie within the social worker communities, which at Nelson Square was an extension of their experiences at the women's university colleges. The settlement movement gave these individual women – albeit socially privileged and economically comfortable, compared to those living in the streets around them – far greater independence, a wider range of life experiences, and a genuine sense of purpose beyond the narrow realm of marriage, homemaking, child-rearing and entertaining that was standard fare for their social background. However severely we choose to judge them now, in the 1880s these were undeniably pioneering women who demanded equality in education to their male peers, and many were part of the drive for female suffrage.* Among the founders of the Women's University Settlement (WUS) at Nelson Square was the formidable Octavia Hill, a campaigner for good-quality working-class housing, later a force behind the establishment of the National Trust, and the equally remarkable Helen Gladstone, daughter of the Liberal prime minister, who led the WUS as warden from 1901 to 1906.

In early February 1888, soon after the WUS was founded, *The Echo* sent a reporter to investigate how this unusual enterprise was surviving in the depths of South London:

> Though it is quite a young establishment, it is one of the most interesting in the Metropolis; and the devotion of these ladies who have taken the highest distinctions that their sex can win at Oxford and Cambridge in coming into dreary, cheerless South London to minister to the wants of the poor and degraded, will do more to silence the taunts of those who find fault with the 'higher education' than an interminable list of mere academic honours could do.[10]

'I have seldom spent a pleasanter time than that I passed in the society of the cultured noble women at the unpretentious "settlement" at 44, Nelson-square, Blackfriars,' the reporter declared, going on to describe the accommodation for the 'five inmates'. The communal spaces included 'a pretty little drawing-room and library'. The bedrooms, also used as sitting rooms, 'are furnished in the style prevalent at the Universities. That is to say, ingenious arrangements of screens conceal wash-handstands and toilet tables; and the small bed rather resembles a couch than anything

---

*It was not until 1920 at Oxford and 1948 at Cambridge that women were awarded degrees. The University of London had been awarding women degrees since 1878.

else, and is covered with a gay, pretty rug, or art serge and embroidery.'[11] As described here, the domestic arrangements at Nelson Square were intended to bring some comfort and familiarity to the women, even as the world beyond differed so extravagantly from the cloisters and quads of Cambridge and Oxford.

In 1891, the year Hannah Chaplin, her sons and mother were living at Barlow Street, *The Gentlewoman* announced the appointment of Margaret Sewell (1852–1937) as the new principal or warden of the WUS, noting she had been a natural science student at Newnham College and was an intimate friend of Helen Gladstone. The article described Margaret – the niece of Anna, the author of *Black Beauty* (1877) and from a Norfolk Quaker family of some means – as a great organiser 'for which she will find ample scope at the settlement'.[12] Sewell had been the agent for the Charity Organisation Society (COS) – the poor-neighbourhood visitors established in 1869 to better 'manage' outdoor relief – in Camberwell, so was already an experienced social worker within the district located just to the south of Walworth, at the time Charlie Chaplin was born there. The article names 'one of her most devoted helpers' as 'Miss Lubbock', the daughter of Sir John Lubbock (1834–1913), the Liberal politician, philanthropist, and supporter of the Elementary Education Act of 1870 and the Electoral Reform Society.*

A further report in *The Echo* of 28 November 1893 highlighted a paper written by Margaret Sewell (1852–1937) and published in the *Charity Organisation Review*, which 'should be read by every woman whose life and interests bring her in contact with the complex difficulties of dealing with the poor'. The warden of the WUS talked about the mental and physical fitness needed for such social work which entailed, after all, daily contact with poverty unimaginable for anyone not born and raised in these streets. Sewell highlighted the plethora of specific knowledge required to be effective in such a role, including the workings of the various charitable institutions active on the ground, trade societies, local

---

*Gertrude Lubbock (1876–1955) was later author of an important study, *Some Poor Relief Questions. With the Arguments on Both Sides ... A Manual for Workers* (London: John Murray, 1895).

wages, rents and much more. She observed that the goal for the social worker was to help the people to arrive at an ideal for living themselves, rather than divining one on their behalf and thrusting it upon them. She concluded by considering the misguided use of social work and the provision of relief as vehicles for religious evangelising: 'If you regard relief as a gospel agency, you are carrying in your hand a two-edged sword, and doing infinite harm to the cause of religion … You may get more members of your church, you will certainly get more hypocrites, and you will certainly not get more religion.' In other words, desperate people will say and do anything for free food and money; whether they believed what they said and did was another thing altogether.

In settling in an area specifically chosen for its deprivation, the women of Nelson Square were exposing themselves to evident physical danger. This can be gleaned from George Duckworth's notebook entries for June 1899, when he was touring the police district in which Nelson Square was located. His companion was Sergeant F. J. O'Dell, who was no longer on active duty pounding the streets but was employed in the clerks' office at the police station. As a result, he knew a 'good deal more about the different parts of the division in their criminal aspects, than most of the policemen who have been round with me – all charges from every quarter pass through his hands every day'.[13] Sergeant O'Dell told Duckworth that juvenile thieving and betting were the most serious issues in the area. The level of drunkenness was no worse than before, but he viewed the general roughness of the streets as markedly increasing.[14]

Under 'General Remarks', Duckworth noted that the block of streets to the south of Nelson Square and across to Borough Road had the reputation of being not only poor, but as rough as any place in the police division, excepting the 'vicious' hidden courts near Borough High Street and Red Cross Street. Sergeant O'Dell spoke of the area near Great Dover Street 'as being as bad as any district in London'. Drunk and disorderly cases abounded, along with juvenile thieves, 'race course roughs' and 'a good proportion of ponces & prostitutes of the lowest class as well'.[15] Little Surrey Street was very poor, Duckworth observed, with nearly every front door open and, standing around in the road, 'heavy bloated faced women', all middle-aged and old mothers. Duckworth saw birdcages in the windows, and houses, outwardly at least, in a fair state of repair, but there was a 'fearful mess' in the street itself, a mix of bread, meat-wrapping, paper and sacking, among which a pack of mangy cats were feeding. The children were 'sore eyed, hatless, some clean', and although an organ was playing nearby, there was 'only one child dancing'.[16] Of Butcher's Row he noted

> all doors open, ice cream vendors, children dirty & ragged, sore eyes but well fed ... all the tenants here are rough poor, plenty of money at times & none at others: women sitting about on doorsteps: a few thieves & prostitutes & betting roughs: men who regularly snatch <the [betting tickets] from> those who come with their slips after a race to be paid; they are in league with the smaller bookmakers.[17]

In Bean Street ('every door open'), the inhabitants were noisy and rough, and 'do a good deal of singing before they go to bed'. The children were well fed and a little cleaner than in the other streets, but the houses were poorer, with 'less furniture to be seen through the doors'. Here we have an example of Duckworth, from the pavement, squinting into the unlit hallways and front parlours of the poor residents: no one on Bean Street was interested in inviting this strange 'toff' inside, particularly when accompanied by a policeman. Finally in Gun Street, Duckworth and O'Dell saw crowds of children, and among them, 'loafing about', were what the sergeant called 'hooligan boys'.[18] These were the people that Margaret Sewell and her small band of university ladies were living among, and these the streets they worked within.

The boom in 'penny dreadfuls' earlier in the century had given way to increasingly lurid reporting on contemporary crime, with attention-grabbing imagery in local and national newspapers – as had been seen with the infamous killings in Whitechapel, occurring only a few years before the Charles Booth investigator was recording the conditions in the Waterloo–Southwark area. Such literature, and particularly that targeted at the working class, was believed to be behind a shift, for the worse, in conduct among the lower classes, and particularly young men who, courtesy of these sensational publications, might consider crime as not only glamorous and an easier way to make money than an honest trade, but encouraging in them an underlying sense that aggressive and intimidating behaviour within gangs brought respect and power.

The Hooligan Boys was one such gang of youths, based in the Southwark area; their leader was Charles Clarke, described in *Reynolds's Newspaper* (a publication not averse to sensationalism) as a 'powerful lad' aged nineteen at the start of his criminal career, who traded as 'a general dealer'. It was said that a 'subscription' of twopence a week was paid to the 'secretary' of the gang, which was used to settle the fines should any members find themselves in court. Clarke was arrested in April 1894 for assaulting a police officer: rowdy behaviour at the South London Palace of Varieties on London Road in Lambeth – a theatre where music-hall stars Dan Leno and Marie Lloyd regularly performed – turned to violence, with bottles and glasses thrown about the gallery. Constable Chappell, hired by the proprietor Mrs Poole, attempted to stop them, but Clarke 'seized a broom and struck him a violent blow with it, felling him to the ground, where he lay in an unconscious condition. The prisoner and his companions then kicked him violently about the body.'[19] 'THE "HOOLIGAN BOYS" AGAIN' was the headline in the *Illustrated Police News* of 19 May 1894; two seventeen-year-olds, the costermonger Edward Holt and Edward Smith, a 'van boy', were arrested for disorderly behaviour and using obscene language. They were part of a gang of 'young roughs' in the St George's Road area. The year before their arrests, Charles Frederick Hill was living at 87 St George's Road; Charlie Chaplin's grandfather would have witnessed any intimidating behaviour, which included, according to the paper, 'coming down the street flourishing sticks and using obscene language and causing foot-passengers to go into the roadway'. Two constables in plain clothes caught the two ringleaders, but 'were then stoned by the rest of the gang, the stones falling about them, to use the words of one of the officers, "like hail"'.

A few years later, on 20 August 1898, the *South London Press* printed an article under the headline 'South London Ruffianism'.

A victim of the now notorious 'Hooligan Gang', Abraham Smith, had received a threatening letter since his case had appeared in the newspapers. The letter read: 'I am well acquainted with you, and also a gang who I swear will murder you! Murder! Yes, we will murder you as sure as I am an Anarchist. Prepare to meet your death.' At the foot of the letter was drawn a skull and crossbones, two swords crossed, plus, for good measure, 'a heart with a dagger through it'. This would be menacing enough, but the contents of the envelope included the press cutting giving Mr Smith's office address and therefore some credence to any threat of grievous bodily harm. Smith told the reporter he had given this letter to the police in M Division, and Detective Sergeant Ottway was handling the case. In the same column there was a further report concerning an assault by the Hooligan Gang on Frederick Jameson, potman at the Salutation Tavern on Stamford Street near Waterloo Station, with one Alex Hulme arrested for the attack. The gang had been thrown out of the tavern for disorderly conduct and returned the following night 'about 14 strong, playing mouth-organs and dancing on the cellar-flap'. They were refused service, 'whereupon they knocked [the] witness down and tore the shirt off his back. They also assaulted the manageress and her daughter.' Hulme was sentenced to two months' hard labour.

The 'hooligan outcry' has a similar feel to the fears of juvenile delinquency in the 1950s that produced Anthony Burgess's *A Clockwork Orange*. Unsurprisingly, given such intense and sustained coverage, in late 1898 there were reports in the *South London Press* that a rate-payers' Protection Association had been formed and that 'a meeting of working men was held under its auspices in the Blackfriars-road'. Local tradesmen had promised their support for such an association, and no one was surprised that working men from South London had joined the response against the ruffianism that now seemed rife in the area: 'They had to think of their wives and children, who were, in addition to themselves, the prey of the gangs that infested many of the most thickly-populated localities of the metropolis.' As part of this local groundswell against the gangs, it was agreed that South London MPs would be invited to attend the next meeting, so that constituents' concerns could be voiced directly to their elected representatives.[20] Working people were more than capable of taking matters into their own hands and punishing alleged offenders themselves, a remnant of the ancient folk justice of 'hue and cry'. Listed in the column next to the report on the Protection Association, and concerning the proceedings at the recent South London Court Sessions, was the case of James Sheppard, a twenty-three-year-old window cleaner who was convicted of 'improperly assaulting' a six-year-old child in Dodson Street off Waterloo Road. The reported details were vague, but the article concluded: 'It was a shocking case, and, before being arrested by the police, the prisoner was soundly beaten by a number of women, who blackened his eyes and drove him out of the neighbourhood.' Sheppard was sentenced to nine months' hard labour.[21]

A year after the formation of the anti-ruffianism Protection Association, Detective Sergeant Ottway was labelled 'The Hooligans' Terror' for breaking up the gang and ending their 'reign of terror' in South London.[22] Even so, no one would have been surprised at the levels of criminality among the poorer lads of the district. But another notorious gang, operating around Nelson Square area in the 1890s, was truly astonishing, for its membership was entirely female.

Although it is thought that the 'Forty Thieves' had existed as an entity, if not under this name, since the late eighteenth century, it was from the 1850s that they turned from a South London criminal syndicate into an urban legend. Their name was likely a reference to the Arabic folk tale *Ali Baba and the Forty Thieves*, made popular through children's literature and then the late Victorian Christmas pantomime circuit. By the 1890s, the acknowledged gang leader was Mary 'Polly' Carr, who lived on Stamford Street, the long broad thoroughfare connecting Blackfriars Road to Waterloo Road and running parallel to New Cut. This was the heart of the music-hall management district, where agents had their offices and, at the junction with Waterloo Road and York Road, the location of 'Elbow's Corner', where desperate variety artists lurked in the hope of begging a turn. It is also the area where Hannah Chaplin and her two young sons were living around 1893. Stamford Street sliced through several parishes, including St John the Evangelist on

Waterloo Road (Charlie Chaplin's grandmother, Mary Ann, had married her first husband here) and Christ Church on Blackfriars Road, with its Marlborough Street workhouse, where Keziah Tinworth had been an inmate fifty years before.

The Peabody Buildings, funded by American philanthropist George Peabody, in Stamford Street were an example of the new multi-storey housing popping up all over London that was attempting to address the issues of accommodation for the poorer levels of society. (Another set of Peabody Buildings had been built in nearby Southwark Street.) Apartments of one to four rooms were made available by application, which required a character reference from employers in order to attract, according to the charity's regulations, only the 'most deserving of the working poor'. Among them, in 1876, was Polly Nichols, her husband and three children, paying 6s 8d a week. But in 1880, unable to bear her husband's adultery, Polly left the relative safety and outward respectability of the Peabody Buildings on Stamford Street for the last time; this began a downward spiral over the subsequent years, which would find her moving in and out of the Lambeth Workhouse on Renfrew Road, and ending in her brutal murder.[23]

Ten years later, in early May 1899, Stamford Street was visited by George Duckworth; the first scribble in his notebook quotes his companion on this occasion, Sergeant Waters, who said that there were a 'great many prostitutes living here: hotels are places of accommodation: some are little else than brothels: girls live in them, walk out & bring men home to them: there have not been so many foreign prostitutes since the passing of the "act against bullies"'. 'Bullies' was a historic term for pimps, men who earned money from prostitution by arranging clients and offering 'protection'. This broadly describes the life of Eliza Grimwood, the sex worker murdered in her own bedroom, in this very area, sixty years before. By 1899, 'rescue work' in the Waterloo area included a 'home' for fallen women, which was under the diocesan management of the Bishopric of Rochester, alongside the activities of a 'ruridecanal' social worker called Miss Packham who lived at 23 Lambeth Walk. 'She appears to be a hard worker,' Ernest Aves observed while interviewing the vicar of the St-Mary-at-Lambeth parish, the Reverend Reeve: 'One extraordinary enterprise of hers was mentioned, and it appeared to excite Mr. Reeve's wonder as much as my own, a weekly service that she held in a doctor's house in Stamford St' – this was the very street where the Forty Thieves' leader Polly Carr resided – 'at which a good many women were living. Permission appears to have been given and the women to welcome the visits, but nothing more incongruous than this congregation of prostitutes can well be imagined. They are said to belong to the older section of the women, passées as a class.'[24]

Duckworth summarised his exploration of Stamford Street and the surrounding roads by noting that 'the bulk of the inhabitants both work & sleep in the district ... The inhabitants make one vast poor family whose lives are well known to one another. There is more street life <than even in the E[ast] end>, more children in the street & more women gossiping at the doors.'[25] This observation, alongside the prevalence of sex workers, provides the context for Polly Carr's influence over the women and girls in the area.

Legend had it that the criminal career of the Forty Thieves' leader began when she was a flower seller on the Strand; because of her fabled beauty, she would often receive more for the flowers than they were worth: gold sovereigns rather than bronze pennies, according to an article written by a decidedly giddy journalist in the *Weekly Dispatch*.[26] (Flower sellers, as poor street workers, were viewed with suspicion because their presence in and familiarity with this urban terrain made them vulnerable to corruption, whether by petty thieving or prostitution.)* Polly came, the journalist records eagerly, from a large family 'well-known in criminal circles in South London'. The article continued:

> A most expert pickpocket she became, about this time known as 'Queen of the Forty Thieves,' a confederacy of young women from the New Cut, the Borough, and Waterloo-road, who nightly frequented the Strand, and who chose as their

---

*Such a context perhaps adds resonance to (that founder member of the Fabian Society) George Bernard Shaw's choice of heroine, the flower seller Eliza Doolittle in his 1913 play *Pygmalion*.

victims elderly gentlemen who were proceeding home after having dined not wisely, but too well. Many a gold watch and 'prop' (pin) found their way into the hands of this gang but when arrested by the police almost *in flagrante delicto*, the victims were not desirous of posing in the police-courts, and consequently the thieves were released.

One of Polly's 'little tricks' was to strike up a conversation with such a gentleman in the saloon bar of a public house on the Strand, and while her prey was flirting with her, she would expertly divest him of his gold watch and chain. A girl gang member would then enter the bar, the goods passed to them unseen,* and the gold watch and chain would be immediately sold to a fence – a dealer in stolen goods – with the money brought back to Polly, all while she was still in the company of the hapless victim. Now in possession of her spoils, Polly, with raffish aplomb, would offer to buy him a drink. When he discovered the loss of his watch, Polly's victim would assume that the theft had occurred before he entered the bar, and his charming companion would encourage him in that assumption. If the item was a valuable heirloom, Polly might arrange to meet the gentleman the following night, having 'bought back' his precious possession; her reward would be, say, £20 expenses, plus £5 'for her trouble'. So, even after paying back the £9 to the fence for the return of the object, Polly and her fellow thieves were still up around £25 – not bad for a few hours' work. On their profits the 'Forty' gang would have a right royal blowout (or, as they called it, a 'flare-up'): a night at the Surrey Theatre on Blackfriars Road, followed by 'whelks and mussels at the stalls in the vicinity', likely from the market on New Cut.

The *Weekly Dispatch* article continued its extensive reporting on Polly, stating that despite being 'brutal and unscrupulous as a thief', she had a soft side when it came to children – and particularly the sons and daughters of fellow criminals. It described her finding children in the street, 'shivering with cold'. She would give them her jacket, wrap them up in a cloak and take them home. This natural generosity was noted by the male journalists who were

---

*Or 'slung', in contemporary street jargon.

regular attendees at police courts: 'Should a thief with a family "fall" (into the hands of the police),' one observed, 'Carr would be the first to find food for them, and to support them while "father" was away.' It is worth pointing out here that such behaviour went beyond the 'thieving fraternity': the broader community had close ties, offering mutual support, for example, in the care of children – encouraged from infancy to call friends and neighbours 'auntie' and 'uncle' – which indeed features in the life stories of both George Tinworth and Charlie Chaplin.[27]

In March 1896, Polly Carr, who, in the court documents was said to have been born in America in 1871, found herself accused of kidnapping a five-year-old boy, 'a bright-eyed, engaging little chap', from the fair booths at the Epsom races the previous April; child abduction was a far cry from her usual criminal activity. According to the article in the *Weekly Dispatch*, Polly had the nickname 'Swan's Neck', and the journalist makes much of her startlingly attractive appearance. She was eventually tried at the Old Bailey. The 'kidnapping' had occurred 'at last year's City and Suburban day', an event during the annual Epsom 'Derby' horse-race meeting, famously depicted by the painter William Powell Frith, and a popular resort for the working class of South London.* The child was identified as Michael Magee, a 'gipsy boy' whose mother was a race card dealer.[28]

The *Weekly Dispatch* article sets out in detail the sequence of events at Epsom, with Polly – dressed, as she recalled at her trial, in 'an electric blue cretonne dress, and a little band round my neck'[29] – offering to buy the boy from his mother. When she refused, Polly had the child spirited away by a male accomplice, who took him to Polly's house on Stamford Street. Ten months later, Detective Sergeants Gray and Brogden found Michael at this address, after a tip-off. One witness at the Old Bailey trial, Mrs Sarah Harman, stated that while at Stamford Street the boy had been renamed 'Billy'. Polly herself was called as a witness, 'where she gave evidence in a very cool and collected manner' to the effect that she was caring for the child on behalf of an acquaintance. The

---

*Herbert Stead (1912) observed that when 'the popular favourite wins the Derby, Walworth is a carnival of bibulous gaiety' (p. 8).

prisoner, the reporter continued, was 'a handsome young woman, with particularly well-chiselled features ... She stated that she was fond of children, and that she had adopted little children before and brought them up'; given her occupation as a gang leader, this potentially established Polly as a sort of female Fagin.

At the Old Bailey trial, the witness Mrs Harman, described as Polly's neighbour and the parent of eight children, some to whom Polly 'stood god-mother', said: 'I know the prisoner very well – I frequently go to her house in Stamford Street – it is a respectable house – I have known her for ten years – she has some women lodgers, single women as far as I know.' If we consider Duckworth's descriptions of Stamford Street – that 'the inhabitants make one vast poor family whose lives are well known to one another' – alongside the comments on prostitution by the local policeman Sergeant Waters, and the work of Miss Packham, Polly was probably offering protection to these unmarried, lone women lodgers, whether in exchange for membership of the Forty Thieves, or simply as a place to live and from where they could ply an independent trade, of whatever type.

It was reported during her Old Bailey trial that, beyond thieving, Polly had a sideline posing for artists. Mrs Harman, under examination, stated that 'I do not know whether she does any work; she used to sit to Arthur Small as an artist's model.'[30] Who 'Arthur Small' was is not known, the name in all likelihood an alias. Earlier in the century, as we have seen, artist models, whether within an institution such as the Royal Academy or privately posing for an artist at their studio, could earn decent wages; in the spring of 1896 a 'Miss May' and a 'Miss Ellsmore' were paid £5 each for posing nude in the Royal Academy's School of Painting, while the 'gypsy' Antonio Corsi, who appears in the paintings of John Singer Sargent and Edward Burne-Jones, was paid £4 by the academy for modelling 'draped'.* By way of comparison, three detectives, hired to mingle among the crowds at the 1896 summer exhibition, earned £4 16s between them.[31] Besides his recollection of the life models at the Royal Academy Schools in the 1860s, in

---

*Corsi went on to become a successful silent film actor in Hollywood.

his memoirs George Tinworth records personally hiring individuals to pose for the figures in his sculptural works in the 1880s and 1890s, including a man 'from near Rome, and had fought under Garibaldi he told me that Garibaldi had got fierce eyes when on the battle field', and a former marine with whom the sculptor chatted amiably about his time at Chatham dockyards.[32]

The *Weekly Dispatch* expanded on this intriguing line of enquiry from Polly Carr's trial, by reporting that 'Mrs H. M. Stanley (Miss Tennant), the daughter of Sir Charles Tennant, engaged Polly on more than one occasion to sit as a model. She has also sat for a celebrated R.A., and her portrait, as a model, of course, has frequently been seen on the walls of the Royal Academy.'[33] The London-born Dorothy Tennant was another pioneering middle-class woman, as a Slade School of Art alumna, who married the celebrated explorer Henry Morton Stanley. She was a regular visitor to the poorer areas of London, sketching children in the streets and using them as models for her artworks; as a result, no matter how worthy her intentions, she can be described as another type of social explorer, documenting life in the mysterious depths of the capital's slums. These images – undeniably tender and empathetic – were published in 1890 as as a compendium of drawings and paintings called *London Street Arabs* (see p. 234). The term 'arab' was everyday parlance in Victorian Britain, as were other forms of casual racism, and was used by the reviewer of George Tinworth's terracotta exhibit at the Royal Academy, *Peace and Wrath in Low Life*, referring to a poor child, a 'gutter snipe'. This would explain the gang-name 'Forty Thieves', now applied to the 'Street Arabs' of South London. The purpose and sentiment behind such projects as *London Street Arabs* are complicated and contradictory, fluctuating between humanity and bigotry.

Dorothy Tennant's more significant paintings, which she would have exhibited at public venues such as the Royal Academy, included the oil on canvas entitled *His First Offence* (1896), depicting a nameless lad, wide-eyed, dirty and dishevelled, standing meekly at the bar of a magistrates' court.* It is therefore highly

---

*It was purchased by Henry Tate and presented by him to the new National Gallery of British Art (now Tate Britain), near Vauxhall Bridge, in 1897.

probable that Miss Tennant hired working-class models, such as this poor child, as part of her studio practice, including, perhaps, Polly Carr. By the 1890s, female artists like Dorothy were regularly attending academy life classes – a major leap forward, given the exclusion of significant commercial artists like Angelica Kauffman and Mary Moser, despite both being full academicians at its foundation in 1768. But, over a century later, their presence before naked models (particularly males) was still considered unseemly.

The prominent Royal Academician for whom it is said Polly likewise posed is thought to have been Frederic Leighton, since 1878 the president of the Royal Academy. Leighton is known to have hired models, including Dorothy Dene (born Ada Alice Pullen) and Mary Lloyd, who posed for him at his spectacular purpose-built home and studio in Holland Park (now the Leighton House Museum). With artists like Leighton, James Abbott McNeill Whistler and John Singer Sargent now seen as deliciously outré, Dorothy quickly became a celebrity in her own right. One of her noted physical attributes was her long 'swan-like' neck: perhaps the journalist of the *Weekly Dispatch*, in alluding to a nickname he assigns to Polly, was hoping to create a connection in the minds of his readership between the Queen of the Forty Thieves and Dorothy Dene. Leighton, conveniently perhaps, had died suddenly just before Polly's trial. Was 'Arthur Small' an alias for one of the most powerful men in the British art world? In any case, these details certainly lent a thrillingly bohemian frisson to the Old Bailey criminal proceedings, even if modelling for artists was a perfectly legitimate and time-honoured form of paid employment for girls and women who needed the income.

But the life of an artist's model was precarious too. Mary Lloyd, whom Leighton used extensively between 1893 and 1895 – she is almost certainly the figure in his celebrated painting *Flaming June* – was tracked down and interviewed by the *Sunday Express* in 1933. Within the front-page article headlined 'THE STORY OF MARY LLOYD, WHO HAD THE FACE OF AN ANGEL BUT OUTLIVED HER LUCK', the former muse of Millais, Edward Burne-Jones, William Holman Hunt, as well as Leighton, is quoted as saying wistfully: 'I lived for the moment, never dreaming that I should ever be in need. But one by one the artists died. Each year I grew poorer and poorer, and moved, as I did so, to humbler apartments.' Now aged seventy and living in a back room in Kensington, the article concludes, 'this woman, whose lovely face adorns the walls of palaces, mansions and famous buildings, will darn your socks or sweep your house to earn a few shillings!'[34]

The *Weekly Dispatch* reporter is certainly glamorising a situation that had very bleak undercurrents. The *Morning Leader* report (of 26 March 1896) was written by someone far less beguiled by Polly's fabled good looks and criminal audacity. He observed that when the boy Michael was inspected at Carr's home on Stamford Street, the 'medical evidence as to the condition of the child revealed a shocking condition of things'. This is supported by the trial transcript; after examining him, the doctor assessed that 'the child was suffering from a foul disease'.[35] It can be presumed that it was a venereal disease, probably syphilis and likely a congenital condition. In Polly's defence, she may have recognised the outward signs when she saw the child at Epsom and decided, in that moment, to rescue him. The reporter recorded that when the little boy was asked 'who he loved', he named Polly and another, a 'Nurse Fisher', the latter the woman, according to this source, who had been fostering him since his discovery at Stamford Street. The unguarded response of the boy might confirm that he had experienced ill-treatment from his mother, who had already passed on a nasty – potentially incurable – disease to her offspring.

As recorded in the trial transcript, prior to her being found guilty, Sergeant Grain informed the court that Polly 'lived with bad characters, who called themselves the "Forty Thieves"' and that she had previously been 'sentenced to Four Months' Hard Labour for stealing a watch and chain' – perhaps the crime fulsomely described in the *Weekly Dispatch*. Finally, before she was removed to the cells at Newgate Prison, the *Weekly Dispatch*, signing off on this touching episode, noted that Polly 'requested that she might be permitted to see the boy before she went away, but permission was refused, whereupon the prisoner burst into tears'.[36] Michael, with the blessing of his mother, was taken into institutional care by the Society for the Suppression of Vice.[37]

This whole account of Polly Carr reads like a blend of fantasy and reality, characterising the Forty Thieves' leader as a criminal folk hero, a female Robin Hood, or the real-life embodiment of Nancy, the soft-hearted gang member from *Oliver Twist*. For all the reported glamour and status, which (no doubt) assisted in swelling the ranks of the Forty Thieves, the reality is that Polly was sentenced to three years' penal servitude: imprisonment in a British gaol with hard labour, which by this date had replaced transportation to the colonies. Two years later, after serving time at Aylesbury Prison, Polly came up for parole. She was discharged as a habitual criminal on 21 March 1898. This was a category that had emerged by the late nineteenth century, assigned to repeat offenders.[38] Here Mary alias Polly (and with yet another named alias, 'Eva Jackson') is recorded as 5 foot 3 inches tall, with brown hair, a fair complexion and light hazel eyes; after her release, she was resident at 32 Charing Cross, closer than Stamford Street to her early haunts in the Strand.[39] But by the time she had emerged from two years in prison, the reign of a new Queen of the Forty Thieves, Minnie Chamberlain, had already begun. The life of a low-born criminal, however it was sensationalised by journalists for the delectation of lower- and middle-class readers, was sometimes fun (perhaps) but far from glamorous and, almost inevitably, brief.

George Duckworth interviewed the social workers of the Women's University Settlement on 7 June 1899. He observed, casting a critical eye, that a Miss Gow and Margaret Sewell were both 'ladies of a certain age', while Miss Sheepshanks was about twenty-six and Miss Kerby 'just below a certain age'. Sewell, whom we have already met, had known the district since 1891 and was 'capable', 'plain', 'rather tall', but 'with a pleasant voice' and 'anxious to do all she can to help'. Having appraised her appearance and manner, he moved on to her clothing: she was 'dressed in shirt, collar & tie', Duckworth noted, 'but' (he continued) the overall impression was 'not too masculine'. Like the warden, Miss Gow had been in the area for eight years and was, Duckworth observed, kindly and rather sentimental. Miss Sheepshanks, also dressed in a 'shirt, collar & tie', with 'pince-nez' and 'rather pretty', had worked at the settlement for four years.[40]

Miss Gow's particular area of focus included Gray Street, which connected Blackfriars Road to the east with Waterloo Road to the west. The western end of Gray Street she considered 'so bad that we cannot go there at all' and 'if a special enquiry must be made then someone is specially chosen, but no girl could be sent there'. At the better end lived lightermen, labourers, cabdrivers, newsagents and cellarmen. The wages of the head of household ranged from 15 to 25 shillings a week – significantly less than Joshua Tinworth's wheelwright business was reported to be generating in the 1860s. In this area, a single house could have two to five families living in it, with pressure on space inevitable.[41] Then there was Gun Street Buildings, 'the worst spot in the area' – as Duckworth had discovered on his walk with Sergeant O'Dell – populated by a 'rough low class of coster'. The residential buildings built by charities like Peabody from the 1860s and the new London County Council in the 1890s had 'a better class in them because rents are more strictly exacted', although this style of accommodation had no back yards (unlike the traditional terraced houses and cottages) so they were not, in the opinion of the settlement workers, as good for the inhabitants. The vestry, Miss Gow told Duckworth, 'neglects all these streets' and, she warned, 'they will probably remain in the state in which you saw them' – covered in rotting bread and whatever else was dumped, through which the rats and cats scuttled and prowled. The weekly rents in Gun Street were between 6s and 6s 6d for just two rooms – a sizeable proportion of the earnings recorded above, and in one case Miss Gow said there were ten people living in such a restricted space; 'It is useless to report any except very extreme cases of overcrowding,' she observed. 'The medical officer told us that he should take no notice of any but extreme cases.'[42] In Little Surrey Street, one room cost four shillings a week and the settlement women knew of one case where a husband, wife and their children were living in a single room here. Then there was Surrey Row, where the women social workers witnessed a lot of drunkenness; the sleep of those in Nelson Square was often disrupted by loud shouting at night from this street, with 'screams of help, murder', the 'cries of children etc'. This already intimidating environment had become notably worse during the recent hot weather, when tempers had become frayed and the overcrowding particularly unbearable. Even the dark cellars in Surrey Row, not intended as accommodation, were occupied by renters.[43]

The courts between Borough High Street and Redcross Street were 'too bad to work in'; in Miss Sewell's opinion, with reference to Booth's 'poverty map' colour coding from gold (wealthy) to black (extreme poverty), these streets were simply shades of black.[44] Octavia Hill managed Stanhope and Mowbray Buildings on Redcross Street, but 'these buildings are so badly planned that they never can be well managed. The dark staircases harbour ruffians at night'; indeed, observed Miss Sheepshanks, they were 'so dark that even by day you could not see the numbers on the doors'.[45] 'As to model Dwellings,' added Margaret Sewell, meaning the newer purpose-designed and built higher rise blocks, 'the worst are those with dark staircases & without gates. They are made sleeping places by the lowest class.'[46] This indicates how brand-new accommodation, intended for 'model' poor tenants, transformed over the years and decades as the national and local economic environment changed.

Improvements were, however, being made by people associated with the settlement, for example in the accommodation owned as well as under the management of Octavia Hill in Loman Street and in the adjoining Orange Street, where Hill and the suffragist Beatrix Maud Palmer, Countess of Selborne, owned Winchester Cottages and Walpole Cottages respectively. Hill also argued that cottages, with adjoining gardens and communal space, had the potential to be a healthy, attractive alternative for working-class renters and their families – in contrast to the large, utilitarian apartment blocks, thrown up by developers, that increasingly lined the streets of London. Hill regularly visited such multi-storey buildings as part of her duties, and as a landlord herself she had first-hand experience of how they functioned in practice. This dense, multi-storey style of accommodation, a response to the rapid increase in demand and the corresponding pressure on limited land, was replacing whole swathes of more diverse housing across the capital (albeit some considered derelict 'slums' by the late nineteenth century), introducing a uniformity of streetscape which became increasingly soulless and, as Octavia Hill would argue, insanitary, unhealthy and dangerous. Prime examples, still in existence, of Hill's enterprising working-class social housing are the Red Cross Cottages and Garden south of St Saviour's in Southwark, designed by Elijah Hoole in an arts and crafts 'Tudor' style and built between 1884 and 1887.

Seven years after the founding of the WUS in Nelson Square, and just over a year since James Keir Hardie's 'lilies of the fields' speech on Walworth Road, the Robert Browning Settlement was established a short walk from the street where Charlie Chaplin had been born in 1889. The public inauguration of Browning Hall (see p. 39), the building previously known as the York Street Chapel, replete with its ground-floor seating and upper-level gallery, occurred on 21 November 1895 with a speech by Herbert Asquith, the Home Secretary in William Gladstone's Liberal government, before a large crowd.[47] The new settlement was named in honour of the poet, playwright and – to date – Walworth's most celebrated son, who had been baptised at the chapel in 1812 alongside members of George Tinworth's family, was a regular attendee in his youth, and who had died on 12 December 1889. As an advocate of universal human rights, Browning was, effectively, the settlement's patron saint: their motto, 'All's love, all's law' (advocating fellow feeling with orderliness) came from his poem 'Saul', regarding the Creation: 'I report, as a man may of God's work – all's love, yet all's law.' Rather than purely philosophical or sentimental, the aligning of this embryonic mission to one of the greatest of modern English poets was very astute. It brought national and international attention to an obscure part of London and, crucially, to their programmes and campaigns on behalf of the Walworth poor and beyond.

The Browning Settlement differed from Toynbee Hall and the organisation on Nelson Square; it was open to self-taught, labouring and working-class volunteers, including the first Labour Party Member of Parliament and leader, Keir Hardie, alongside future Labour leader and British prime minister, James Ramsay MacDonald. By design, and again to distinguish it from other foundations, the Browning Settlement had an overt interest in the broader labour political and social movement, embedded in a specific approach to Christian service: springing from a Nonconformist tradition but separate from the dogma of *any* organised religion. It is worth recalling here the Reverend Edward White's memories of Robert Browning, which were read out at the inauguration of the new settlement, in particular his discomfort at the segregation of the York Street Chapel members in the 1830s according to their relative wealth and income; the future poet and his family were in the gallery, alongside the young Jane Daniel – later Mrs Joshua Tinworth – looking down on the heads of their more august, that is moneyed, brethren.

The Browning Settlement's entry in the *Directory of Settlements* (1898) stated: 'We stand for the Labour Movement in religion. We stand for the endeavour to obtain for Labour not merely more of the good things of life, but most of the best things in life. Come and join us', it implored, 'in the service of Him who is the Lord of Labour and the soul of all social reform.'*[48] In emphasising Jesus as the carpenter of Nazareth, the humble worker and, through his words and deeds, the champion of all who labour, the potential of this settlement to attract the poor working-class population of Walworth becomes obvious. Its substance was echoed by a manual worker from Walworth, George Tinworth, who, like Keir Hardie, was deeply religious, when he wrote of generations of his fellow workers at the Day of Judgement before the 'great master': 'What thousands of lives healp to make up the mighty play that is acted in this world, and most of them after they have done there part, pass on before the great master that neads no recommendation, for he [h]as been a worker himself.'[49] George carried this conviction, alongside a personal relationship with the 'Lord of Labour', throughout his life and his art.

Among the first residents of the settlement's house at 92 Camberwell Road was the warden and founder, Francis Herbert Stead, his wife and fellow social worker Bessie, and their three young children. Originally from a Northumberland, Nonconformist,

---

*'The Lord of Labour' alludes to the New Testament Gospel of Matthew: 'Come unto me, all ye that labour and are heavy laden, and I will give you rest' (11:28).

middling-sort family, Francis Herbert (usually called Herbert) and his elder brother, William Thomas, were remarkable characters. Prior to relocating to London, Herbert established the Gallowtree Gate Congregational Church in Leicester, but then saw his calling lay among the poor of the British capital city. *The Christian* (15 June 1899), observed that 'there are many sincere Christians who do not feel able to dogmatise as to what Jesus would do in any given set of circumstances. Mr. Herbert Stead ... feels convinced, however, that Jesus if He came to London in person, would settle down in a central district, and work among the poor there.'[50] William Stead was a radical journalist, editor and social campaigner, whose activities over the 1880s highlighting the circumstances around prostitution, had included an investigation into child exploitation, published in a sequence of articles under the title 'The Maiden Tribute of Modern Babylon'.* As a result of his unconventional investigative methods, William would spend time in Holloway prison for the 'purchase' of Eliza Armstrong, the thirteen-year-old daughter of a chimney sweep. Observers (then as now) would query William Stead's motivation, even as his social status and public forum as a journalist and newspaper proprietor drew vital attention to the cause and changed the law, for better or worse, as a result.[51]

Another resident at Camberwell Road was Thomas Albert Bryan (1865–1917), the assistant and sub-warden to Herbert Stead, who was born in Leicester and had been a member of Stead's Gallowtree Gate Congregational Church. Unlike Herbert, Bryan was a working-class man, a former labourer who had earned a Master's degree from London University. After rising through assorted civic positions in Walworth and then in various posts within the district – elected to the vestry in 1896 and then chairman of the Public Health Committee – Bryan, an example of the more socially diverse membership and the fresh thinking that ensued, would become mayor of the newly formed Metropolitan Borough of Southwark from 1902 to 1903. This role, as continued to be the case for Members of Parliament also until 1911, was unpaid,

---

*'Tribute' is here used in its classical meaning of human sacrifice.

which had kept such influential civic positions beyond the reach of working men and women and firmly within the orbit of those with private income or wealthy patrons. When asked how he would be able to afford the expenses usually associated with such an elevated public function, Tom Bryan reportedly answered, 'By not incurring them.'[52] He also declared that in his position as mayor he hoped 'to do something for the poor, the helpless, and the suffering, more especially for the cripples and those suffering from consumption.'[53] *The Arena*, a liberal literary magazine advocating social reform and based in Boston, Massachusetts, would declare Mayor Bryan a different sort of political animal, 'a fine type of the new statesmanship', who 'represents the type of men whose brains are aflame with love for humanity and moral enthusiasm, that the Browning Settlement is pushing forward into public life, to the immense benefit of the community'.[54]

When George Duckworth interviewed Herbert Stead and Tom Bryan at Browning Hall, he declared: 'Of Mr Herbert Stead it may be said that both in appearance and character he is like his more famous brother, though no doubt he is less of a crank.'[55] Herbert was, as Duckworth described, less scandalous in his drive to highlight social wrongs, but he was as strident, determined and unwavering as his elder brother in the rectitude of his cause. The sub-warden Tom Bryan, Duckworth goes on to record, was 'a man of different type: he is a working man in origin, appearance and manner'. Bryan 'got educated', Duckworth continued, 'is an M.A. of London Uni[versity] and lectures to the working men of Walworth on Plato and Aristotle. But', he continues, less patronisingly, 'with all his culture he remains essentially one of themselves, and his influence among the working men is probably great.' Duckworth's short pen portrait concluded: 'If he has not Mr Stead's red hot enthusiasm for righteousness, he too is an enthusiast in his way: but he approaches questions I imagine with a more balanced mind than his Warden.' Duckworth then quotes Herbert Stead in describing his purpose in settling in Walworth: 'We did not come ... to bring education to the educated, or a church to the religious but to lighten the lot and to brighten the lives of those who have hitherto been outside all organisations.'[56]

By the end of 1898, various programmes around and within the Browning Hall site were gradually integrating into and impacting on the lives of local people. Meanwhile, other ambitious projects were being considered, such as a club house for the working men of Walworth (eventually opened by Charles Booth in 1902). All were discussed and promoted in the annual report for that year, in the hope of further support from current donors, to energise ongoing fundraising campaigns, as well as to encourage new volunteer social workers to join the settlement and move with their families to Walworth.[57] In 1898, Tom Bryan's new wife, Frances, became a member of the settlement's management committee, alongside Bessie Stead, and with her brother-in-law, William, as a vice-president. The equality of women within the settlement was matched by another core aim, that the settlement should not rely on young single people – Herbert Stead called them 'celibates' – but rather be populated by married couples and families, who would set down permanent roots within the district. The Steads and the Bryans led by example.[58]

Browning Hall, the hub of the settlement, hosted evening lectures and programmes directly associated with the settlement's core beliefs. In 1898 Tom Bryan – a working man who had grasped with both hands the opportunities available for education and 'betterment' – was addressing the people of Walworth on a variety of subjects germane to their everyday experience. 'What 1848 can teach 1898' was one example, presumably drawing lessons from the year of revolutions across Europe and the Chartist mass meeting on nearby Kennington Common, as potentially witnessed by Joshua Tinworth. The subject of the sub-warden's 'Men's Adult Club' winter course was 'The Industrial Revolution: Its Poets and Workers' and, prior to Christmas, he had 'dealt with the chief inventors and promoters of the steam, cotton, steel, canal, and bridge-building industries', and covered the spiritual messages within the poetry of William Cowper, Thomas Gray, Oliver Goldsmith, Robert Burns and John Keats. Attendance had ranged from twenty to thirty people, and the annual report declared that 'great interest has been evoked'.[59] Bryan had also presented an atmospheric lime-lit Sunday night lecture on Burns's 'The Cotter's

Saturday Night' (1786), which described a poor peasant family at the end of a week's labour, and Gray's *Elegy Written in a Country Churchyard* (1751):

> Let not Ambition mock their useful toil,
> Their homely joys, and destiny obscure;
> Nor Grandeur hear with a disdainful smile
> The short and simple annals of the Poor.[60]

In tandem, the subjects covered in Herbert Stead's lectures included 'The Jubilee of Chartism', 'The Service of Mammon' and 'Mr. Charles Booth on Old Age Pensions' – a proposal that the Browning Settlement would actively support. Meanwhile, G. E. Anstruther (there being nothing new under the sun) had addressed the thorny issue of 'Levelling Up'.[61] Such subjects and lectures were not for everyone, and no one was forced to attend: the modest audiences hint that most Walworthians had other ways of spending what little spare time they had.

Of the various programmes already in train by the time the annual report was published in 1899, the 'medical mission' was one of the most popular. Supervised by Dr G. W. Richards, who gave his services free of charge, by the end of 1898 it was seeing between seventy and eighty sick people every Tuesday and Friday. (If such a service had existed half a century before, the young George Tinworth would no doubt have been among them.) The data provided by Dr Richards for the annual report included the following: 1,167 different patients had been treated, 884 homes had been visited, and there had been 4,318 patient attendances at Browning Hall – and all for the total outlay of less than £70. Dr Richards also noted that this medical provision had filled the gap that existed between the private practitioner and the provident dispensary (a charity) on the one hand, and the state medical officer on the other. 'Many people', Dr Richards observed, 'with quite intelligible pride object to apply for medical relief to the Poor Law';[62] usually, like Keziah Tinworth, Mary Ann Hill and Hannah Chaplin, they attended workhouse infirmaries which might lead to a worse fate – admission to the workhouse proper. Indeed, even as Dr Richards was assisting hundreds of Walworthians locally and in their homes, their neighbours Mary Ann Hill and Hannah Chaplin were undergoing treatment in institutions many miles away from their family and friends.

Then there were those, Dr Richards continued, who did not bother to prepare for the future – for themselves, or their family – simply living day by day: 'Others, again, through lack of thrift, or through ignorance or selfishness, disregard the needs of those dependent upon them who are unable to assist themselves. Hence,' Richards concluded, with reference to the demand on the medical mission at Browning Hall, 'the patients consist almost exclusively of women and children.'[63] Again the tragic figure of Joshua Tinworth, slumped in a local hostelry, comes to mind.

The 'poor man's lawyer', inspired by a similar scheme at Toynbee Hall, offered legal advice every week to those who needed it.[64] Herbert Stead later observed that the 'majority of cases are, alas! those of matrimonial difficulty', followed by cases of compensation for injury, or the death of relatives: 'Again and again has substantial redress been secured for wounded workmen or desolate widow[s] who, but for the aid of our lawyers, would have no remedy.' Breach of contract and wage disputes were also regular issues brought to the settlement lawyers, as were 'questions of seizure of pianos and sewing machines under purchase by instalments, and other incidents in the sad story of the wrongs of the poor.'[65]

The settlement also encouraged gatherings on a sociable basis. A weekly men's meeting called the 'Pleasant Sunday Afternoon' club, or PSA, had been established, where readings from Charles Dickens were favoured, while the women's meetings – the 'Pleasant Tuesday Afternoon', or PTA – were managed by the wife of Lawrence Briant (treasurer to the Medical Mission), Mrs Morgan and Bessie Stead. Starting with just seven attendees and two babies, offering a slice of cake and a cup of tea to every woman present, by 1898 – after observing (a standard idea among middle-class reformers) 'that a neighbourhood will only rise to the level of the homes it contains; and also that it is the woman who makes the home' – the settlement workers felt 'no small measure of thankfulness that the membership of our Women's Meeting', held at Browning Hall, 'has grown to the number of 763, with an average weekly attendance of 400'.[66] The helpers 'who have the best opportunity of judging say that, especially among the poorer members, there is an effort after much greater cleanliness and order in personal appearance',[67] and the presence of a crèche for the babies and infants was an enormous boon for the working mothers. Among the popular activities organised by the PTA over the coming years were the Thrift Club, the Clothing Club (where women could buy cheap new and old ready-made clothes), the Coal Club and the Goose Club, all based on members pooling their financial resources to get a far better unit price – a practice akin to the Cooperative Consumer Societies, the first successfully established in Rochdale, Lancashire in 1844. For example, in the Goose Club, which by 1898 had 388 members, a weekly sum was collected from participants, accruing to 6s 6d each over the year (£126 2s in total), which purchased a large goose or a turkey, half a pound of tea and a plum pudding for the Christmas table.*[68] Charlie Chaplin would recall the importance and pride within working-class communities of having a home-cooked Sunday meal; the provision of a Christmas feast, as George Tinworth's memoir revealed, was something people considered a greater symbol, and, for the Goose Club members, who, by the turn of the century, would be numbered in their thousands, a worthwhile investment.

Among the many high points over 1898, all recorded in the settlement's annual report, was the opening of a public garden, funded by private donations and the Metropolitan Gardens Association; the latter provided the design and planting. The site selected was a disused graveyard, 'an abomination of desolation' as Herbert Stead described it, adjoining the former York Street Chapel, now Browning Hall, which had become a dumping place – including of dead cats – for those living in the vicinity. It was also home to an 'animated gargoyle of a dog', as Stead recalled, 'which lived in a vault and grew unwholesomely fat on its decaying contents'. Adding further Gothic flavour, he continued, regarding this dog: 'Human

---

*A similar goose club features in the Sherlock Holmes story, 'The Blue Carbuncle' (1892).

bones dragged out by it or by some other means became the playthings of Walworth children.' One of the first acts of the settlement was to organise the local unemployed men to clean up this graveyard.[69] The mid-1890s was a period of acute distress in Walworth, when the settlement, rather than handing out doles, employed men to do such work around Browning Hall.[70] This would eventually develop into an agitation for some form of national programme of paid work for the unemployed, including developing skills to vary employment prospects among the unskilled labourers.

The laying out of the settlement garden had been preceded by the 'Flower Mission', organised by members of the Young Women's Bible Class, which was led by Frances Bryan. Every week they bought cut flowers on Saturdays (likely from the East Street market), arranging them into small posies, and attaching a handwritten message with (in a subtle form of evangelising) a quotation from scripture, to be delivered to the aged and sick of the area. These small gifts, the warden believed, represented 'brief happiness to many an aged heart', including a poor old lady who had been born in the countryside, but now 'has come, old and blind, to end her days in Walworth'. This lady 'never fails to recall the beautiful home of the younger days when our visitor calls with a bunch of flowers'.[71]

In a similar vein, Herbert Stead also encouraged the revival – or, perhaps a better description, the repackaging – of Walworth's May Day celebrations, which had been recalled by George Tinworth in his memoir as joyful interludes in an otherwise fraught childhood over the 1840s and into the 1850s. George would have recognised some elements, which no doubt stimulated a tinge of nostalgia in the older members of the community. There was no hint, however, of the bawdy misrule of the Jack-in-the-Green (which, in parallel, continued to be performed locally) in the celebrations stage-managed by the well-meaning reformers of Browning Hall. These included the crowning of a May Queen from among the girls attending the settlement's Sunday School. In 1898 this honour had gone to Emily Rivett, who had just turned fourteen. As reported in the local press, Emily 'with her maids of honour was dressed in white, & prettily bedecked with spring flowers'. That Monday

Emily Rivett as May Queen, 1898. According to the 1901 census, Emily lived at 63 Faraday Street with her parents George, a hop porter and Emily, a housewife. Emily junior was the eldest of four children (her siblings were George, Ethel and Herbert) and, aged sixteen, she is listed as an apron machinist.

morning, the enthronement was held in front of a large audience in Browning Hall, with the warden as master of ceremonies. The front of the platform where Emily sat with her attendants, was 'almost hidden by a profuse display of bud and blossom, sent by generous friends in the country'. Emily was crowned by a girl representing the 'spirit of spring', and afterwards a bugler from the boy's brigade band sounded a 'royal salute'. The bunches of flowers that had been laid at the May Queen's feet were afterwards distributed among the sick and poor of the neighbourhood. Finally, Emily and her handmaids were conveyed through the streets of Walworth to her home 'by a cart adorned with flowers and drawn by a well fed and groomed donkey', followed by the boys' brigade band and company, holding aloft the Union Flag and the banner of the Browning Settlement.

The Browning Settlement, whether or not we agree with their methods, had an agenda to transform the streets of Walworth and the lives of its inhabitants. The evident pride and sense of community engendered by such apparently trivial celebrations stayed with participants long after the floral tributes had wilted. In the years to come, Emily Rivett would gain further local fame by becoming a teacher at the Browning Settlement and winning a recitation competition on behalf of the Sunday School: her poem was Rudyard Kipling's 'If'. She married another member of the settlement, James Blake, in June 1916, just prior to her husband leaving for the Western Front, on which occasion she was presented with a silver rose bowl, 'as an expression of their love & regard', as its inscription read, 'by her fellow workers in Browning Hall Sunday School'.*[72]

The development of the garden, many years in the making, came out of this desire to bring beauty and pride to the people: the letter and spirit of Thomas Burke's declaration, 'The more foul the environment, the more people will fight, the more they will laugh, and the greater is there capacity for joy in little things.' And, with the influential presence of Tom Bryan, this cannot be

---

*These fellow workers included Emily's helper and close friend Winnie Freeman, after whom she named her daughter. The latter provided the Browning Settlement with these family recollections in the 1980s.

dismissed simply as a top-down imposition of middle-class attitudes: working-class people had driven a demand for learning and betterment through education for over a century, alongside, as both George Tinworth and Charlie Chaplin recalled, a need for delight and beauty in whatever form it might take.

The garden was also a restful open space, away from the rowdy market in nearby East Street and the bustle of Walworth Road. Under the heading 'OPENING OF THE BROWNING GARDEN: An Anglo-American ceremony at Walworth', the *South London Press* provided an extended report on the launch event, which caused quite a stir. It was not very often, after all, that the American ambassador to the United Kingdom, at this time Colonel John Hay, found himself standing on a patch of greenery in South London, let alone a former abandoned graveyard in the vicinity of East Street and Walworth Road. However, the work of the Browning Settlement had brought this district of South London to the attention of social reformers across the Atlantic; according to Boston's *Arena* magazine, the settlement was known as 'a Victorious Social Experiment' in 'the very heart of darkest London' ('that gloomy hive of labor's children'), and where 'the atmosphere of despair was felt on every hand. Poverty and misery jostled with vice and crime, and into this ocean of human wretchedness and sin were constantly being wafted a multitude of innocent lives.'[73]

The international reach of the settlement was a conscious strategy by its management. An article in the *Daily News Weekly* declared that the Browning Settlement stood 'for a great deal in the life of the neighbourhood', but was also 'known far beyond the confines of Walworth',

> and therein lies one of its most potent influences upon the people. It is the connecting link joining together this dark and poverty-stricken district with the great world outside. In the Hall the men and women of the most widely differing classes are brought into close contact. There is not a movement in the world which makes for progress but Mr. Stead does not get one of its leaders to come down and address the people of Walworth. Many a speech has been followed up by

action, and in this way Walworth in its turn is able to impress its ideas upon the world.[74]

As noted by the reporter from the *South London Press*, the garden had been created for the people of Walworth, and thanks 'to the energy and kindliness of Mr. F. Herbert Stead and his earnest colleagues of the Browning Settlement, the children of overcrowded Walworth can now enjoy an oasis of grass and flowers in the arid desert of York-street'. The reporter described the illustrious history of this modest plot next to the old Nonconformist chapel. Not only, he noted, had the great Robert Browning been baptised there in 1812, and the missionary explorer Dr David Livingstone and his wife worshipped there, but other illustrious individuals associated with the chapel included both 'Sir Henry Doulton' and, coupled with his employer and sponsor, 'George Tinworth, the sculptor'. 'It is a source of great pleasure,' the report continued, 'to those who know the history of the place to feel assured that the Browning Settlement is keeping up the best traditions of a glorious past.' York Street was decorated with bunting for the occasion, and two large flags, the Union Flag and the Stars and Stripes of the United States of America, were draped over the garden entrance. Further festive decoration was provided by hawthorn branches, 'festoons of yellow laburnum and boughs of copper beech' that 'gave Walworth quite a floral appearance'.

The gathering moved to Browning Hall, where the American ambassador gave a powerful and heartfelt speech, in which he celebrated Robert Browning and the good work that was now being done in his name, a name that 'stands as a symbol of intellectual energy and moral earnestness'

> and it is most fittingly upheld in any work which tends to the uplifting and enlightenment of humanity. Especially appropriate is that name as a symbol of any work which is intended for the benefit of the people. Because, although he, of course, belonged to the higher aristocracy of genius and character, yet he was one of the most uncompromising democrats that ever lived – in all the essentials underlying the principles of true

attend it. An hour is spent in chat, and then tea and cake are served, being provided by the generosity of Mrs. Lawrence Briant, and a short religious service is held. The boon is appreciated. There are over 900 women on the roll of membership, with an average attendance of about 450. There were nearly 500 women, some of them with tiny children in their arms or at their feet, in Browning Hall on the Tuesday when I was present. Some of them were knitting or sewing, and all, I think, were talking when I entered. Mrs. Lawrence Briant gave out a hymn, which was heartily sung. Then a portion of Scripture was read by Mr. Stead, and a short prayer was offered, followed by another hymn. Mrs. Briant then sang "Love's old sweet song," and after she had sung the refrain, It was repeated as a chorus by the women:

MRS. LAWRENCE BRIANT.
(*From a Photograph by C. F. Treble.*)

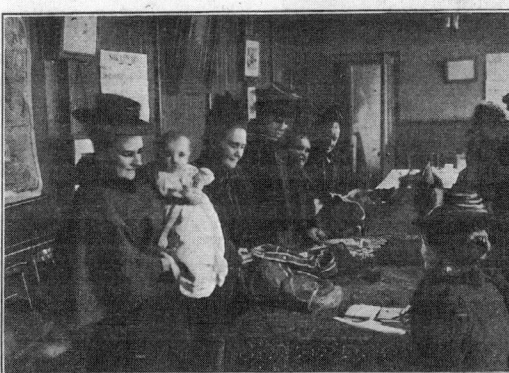

BUYING READY-MADE CLOTHING, ETC.

But the P. T. A. is more than a meeting for speech and song and rest—helpful though each of these may be. The women bring their pennies to the Thrift Club, the Clothing Club, the Goose Club or the Coal Club. Here are two sentences from a recent report:—"The Coal Club, with a year's total of £227 receipts, enabled its members to get coal at 1s. 3d. a cwt. instead of the current retail price of 1s. 9d. The women's Goose

"Just a song at twilight,
when the lights are low,
And the flick'ring shadows
softly come and go;
Though the heart be weary,
sad the day and long,
Still to us at twilight comes
Love's old song,
Comes Love's old
sweet song."

The singing was most sweet and touching. I could not help thinking of *Mord Em'ly*. Then followed a short address by a visitor, and another hymn brought the meeting to a close.

THE GARDEN: CHILDREN ARE TAKEN CARE OF WHILE THEIR MOTHERS ATTEND THE P.T.A.
(Captain James Wilson's Tomb in Background.)

A page from *Men who Reach the Masses*, c.1900, with photographs of the Clothing Club (centre) and the creche held in the new garden (bottom) while mothers gather for their PTA meeting led by Mrs Briant (top). By 1900, PTA membership had risen to 900, with knitting, sewing, singing and chatting among the activities.

democracy – to whom, in the sight of God, all men were equal. He believed in the equality of rights, the equality of opportunity, equality in the individual sacredness of soul of every man and every woman. It is for these reasons, and because, also, the greatest of all rights – the right to truth, and the right to life – was the principle he upheld and vindicated, not only by the marvellous power of his poetry, but by the example of his laborious and blameless life, that I am glad to be here.[75]

The veneration for the late poet extended to programming organised by the settlement:[76] 'It is satisfactory to know,' wrote A. E. Fletcher, 'that Mr. Stead has done much to inspire many of the poor hard-working people of Walworth with a reverence for Browning, and to assist them to take an intelligent interest in his works. One of the most delightful features of last Saturday's programme was the series of recitations by children of some of the more popular of Browning's poems.'[77]

After the ambassador's uplifting speech, Miss Hay, his daughter, with a 'beaming smile', declared the garden open.

A separate ceremony was held to celebrate the local association with the Doulton family and their Lambeth Pottery. The *South London Press* reported that Herbert Stead officially accepted, on behalf of the people of Walworth, 'a beautiful drinking fountain of salt-glaze vitreous Doulton ware', which the reporter described as a 'fine specimen of Lambeth art'. It was presented by Lewis Doulton in memory of his father, Sir Henry, who had died in 1897. The first draught of water was put aside for the baptism of Frances and Tom Bryan's first child, who had been born that very day.[78] The reporter reminded the readership of Sir Henry's baptism at the chapel in 1821, and that he had been 'a great admirer of Browning's poetry.' The report concluded by noting again that 'Mr. Tinworth', as the fountain's creator, 'was present at Monday's ceremony but, with his usual modesty, he did not make his presence known.'[79] Fifty-five years after his birth in a humble cottage in nearby Milk Street, George Tinworth, alongside Henry Doulton and Robert Browning, was the pride of Walworth.

In his memoir, George records that after Sir Henry Doulton's death he suffered from what he calls 'a nervous break down'. 'I used to sit before my work,' he went on, 'and my arms would drop at my side and although I wanted to work I could not.'[80] For all George's grumbling about how he was treated by the contemporary art world and commercial art market, and his desire to be independent of Doulton's employ, this confirms Sir Henry's importance as the modeller's supporter, as well as his employer. In the process Doulton may have become an emotionally significant figure too, like a father, in George's mind. Certainly the sequence of events suggest this: the death of Joshua, the returning hell of back-breaking work in the wheelwright shop, followed by his deliverance by Doulton (encouraged by John Sparkes) and the paradise of his pottery studio.

Rather than sitting in a listless and morose state at Doulton's pottery, however, George 'decided to go to Rome', paying £17 at Thomas Cook's travel agents for a return train ticket via Paris and Turin – and off he went. He later recorded the wonders of the art he saw at the Louvre and the Vatican, among many other locations.[81] Unfortunately, after the extensive recollections of this trip, George's memoir trails off.

Herbert Stead may have been thinking of the likes of George Tinworth when he observed of the area, fourteen years after the garden ceremony, 'The more enterprising workers, as they better their position, soon flit to pleasanter neighbourhoods, while the more timid and disheartened remain.'[82] The vicar of St Mary-at-Lambeth, the Reverend Reeve, had made a similar comment in 1899, regarding the Doulton workers resident in the area around the factory, that 'nearly all Doulton's good people lived at a distance', leaving the poorer workers (furnace-men and carters among them) in the immediate environs.[83] By 1898 George Tinworth had been living in leafier Richmond for several years. The 1891 census records the Tinworths at 8 Maze Road in Kew, with the then forty-eight-year-old George listed as an 'Artist in Clay', and Alice's single sister Ellen Digweed now living with the couple, her occupation recorded as 'companion'.[84] The nearest train stations were at Kew Gardens and Kew Bridge, offering transport by overland train to Waterloo. Vauxhall was the nearest station to Doulton's in Lambeth and the station George travelled to and from on his daily commute to his studio, after which he would have walked from the station along Albert Embankment, with views of the new Palace of Westminster, to Doulton's on Broad Street.

It may be that by 1898 George had resigned himself to his current position and status: a decade since his depression, brought on by the thwarted ambition to move beyond his role as modeller at Doulton to achieve success and renown as an independent artist, followed by Sir Henry's death, which caused another collapse and his impromptu trip to Italy. It is the fate of ambitious people, from whatever background, never to be satisfied. Given the rarefied, snobbish nature of the art world, George may have suffered from imposter syndrome; worse, perhaps, like many born in 'low life' but now firmly within the middling classes, he may have felt he did not belong to either group; he was neither fish nor fowl. He most certainly displayed a bitter belief that he and his art were consistently misjudged, underrated and under-appreciated. On the very first page of his memoir, opposite the title, is written the following inscription in Alice's hand, with George's emphases in capitals: 'When the Smith takes the hot iron out of the fire he bruises it and bends it this way and that way according to his will, and then lets it get cold'; it concludes, 'If you see in me some thing you do not like, remember it is the treatment I have received from MEN in this world, I HAVE BEEN BENT SO.'[85] Perhaps George had simply reached the limit of what he could achieve, given where his life journey had begun. As he stood in the new Browning Settlement garden, quietly observing the inauguration of the beautiful fountain he had made, dedicated to his late patron for the benefit and delight of the working people of Walworth – his people – George must have allowed himself a moment of pride, accompanied by a profound sense of achievement.

To reflect how such a simple change in the local environment could cause a ripple effect in the behaviour of the community at large, Herbert Stead recalled one meeting of the men's PSA club which included among its members a local knife-grinder. A Chartist in his youth – and, five decades on, still without the vote – he was attracted to this open-air gathering of fellow workers because of the songs the members sang and the speeches they and others delivered, 'the like of which he had "never 'eard since

Chartist times'". It is an important reminder that the settlement was not only tapping into existing working-class networks, but the memory of political solidarity from half a century before. At this meeting, the knife-grinder rose to his feet before his companions, they no doubt trailing off from their conversations, one by one, as they turned towards him expectantly: 'Look 'ere, men!' the knife-grinder began (as transcribed by Herbert Stead):

> At Browning's 'All I 'eard a lot about makin' Walworth brighter. Well, I went 'ome and I looked outer my back winder, and see my backyard full o' rubbish. I says to myself, 'Yer can't call that bright, nohow'; and I thought, 'Why shouldn't I turn it into a little garding? So I never said nothink, 'cause I knew the missis 'ud only kid me if I was to tell 'er afore it was done. I waited till Easter Monday. Me and the missis generally goes over the water of a Easter Monday to see a daughter of ourn. When the missis gits up I says, 'I don't feel up to the mark to-day; I'll jist lay abed a bit. You take the 'bus over yerself.' Then, as soon as I thought she was safe away in the 'bus, I gits up, dresses myself, clears up the yard, goes down to the cabyard, borrers a barrer and fills it full o' dung, and had jist got it inter the doorway of my own house when, lawk-a-mercy! back come the missis! She'd forgot somethink. Then the fat was in the fire, I can tell yer! But I stuck it. I got a pal in the buildin' trade to give me some cement an' I made a nice balusterrade acrost the end o' the yard. I put in muck and dung, an' I sowed a few seeds and put in a few plants, and now – why, it's the very brightest spot in Walworth!⁸⁶

The knife-grinder's garden was visited by the warden and sub-warden, and the thought promptly occurred to those standing in this little oasis: 'If a backyard in such a street can be transformed into a pretty little garden, why should not similar transformations be made in other, and possibly less difficult, quarters?' The idea was announced at the next PSA meeting, 'to the great amusement of the men', who joked about a fine crop of cabbages growing on their concreted yards. 'But,' Herbert Stead recalled, 'however Utopian and even ludicrous the idea appeared at first, that speech of the aged knife-grinder was the beginning of the gardening movement in Walworth',[87] which came to include an extremely popular annual garden competition that, a decade later, received hundreds of entries.

This broader movement – the May Queen, the posies, the gardens – was very far from trivial. 'I used to laugh at my mother for thinking so much about flowers,' George Tinworth noted, 'but I should not laugh at her now, for I see there is a power', recollecting that when he was sixteen he made Jane 'an ornamental stand to fix on the window sill at Hope St and she used to take it out every morning and fill it with pots of flowers'. The local children, to George's surprise, never picked the flowers.[88] When Vincent van Gogh lived in North Brixton and then near the Oval in the 1870s, he walked through Lambeth to his work at an art dealer's in Covent Garden via Westminster Bridge in the morning, and then back again in the evening. One spring he wrote: 'There are lilacs and hawthorns and laburnums &c. blossoming in all the gardens, and the chestnut trees are magnificent. If one truly loves nature one finds beauty everywhere.'[89] As Thomas Burke declared, thirty years later:

> The desire for beauty is not the gift of intellectuals or divines. Everywhere it manifests itself. Every working woman in the slums who puts a coloured almanack on the wall, every clerk that potters in his garden, is satisfying the yearning for beauty. The girl who saves up for a feathered hat of clashing colours is striving for beauty as she sees it. The working man who spoils his cheap furniture by painting it with flowers is striving for beauty. This instinct has nothing to do with culture; it is an inward force.[90]

And finally, consider the inclusion of flowers, among other incidental, frivolous items such as coloured omnibus tickets and children's balloons, which Charlie Chaplin recalled, decades after leaving these very streets, perhaps filtered through the romantic gloss of the exile, as the colours, sights and smells of a Lambeth spring that accompany his memories of 'riding with Mother on top of a horse-bus trying to touch passing lilac-trees':

> Of the many coloured bus tickets, orange, blue, pink and green, that bestrewed the pavement where the trams and buses stopped – of rubicund flower-girls at the corner of Westminster Bridge, making gay *boutonnières* ... of the humid odour of freshly watered roses that affected me with a vague sadness – of melancholy Sundays and pale-faced parents with their children escorting toy windmills and coloured balloons over Westminster Bridge; and the maternal penny steamers that softly lowered their funnels as they glided under it. From such trivia I believe my soul was born.[91]

In addition to the convivial PSA meeting, the Adult School was run on Sunday mornings, and in the summer of 1898 the men had read and discussed Thomas Carlyle's *Chartism* (1840) and John Ruskin's *Sesame and Lilies* (1865) and *The Crown of Wild Olive* (1866),[92] and Herbert Stead would later recall that the language of the Adult School members 'may be rugged at times, but it comes straight from the heart. And the new phrases which are minted out of the pure gold of the men's inner life are of a kind to set theologians thinking.'[93] Education and discussion were important, but so too were recreation and relaxation. Stead accordingly made an appeal to the readers of the 1898 Annual Report to support the building of the new club house, planned for a prominent site at the corner of York Street and Walworth Road, which would cost £4,000 to build and furnish. The proposed club house was seen as a vital space for the men of Walworth, given the area's population density, and because 'the provision of a cheery and comfortable Clubhouse as an auxiliary to the sadly depressed home-life of the people ranks among the most elementary of human duties'.[94]

The sad fact was that, despite positive steps in the four years since it had been established, the 1898 Browning Settlement report included some shocking statistics about the area it served, not least the 'forlorn condition of the Aged Poor' under the jurisdiction of the St Saviour's Union, showing the highest percentage of aged pauperism of any Poor Law Union in England and Wales. According to the report, 84 per cent of the population over the age of sixty-five were in receipt of indoor or outdoor relief; the 'fate of honest, industrious, and often God-fearing men and women, who for no other fault than that of age have been flung out of employment, to spend their days and nights in dread of the alternate horrors of starvation and the workhouse, has been a continual heartbreak to us.'[95]

In fact, the workers of the Browning Settlement were not simply highlighting the issue of those no longer able to work, but were at the forefront of addressing the needs of the poor in old age. The question of an old age pension scheme had been raised in the general election of 1895, and there appeared to be cross-party agreement that something needed to be done. The 1898 Browning Settlement report noted the deliberations of Lord Rothschild's Parliamentary Committee, which had sat for two years assessing different schemes with the aim of, finally, resolving the issue. However, this committee had reported the previous summer that 'none of the schemes presented were free from grave inherent disadvantages', a conclusion that, as Herbert Stead declared in his survey of 1898, 'fell on waiting hearts like the knell of despair'.[96] For as Rothschild and his fellows deliberated, themselves free from the acute financial concerns of the vast majority of the population, every day the poor were dependent on the limited wherewithal of family members, or forced onto the mercy of Poor Law Unions.

Yet there was still hope. In a speech at Browning Hall in November 1898 the agent-general of New Zealand, the Hon. William Pember Reeves – husband of Maud and another indication of the settlement's international reach – explained the core aim of the former colony's recently passed Old Age Pension Act, whereby each poor person over the age of sixty-five received a shilling a day. In December 1898, a conference held at Browning Hall addressing the need for some form of old age pension had developed into the National Committee of Organised Labour. The 1898 report summarised what had happened at the event in December, where Charles Booth, a great supporter of the Robert Browning Settlement, addressed forty trade union representatives on behalf of over 250,000 members from Newcastle, Leeds, Hull, Manchester,

Leicester, Bristol and London: 'All present endorsed Mr. Booth's condemnation of contributory schemes, and his demand that every old person should be entitled to a pension from the State.'[97] (The UK's Old Age Pensions Act would finally pass in 1908.)

Leafing through the 1898 Browning Settlement report, the author and popular historian Walter Besant noted the various innovations and support offered to locals from the settlement's headquarters in the heart of Walworth.[98] 'The keynote,' he later wrote,

> of all such work as this is, for the workers, personal service; for the people, the influence of examples, the attraction of things which they understand at once to be a great deal more pleasant than the bar and the tap-room; such a variety of work and recreation as may drag all into the net except the substratum of all, whom nothing can lift out of the mire.[99]

But, Besant wondered, how large an area could a single settlement cover, particularly one so densely populated? Quoting statistics from the report, he observed that the Walworth area alone (as the nineteenth century drew to a close) had a population of 120,000. Besant calculated that, for the whole of South London, around 1,500 voluntary workers would be required 'in order to cover this land of slums with an effective string of settlements'.

The 1898 Browning Settlement report signalled that the pressure was being felt; considering it as 'painfully evident the strain which the work involves on the strength and life of our limited staff. If only the number of our Residents had grown with the increase of opportunity and the multiplication of imperative demands on the resources of the Settlement, we should have had a far more cheering tale of progress to recount.'[100] Walter Besant had acknowledged the stress on those attempting to alleviate the suffering, but concluded on a note of optimism, tempered by the sheer scale of the challenge:

> There never was a time when more determined efforts have been made for the elevation of the submerged, and there never was a time when so many young men and young women have

been found ready to give the whole of their time, or all their spare time, to the work. Whether they will succeed in effecting a permanent improvement remains to be seen; whether the attraction of personal devotion which is now passing over the minds of the young will continue and remain with us has also to be proved.[101]

No matter how idealistic and upbeat Herbert Stead appears to be, his outlook was also tempered by pragmatism and a knowledge of the people he served that came from experience.

As a general approach, Stead observed, to George Duckworth, that 'to win the friendliness and sympathy of the working classes is the first object of the staff, and if this is done they are prepared to chance some measure of fraud and imposition'.[102] The sentiment was echoed in an article in the *Daily News Weekly*: 'Statistics are very poor guides to the value of work such as this. Sympathy and a kindly handshake cannot be measured by the multiplication table or a sum of addition.'[103] Tom Bryan, in his conversation with Duckworth, supported money-giving, making the humane observation, 'It is not possible when you go into a home and see evident want to come out without giving.' There was no attempt at any investigation into how needy the people they visited were: '"We prefer", Herbert Stead stated, "to run the risk of imposition rather than to break through the enamel of self respect by any elaborate enquiry."' The people they served, both interviewees declared, were 'kindly, genial', 'wonderfully kind, extremely good natured', 'very charming', but, Stead admitted, 'their really grave fault' was 'laxity as to truth'. According to Stead, lying was constant, in order to qualify for 'treats or other advantages'. Duckworth offered a side note regarding the social work at the Browning Settlement, opining 'that it is I think pursued much more as an end in itself than is usual'; Stead 'really wants the people to have a better time than they have had quite irrespective of whether or not they come to church'.[104]

Just a few months after this interview, the *Daily News Weekly* described the Robert Browning Settlement as at 'the very centre of the poorest borough within the limits of the greatest city of the world'. By this date Walworth and its surrounding districts had been integrated into the new Metropolitan Borough of Southwark (after the 1899 Local Government Act) and within 'its limits will be the poorest districts in the whole of London, and yet it is but a stone's throw from all the important centres of a world-wide Empire'.[105] The pseudonymous author DULCIMA in their article 'Darker Surrey' for *The Surrey Magazine*, declared that Southwark Borough was, 'in a word, the metropolis of "Les Miserables"', encouraging readers to 'come and look with kindly eyes into the faces of these men and women, and give them an honest grip of the hand; they will respond to brotherhood whilst they curse patronage'.[106]

In late 1901, James Keir Hardie, now MP for Merthyr Tydfil, and Tom Bryan of the Robert Browning Settlement were the principal speakers at an event in Cambridge promoting social settlements, in the hope that some in the audience might be inspired to come to Walworth. The subject under discussion was 'The duties and responsibilities of the Universities to the industrial classes'. Keir Hardie, addressing the company, believed that the claim the poor had upon his audience, as quoted by a reporter from the *Cambridge Independent Press*, many of them students and graduates of Cambridge University, was not 'because of any menace they' – the poor multitudes – 'might make to their peace and prosperity, but because of the duty which their position placed upon them to go to their aid and assistance'. He continued: 'When they remembered what the life of the poor was – he did not mean the slum poor, but the average man, who had to earn his livelihood by the labour of his hands – and the more thinking he was, and the more developed his faculties, the harder was his lot and the more he felt estranged.' This is a statement for which George Tinworth, now existing in a state of limbo between the traditional idea of 'worker' and 'professional', would have had some sympathy. 'Hear, hear!' came the cry from the room.

Keir Hardie then observed that a knowledge of the conditions in which the great bulk of the population lived should stimulate those present 'to noble effort and high endeavour':

> The life of the working man was one perpetual thought of how to obtain the necessaries of life. The conditions were such

PLACED IN SHAFTESBURY AVENUE

THE THREE RELIVES IN THIS PANEL REPESENT N° 1 FINDING THE BOY ON THE DOOR STEP. N° 2 SHAFTESBURY WITH THE BOYS AND GIRLS AT EXETER HALL. N° 3 BOYS ON BOARD NAVY SHIP.

DESIGNED AND MODELED BY ⟨monogram⟩

ONE THAT THE WORKING CLASSES MAY THANK FOR A GOOD DEAL BUT WHAT I CAN HEAR IT WAS THE WORKING CLASS WOMAN HIS PARENT HOUSE KEEPER THAT MADE HIM WHAT HE WAS.

Unnumbered page from George Tinworth's autobiography, with a photograph of his panel in memory of Lord Shaftesbury. George writes that this relief was placed in Shaftesbury Avenue, near the famous fountain memorial to 'the poor man's earl' adorned with the figure of 'Eros' (Anteros) by Alfred Gilbert, at Piccadilly Circus. In his accompanying text, George describes Shaftesbury as 'one that the working classes may thank for a good deal'.

as tended to continually degrade, to demoralise, weaken the will power, and render people easy victims to temptations at which strong men could afford to laugh. The real problem was as to how each class in society could be made of service to the other. The most important aim was to make the working man think, to train him into habits of self-respect – not to make himself a prig, much less a sycophant – to make him feel that those who were working amongst them were human beings like himself. Settlements existed, as he conceived, to develop the human relationship, which was the only bond that bound society together. (Applause.) Their present conditions of life, especially the industrial conditions, stifled human relationship. (Hear, hear.) ... They saw on either side of them a great multitude going on its way as if there was no to-morrow.

A nation, he concluded, to loud applause, 'could not pursue those lines and continue to exist as a great nation ... Greatness, first of all, meant character, individuality, and self-respect on the part of its citizens':

Selfishness was the ruin of the race; there could be no happiness amongst any part of the nation so long as there was a great festering part of misery away down at the bottom of the social scale. If the idea he had spoken of could take hold upon the nominal Christian life of the nation, there could be raised in England again, as there had been raised previously, a race of people who would be great in the truest sense of the word, because they would be great in the greatness of character.[107]

Keir Hardie then sat down, to the cheers and loud applause of his audience.

It will become clear, as we return to Charlie Chaplin's autobiography, that despite the existence of settlements and social workers doing extraordinary things for the poor in the very areas, indeed the very streets, where he, his mother and his brother were living, none of this practical activity and emotional support seems to have reached them directly, at a time when they were at their most desperate.

Fred Karno in 'petticoats', c.1888. This photograph was probably taken while Fred was part of a gymnastic act called 'The Three Karnos' prior to his marriage to Edith.

7

LAMBETH WALK

'Girls and their Lovers'

Frederick John Westcott married Edith Blanche Cuthbert on 15 January 1889 at Lambeth Register Office on Lambeth Square, three months before Charlie Chaplin was born. Frederick, or Fred as he was known, was twenty-three, a 'gymnast' living at 14 Little Canterbury Place, off Lambeth Road in the parish of St Mary-at-Lambeth, and his father was a journeyman French polisher originally from Exeter in Devon. Like his exact contemporary Charles Chaplin senior, then married to the pregnant Hannah, and about to achieve success in New York City, Fred was trying to establish himself as a performer in the music halls and variety theatres. Edith was aged twenty-one with no profession, living at 118 Kennington Road (literally around the corner from her fiancé) and her father, John, was a journeyman rope maker.[1] Two years later, in the census of 1891, Fred's status had improved significantly to that of 'Professional Gymnast' and he was the head of the household resident at 115 Page Street, located across Lambeth Bridge from where he and Edith had both been living. Edith was the only other occupant of their one-room dwelling, but their fellow lodgers within that address included a labourer, a dressmaker, a clerk, a housemaid, an electric wireman, a coachman-groom and a cook.[2]

By 1895, Frederick Westcott had transformed himself into Fred Karno, impresario of variety theatre. Eventually he would establish his company headquarters, nicknamed 'The Fun Factory', on Vaughan Road off Coldharbour Lane in Camberwell. He would be the acknowledged presiding genius of British 'Golden Age' music hall: the man who discovered Charlie Chaplin and Stanley Jefferson, better known to history as Stan Laurel.

In the six years since his marriage, Fred Karno had become famed across Great Britain for a particular form of speechless theatrical sketch: reflecting recognisable character-types, relationships and contemporary issues, in the mode of traditional pantomime, but grafted onto a performance style that was, as Charlie later observed, 'cruel and boisterous, filled with acrobatic humor and low, knockabout comedy'.[3] One sketch from 1898 called *The New Woman's Club* was a skit on the women's emancipation movement, epitomised in the national consciousness by Millicent Fawcett, who had become president of the National Union of Women's Suffrage Societies in 1897, and Emmeline Pankhurst, founder of the Women's Franchise League, later president of the militant Women's Social and Political Union, or 'suffragettes'. In the sketch Karno appeared as a butch lady-cyclist in bloomers, jacket, shirt and tie and straw boater – the sartorial epitome of 1890s female independence. The twist was that, rather than middle-class women seeking careers or demanding formal education, Karno's 'new women' were gamblers and pickpockets, their apparent refinement, social causes and political activism a veneer hiding a multitude of illegal activity.

Karno, effectively, had melded two female 'gangs' of the Southwark–Lambeth districts. The first was the Women's University Settlement in Nelson Square, which, in 1897 had paved the way for another all-women settlement in Kennington Road named after Lady Margaret Hall, Oxford. All were independently minded, and some were involved in the struggle for women to get the vote. The second was the infamous all-female criminal gang who operated from the area around Blackfriars Road and New Cut, close to Nelson Square, known as the Forty Thieves. Later the gang once led by Polly Carr became associated with a violent male gang from the Elephant and Castle area, but remained distinct from them in membership and activities. Both groups, it could be argued, were examples of unusual female behaviour: both, it could also be argued, were aiming for female independence in a desperately unequal society. Like many of his fellow residents of South London, Fred Karno would have had knowledge, even some experience of both. *The New Woman's Club* revealed how variety sketches quickly adapted to respond to shifts in contemporary politics and society, whether remarkable events and current affairs or personalities and celebrities, all for the entertainment of working-class audiences.

In the year 1897, Charlie Chaplin and his brother Syd were in their respective parts of the Hanwell School for Pauper Children; Charlie was at the Cuckoo School, while Syd was on the training ship *Exmouth*. Hannah Chaplin was suffering bouts of ill-health, while her errant husband, by now living with his mistress and their child on Kennington Road, was avoiding increasingly insistent missives from St Saviour's Board of Guardians. In that year, the Lady Margaret Hall Settlement was established at 129 Kennington Road, in one of the early nineteenth-century terraced houses once occupied by the families of middle-class professionals.* This new settlement, led by Edith Langridge, was inspired by the work of Margaret Sewell and her fellows in Nelson Square. It worked in close association with two local parishes within which the extended Chaplin family lived: St Mary-at-Lambeth and St Mary-the-Less. Both parishes sat to the west of Kennington Road, extending from St Thomas's Hospital and Lambeth Palace in the north, via Doulton's Pottery complex, the Queen's Head public house and Lambeth Walk market, to Vauxhall Bridge to the south.

Katherine Thicknesse joined the new community two years after its establishment, beginning her time at the LMHS working four days a week at the Battersea branch of the Charity Organisation Societies followed by a busy weekend in Salamanca, an area within the parish of St Mary-the-Less to the west of Vauxhall Walk.[4] In her first winter, Katherine also assisted a Miss Hodson at a boys' club in the crypt of St John the Evangelist in Waterloo, which she described as 'a pretty rough affair'. This was the area where Polly Carr had lived a few years before, and from where she had led her gang of thieves on raids across Waterloo Bridge to the rich pickings on the Strand and around Covent Garden.

---

*The adjoining No. 131 was added to the settlement in 1900.

The modest comforts of the settlement accommodation on Kennington Road acted as a respite from the hardship witnessed on the streets beyond: hardship that was experienced daily by Charlie Chaplin and his family.

After Hannah had collected Charlie and Syd from 289 Kennington Road, with the jubilant Louise looking on, the three moved briefly to lodgings at 39 Methley Street, just to the east of Kennington Cross and next door to Hayward's Pickle Factory. By 26 December 1898, Charlie was performing with the Eight Lancashire Lads, a clog-dancing troupe founded and run by William Jackson, an acquaintance of Charles Chaplin senior. As he recalled:

> Father knew Mr Jackson, who ran the troupe, and convinced Mother that it would be a good start for me to make a career on the stage and at the same time help her economically: I would get board and lodging and Mother would get half a crown a week ... When touring the provinces we went to a school for the week in each town, which did little to further my education.[5]

According to Alfred Jackson, when Charlie joined his father's troupe, he was living with Syd and their Aunt Kate above a barber's shop in Chester Street off Kennington Road: 'He was a very quiet boy at first ... My first job was to take him to have his hair, which was hanging in matted curls about his shoulders, cut to a reasonable length.'[6] Charlie's eldest son, again using his father's childhood recollections, observed that, prior to joining the Eight Lancashire Lads, he

> became scarcely more than a London street waif, begging for a living, sleeping heaven knows where, and just barely keeping body and soul together. His natural wiry body became so wizened that his great handsome head, with its black curls, looked grotesque perched on top of his thin shoulders. There in the tough and ribald slums, where incongruities are often considered fit objects for ridicule, his appearance evoked

ribald jokes and jeers. He was knocked about, too, but at least he had his freedom.⁷

In the chapter 'The Haunts of my Childhood' from his early travel memoir *My Wonderful Visit* (1922), which is based around his first return to London since becoming an international star, Charlie Chaplin refers to a 'Kennington "pub"' on Chester Street (possibly the Chester Arms, on what is now Chester Way) 'where I used to sleep ... There is the old tub outside the stables where I used to wash. The same old tub, a little more twisted.' In 1921, he recalled how, walking along the street where children were playing, 'I see myself among them back there in the past.' He then declared: 'Oh, if only I could do something for them. These waifs with scarcely any chance at all ... I want to shriek with laughter at the joy of being in this same old familiar Kennington. I love it.'⁸

According to David Robinson, Charlie toured with Jackson's troupe through 1899 and into 1900, his first continuous engagement on the stage, which brought in vital income for his mother (although it was Hannah who terminated the arrangement, fearing how her son was being treated).⁹ During this time, Grandfather Hill came back into Hannah's life. In July 1899, Charles Frederick had become homeless, having moved lodgings many times since separating from his wife Mary Ann. He moved briefly into Methley Street with his daughter, before entering the Lambeth Infirmary on Renfrew Road, followed by full admission to the workhouse. According to his grandson, Grandfather Hill worked in the kitchen of the infirmary and would smuggle out eggs, which he gave to Charlie when he visited between tours with The Eight Lancashire Lads.¹⁰ Charles Frederick Hill would repeatedly be discharged and then readmitted to the workhouse for years to come.

Charlie Chaplin described the year 1899 as an 'epoch of whiskers'. He noted that at the age of ten he was vaguely aware of the Boer War through 'patriotic songs, vaudeville sketches and cigarette pictures of the generals ... One heard dolorous news about the Boers surrounding Ladysmith and England went mad with hysterical joy at the relief of Mafeking.' The patriotic songs sung in public houses and music halls were part of the propaganda to

The test match at the Oval between England and Australia was played from 14 to 16 August 1899. The crowd, including a woman (far right) sport a variety of headwear suggesting a mix of social classes. Top right is the pavilion, designed by Thomas Muirhead and completed in 1897.

swell the ranks of the British Army fighting in South Africa. In fact, half the working men who attempted to enlist were rejected because of poor health and weak overall physical condition. It was this that stimulated a concerted interest in public health, alongside an upsurge in advocacy for social engineering and eugenics. 'All this,' Charlie concluded, 'I heard from everyone but Mother. She never mentioned the war. She had her own battle to fight.'[11] According to her son, Hannah was earning a mere 6s 9d a week doing piecework on her sewing machine – on average she was producing fifty-four women's shirts a week – and she had pawned every possession she could.

As the nation moved from the Victorian epoch to the Edwardian (the old queen died in 1901, to be succeeded by her wayward son Edward VII), the instability for Charlie, Hannah and Syd reached such a pitch that it is impossible to chart with any accuracy where they were living and when between 1899 and 1903. Again, the residencies listed every ten years via the national census, even if supplemented by other official documentation, is just the tip of the iceberg for some – if not most – poor working-class families. 'My memory of this period goes in and out of focus,' Charlie recalled. 'The outstanding impression was a quagmire of miserable circumstances. I cannot remember where Sydney was; being four years older, he only occasionally entered my consciousness. He was possibly living with Grandfather to relieve Mother's penury. We seemed to vacillate from one abode to another'; but eventually they moved into a small garret in Pownall Terrace, a row of houses set back from Kennington Road.[12]

No. 3 Pownall Terrace is the one address that left an indelible mark on Charlie – he returns to it again and again, whether in his writings or in person during his several trips to London while living in America and then Switzerland. On one such occasion, he recalled standing before his old home and mounting 'the rickety stairs that led to our small garret':

> The house was depressing and the air was foul with stale slops and old clothes ... The room was stifling, a little over twelve feet square, and seemed smaller and the slanting ceiling seemed lower. The table against the wall was crowded with dirty plates and tea-cups; and in the corner, snug against the lower wall, was an old iron bed which Mother had painted white. Between the bed and the window was a small fire-grate, and at the foot of the bed an old armchair that unfolded and became a single bed upon which my brother Sydney slept.[13]

This attic would be replicated, literally, metaphorically and emotionally, in *The Kid* (1921).

On a fundamental level, Pownall Terrace signified, more than any other lodging, Charlie and his mother's lowly status, even among the poor of Lambeth at the turn of the century. In an audio interview recorded in February 1983,* the ninety-two-year-old Effie Wisdom, with a wonderfully rich, vowelly London accent, reminisced about the regular visits she made as a child to her aunt's lodgings in the Kennington Road area over the last years of the nineteenth century. In fact, as one of nineteen children, she was effectively living part-time with her aunt, who had no children, to take some pressure away from her parents: 'Well they had a lot of kids those days, they had nothing else to do did they ... there was no wireless, no television ... they got up to mischief, didn't they.'

---

*With the documentary film maker and Chaplin specialist Kevin Brownlow.

A fair appraisal, although there was plenty for poor working-class women to do other than bear and raise children. Effie resumes her narrative: 'My aunt lived in Kennington next to Mrs Chaplin, and the two boys ... I first saw Charlie when he was about five.'[14] Effie gives her aunt's address as 'at the back of Lambeth Walk' on Fitzalan Street, which emerges from the west side of Kennington Road, near to Walnut Tree Walk, Chester Street and Pownall Terrace, so she could be referring to any number of residences occupied by Hannah, Syd and Charlie over these years. Effie continues, supporting the assessment from Charlie's eldest son: 'Before the First World War I'm talking about ... he used to call me his cousin, he used to say "When's me cousin Effie comin'?" ... Of course I felt sorry for him really, all ragged clothes he had on, always filthy, he had a terrible life, and his brother Syd, had a terrible life.'[15] To the question, 'What was he like?' Effie replied 'Oh, he was a lovely little kid, but very temperamental. Very, very temperamental.'[16]

So, according to Effie Wisdom, her childhood friend existed in a far worse state of poverty than did she and her very large family, who were themselves scraping along. In an age of trimmed hair, neat moustaches or beards, matted locks hanging to the shoulders – as Alfred Jackson had described Charlie's appearance – would have been one obvious signal of neglect and privation. And Charlie himself was sensitive to even the smallest signs that indicated degrees of hardship and a corresponding hierarchy of want within a working-class population. As he recalled:

> I was well aware of the social stigma of our poverty. Even the poorest of children sat down to a home-cooked Sunday dinner. A roast at home meant respectability, a ritual that distinguished one poor class from another. Those who could not sit down to a Sunday dinner at home were of the mendicant class, and we were that. Mother would send me to the nearest coffee-shop to buy a sixpenny dinner (meat and two vegetables). The shame of it – especially on Sunday! I would harry her for not preparing something at home, and she would vainly try to explain that cooking at home would cost twice as much.[17]

This quote captures succinctly what some middle-class reformers failed to understand about how the cost of living worked among those near the bottom of society. Charlie is recording a recognised phenomenon among the poor: firstly to 'sit down' to a meal, to quote Ellen Ross, where 'food was served and eaten properly', meant 'respectability for everyone at the table'; and secondly how 'exceptionally meaningful', as Ross describes it, this particular meal was: the 'Sunday dinner' or Sunday lunch. Indeed, a mother might scrimp throughout the week in order to provide a good meal on Sunday.[18] This reiterates the experiences around food and meals as recalled by George Tinworth earlier in the century, as well as the popularity of the Browning Settlement Goose Club; it was at meal times in general and special meals in particular that a family's poverty became most apparent.

Recalling George Duckworth's tally of costs for basic food at New Cut and Lower Marsh markets, half a cooked chicken was between eight- and ninepence, even though at that price these pre-cooked birds were 'not appetising to look at'. Hannah's weekly income of 6s 9d would not stretch far, but she eventually succumbed to pressure from her son and attempted to cook a Sunday lunch at home; as for many renting a single room Hannah had to use the landlady's oven on a lower floor. The lunch was not a complete success – the joint of beef had shrivelled to the size and consistency of a cricket ball. Even so, because it was home cooked, Charlie recalled, 'I enjoyed it and felt the gratification of having lived up to the Joneses.'[19]

The reminiscences of the settlement social worker Katherine Thicknesse from 1899 put Hannah and Charlie's experiences into the context of what she calls 'the instances of greatest poverty and need'. Writing in the 1940s, Katherine states that her 'remembrances of things you would never see now are very vivid'. For example, it was 'more usual than not to see children with broken boots & shoes – or odd shoes or sometimes none'. The local babies 'all looked about 90! Little white wizened faces – heart-breaking to see.' But it was 'wonderful how those who survived improved after about 2 years old when they were running about in the street'.[20] In Katherine's experience, very few of these children had left that part of London in which they had been born; the 'rare appearance of a cow or sheep in the street caused a wild mob'. She recalled accompanying one Lambeth child on a train ride into the countryside for the first time, and 'when she saw the fields & flowers & cows' she 'turned from the window & flinging her arms round me said "Oh Miss, I WILL be good, I <u>will</u> be good."' The girl's response chimes with Charlie Chaplin's description of his first glimpse of the sea at Southend, which he described as 'hypnotic': 'What a day that was – the saffron beach, with its pink and blue pails and wooden spades, its coloured tents and umbrellas, and sailing boats hurtling gaily over laughing little waves, and up on the beach other boats resting idly on their sides, smelling of seaweed and tar – the memory of it still lingers with enchantment.'[21] And the sense of enchantment in the recollection is the key, even if the reality would fall somewhat short when Chaplin returned to Southend decades later.

The garden at the settlement on Kennington Road, like the one next to Browning Hall, was used by many different local groups: 'One of the first things undertaken,' recalled Thicknesse, 'was the Invalid Children's Aid':

> There were only 30 cases handed over for the whole of the N[orth] Lambeth area ... & out of it grew a tiny class for invalids & cripples. This very soon became too large for our quarters & was carried on in some church hall & was one person's work with such helpers as could be found. This little school & the one at Nelson Sq[ua]re were the first attempt at 'Special Schools' which later became such a regular part of the education.[22]

'The little invalid class met there when fine,' she continued, 'individual cripples or invalids spent long afternoons', and 'in school holidays in August there were many to enjoy rocking-horses and dolls prams. Later on we organised a regular holiday play hour in August.' Every resident social worker brought her own special group, 'and we were fairly often asked to lend it by other Lambeth social and church workers'.[23] At the same time, Katherine

Thicknesse also observed significant changes for the better during her early years at the Kennington Road settlement, notably the provision for maternity, newborn and infant care.*

William Somerset Maugham, before achieving fame as a writer, studied medicine at St Thomas's Hospital Medical School: he would channel his experiences serving the poor of the area into his first published novel, *Liza of Lambeth*. After spending time in the out-patient departments, to complete his studies he moved on to obstetric work. At this time, to obtain their certificates, students had to attend twenty confinements. Maugham was appointed obstetric clerk for three weeks and to be on hand both day and night he rented temporary lodgings opposite the hospital's main entrance. At night, if needed, a porter with a key woke him up: 'You dressed and went to the hospital where you found waiting for you the husband or perhaps the small son of the patient, with the card which the woman in labour had earlier obtained from the hospital.'[24] For the first confinement the student was accompanied by the senior obstetric clerk, but after that they were on their own. Maugham recalled, in the preface to *Liza of Lambeth*, the student, 'was hard worked and often very tired so that if you dragged him out of bed without good reason you were liable to hear some unpleasant truths about yourself'.[25] He then describes the following, with a thrilling sense of drama, for the vicarious enjoyment of his readers:

> The messenger led you through the dark and silent streets of Lambeth, up stinking alleys and into sinister courts where the police hesitated to penetrate, but where your black bag protected you from harm. You were taken to grim houses, on each floor of which a couple of families lived, and shown

---

*The General Lying-In Hospital, a charity serving mothers mostly from North Lambeth and Borough (some of the poorest areas in inner London) recorded from 1877 to 1882 that 62 per cent of women aged thirty-five and over had had two or more children die, and that 40 per cent of this group had lost three or more babies and children. From the figures quoted earlier (p. 35) child mortality remained static until 1905 to 1910. (See Ross (1993), pp. 182–3.)

into a stuffy room, ill-lit with a paraffin lamp, in which two or three women, the midwife, the mother, the 'lady as lives on the floor below' were standing round the bed on which the patient lay. Sometimes you waited in that room for two or three hours, drinking a friendly cup of tea with the midwife and going down in the street below now and then to get a breath of air. The husband was sitting on the step and you sat down beside him and chatted.[26]

Less than ten years later, the improvements noted by Katherine Thicknesse were largely down to the pioneering work of Anne Emily Cummins (1869–1936), the first almoner (hospital social worker) appointed by St Thomas's Hospital in 1905: 'Miss Cummins was a very fine and notable woman and a great gift to Lambeth. She would have nothing to do with a second rate makeshift. The best was the only admissible thing.' Katherine then continues, supporting Maugham's grim assessment: 'Before her appointment babies in Lambeth arrived in their own miserable homes with no supervised preparation whatever. The mother put her name down at St. Thomas's and was attended by a young doctor. There was no guarantee of sufficient clothing for the new arrival!' Thicknesse offers the following example: 'As a comment on this state of things I will add my memory of a family (living in "Provident Place") where I visited a delicate child called Rebecca. I shall be accused of exaggeration but I know it was over 10 babies in that family who died under one year old!' Returning to the innovations under Anne Cummins: 'Let it be added at once that the younger mothers welcomed and worked well with the first Clinics.'[27]

Although she was active around the whole Kennington Road area, Katherine's main geographical focus was the district called 'Salamanca' within the parish of St Mary-the-Less to which St Saviour's, Salamanca, was an associate chapel. It is one area where Doulton's workers lived, where George Duckworth had visited, while Katherine was working for the settlement, and where he had noted the presence of long-term residency stretching back generations.

Katherine recalled: 'Salamanca was rather an obscure little

corner and had many families living in the houses their grandparents had been in – and it had a curiously mixed population, that is, some very rough and low class people, in and off Vauxhall Walk, but some much superior sort, chiefly living in lovely old 18th century houses in Andersons' Walk.' The curate at St Saviour's was the Reverend A. Shirley, then resident at 55 Upper Kennington Lane.[28] He was described by Katherine as 'remarkable and devoted'. There was 'both a Boys and a Girls Club', she continues. 'I helped with the latter three nights a week ... owing to the strong neighbourhood sense of belonging to Salamanca, partly to Mr. Shirley and the influence of the Mission Room and Clubs these different elements mixed to a quite unusual degree and the running of the Clubs was much indebted to this fact.'[29] The mission room at Salamanca had opened the previous February, after a refurbishment that had cost a considerable £1,325, raised through local donations.[30]

According to Thicknesse, the social workers ran the boys' and girls' clubs with the assistance of the young members themselves, 'who were really helpers and were of sufficiently high standards to be natural leaders'. Among a varied programme, the girls' club ran sessions for physical exercise. Katherine recalled the popularity of this weekly 'drill class', which she described as 'the backbone of the Girls Club' and 'immensely enjoyed though equipment was meagre'. Drill class was the Victorian equivalent of PE, often set to music. Jumping 'was the high light', Katherine, a regular hockey player, declared, 'and I too was able to enjoy this, but my place was the piano much of the time'. She continued: 'It was wonderful how the girls enjoyed this drill evening and loved their teacher, Miss Summerscales, for very often some came in looking dead tired and not up to much activity till late in the evening.' She observed that, as a church-related club, the evening would end with brief prayers, 'and sometimes the wilder spirits made them a difficult moment and one perhaps wondered if it would be better not to attempt it'. This chimes with the comments from the local Lambeth clergy, who perceived that the youth were reticent, even hostile, to the idea of being associated with the religious purpose of the church, even as they enjoyed the activities and clubs organised through the parish. In this you can sense further examples of working-class independence: picking and choosing for themselves, from the gamut of opportunities and activity on offer. That said, according to Thicknesse, these classes had a lasting impact on the participants, describing how 'not so very long ago' (sometime prior to the 1940s):

> a friend of mine was working at LMHS for a time and in her visiting came across an old girl of the Club whom I had lost sight of. She was a middle-aged married woman and had been through some very hard times. She spoke with great happiness and affection of Salamanca Club and told my friend she still said every night the Club prayer we used to repeat together.[31]

The LMHS was also active in the adjoining parish of St Mary-at-Lambeth. Ernest Aves had ventured to the rectory at 214 Lambeth Road in late 1899.* He noted that the Reverend Reeve had arrived in Lambeth from Cornwall four and half years before, and his experience of London was, therefore, limited – certainly in comparison to other clergymen Aves had interviewed. The Booth investigator considered that some allowance should be made for the opinions the clergyman expressed. Conversely, Reeve may have cast a usefully fresh eye on the prevalent issues occupying his new flock – and Cornwall, too, had its share of hardship and deprivation. Aves described him as 'a very human soul': 'touches of humour flash from time to time, he is full of sympathy, and of generous appreciation, even wonderment, at the <goodness> and the good work of other people.'[32]

The Reverend Reeve confirmed that several 'ladies' were working with the clubs organised through the church, including the Hercules Club for young men. Indeed, observed Aves, 'much of the amiability of Mr. Reeve's character show[ed] itself when he was enlarging on the affection that his ladies were able to elicit, and the influence they were able to exercise' among the local people and particularly the youth.[33] 'The SOCIAL AGENCIES are numerous,'

---

*Originally built in 1778, one former resident was Christopher Wordsworth (1774–1846), brother to the famous poet, and rector of St Mary's between 1816 and 1820.

Aves noted, 'but the Clubs ... appear to be [the] most important and distinctive.'[34] As elsewhere, the clubs were more enticing to the local boys than regular church attendance. In the parish of St Mary-at-Lambeth, the Hercules Club membership focused on lads between the age of fourteen and twenty-one: the age when 'hooligan gangs' might otherwise be attractive. The name, conjuring up a manly image of strength and physical fitness, related to the nearby Hercules Buildings. Based at 21 Paradise Street, the club had a room for academic classes, a gymnasium, two club rooms, one with a bath (available to the lads for a small additional charge), and a hall for billiards and boxing. The latter sport had a long tradition in the area, noted by Jack Butler Yeats, the artist-brother of the poet, who was born in London in 1871. He recalled that the Lambeth School of Arms on Old Paradise Street 'was an extraordinary place – like a little pit – the seats raised up all round the ring. The ring was very small, the people, as they used to say then, had to "fight on a piece of toast", and it was very exciting.'[35] Outdoor games, including cricket, football, swimming and running, were organised through the Hercules Club, and the club even had its own savings bank 'to which fully ¾ of the lads belong.'[36] In its modest way, the Hercules Club was challenging the idea that the working class was inherently unruly and unhealthy; perhaps planting the seed of thrift, and the pooling of resources, to be better prepared for whatever fate threw at its members, rather than having to live day-to-day, as had their parents and grandparents. Such activities – from sport to saving schemes – had seen huge success, too, at the nearby Robert Browning Settlement.

The main female club hosted by St Mary-at-Lambeth was called 'The Daisy Club for Working and Factory Girls', which numbered about 80 juniors and 250 senior members, several of whom were married. One of the volunteers was Kathleen Courtney, later an active suffragist. The club, according to the organiser, Mrs Bennett, had 'a drawing room for social purposes & for classes, a small garden for games, accommodation in Lambeth for a few homeless girls, rooms at the Seaside all the year round', and 'an organised band of ladies to visit & teach'. Regarding social events, the Daisy Club 'gives invitation dances to girls & men, it opens its drawing room once a week to both'. More extraordinarily, in recent years members had begun to assist local authorities in 'sanitary work'.[37] The embanking of the Thames had occurred from the 1860s, with the old wharves, warehouses and factory buildings, including Doulton's, swept away by the new Albert Embankment. At the same time Joseph Bazalgette's new sewers were laid. Ernest Aves noted that the 'Sanitary Aid Committee' had, again, stirred Reeve's admiration for his club ladies. 'It has also', Aves added, 'mightily amused him.' He then quotes the clergyman himself: 'I went down the other evening,' he said,

> and found them hard at work, talking out their cases, drains, and smells, and defective flushings and all the rest of it. Mrs. Bennett has started it, and the Daisy Club supplies the nucleus of the members. But the young men have been brought in too – just fancy, the girls and their lovers taking this sort of work in hand! Wonderful![38]

The proximity of Doulton's offices and factory around Broad Street and Lambeth High Street, which produced the ceramic pipes and other sanitary wares for the new drains and water supply to the homes of the Daisy Club's members, may have encouraged this very local enthusiasm. And such activity would have prepared these young working-class women for the type of public, school and local authority work that had already been available to their middle-class sisters for years.

Around the turn of the twentieth century, Charlie Chaplin recalled walking past the Three Stags public house near the Bethlem Asylum, at the crossroads of Kennington Road and Lambeth Road, and a short stroll from the Reverend Reeve's church and vicarage. Something made the youngster push open the snug door and peer inside. There, sitting in the corner, was Charles Chaplin senior, looking desperately ill: 'his eyes were sunken, and his body swollen to an enormous size. He rested one hand, Napoleon-like, in his waistcoat as if to ease his difficult breathing.' That evening Charles, sensing his end was near, asked after Hannah and Syd;

before his young son left, he took him in his arms 'and for the first time kissed me. That was the last time I saw him alive.'[39]

On 6 April 1901 the enterprising Syd, after a series of barman jobs, embarked on a steamer heading for the Cape, as assistant steward and bandsman. Three weeks later, Charles Chaplin was admitted to St Thomas's Hospital. Charlie recalled that his father's friends had to get him drunk, before they were able to manoeuvre him there. For a few weeks, as he lay dying, Hannah visited him.

When Charles died on 9 May aged just thirty-seven (immediate cause of death cirrhosis of the liver), the hospital officials wanted to know who was organising the funeral and how it would be paid. Hannah, with barely a penny to her name, suggested one of the professional societies, like the Music Hall Benevolent Fund run by Frank Hall from his offices in York Road. This suggestion, according to Charlie, 'caused uproar with the Chaplin side of the family – the humiliation of being buried by charity was repugnant to them'.[40]

This fear of being buried by charity was doubled if by the parish – as had happened to Joshua Tinworth and his sister Keziah – and the corresponding desire to provide a dignified end for loved ones was the subject of several recollections by the LMHS social worker Katherine Thicknesse.* She recalled that some 'shocks remain very vivid to me: the block of flats in Vauxhall where the staircase did not allow of a coffin to be carried down and it was swung down over the balcony. The visit I paid once to a big family of very charming children in a two-roomed home.' The child whom Katherine had been helping had died, and when she arrived at the family's lodgings, 'I found the others at tea with their little legs dangling round the table and underneath was the little white coffin'. And another time, when the mother of 'one of Vauxhall's immense families died', on enquiring after the family, 'the chief thing, eagerly told, was that Dad had said: "Kids 'ow'd it be if we was to pray till Monday as Mum would come out top?"' By which the father meant that the family should pray for his wife's coffin

---

*The story was included under the heading, 'The sorrows and troubles of the other end of life'.

to be placed last, within a deep communal grave, on top of all the others who had died over the previous days, weeks and months before the plot was deemed 'full' and covered over. Katherine concluded her anecdote: 'With awe the child added, "and Miss, she did come out top!"', revealing, noted Katherine 'the misery of a huge common grave'.[41]

On the day of his father's funeral, Charlie and his mother arrived early to St Thomas's Hospital; Hannah wanted to see her husband laid out before the coffin was closed and nailed down. Peering in, Charlie saw that his father's head was surrounded with little white daisies: 'Mother thought they looked so simple and touching and asked who had placed them there. The attendant told her that a lady had called early that morning with a little boy. It was Louise.' The burial, at Tooting Cemetery, was paid for by Charles's younger brother Albert.[42] By the end of the nineteenth century, large municipal cemeteries had been established for burials in areas beyond the centre of London, such as at Tooting and West Norwood (where Jane Tinworth had been interred in 1881). Katherine Thicknesse recalled travelling with a poor man's funeral cortège, the coffin carried by a cart through the streets of Lambeth to Tooting. The family, she writes,

> had managed all the arrangements in their tiny cottage in a court with great care and dignity. What struck me most was their reaction to the signs of lifting a hat or standing quietly to let the car pass. It was so utterly unusual to have such attention shown. The only words spoken on the long drive were: 'It's nice to see what respect people show.'[43]

As his legal spouse, Hannah collected Charles's belongings, consisting of a black suit 'spotted with blood', a shirt, a tie, a dressing gown and some slippers, the latter 'with oranges stuffed in the toes'. When Hannah removed one of the oranges, a half sovereign, a gold coin worth 10 shillings fell out. 'It was a godsend!'[44] Only later would Charlie discover what had happened to Louise and her child.

After his father's death, Charlie recalled leaving school

completely to get various jobs to bring in money: an errand boy in a chandler's shop, a glass blower, a shop boy for W. H. Smith's (before they realised he was underage), odd jobs for Straker's Printers and Stationers. Straker's paid twelve shillings a week and Charlie described the 'romance and adventure about getting out on those cold mornings, before daylight, and going to work, the streets silent and deserted except the one or two shadowy figures making their way to the beacon light of Lockhart's tea-room for breakfast'.[45] This recalls the range of casual jobs – from laundry delivery boy to gunpowder carrier – that George Tinworth undertook as a child half a century before, simply because the family was so poor. Once again, the need to work for money had removed another child from the benefits of a basic education.

By the beginning of May 1903, however, still resident in the one-room garret of 3 Pownall Terrace, Charlie could see that Hannah was ill again. Syd had returned from his travels, and then left again on another voyage, but the adventurer was now late coming home, and there had been no word from him in weeks. The money Syd left for his mother and brother had been spent, and Hannah was not earning enough from sewing to make up the shortfall: they were again in crisis.[46] One Saturday morning, Charlie gathered up some old clothes and took them to Newington Butts, where there was a weekly market. Laying them out on the street he started shouting out, 'What will you give me? – a shilling, sixpence, threepence, twopence?' But 'not even at a penny could I make a sale. People would stop, look astonished, then laugh and go on their way.'[47] Six decades later, Chaplin could still recall the humiliation he felt.

The additional strain explains Hannah's relapse. Charlie had made friends with a lad called Walter McCarthy, whose family lived in Walcott Mansions, just north from Pownall Terrace on Kennington Road. Charlie was constantly back and forth to the McCarthys' house, giving no thought to his mother's state of mind: 'I might have noticed that for several days she had been sitting listlessly at the window, had neglected tidying up the room, had grown unusually quiet.' He might have, he later recalled regretfully, shown some concern when the business for which Hannah had been making shirts for a few pence apiece had stopped giving her work and eventually took away the sewing machine they had loaned her.[48] Despite these calamities, Hannah showed no distress; rather, she 'remained indifferent, apathetic'.

Charlie's attitude suggests some suppressed anger towards his mother, to which his eldest son made reference in his own memoir. As Charles Chaplin junior mused decades later:

> 'Only mother love lasts,' he was once quoted as saying. But I don't think he was ever convinced he had truly possessed that love. He frequently told the outside world that it was poverty that had caused all his childhood unhappiness, but to my maternal grandmother he admitted an even deeper source of hurt, a feeling that his mother had failed him when he had needed her most.[49]

One day, Charlie returned to Pownall Terrace from visiting the McCarthys, to find some children standing in the street outside. They informed him that his mother had 'gone insane'. One told him: 'She's been knocking at all our doors, giving away pieces of coal, saying they were birthday presents for the children.' Charlie was sceptical of the truthfulness of this yarn. 'You ask my mother,' the child responded indignantly. Charlie ran up the stairs of 3 Pownall Terrace to the garret room, to find Hannah sitting at the window – she 'turned slowly and looked at me, her face pale and tormented.' She explained that she had been looking for Syd, but the neighbours were hiding him from her. The landlady had sent for a doctor, who, after listening to Hannah's story, declared her insane: 'Send her to the infirmary' were his parting words.[50] The Lambeth infirmary documentation for 'Lily', corrected to Hannah Harriet Chaplin (aged '40'), confirms she was accompanied by her twelve-year-old son, who was cited as her next of kin.[51] After leaving Hannah in their care, Charlie returned to the Pownall Terrace garret. The following day, the landlady told him that Hannah had been transferred to Cane Hill Asylum: 'This news relieved my conscience, for Cane Hill was twenty miles away and I had no means of getting there.'[52] Charlie kept his head down, fearing he would be sent to a pauper school at Hanwell or Norwood if anyone realised he was living on his own. Based on recent experience, Hannah could be away for weeks, even months.

In her reminiscences, recorded on tape by Kevin Brownlow, Effie Wisdom stated: 'Mrs Chaplin had a nervous breakdown and of course there was no one to look after the boys.'[53] "Terrible, you know, the way these boys suffered."[54] After saying, 'I tell you this much, he was always hungry,' she is asked about shoplifting and Effie replies: 'He used to pinch, he used to go up Lambeth Walk and pinch.' She particularly recalled occasions when he stole eggs and a pair of boots, all of which, according to Effie, her aunt forced him to return to the shopkeepers.[55] However he was surviving, it is certain that Charlie's situation now, with his mother and brother absent and his father dead, was perhaps as bad as it had ever been.

Eventually, Syd returned to England, having sent ahead a telegram to Pownall Terrace to say he was arriving at Waterloo Station the following morning.*[56] Charlie walked to Waterloo to meet the train: 'I was not an imposing sight to greet him ... My clothes were dirty and torn, my shoes yawned and the lining of my cap showed like a woman's dropping underskirt.' Hiding his shock at his brother's appearance and after buying Charlie new clothes, Syd treated the two of them to an evening at the South London Palace at 92 London Road, to the north of Elephant and Castle. The following day they visited Hannah in Cane Hill, where the doctor told them 'her mind was undoubtedly impaired by malnutrition, and that she required proper medical treatment, and although she had lucid moments, it would be months before she completely recovered'.[57]

At the end of April 1904, Fred Karno and his ensemble were playing the Royal in Holborn. By this date, after some years performing under the name of Winnie Warren, the 'Premier Tyrolean Vocalist and Serio', his wife Edith's stage career had effectively ended after the birth of their son, Frederick Arthur. But for Fred, things were going from good to better. The proprietor of the Royal,

---

*Syd's delay home was due to his falling ill, followed by months of medical treatment in Cape Town.

Mr Walter Gibbons, had introduced a 'two-houses-a-night' plan, which was proving successful: 'The current programme ... contains the names of new and old favourites, and has a strong attraction in the speechless fares presented by Fred Karno and troupe entitled *Jail Birds*. This is built up for the purpose of fun, and the drollery of incident and the knockabout business keep the audience shouting with laughter.' The scenario for *Jail Birds* was described in *The Era* as follows:

> A simple-minded curate of seemingly effeminate manners is a conspicuous character in the 'rallies', which commence in a dining-room, with a number of burglars looting the plate and being caught in the act. They are supposed to be doing time in the second act, the drop scene of which discloses a number of cells. Here the fun becomes somewhat conventional; but it vastly improves in the final scene – representing the convict settlement at Portland. The gang make light of their responsibilities, and matters become very warm for the aforesaid parson and his lady, who are on a visit to the settlement.[58]

The jokey references to a 'simple-minded curate', 'visiting a settlement' and wily criminals literally running rings around him, may allude to the occupational hazards of providing pastoral care to the poor, as experienced by vicars like the Reverend Reeve and settlement workers like Margaret Sewell, Katherine Thicknesse and Herbert Stead: middle-class do-gooders, ridiculed by working-class performers to an audience of their peers. Surely this was entertainment by the people, for the people? As a publicity stunt, the wily Karno had promoted *Jail Birds* with a 'Black Maria', a police vehicle purchased from Wandsworth Prison, in which the entire company had travelled to the Derby at Epsom.[59] Karno was the master of promotion, and his variety empire was dominating the national circuit.

Two months later, however, all was not well with his marriage. Edith had filed a petition for judicial separation, a legal status one step away from full divorce and therefore more readily achievable for a woman in the early twentieth century.[60] The Marriage Act of 1895 (following on from the Matrimonial Causes Act of 1857, which established a path for divorce, of which more below) had made terms more favourable for women seeking a judicial separation and in many instances it could be dealt with by a magistrate, rather than having to apply to the divorce courts. However, women who separated from their husbands could not remarry, and separation was at the discretion of the judges, who sometimes liked to play the role of marriage mender. Despite all this, magistrates were issuing separation orders at about ten times the rate that divorce courts were issuing divorce or separation decrees.

The details of the Westcott–Karno (Westcott vs Westcott) case were 'closed' until 2006, so any reference to the disintegration of the Karno marriage prior to this was reliant on other material, including the subjective recollections and testimony of friends and supporters on both sides. Edith had moved out of her home at 28 Vaughan Road, to live with the comedian Charlie Bell and his wife Clara.[61] By the autumn of 1904 she was renting a house on Brixton Road, where the music-hall celebrities Marie Lloyd, Marie Kendall, Marguerite Broadfoote, and the dancer Ida Crispi were regular callers.[62] The novelist Naomi Jacob, with reference to Edith, later declared: 'I believe that a more saintly woman never lived ... Yet such a woman was regularly subjected to incredible degradations by her husband, indignities which even in these days of frank writing could not be publicly described.'[63] The validity of Naomi's assessment to an extent can be tested against the information presented within the court documents. But the truth of the following description of Edith, given her public role as performer and the wife of a theatrical entrepreneur, must surely be accepted: 'She was very fair, with natural golden hair, a beautiful skin and very wide laughing blue eyes. Her figure was trim with small, fine-shaped hands and feet. She had a great sense of humour.'[64]

The folder of documents associated with the case for separation include the original petition by Edith and the counter petitions by Fred, with Edith's responses. The judge, Sir Henry Bargrave Deane, one of the Justices of the High Court at the Royal Courts of Justice on the Strand, had decided to take all claims and counterclaims as one single entity: this was a far more complex case, and therefore process, than would be overseen by any magistrate.

Edith's original petition, dated 24 June 1904, stated that in early May of that year, at their home, 28 Vaughan Road in Camberwell, Fred had violently assaulted her 'by knocking her down and putting his heel on her face giving her a black eye and causing her to bleed very much and bruising her severely on the limbs'. Another alleged physical assault occurred in June 1904, when, according to Edith, Fred struck her on the face.

As already explored above, culturally working-class women had little choice but to accept some domestic violence in exchange for financial security, or, at the very least, a hope of regular income from the main breadwinner. This, it can be assumed, was the case for Jane Tinworth. Charlie Chaplin described a situation he witnessed in the few months he was resident with his father and Louise. Charlie had been locked out and was walking around the area of Kennington Cross, waiting for the landlady or any of her lodgers to arrive at 289 Kennington Road. Then he noticed someone walking up the garden path towards the house: 'It was Louise – and her little son running ahead of her.' He saw that she was limping and listing to one side and 'I realised she was very drunk. I had never seen a lopsided drunk before.'[65] Louise told Charlie, in no uncertain terms, to go away, so he wandered along Prince's Road towards the Queen's Head in the hope of finding his father. Charles Chaplin had spent the day with his brother Spencer and, like Louise, was very drunk. Father and son returned to the house together and climbed the stairs to the first-floor front room. Charlie described the scene. Louise was swaying unsteadily by the fireplace, while his father demanded to know why she had not let his son into the house. Louise mumbled: 'You too can go to hell – all of you!' At this, Charles seized a heavy wooden clothes brush and threw it at Louise with great force. The flat side hit her on the face, and her eyes closed as, Charlie recalled, 'she collapsed unconscious with a thud to the floor as though she welcomed oblivion'. Charles and Louise had already argued that morning because he wanted to spend the day with his brother. Louise, 'being sensitive to her position' as Charles's mistress, did not like to visit his family.

So Charles had gone alone, and in revenge Louise spent the day elsewhere, leaving Charlie to fend for himself.

The situation was not assisted by the additional stress of Charles's other dependants being resident at their two-room lodgings; despite the occasional violent outburst, Charlie assessed the relationship between Charles and Louise as a good one. He even recalled Louise with empathy: 'She loved Father. Even though very young I could see it in her glance the night she stood by the fireplace, bewildered and hurt by his neglect.'[66] This may seem surprising, given her hostility towards him and particularly his brother Syd, but this is the adult reflecting maturely on what he had seen as a child. Of his father, Charlie stated, 'I am sure he loved her. I saw many occasions of it. There were times when he was charming and tender and would kiss her good-night before leaving for the theatre.' Drinking with punters to help the bar takings was expected of music-hall performers, so Charles Chaplin, an alcoholic, was on a hiding to nothing – unlike Joshua Tinworth, who made a conscious decision to spend time drinking in a local tavern, even when he and his family could least afford it.

In his autobiography, Charlie Chaplin also considered the relationship between his mother and father, despite (apparently) having never seen the two together and basing it on information he had gleaned from Hannah: 'Whenever she spoke of him it was without bitterness, which makes me suspect she was too objective to have been deeply in love.' This suggests that Hannah and Charles had married for mutual support and companionship; and, for Hannah, it was a means of achieving respectability after the birth of Syd. Charlie continued: 'Sometimes she would give a sympathetic account of him, and at other times talk of his drunkenness and violence.' And then, years later, when Hannah was angry with Charlie, 'she would ruefully say: "You'll finish up in the gutter like your father."'[67]

The sound of couples arguing must have been a familiar occurrence within working-class communities. As Herbert Stead had observed of the 'poor man's lawyers' assigned to cases of 'matrimonial difficulty' by the Browning Settlement ('some ludicrous, other tragic'), to 'novelists in search of a plot the lawyers could give many thrilling suggestions from real life'.[68] Walnut Tree Walk, off

Kennington Road, is featured in George Gissing's novel *Thyrza*, where a woman with a 'bell-clapper tongue' is described haranguing her husband in the street, for the entire neighbourhood to hear:

> They became aware that a common incident of Saturday night was occurring in the street below. A half-tipsy man and a nagging woman had got thus far on their way home, the wife's shrill tongue running over every scale of scurrility and striking every note of ingenious malice. The man was at length worked to a pitch of frenzy, and then – thud, thud, mingled with objurgations and shrill night-piercing yells.[69]

This recalls the description from the women social workers living at Nelson Square, where a night's rest was disturbed by screams of 'Murder!', and Charlie's description of his thirteen-year-old brother threatening a drunk Louise with a sharpened button hook. Even so, Gissing presents a social cliché, the nagging wife. The familiarity of such a scene would have inured those listening to the level of violence, although one of Gissing's female characters is herself silenced by what she can hear happening in the street below.

While making his notes for lower Kennington Lane and its immediate environs, George Duckworth referred to a recent event he called the 'Kennington Murder', which had happened just three weeks before his visit in mid-1899.[70] Frederick James Andrews (aged forty-five) had been living with the widow Elizabeth Frances Short, ten years his senior, for eight or nine years at her dwelling, 4 Garden Cottages, a group of wooden buildings on Garden Row (a narrow alley off Opal Street near to Lambeth's Renfrew Road workhouse). Duckworth noted that the woman had been 'stabbed in 54 places by her coster husband, who then undid a flock mattress & put her into it: he was discovered a day or two after wards trying to wash the stains from his coat in a public house in Covent Garden'.[71] The case caused a sensation for several weeks and was reported in the major London newspapers and across the country, as well as the more colourful publications, like *Lloyd's Weekly Newspaper*, for whom murder was a stock-in-trade and popular among their working-class readership. Elizabeth Short kept a greengrocer stall on Newington Butts (where Charlie Chaplin had attempted without success to sell the old clothes) and Frederick Andrews assisted her. One night, their immediate neighbours heard ferocious quarrelling from the cottage, but 'in view of the frequency of such proceedings no special notice was taken'.[72] Early the next morning, the couple were seen in the alley as usual, preparing the barrow for market. Both returned to the cottage at the end of the day, but 'angry words were heard up to nine o'clock'. Andrews was seen hurrying from the cottage and, suspicious, Mary Ann Sawyer, from No. 5 next door, entered Short's cottage with another neighbour. What they found was Elizabeth Short slumped in the corner of the room used as a bedroom, with a wound in her throat: 'An attempt had been made to conceal the body by piling up in front of it the bedding, some old clothes, and a quantity of vegetables. The woman's clothing was saturated with blood.' A pocket-knife stained with blood was discovered in the room.[73]

Duckworth seemed to have muddled two recent murders in his description; the other, where the blood-stained body had been hidden in a mattress, referred to a newborn murdered by their mother. But he was correct regarding the discovery of Frederick Andrews in a Covent Garden pub, the Horse and Groom on Neal Street. Mary Ann Sawyer further informed the court that, on several occasions prior to her death, 'she had seen the woman Short with black eyes, and she had shown her bruises on her chest. On Wednesday morning, at 4.15, she came to [the] witness, crying, and said, "Did you hear that pig on at me last night?"' (The main cause of their arguments seemed to relate to Elizabeth's grown-up son and his attitude towards her live-in partner.) Her neighbour responded that she had heard Andrews 'on at her' and, given he was not Short's husband, she advised Elizabeth to get him locked up by the police for assault. In fact, even if living as husband and wife, the police may have taken Andrews's assault on Elizabeth more seriously because they were 'merely' cohabiting.[74]

At that moment, Andrews was heard walking towards them in the alleyway. Short accused him of spending her money in the public house. He remained silent and the two entered the cottage. Later Mrs Sawyer heard a 'faint scream', followed by silence. Frederick Andrews admitted being drunk and confessed to murdering his partner. The policeman interviewing him stated in the Lambeth Police Court that Andrews had said, 'It's no use my denying it ... This is a bad position to be in. I done it in drink. I have been drinking heavily. I had better be hung and get out of it.'[75] The case highlighted the casual way into which some relationships were entered, and the vulnerability of women to extreme aggression. Of particular interest is the suggestion, from Elizabeth Short's neighbour, that such treatment should only be suffered by her if Short and Andrews had been married. Cohabiting women in some respects could be seen as having more choice than married women: they could, after all, more easily leave a relationship.[76] The costermonger's sober regret may have been genuine, but the verdict was guilty; he was hanged at Wandsworth Prison on 3 May.[77]

In the same year, the Reverend Bromfield of St-Mary-the-Less, during his interview with Ernest Aves, offered various explanations as to why couples would live together rather than marry. He observed that there was a 'good deal' of cohabitation within his parish, 'but he thought that in most cases there was a legal obstacle to marriage'.[78] This could be that either one or both were already married – as was the case for Charles Chaplin and Louise – and divorce was to all intents and purposes impossible. The Matrimonial Causes Act of 1857 had established clear routes to divorce: men needed to prove adultery, whereas women had to prove aggravated adultery, 'aggravated', that is, by bigamy, incest, bestiality, sodomy, desertion, cruelty or rape (this was the case until 1923). And that is before the obstacle of cost which – at between £40 and £500 – was beyond most people's reach. One consequence of the 1857 Act, and the corresponding need for evidence of domestic abuse, adultery, bigamy and much else, was the employment of women as private detectives working undercover as servants, hotel maids and street hawkers.[79] Another obstacle to marriage was when one or other in the relationship was too young: the age of consent and marriage had been raised from twelve to thirteen in 1875, and then to sixteen in 1885, as part of the Criminal Law Amendment Act.* Bromfield

---

*It had been twelve since the year 1275.

further stated that the 'couples [who] married are generally young, and a certain number are forced'.[80] The parish newsletter advertised the availability of marriage services on Sundays at 9.45 a.m., weekdays at 9 a.m. 'or by special appointment'.[81] He then recounted a situation in which a woman was attempting to marry off her eighteen-year-old daughter to a seventeen-year-old boy 'by whom the former was enceinte' (that is, pregnant). The cleric asked whether permission had been received from the boy's parents;* as it had not, he returned the banns money and offered Aves the observation that in all likelihood, the couple would now get married at Lambeth Register Office, with or without parental consent. Aves noted that Bromfield was particularly irritated by the churches in Walworth, who had lowered marriage fees to 'too low and too tempting a scale': 'the careless admission to the rite (and he thought that many of the clergy had been careless in the past) made legality very uncertain, and risked constant breaking of the table of consanguinity'.[82] This last comment relates to the degrees of blood relationship between individuals who could marry – the Reverend Bromfield seemed to infer that incest had occurred, whether knowingly or unknowingly. Commenting on the Walworth district, Herbert Stead had observed in his account of the Robert Browning Settlement (1912) that prostitution 'is almost wholly absent', but 'overcrowding bears its deadly fruit in immature and illegitimate motherhood and sometimes in incest'.[83] Stead would have given his honest perception of what was happening on the ground, from his experience of the community in which he lived, albeit, because of his background and particular circumstances, from a position of relative privilege. Nonetheless, this puts Hannah Chaplin's chequered history of romance, sex, marriage, cohabitation and motherhood into a broader context: her experience was not unusual.

Returning to the alleged violence highlighted in the Westcott vs Westcott court papers, Fred had certainly (according to Edith) gone a lot further than Charles Chaplin (as far as we know); and

---

*Parental permission was then required for any participants in a marriage under the age of twenty-one, a legal restriction that was not reduced – to eighteen – until 1987.

as a teetotaller, Fred Karno, if indeed guilty, could not point to the negative effects of excessive alcohol consumption that both Chaplin senior and Frederick Andrews could offer as an explanation (or excuse) for their aggression towards their womenfolk. Edith's petition nevertheless outlined further cause for complaint beyond her husband's alleged physical violence: his adultery, which Edith claimed had begun in or about the month of August 1903 until the present time, whether in London, Birmingham, Manchester, 'and the various other provincial towns in which he has been performing in his Theatrical pieces and sketches during that period'. The woman in question was 'known to your Petitioner as "Marie Moore" a member of one of his Companies'.*

To be clear, this is a petition for a separation and not a divorce. If the latter, Edith would have had to prove the adultery as well as violence, since a woman could not divorce a violent husband: she needed to prove aggravated adultery. But for a separation, a wife needed to prove adultery, or cruelty and (or) violence, or desertion without reasonable cause. Edith, in the event, may have had enough grounds for a divorce, but she is choosing separation; it appears she is flagging cruelty and (or) violence, as well as adultery, in order to get a decent maintenance payment on top of a successful custody claim.

In her petition Edith had accused Fred of cohabiting and committing adultery with 'Marie Moore' during January and February 1904 at 28 Vaughan Road. This was the last straw: Edith, by this point, had moved out. The petition concluded by requesting custody of Leslie Karno Westcott, just sixteen months old, and such 'further and other relief as the nature of the case may require'.[84]

So who was Marie Moore? One 'Maria Theresa Laura Moore' was listed in the register of baptisms at St Anne's Liverpool for the year 1881. The child, called 'Marie' by her family, was born on 24 August to Thomas William Moore and his wife Elizabeth

---

*Fred Karno's Company was certainly on tour in England's West Midlands and North West in the late summer of 1903, when he was appearing at Liverpool's Royal Hippodrome on and around 4 September (*Music Hall and Theatre Review*, 4 September 1903).

Winifred, and can be traced through census details from 1891 to 1911. In 1891 she is listed among the Moore household of five individuals: her parents, Thomas, an 'Ex minstrel performer' aged thirty-five, and Eliza (no profession listed) aged twenty-four, plus two siblings, who were occupying four rooms at 24 Victoria Road in Battersea. A total of three separate family groups occupied No. 24 at this date.[85] By 1901, the Moore family had moved to 55 Queens Road, East Battersea. Thomas was listed as a 'Comedian Act' from Boston, USA, while Eliza was described as a wardrobe mistress and Marie Theresa as a wardrobe assistant.[86]

Given this family's connection to variety theatre, it is likely the very same 'Marie Moore' who performed in a new melodrama, *The 10.30 Down Express*, at the Royal Court Theatre Bacup in Lancashire, on 21 February 1903. Marie's performance, playing the part of a maid, 'Letitia Leigh', was described in *The Era* report as 'amusing'.[87] On 6 April 1905, she was in the cast of *Queen of the Night*;[88] by 12 August, likely the same actress was playing 'Countess Daphne' in *The Branded Woman*, a 'Drama, in Four Acts, by F. Wybert Clive, produced for the First Time on any Stage at the Gaiety Theatre, Burnley'.[89] Finally, Marie Moore's name appeared in an advertisement in *The Era*, dated 9 December 1905, for Fred Karno's *Early Birds* sketch at the Scala Theatre in Antwerp.

In his 'answer' (dated 20 July 1904) as 'respondent' to the accusations, Fred denied the cruelty Edith alleged, and he also denied adultery. He stated that 'if on any occasion he has been guilty of violence to [the] Petitioner, such violence was provoked by the drunken and violent conduct of [the] Petitioner to himself on each of such occasions respectively'. This sounds contradictory at best. Having denied the adultery, Fred then declared that 'the adultery alleged in the said Petition has been condoned by the Petitioner [that is, Edith] by co-habitation with the Respondent as her husband at 28 Vaughan Road from March to the 10th day of June 1904'. In other words, if you live with your husband while he is committing adultery, then you are condoning the situation. Finally, Fred rejected all points of Edith's petition; for judicial separation, for custody of the youngest child, Leslie Karno, and finally for any alimony to provide for herself and her son.[90]

Fred followed this response with a further counter petition dated 23 July 1904, in which he elaborated on Edith's alleged drunken and violent behaviour and ratcheted up the allegations against her. Fred declared that his wife was a woman of violent and intemperate habits, 'that she has been for many years', and was constantly 'under the influence of drink'. He accused her of frequently threatening his life 'and the life of the aforesaid child Leslie Karno Westcott'. He accused her of being very drunk and violent in May 1904, throwing a glass soda-water syphon at him. The next paragraph details an incident Fred alleged happened on 12 June 1904, when Edith 'was very violent and took up a knife and threatened to kill your Petitioner saying she would "rip his b— guts out"'. According to Fred, his wife 'broke up the furniture in the house and set it on fire and was so violent that the servants would not stay in the house with her alone'. The final paragraph reiterated that Edith 'is unfit by reason of her intemperate habits to have the custody of the children'. He concluded that he hoped the judge would 'be pleased to decree that he may be judicially separated from the said Edith', and further, that he should have custody of both sons.[91]

During an interview, many years later, for the *Picturegoer Weekly*, Charlie Chaplin described Fred Karno as having 'a kind of pathetic stout-heartedness; a take-it-and-come-up-for-more attitude to life'.[92] He also observed, admittedly decades on, that Fred Karno 'could be cynical and cruel to anyone he disliked. Because he liked me I had never seen that side of him, but he could indeed be crushing in a vulgar way.'[93]

Chaplin's observations characterised Fred Karno as vindictive towards his opponents, with a desire to 'crush' them. In 1904, as the husband, Fred held all the cards under the laws of separation, divorce and child custody. In his counterclaim, he had played on the generally held view that the drunken, nagging, violent working-class wife was not just a cliché of music hall, popular fiction or the penny dreadfuls, but a real societal type epitomised by Edith. Objectively, Edith comes across as a strong, determined character and it is not difficult to imagine a wife lashing out (whether verbally or physically) at an errant spouse in frustration and despair, perhaps fuelled by drink, as had Louise, the partner of Charles Chaplin senior. In his recent biography of Fred Karno, David Crump details the period leading up to and including the court case, challenging the manifestly one-sided interpretation of Karno's earlier biographer, Joseph Gallagher, which relied heavily on the testimony of Naomi Jacob, as noted, one of Edith's closest friends and supporters. Here, in Gallagher's words, Edith is portrayed as 'blonde, petite, gentle in nature and with an almost virginal mind'.⁹⁴ Crump, in contrast, describes Edith as 'a woman scorned – understandably hurt, resentful and turning to drink'. He also posits an intriguing case for Edith's sexuality, that she 'may have been gay or bisexual', possibly with Jacob or Marguerite Broadfoote.⁹⁵ Whether true or not, none of this, other than the alleged drinking and violence on both sides, was aired in court. Fred simply appealed to the judge's likely biases as a man, as well as an upper-middle-class professional, with the aim of swinging the judgement in his favour. On a purely personal level, official documentation revealed that over the course of her life Edith had experienced five live births, of which only two had survived into childhood: Frederick Arthur (born 1891) and Leslie Karno (born 1903).*⁹⁶ Attempting to take away both of her children, in the light of such a family history of newborn death, was, by any reasonable measure, unjust.

A story told by Naomi Jacob and repeated by Gallagher describes how, after the birth of Leslie Karno, Edith received a package of compromising (some described them as pornographic) photographs of Fred and another woman – perhaps the elusive Marie Moore. The veracity of this story cannot be supported by the court documentation, but a photograph of Fred sitting in his office at the Fun Factory has some interesting details, not least the pictures hanging above the mantelpiece. Two appear to be photographs of the same woman, probably Edith, or even Marie. Above these portraits is a picture of a reclining, possibly naked woman: a standard example of Victorian–Edwardian erotica, or

---

*The 1911 census was the first to include such details, due to government concerns about declining national birth rates.

a saucy portrait of Fred's mistress? But if Edith had photographic evidence of adultery, as argued by Gallagher, it is unclear why she would not be willing to use it. Either these pornographic photographs never existed, surely the more likely scenario, or Edith was confident enough of success to not stoop to utilising them. After all, such disclosure would have resulted in the public humiliation of her children's father, and as a result may have impacted on his earnings, a source of her future income via alimony.

In her reply (dated 10 August) Edith denied Fred's accusations, including the incident with the soda water syphon, and the violence and intemperance said to have occurred on 12 June 1904, that is the incident where the furniture was allegedly broken up and burned. Indeed, according to Edith, on that very date and at 28 Vaughan Road, Fred struck Edith 'violently on the face and taunted her by boasting of his adultery with a woman named Marie Moore'.[97]

On 25 May 1905, the judicial separation was finally granted, the main cause given as Fred's adultery, with Leslie Karno Westcott ('the youngest child') to remain with Edith and Frederick Arthur Westcott ('the eldest child') to remain in the custody of his father. Further, 'with consent the husband and wife have mutual access to the children with liberty to apply but it is directed that such children be not removed out of the jurisdiction of the court without its sanction'. Fred was ordered to pay Edith the sum of £10 a week 'by way of permanent Alimony during their joint lives'.[98] The 1911 census reveals that Edith (by then aged forty) was living at 93 Oakleigh Park Drive, Leigh-on-Sea, Essex – a spacious seven-room house – with her younger son Leslie Karno (then aged eight); she is recorded as living by 'Private Means'.[99]

Soon after the official separation from his wife, a redevelopment at the Fun Factory required Fred's move to his houseboat, the *Highland Lassie*, which was moored on the Thames at Tagg's Island, near the picturesque village of Hampton.[100] Living with Marie, as husband and wife, might have been easier to manage from the privacy of rural Middlesex; in densely urban Camberwell and within a lively business where the domestic and professional combined, people knew exactly the nature of his marital circumstances.

Indeed, the Westcott vs Westcott case was sufficiently interesting to have been the subject of a short article, on the day following the granting of separation, in the London paper the *Daily News*. Under the heading 'PERMANENT ALIMONY' and another, 'LARGE PROVISION FOR A WIFE', the report stated that of the various 'cross suits of Westcott v. Westcott ... only one was tried, that of the wife, Mrs. Edith Westcott, who sought a judicial separation by reason of the adultery of her husband, Mr. Frederick John Westcott'. This report noted that in August 1903, a deed of separation had been executed and that

> the following September the respondent lived with a woman of the name of Marie Moore, at the Washington Hotel, Liverpool. A decree of judicial separation was granted to the wife, with costs, and custody of the youngest child. It was stated that Mrs. Westcott would receive £10 a week as permanent alimony, and that a lump sum of £250 would be given to her.[101]

On the same day, the *Morning Leader* reported most of these details, without naming Marie Moore as the woman staying with Fred Westcott at the Washington Hotel. It added that 'Mr. Frederick John Westcott ... is known as a member of the Karno troupe of sketch artists', which rather underplays his role as leader and impresario of the company and therefore avoids identifying him under his well-known stage name. The short report was heralded by the title 'GRANTED A SEPARATION', and then 'PETITION BY THE WIFE OF A WELL KNOWN SKETCH ARTIST'.[102] Even with this scant information, readers could have surely joined the dots.

Despite, apparently, living openly with Fred at Hampton, in the 1911 census the Marie Moore here presented as his mistress is listed as still resident at 55 Queens Road in Battersea, with her parents and her twenty-eight-year-old sister Winifred Brammall, a married actress. Marie is also recorded as twenty-eight and an actress, but unmarried.[103] If she was Fred Karno's mistress, then being registered in Battersea is hardly surprising: propriety, in the official record, is maintained. The only question is why Fred did not attempt to secure a full divorce in 1905, so that he and his lover could marry.

The answer, if Marie Moore of Battersea was his mistress, is revealed through her baptismal record from 1881; her family were Roman Catholic and she was baptised into this faith, where marrying a divorced man was forbidden. This hypothesis is supported by the fact that Fred and Marie were indeed married, on 16 June 1927, just days after Edith's death.[104] Their marriage, to all appearances affectionate, and after decades as cohabiting partners, survived further ups and downs – including Fred's bankruptcy in October 1927 – until his death in 1941. Marie died three years later.[105]

After Hannah's admission to Cane Hill Asylum (where she remained from 11 May 1903 to 2 January 1904), Charlie's life took an unexpected turn for the better. His persistence, since touring with the Eight Lancashire Lads, in contacting a Covent Garden theatrical agent led to him performing in a new play called *Jim, the Romance of a Cockney* (a flop), followed by the part of a pageboy in William Gillette's stage version of *Sherlock Holmes*: a roaring success. As Charlie recalled, after he had been offered both parts, 'I went home on the bus dazed with happiness and began to get the full realisation of what had happened to me. I had suddenly left behind a life of poverty and was entering a long-desired dream – a dream my mother had often spoken about, had revelled in. I was to become an actor!' During the bus ride, he continues, 'I realised I had crossed an important threshold. No longer was I a nondescript of the slums; now I was a personage of the theatre. I wanted to weep.'[106] Despite this good fortune, Syd and Charlie remained for the time being at Pownall Terrace, and soon afterwards Hannah was once more released from Cane Hill Asylum.

One of the most striking anecdotes in the early part of Charlie's autobiography related to a former star of the music hall who, in her pomp, according to Charlie, had been a close friend of his mother. The event in question apparently occurred while he and Hannah were living at Pownall Terrace. At the time, Charlie was suffering from acute asthma and was being treated in hospital. Returning to Kennington Road, and as the two of them were walking along the pavement, Hannah paused to scold some boys who were 'tormenting a derelict woman who was grotesquely ragged and dirty.

She had a cropped head, unusual in those days, and the boys were laughing and pushing each other towards her, as if to touch her would contaminate them. The pathetic woman stood like a stag at bay until Mother interfered.' As Hannah did so, 'a look of recognition came over the woman's face': 'Lil,' she said, feebly, referring to Mother's stage name, 'don't you know me – Eva Lestock?' Hannah now recognised her old friend from their music-hall days. Charlie, on the other hand, out of irritation and embarrassment, continued walking and then waited for his mother at the corner of the street:

> The boys walked past me, smirking and giggling. I was furious. I turned to see what was happening to Mother and, lo, the derelict woman had joined her and both were walking towards me. Said Mother: 'You remember little Charlie?' 'Do I!' said the woman, dolefully, 'I've held him in my arms many a time when he was a baby.' The thought was repellent, for the woman looked so filthy and loathsome. And as we walked along, it was embarrassing to see people turn and look at the three of us. Mother had known her in vaudeville as 'the Dashing Eva Lestock'; she was pretty and vivacious then, so Mother told me.[107]

This 'derelict' woman, through the information Charlie gives, is generally thought to be a moderately successful music-hall performer called Eva Lester (also known as the 'Dashing' Eva Lester) whose career can be traced through the press over a twenty-year period.

On Saturday, 16 August 1884, for example, the year before Charles and Hannah Chaplin were married, the *South Wales Daily News* reported on a 'Theatrical Quarrel' between Wolf Goldstein, a theatrical agent on Waterloo Road, and Rosa Pritchard, 'known in musical circles as Eva Lester'. Goldstein had appeared at Southwark Police Court accused of assault, found guilty, and ordered to pay £10 compensation, as well as fined £1 plus £3 costs. The following year, Eva was named as performing at the famous Gatti's Palace of Varieties on Westminster Bridge Road;[108] by 1886, she had transformed herself into 'Dashing Eva Lester', 'The Californian Gem' and 'England's Queen of Song', then performing at the Oxford, the Metropolitan and the Standard music halls in London, before touring England, returning to the Canterbury on Westminster Bridge Road for the Christmas season.[109] She could then be seen at the Royal Standard in London's Victoria district in 1892, the same year at the Empire in Hull, East Yorkshire, appearing as 'The Dashing Burlesque Artist, with Dashing song and Dashing Dressed', and at the Parthenon Theatre, Greenwich, in 1893.

But in November 1894, 'Miss Eva Lester, well known in the music-halls', appeared at the Lambeth County Court 'to explain why she had failed to pay a judgment debt'. She was described in the *Evening News* as stylishly dressed for her day in the dock, where she explained that she had not paid the debt because she had been ill and was unable to work. In this instance the judge gave Eva six weeks to pay what she could.[110] By late 1897, while Hannah Chaplin was spending her first months as an inmate at Cane Hill Asylum, and Charlie and Syd had been sent to the Hanwell Pauper 'Cuckoo' Schools, Eva Lester was living in Appach Road, Brixton.[111] As reported by the *South London Press*, she was the persistent victim of an 'uninvited guest' by the name of Louis Holmstock, here described as a well-dressed animal-fur dealer. Eva, in this report styled 'an actress', said she had had only business relations with Holmstock, but in recent days he had proposed marriage and, in response, Eva would have nothing to do with him. However, 'the prisoner would persist in coming to her home and annoying her'. It all came to a head when, the Saturday before his appearance in court, Holmstock had followed Eva about 'the Halls' all evening, and then 'after midnight he came to her house and began ringing the bell and knocking at her door'. In court, Holmstock promised not to offend again, upon which he was ordered by Mr Denman, the same magistrate who had sat in judgement of Charles Chaplin in 1898, to recognise the sum of £10 and 'to be of good behaviour for six months'.[112] Louis Holmstock sounds like a besotted and thwarted lover, of whom the Dashing Eva had grown bored. But from his evident desperation, it could be deduced that Eva Lester was quite a catch.

Two years or so later, as Charlie continued: 'The woman said that she had been ill in the hospital, and that since leaving it, she had been sleeping under arches and in Salvation Army shelters.' Hannah sent her to the local public baths, likely the Lambeth Baths and Washhouses on the corner of Lambeth and Kennington Roads (opposite the Three Stags public house), which had opened in 1897, offering, for a small fee, a swimming pool and a laundry, as well as facilities for bathing. But then, to Charlie's horror, Hannah brought Eva back to their tiny Pownall Terrace garret:

> Whether it was illness alone that was the cause of her present circumstances, I never knew. What was outrageous was that she slept in Sydney's armchair bed. However, Mother gave her what clothes she could spare and loaned her a couple of bob. After three days she departed, and that was the last we ever saw or heard of 'the Dashing Eva Lestock'![113]

This poor, distressed woman could have been a friend from Hannah's music-hall days – the profession was certainly precarious enough – but that she was Eva Lester seems unlikely, for the reason that another unusual episode from Charlie's childhood also occurred around the time he and his mother were living in the garret at Pownall Terrace. In a similar scenario, Hannah had met up with an unnamed friend, but this ex-performer 'had become very prosperous' and was 'a flamboyant, good-looking, Junoesque type of woman'.[114] This friend had exchanged her theatrical career for life as the mistress, so Charlie recalled, of a wealthy retired army colonel with a jovial red face and full mutton-chop sideburns. She had been set up by the old colonel in Lansdowne 'Square' (or Gardens) in Stockwell, a relatively affluent part of South Lambeth with well-appointed late-Georgian terraced houses and villas.* The friend invited Hannah and Charlie to stay with her over the

---

*Between 1895 and 1898 Ralph Vaughan Williams had been the organist and choirmaster at the local church of St Barnabas, living at 2 St Barnabas Villas, earning £50 a year. He suggested his friend Gustav Holst to replace him. (British Library, MS Mus. 158, fol. 10–11: Letter VWL245, RVW to GH, July 1897; www.vaughanwilliamsfoundation.org).

summer – Syd, like many Londoners during the summer season, was on a working 'holiday' hop-picking in the country, likely Kent or Essex.[115]

The curious thing about this entire episode is that, according to the 1901 census, an Eva Lester had been living at 36 Guildford Road, adjoining Lansdowne Gardens. This Eva Lester was described as the head of household, single, aged twenty-eight and an 'actress'. Her place of birth was recorded as America. She was living with a domestic servant called Edith Pickett, aged twenty-six, from Norwood in Surrey. Also resident on census night was an Olive Gwynn, described as a visitor, single and aged fifteen. Olive had been born in Worcester and appeared to have been Eva's pupil.[116]

In assembling the colourful characters of his autobiography, over sixty years after the event, might Charlie have melded two women together – both friends of Hannah, both former artistes – for dramatic effect? Or had his memory, in this rare instance, come to fail him? He had misremembered the surname of the real 'Dashing Eva' as 'Lestock', and he may have been thinking of Lestock Place, near East Street in Walworth.[117] On the other hand, the fact that Eva Lester's former lover – and later nuisance – was called Holmstock might also be of relevance, since the two names (Lester and Holmstock) precisely conflate into Charlie's memory of this striking episode. Might the army colonel's flamboyantly comely Juno, and the music-hall actress Eva Lester, the focus of Mr Holmstock's obsessive ardour, be one and the same person?

Sometime around 1904, another retired female music-hall performer fell on hard times: Charles Chaplin's partner Louise. While Charlie was still touring with *Sherlock Holmes*, Hannah Chaplin was discharged from Cane Hill Asylum on 2 January 1904 and had moved, once again, to the area of Kennington Road, and lodgings on Chester Street.[118] In a letter to her son, as Charlie recalled later, Hannah brought him the news that Louise had died, 'ironically enough, in the Lambeth Workhouse, the same place in which we had been confined. She survived Father only by four years, leaving her little son an orphan.'[119] The unnamed child, again according to his half-brother Charlie, had been sent to the same Hanwell Schools as the older Chaplin brothers. If this is correct, then the workhouse to which Louise and her son had been admitted would have been Newington Workhouse on Westmoreland Road. (It is also possible that by the early 1900s the Lambeth Board of Guardians were sending children to the District Schools at Hanwell.) Hannah then informed her son that she had visited his half-brother, in her words 'a very handsome boy, very quiet, and preoccupied', who remembered very little of what had happened in 1898, when he was four years old and briefly living with Charlie and Syd. And, tragically, just a few years after Charles Chaplin's death, the lad had no recollection of his father at all. 'He was registered under Louise's maiden name,' Charlie recalled, 'and as far as Mother could find out he had no relatives.' Hannah visited Louise's son until she herself fell ill again and was readmitted to Lambeth Infirmary on Renfrew Road and then transferred to Cane Hill Asylum in March 1905.[120] Until the full name of the woman Charlie called Louise can be discovered, or there is a lucky find in the extensive archives of the Lambeth or Southwark Guardians, her son with Charles Chaplin will remain unnamed and untraced.

'The news of Mother's relapse came like a stab to the heart,' Charlie would recall: 'We received a curt official notice that she had been found wandering and incoherent in the streets. There was nothing we could do but accept poor Mother's fate. She never again recovered her mind completely.'[121] There are four letters datable to 1905 in the Charlie Chaplin Archive from Hannah to her sons. One includes a request for regular issues of *The Era*, one of the theatre profession's key newspapers, to be sent to her at Cane Hill: perhaps out of habit, Hannah wished to keep abreast of the theatre and music-hall world.[122] Another, dated 20 August, reads: 'Dear Children just a line thanking you for the "wire" on my Birthday many thanks for remembering me – trusting you are all in the best of health & that,' concluding: 'Why do you not send me a little pin money? Fondest love to my dear Boys a few xxxx do write soon.'[123]

The experiences of Hannah Chaplin, 'Dashing Eva Lestock' and Louise might suggest that working-class women at the turn of the twentieth century were simply flotsam, buffeted by life's ebb and flow and with no individual or collective agency. (Until she took her husband to court, and won, Edith Karno's life was not her own.) In his memoir of the early years of the Robert Browning Settlement, Herbert Stead recalled that an idea emerged from one of the Women's Pleasant Tuesday Afternoon meetings at Browning Hall: the women of Southwark should form a deputation to Queen Alexandra, consort of Edward VII, at Buckingham Palace and bring to her attention the suffering of the area's unemployed. It was suggested that the women of Poplar in the East End of London should join them, a plan enthusiastically supported at the PTA meeting. A mass march on a royal palace, peopled by desperate, poor but determined women, had historic precedent: 'What was intended', Herbert Stead recalled, 'was in complete and striking contrast with the raid of Paris women on the palace of Versailles at the beginning of the French Revolution. It would be no menad [frenzied] march of menacing despair: it would be a procession of loyal and touching confidence in a Royal sympathy certain somehow or other to bring about relief.'[124] British working-class women, independent from their menfolk, had formed themselves into political associations in the past. The Female Reform Societies of Lancashire had joined the processions to St Peter's Field in Manchester in August 1819, and the leader of the Manchester Female Reform Society, Mary Fildes (grandmother of the society portrait painter Sir Luke Fildes), had been on the hustings with Henry 'Orator' Hunt when the cavalry attacked.[125] As a natural progression, working-class women had been active supporters of Chartism and organisers of female Chartist associations in the 1830s and 1840s: such activity, and the embracing of popular rights, as earlier in the century, was seen, Susie Steinbach assesses, 'as an extension of their domestic duties, thereby recasting themselves as both respectable women and political beings'.[126] And more recently, there had been the 'Match Girls' Strike' of 1888 at the Bryant & May Factory in the East End. Annie Besant had published an article equating the awful working conditions at the factory with slavery, including fourteen-hour days, low pay and the prevalence of the disease known as 'phossy jaw', where the phosphorus inhaled by the workers caused abscesses, facial disfigurement, brain damage and death.[127] The women and girls at the factory in Bow went on strike, supported and publicised by Besant, William Stead (as editor of the *Pall Mall Gazette*) and Emmeline Pankhurst; the industrial action resulted in an improvement in pay and conditions and the formation of the Union of Women Matchmakers, which in turn encouraged the mobilisation of other industrial workers.

The opening up of local and public service to women, in tandem with their greater visibility in politics (notably via the suffragist and suffragette movements), further meant that, by the turn of the century, collectively women had, arguably, never been more powerful and more present on the national stage – despite a woman occupying the highest position in British society for sixty years.

In 1905, allowing such a mass demonstration of poor working people was deemed unwise, so a more contained parade was approved for 6 November 1905, starting from the embankment near Doulton's Pottery, and passing over Westminster Bridge to Whitehall, with an address sent in advance to Queen Alexandra at Buckingham Palace. This had echoes of the mass petitions, meetings and parades in support of the Chartist six points. It read: 'We appeal to your Majesty to use your vast social influence in order to induce those who have the means to provide what is needed for the employment of the Unemployed of London ... We appeal to your Majesty as Queen, as woman, as mother, to save us from despair.'[128] Some 3,000 women and 2,000 men marched: *The Times* reported the following day that the demonstration 'was, perhaps, the most striking and significant of the kind that has been held in London for several generations'.[129] Herbert Stead recalled that the 'spectacle of that sombre procession of poverty-stricken womanhood made a profound impression on the metropolis', and concluded, with well-intentioned paternalism:

> To those who, like the Settlement, knew the working womanhood of London the scene was bright with the glory of a social resurrection. The working woman long buried in drudgery and ignorance and lethargy had at last risen to the idea that

Government could help, and that pressure at the heart of Government might mean food and warmth for her starving children. The elemental force of motherhood had burst out at last in politics ... A tigress with famished cubs may yet prove less formidable than the human mother whose children are starving and who is out on the prowl for prey in the political jungle.[130]

Even so, it was not the old or new British government* who acted, but the Danish-born Queen Alexandra: 'Her Majesty took the country and the Court by surprise when with magnificent promptitude she opened the Queen's Fund for the Unemployed with a donation of £2,000.' Large contributions began to arrive from companies and grandees like Coutts & Co. (£500), the owners of *Lloyd's Weekly News* (£1,000) and the Duke of Norfolk (£1,000), alongside single donations of between £10 and £100 from thousands of individuals.[131] After a few months, this fund had attracted a staggering £150,000. But not everyone was impressed: in mid-November 1905 the *Daily News* interviewed James Keir Hardie MP, who, in his usual forthright manner, declared: 'The muddle of this unemployed movement ... is due to two causes – the incompetence of the Government and the maudlin, mawkish, sentimental appeals made to the King on behalf of the unemployed. When the unemployed become a terror and a menace to the peace of the realm', he continued – looking back to 1789, 1848 and, more urgently, to the ongoing unrest in Russia directed at Tsar Nicholas II, Edward VII's nephew – 'they will be in a fair way to get something done for them.' However, in conclusion, he admitted that by launching a national fund, the Queen's gift 'would for the first time enable a systematic attempt to be made to deal with unemployment all over the country'.[132] On this Herbert Stead agreed: 'Work at last was provided for the workless and on a national scale.'[133] The first national provision for the unemployed, he observed, 'was made

---

*Conservative until December 1905, then a minority Liberal administration. The ensuing general election of early 1906 was a Liberal landslide, with the Conservative leader and former prime minister, Arthur Balfour, losing his seat.

practicable, not by Statesmen or legislators, but by the Woman upon the Throne, in response to the cry of working women in distress, and that cry, which produced so memorable and historic a result, was voiced by the Browning Settlement'.[134]

A year later, in 1906, Edith Karno was renting a property near Battersea Park. And here at 69 Primrose Mansions, a late-Victorian development on Prince of Wales Drive, she helped to set up and manage a new organisation, the Ladies Music Hall Guild (LMHG), with Marie Lloyd as president and Anna de Grey as secretary. Edith acted as the first treasurer, with Belle Elmore honorary treasurer.* This new society was created in imitation of the Theatrical Ladies Guild, established by Kittie Carson on 13 November 1891. 'For some time past,' Kittie had stated, 'I have been very grieved to hear of many sad cases of distress among our sisters in the profession.' With an identical impetus, the objectives of the LMHG were set out in *The Era* as follows: firstly, to assist the wives of artists 'who through lack of employment, illness, or confinement are in want of help by supplying proper medical aid, food, coal, or other necessaries as may be required'; and secondly, to 'assist widows of artists to find suitable employment'. Both objectives echoed the activities of the Robert Browning Settlement and would have provided for the 'derelict' former music-hall performer, the former chorus girl Louise and her son, and, of course, Hannah Chaplin herself. But the Guild came too late for them. By 1906, Louise was apparently dead and Hannah was in permanent residence at Cane Hill Asylum.

The third aim of the LMHG focused on the children of artists, thereby addressing the circumstances in which both Syd and Charlie Chaplin had consistently found themselves, namely 'to find employment for children of poor artists and orphans as programme sellers and call boys', or office work, 'or other suitable employment: in cases where possible to assist them in obtaining parts in sketches where children's rôles are included'. What an opportunity this would have been for the Chaplin brothers.

---

*Until she was brutally murdered in 1910 by her husband, Dr Hawley Harvey Crippen.

A further aim concerned supplying 'necessitous artists with free clothing', and another to 'sell stage and other clothing to artists who may require them at a very nominal cost'. Finally, the Guild pledged to 'visit the sick; and give toys, books, and games to the sick children of artists'.[135]

The existence of such a society is testament to the fact that Hannah Chaplin's circumstances were so common. A career on the stage was as fragile an existence as any other, and certainly no guarantee against destitution. If Syd and Charlie were sending their mother issues of *The Era* as she had requested, and if Hannah was reading such reports while resident in Cane Hill Asylum, we can only wonder what her reaction might have been.

On 27 November 1906, the *Morning Leader* reported that 'over forty women artists are to take part in a concert in aid of the "Ladies' Guild", a benevolent organisation which gives to artists who have fallen on hard times. The entire management of the concert is by women, the selling of tickets and the giving of cheques is all that men have been allowed to do.' The concert was to take place at the Canterbury Music Hall on Westminster Bridge Road. The short article included portraits of the four women 'prominent in the work', among them Mrs Fred Karno.[136] The event was covered in *The Stage* two days later:

> A packed house and prevailing enthusiasm gave promise of a prosperous future for the newly-formed institution. From entering the building there was a novelty invested in the entire arrangements, which, let it at once be added, were admirably carried out by the executive. Fair ladies replaced the male janitors at the door, whence visitors were conducted to their seats through an avenue of pretty beggars, who enticed handsome sums for programmes and flowers. Within the hall the orchestra was peopled by ladies again, Mdme. E. H. Angless's band discharging their duties admirably. Miss Constance Moxton occupied the onerous post of stage manager, no grateful task on a benefit occasion.[137]

Midway through the event, the curtain came up to reveal the

founders and executive of the Guild. The president, Marie Lloyd, had sent a telegram apologising for her absence through illness, but she trusted 'the performance will be a gigantic success'. The secretary, Anna de Grey, then made a speech, setting out the purpose and aims of the organisation, declaring, as reported in *The Stage*, that there was 'much distress in the profession, and the ladies present had banded themselves together to help in distributing food, coal, and clothing, and to tend to the sick'. Echoing the approach of the Women's University Settlements, she observed that a woman 'could minister to another where it would be improbable that a woman would reveal her distress to a man'. Of course, the major difference was that these were working-class women helping their own, and all they asked from men 'was a subscription'.

The afternoon included a 'cakewalk', 'which provoked roars of laughter and volleys of applause'. This style of dancing – with couples in procession, and usually with a comic twist – had developed from dance competitions on slave-owning plantations in America. Then the Guild's founder, 'Lovely Lively' Lily Burnand, dressed in a purple velvet gown, sang 'Since She's Had Her Photo on a Picture Postcard', Millie Payne (who would have a hit in 1910 with 'Has Anyone Seen My Tiddler?') followed with a rendition of the traditional folk song 'Jenny Jones', and Lil Shaw, a child of four and a half years, top-hatted and gloved in Eton boy costume, 'gave an impersonation of Miss Vesta Tilley in "Following in Father's Footsteps"'.* The reporter declared Miss Shaw's impersonation of the male impersonator was done in 'admirable style' and 'the mite was showered with nose-gays at the finish'. It was to be hoped, declared *The Stage*, 'that the Guild, which had enjoyed such an admirable send-off, would enjoy perennial prosperity'.[138]

On 14 February 1907 another benevolent society, the Music Hall Artists' Railway Association, held its annual dinner at the Horns Assembly Rooms on Kennington Road, but in the face of a 'critical struggle' within the profession, there were fewer attendees than had been expected: the 'struggle', or strike, by music-hall

---

*Vesta Tilley was a popular male impersonator, who by this date was the highest paid female performer in music hall.

employees and artists, against London theatre owners' attempts to extend hours, add performances, remove perks and withhold pay, occurred across the country. Still, members of the LMHG executive, including Edith Karno, were present at the dinner. The death, since the last gathering, of the great Dan Leno was noted with sadness by those present.

While Mrs Karno was active in good causes, her errant husband was building his empire. In the wake of the redevelopment of the Fun Factory, *The Era* published an article in August 1905 promoting a new idea for his enterprise in Camberwell: a one-stop shop for the creation of comic musicals, alongside his own productions. The reporter described visiting the establishment, comprising 'three residences freshly constructed to meet the requirements of the gentleman who looks like becoming a theatrical Whiteley' – a reference to William Whiteley, a Yorkshire-born draper-turned-London department-store entrepreneur who had left £1 million in his will. The article then described how Karno was 'endeavouring to secure the freehold of adjoining property, and rumour goes forth in the neighbourhood that every house in the street will soon form part of the Karno Combine'.[139] This signalled an amazing shift in status for a working-class man, from gymnast, via showman extraordinaire, to major property owner and employer.

As he entered the premises, the reporter could hear the rapid clicking of the typewriters and scribbling of pens from the ground-floor general office. In the company of Herbert Darnley, the general manager, he walked up the stairs to 'a really beautiful room, furnished in the cosiest style, and embellished with oil paintings, engravings, and photographs of famous theatrical people'. This appeared to be Karno's former office – and was now the office of Darnley, himself a music-hall performer who had written songs for the stars, including Dan Leno.

The two men then walked past the wardrobe mistress's room, and arrived at an impressive, top-lit space which was the scene-painters' studio. Two artists were painting a night scene representing Piccadilly Circus, with the new memorial fountain

(1893) dedicated to Lord Shaftesbury, topped by the Greek god popularly known as 'Eros'* on a frame measuring forty feet by thirty, 'and there is a fine long bridge which is worked up and down by the operation of a winch. Here, too, other men are tacking sheets of canvas upon shapeless wooden skeletons.' Next was the carpenters' workshop, where the wings and other 'props' were made. The props master was 'giving the finishing touches with his paint-brush to a trick piano – that is, a wooden concoction cut out and put together so as to represent the familiar musical instrument'. Looking down into an outside courtyard, the reporter saw seven or eight 'well-groomed horses, and in the coach-house hard by is a number of vehicles, including three motor-cars, two "Royal" coaches ... omnibuses, broughams, lorries, and traps'. Within this brief summary alone are described trades as diverse as scene painters and coachmen – revealing the importance of music hall and variety theatre as an employer of a wide range of skills, crafts and people.

Continuing upstairs, they arrive at the rehearsal room, which, as mentioned in a 1906 advert in *The Era*, due 'to its exceptional height (26 feet 6 inches) can be used as a Practice Room for any Gymnastic or Aerial Acts'.[140] Here there was abundant light, 'for the sun shines through the glass roof, and ample ventilation there is likewise. Storage rooms, toilet apartments, and lavatories are near at hand, and the whole establishment could not have been better planned and appointed for the use to which it is to be put.' Finally, the journalist noted that the exterior facing the street was very handsome, 'and an electrically-lighted figure of Mercury' – much like the Royal Standard over Buckingham Palace – 'in the centre of the roof tells the visitors that Mr. Karno is at home'. The imminent departure of one of his troupes to Paris was also recorded, for which the wardrobe mistress was busily working on costumes – and from which Karno hoped to develop a company based in mainland Europe. Even as this major ambition was coming to fruition, 'another troupe will find their way to America, with his full repertoire of pantomimic sketches'. In addition, pantomimes

---

*In fact Anteros, his brother, the God of selfless and requited love.

Wal Pink's *Repairs*, postcard (possibly with Charlie Chaplin's handwriting), 1906. Walter Augustus Pink was a London-born music hall performer and writer for famous acts including Vesta Tilley and Marie Lloyd. *Repairs* focused on the antics of inept workmen redecorating an interior.

in Liverpool and Dublin had been booked. With all this activity it would come as no surprise that Karno employed some two hundred people; as the report noted, Mr. Darnley 'tells us that the majority of his people remain with him in spite of tempting offers from other quarters. This in itself is an excellent testimonial.'[141]

In February 1908, Charlie Chaplin joined his brother Syd as a performer with Fred Karno's company, becoming a regular visitor to the Fun Factory; he would tour in Karno's *Mumming Birds* to Paris that year. Karno, known to all his employees as the 'Guv'nor', had not been interested in hiring the younger Chaplin, despite Syd imploring him to do so on behalf of his then unemployed brother: after Charlie had finished the run of *Sherlock Holmes* in the West End, he joined Syd in Wal Pink's company, performing the sketch *Repairs*, then left to join Casey's Circus (where he played Dick Turpin) and then, with money he had saved, he decided to relax a little ('Whores, sluts and an occasional drinking bout weaved in and out of this period').[142] In later life, he looked back on his teenage self with some indulgence, observing that the 'word "art" never entered my head or vocabulary. The theatre meant a livelihood and nothing more.' Meanwhile, the diligent Syd had remained with Wal Pink's knockabout troupe, which brought him to the attention of Fred Karno. In his autobiography Charlie confirmed that Karno's was the 'outstanding company' of the day, rotating 'a large repertoire of comedies' and on the proceeds of his three main sketches, *Jail Birds*, *Early Birds* and *Mumming Birds*, had 'built a theatrical enterprise of more than thirty companies'.[143]

When Charlie arrived at Vaughan Road for the first time, he was met by Fred Karno junior in the entrance hall, who then took him up to his father's office.*[144] According to the elder Fred Karno, at their first meeting Charlie Chaplin appeared to him as 'a pale, puny, sullen-looking youngster. I must say that when I first saw him, I thought he looked much too shy to do any good in the theatre, particularly in the knock-about comedies that were my speciality.'[145] At full height Charlie was between 5 foot 4 and 5 foot 5 and – as Fred Holden, the music-hall manager, had described him – painfully thin, with distinctive pale blue eyes and a mop of short curly black hair. His surly expression, arms folded, in the promotional photograph of the *Casey's Circus* cast, taken a year or so before his interview with Karno, backs up the Guv'nor's uncomplimentary first impression.† In his more favourable assessment, years before, Holden had detected an intense single-mindedness – rather than hostility – reflecting a spirit 'unbroken' by poverty. 'You have to believe in yourself,' Charlie's eldest son recalled his father telling him once; 'that's the secret.'[146] Even when he was an inmate of the pauper schools, or, Charlie continued, again quoted by his son, 'roaming the streets trying to find enough to eat to keep alive, even then I thought of myself as the greatest actor in the world. I had to feel that exuberance that comes from utter confidence in yourself. Without it you go down to defeat.'[147]

In addition to the three sketches named by Charlie, Karno

---

*Fred Karno junior would later travel with Charlie Chaplin and Stanley Jefferson (aka Stan Laurel) to America.
†See the cover of this book.

was keen to try out a new lead man in another, called *The Football Match*. When Charlie walked into the office, Fred Karno looked him up and down, was unimpressed at what he saw, and then asked the small, slight, surly individual whether he could manage a lead role. Charlie recalled his response to this question: 'All I need is the opportunity.' At which Karno smiled, observing out loud that Charlie was not only young – he was eighteen at the time – but that he looked young for his age. Charlie simply 'shrugged off-handedly' with the bold retort, 'That's a question of make-up.' Karno apparently laughed, later telling Syd that it was the shrug – soon a signature gesture of Charlie Chaplin's Little Tramp – that got his brother the job.[148] The years of observing and imitating the characters around the South London streets had swayed Fred Karno, who now sensed the younger Chaplin's comic potential. But Charlie's oldest son, when referring to his father's most famous creation, argued that it 'wasn't a studied character', rather it sprang from somewhere innate and intangible: 'It was just released whole from somewhere deep within my father. It was really my father's alter ego, the little boy who never grew up: ragged, cold, hungry, but still thumbing his nose at the world.'[149]

On the back of mutual success and regular employment, Syd and Charlie moved into a flat in a new purpose-built mansion block on Brixton Road, just around the corner from St Mark's Church at the Oval and near Kennington Park. Charlie's new contract offered a year's employment at £3 10s a week, with a second year at £4, while Syd's second year had already arrived and his pay had risen to £4 accordingly. The years of uncertainty, distress and suffering seemed to have ended, thanks to their resilience, opportunism and talent. It proved again that music hall and variety could lift some out of extreme poverty, providing routine and stability, as well as an income that could only be dreamed of by most in such desperate circumstances. Number 15 Glenshaw Mansions, was on the top (third) floor, overlooking the long main road that started at Kennington Park in the north, and led to Brixton itself. Just as 3 Pownall Terrace signified despair and failure, so Glenshaw Mansions became totemic of current success and optimism for the future. The two young men took great delight in decorating what was their first real home and sanctuary, contrasting sharply with the ad hoc lodgings (whether with Hannah or while touring) or pauper school–workhouse accommodation they had become used to. They were now independent professionals, not the helpless recipients of grudging local charity and stark forms of pauper relief.

According to Charlie, they furnished the flat, which had four rooms – more than any of the lodgings the brothers had shared with their mother – with a princely £40, spent in a second-hand furniture shop on Newington Butts, the area where, just a few years before, Charlie had failed to sell a single piece of tatty clothing from a pitch in the street. Having informed the owner of their requirements, Charlie, decades on, still took delight in observing that the shopkeeper showed 'personal interest in our problem and spent many hours helping us to pick out bargains'.[150] There is a strong parallel between this scenario and George Tinworth's anecdote, described earlier, concerning another shopman 'sir-ing' a man's clothing. Again, there was the temptation, justified in the circumstances, to enjoy the moment of success that the purchase of such things represented. There might even be a hint that Charlie was returning to a shop that had rejected their custom in the past or, at the very least, from where their mother would have had no hope of purchasing anything at all.

The home clearly meant something very special to Charlie, who decades on could still recall the precise details of the furnishings. The main sitting room was carpeted, while the other rooms were laid with linoleum, an alternative to oilcloth invented and then patented by Frederick Walton in the mid-nineteenth century. The pattern books for 1908 offered an array of designs, some imitating geometric tiling, others patterned rugs, some plainer, but, as a material that was comfortable to walk on, durable and, crucially, easy to clean, it seemed that the Chaplin brothers were setting up home for the longer term. The furniture included a sitting-room suite (a sofa or 'couch', and two armchairs), around the fire was a raised brass fender with red leather seating, like those in a Pall Mall gentlemen's club, and in one corner was a wooden fretwork 'Moorish' screen. Opposite was a gilt framed 'pastel' of a nude model – perhaps originally from the Lambeth School of Art. The final expense was an upright piano at a cost of £15 – 'and although ... over our budget, we had value for it' during musical evenings together with friends. Charlie concluded that the overall effect was a cross between 'a Moorish cigarette shop and a French whorehouse'.[151] But 'we loved it.' As a 'cherished haven', he described how they both looked forward to coming back home to Glenshaw Mansions after touring with Karno's company: 'Sydney and I would sit in our bulky armchairs with smug satisfaction', and then Charlie would move from his armchair to the leather cushioned fender, 'testing them for comfort'.[152] While her sons were enjoying the fruits of their success, Hannah continued to languish in Cane Hill Asylum.

Fred Karno did not simply hire talent; he rigorously trained his performers in every skill required for his specific brand of variety entertainment, from singing and playing musical instruments, roller skating, juggling and acrobatics, to techniques for fake fighting and safely falling down several flights of stairs. Over 1908 and into 1909, Charlie was performing regularly in *Mumming Birds*. Effie Wisdom recalled seeing her childhood friend in this 'show within a show', with the various acts disrupted by rowdy audience members, including Charlie's 'Inebriated Swell', a part Syd had earlier played.[153] This sketch would be a hit in America, with the young Stan Laurel as Chaplin's understudy.

According to Charlie, it was during a run of *Mumming Birds*, at the Streatham Empire, that he first fell in love. The object of his affection was Hetty Kelly, fifteen years old and a dancer with Bert Coutt's 'Yankee Doodle Girls', who were performing at the same theatre.[154] Dressed as the drunk, in heavy make-up, looking decades older than his nineteen years, Charlie was standing in the wings absently watching the dance troupe's performance when he 'was suddenly held by two large brown eyes sparkling mischievously, belonging to a slim gazelle with a shapely oval face, a bewitching full mouth, and beautiful teeth – the effect was electric'. Hetty lived in Camberwell and for their first night out together, the two met at Kennington Gate, had a fraught dinner at the Trocadero in Piccadilly Circus, and then walked home towards Kennington

Florence Henrietta 'Hetty' Kelly, possibly photographed by Ernest Walter Histed in New York in 1911. Hetty's sister, the actress Edith Kelly married Frank Jay Gould (son of the American millionaire) in 1910 (hence Hetty's presence in the United States at that time). The year after the outbreak of the First World War, Hetty married Lieutenant Alan Edgar Horner and they lived in London's Mayfair. After Charlie Chaplin founded United Artists (with D. W. Griffiths, Mary Pickford and Douglas Fairbanks) in 1919, Hetty's brother, Arthur, became an executive.

Park via the Embankment. 'Camberwell Road', Charlie recalled 'was now touched with magic because Hetty Kelly lived there ... Shabby, depressing Camberwell Road, which I used to avoid, now had lure as I walked in its morning mist, thrilled at Hetty's outline in the distance coming towards me.'[155] When their 'affair' quickly fizzled out, Charlie later stated it was 'inevitable': 'After all, the episode was but a childish infatuation to her, but to me it was the beginning of a spiritual development, a reaching out for beauty.'[156]

Hetty Kelly became Charlie Chaplin's female ideal, which seems to have affected his relationships with women for the rest of his life. By his own admission he had hired sex workers, who had been a highly visible presence around the streets where he lived from childhood. This environment included the social habits formed around an official age of consent, which had only risen to sixteen in 1885 (as a result of William Stead's investigations into child prostitution), and the regularity of young motherhood (in and out of marriage) suggests that the Hill and Chaplin family's sexual attitudes and experiences were commonplace. This is not to excuse, but rather to place Charlie Chaplin's relationships into a broader historical as well as personal context.

Charlie's comments – reported by his eldest son in *My Father, Charlie Chaplin* – about his mother Hannah and her neglect (as he then saw it) would be tempered by the time his autobiography was published (a few years after Charles Chaplin junior's own memoir), but even so, his complex and contradictory feelings towards Hannah are still perceptible.

While his first feature-length movie *The Kid* was being filmed in 1920, Charlie's wife, Mildred Harris Chaplin, began divorce proceedings, citing 'mental cruelty.' The previous year the couple's infant son, Norman Spencer, died aged just three days; a tragedy that put enormous strain on their relationship. Charlie's eldest surviving son recalled reading 'poignant newspaper articles' by Mildred, for which, decades on, he reveals some sympathy, even empathy: 'She told of my father's moodiness, his periods of abstracted silence, his intense need to be alone, his long, lonely walks at night, the weird, sad music he used to improvise by the hour.'[157] Lita Grey, Charles Chaplin junior's mother, appeared in

The Kid when she was twelve and then, some time later, returned to star in *The Gold Rush* of 1924. During filming she and Charlie began a relationship and when she became pregnant, aged sixteen, they were married. As described by her eldest son, Lita was 'a lively young girl who should have still been in high school, enjoying parties and dates and all the things that go with teenage living'. Reflecting what his mother had told him, Charles Chaplin junior recalled how she was in awe of this older, 'great figure', and could not understand, much less cope with, his father's 'complex nature with its strange blend of introverted darkness and extroverted gaiety, or his almost fanatic devotion to work'. She, like Charlie, soon began to feel trapped in a prison 'in which she found nothing that resembled her romantic teenage dreams of love and marriage'.[158]

When Lita, too, filed for divorce just three years later, the published lurid accusations concerning the couple's sex life, as well as the fact that she had been young when their relationship began, caused a media storm about the star's 'School Girl Wife' that followed Charlie Chaplin until his death. J. Edgar Hoover, hell-bent on ridding America of 'Reds', discovered that Chaplin's turbulent private life was a more effective source of outrage than whether he was, or was not, a communist.

While her ex-husband was still alive, Lita published *My Life with Chaplin* in 1966: two years after *My Autobiography*, within which their marriage and aftermath is very briefly described. In one episode from Lita's book, set during the train journey back from their wedding in Mexico forty years before, she recalls Charlie saying to her: 'We could put an end to this misery if you'd just jump.'[159]

Soon after his brief liaison with Hetty Kelly, Charlie left for Paris with Karno's company and a season at the Folies-Bergère. After one performance, a 'celebrated musician' congratulated Chaplin, describing him as a 'true artist'. When Charlie asked who it was he had been speaking to, he was told it was Claude Debussy; 'Never heard of him,' he remarked.[160] The company returned to England and spent many months touring Britain: this period is quickly passed over in Charlie's autobiography. There was a rumour that Karno's American company manager was looking for a new lead comedian, and he alighted on the rising star Charlie Chaplin: 'This chance to go to the United States was what I needed. In England I felt I had reached the limit of my prospects; besides, my opportunities there were circumscribed. With scant educational background, if I failed as a music-hall comedian I would have little chance but to do menial work. In the States the prospects were brighter.'[161] Charlie hated saying goodbye, so, on leaving Glenshaw Mansions, 'I did not bother to wake Sydney, but left a note on the table stating: "Off to America. Will keep you posted. Love, Charlie."'[162]

Charlie returned from a successful American tour in June 1912, just two months after the RMS *Titanic* disaster had claimed over 1,500 fatalities, including Herbert Stead's brother, William. In a letter sent before his return to London, Syd had informed him that their grandfather, Charles Frederick Hill, was living in the Glenshaw Mansions flat – but by the time he arrived, Syd had married Minnie, a fellow performer, and given up the flat completely: the newly-weds were now lodging elsewhere on Brixton Road. Soon afterwards, the two brothers went to Cane Hill Asylum, but only Syd saw their mother in person. Hannah, Charlie later recounted, 'had just got over an obstreperous phase singing hymns, and had been confined to a padded room'. Syd told Charlie that she 'had been given shock treatment of icy cold showers and that her face was quite blue'. They decided then and there to transfer her to a private asylum, 'the same institution', Charlie recalled, 'in which England's great comedian, the late Dan Leno, had been confined'.[163] This was Peckham House in Camberwell. The Lambeth Board of Guardians and Cane Hill Hospital records confirm that Hannah was discharged from the asylum on 9 September 1912 to a 'private class' establishment, with a further note in the Cane Hill records that by 20 September she had 'Not improved'.[164]

Since returning to London, Charlie had been feeling rootless: the loss of the Glenshaw Mansions flat had added to his melancholy. In this troubled state, he later recalled, an episode confirmed his determination to return to America as soon as possible. He had joined Fred Karno and a party of guests for a weekend on the Guv'nor's new houseboat, *Astoria*, acknowledged as the finest craft of its type on the Thames. Some sense of its impressive appearance can be gleaned from an advertisement in the *Pall Mall Magazine* when the houseboat was put up for sale in 1913. Built of teak and mahogany, with steel girders and supports, the *Astoria*, as stated in the advertisement,

> comprises four bedrooms, bathrooms, with marble walls, dining salon, drawing-room, tiled kitchen, and scullery. The upper deck is covered by a span glass roof. There is an automatic water-tank filler and electric light installation. The principal rooms are fitted with fireplaces, and the owner lives on the boat all the year round, and there is absolutely no sign of dampness. The telephone is installed, and there is every possible comfort imaginable. The boat is magnificently fitted and furnished regardless of cost. It will be sold as it is, fully equipped, at a low figure.[165]

This magnificent houseboat, fitted out with all the modern conveniences and with more than a sprinkling of ostentation, represented Fred Karno's larger-than-life character and the measure of his success. Charlie recalled that at night the swags of brightly coloured electric lights looping around the entire boat were 'gay and charming, I thought'. But one man's beauty is another man's tat. As Charlie continues, after dinner the company drank coffee and smoked cigarettes on the upper deck, enjoying the warmth of an English summer evening:

> Suddenly, a falsetto, foppish voice began screaming hysterically: 'Oh, look at my lovely boat, everyone! Look at my lovely boat! And the lights! Ha! ha! Ha!' The voice went into hysterics of derisive laughter. We looked to see where the effusion came from, and saw a man in a rowing-boat, dressed in white flannels, with a lady reclining in the back seat. The ensemble was like a comic illustration from *Punch*.[166]

Pure snobbery, lack of grace, and delicacy: certainly no gentleman. Those on the receiving end of this derision responded as only they knew how: 'Karno leaned over the rail and gave him a very loud raspberry, but nothing deterred his hysterical laughter.' Then it was Charlie's turn: '"There is only one thing to do," I said: "to be as vulgar as he thinks we are." So I let out a violent flow of Rabelaisian invective, which was so embarrassing for his lady that he quickly rowed away.'[167] Charlie Chaplin concluded his recollection by observing: 'The idiot's ridiculous outburst was not a criticism of taste, but a snobbish prejudice against what he considered lower-class ostentatiousness ... This ever-present class tabulating I felt keenly while in England. It seems that this type of Englishman is only too quick to measure the other fellow's social inferiorities.'[168] Charlie sensed, like George Tinworth before him, that he now fell between two stools: at his very lowest ebb, as described by his son, he had been mocked by his poor working-class fellows for being even poorer than they; and now he was being mocked by a man of privilege, simply for enjoying the spoils of working-class prosperity.

Charlie, with the troupe that had recently toured America, began playing the halls around London. The show was a success, 'but all the time I was wondering if we'd ever get back to the States again. I loved England, but it was impossible for me to live there; because of my background I had a disquieting feeling of sinking back into a depressing commonplaceness.' So when he was told that the company had been booked for another US tour, Charlie Chaplin 'was elated'.[169] He sailed with the company on the *Oceanic* on 2 October 1912, never to live in London again.

A year later, George Tinworth left his home in Kew at ten past eight in the morning, as usual, and boarded the commuter train to Waterloo. When the train pulled into Putney, en route to Vauxhall Station, the modeller was discovered in a carriage, tipped forward uncomfortably on the seat. He was swiftly moved to the platform, but he was already dead before a doctor could reach him. He was a few months shy of his seventieth birthday. At the coroner's inquest, Ellen Digweed, his sister-in-law, said that George had been ill for some months, complaining of the cold and sitting in front of a fire covered in a shawl. He had not seen a doctor for three months: 'Mr. Tinworth leaves no family. For some years he was deeply concerned over the severe illness of his wife, who survives him.'[170] His wealth at death, following probate, was £549 9s 6d.[171]

George Tinworth's death was reported in national as well as local papers, including the *Daily Mirror* and *Daily Express*. The *South London Press*, which had long covered his career with tangible local pride, announced with regret that this 'FAMOUS WALWORTH BOY' had suffered a heart attack and this 'DISTINGUISHED ARTIST' was 'DEAD'.[172] Robert Wallace Martin attended the funeral at West Norwood Cemetery, arranged by George's younger brother Tom as executor. In a letter dated soon after, where he described meeting George at the Lambeth School of Art, Martin also records that 'G.T.' only had one other brother, Charley, whose 'widow & 4 or 5 grown up children & some of Tom's made up the mourners with some of GT's wifes relatives'. It is not clear whether Alice was present, but the 1911 census may offer an explanation: under 'infirmity', Alice is described as 'feeble minded'.*[173] A few Doulton workmen were also present. During the short ceremony, with his thoughts turning (inevitably) to the human predicament – how we live and then, all too soon, we die – Martin describes 'the Hill covered with thousands of tombs & all round outside the Cemetry thousands of houses'.[174] Several obituaries repeated the following anecdote as an indication of the man and his life. The Duke of Bedford was one of many visitors to George's studio at Doulton's Art Pottery. Indicating a terracotta relief of the Prodigal Son – the scene where, after a period of trial and financial failure, the son returns to the bosom of his family – the duke declared that George had made the figure, a young man in the Bible story, too old. 'Well, your grace,' replied George Tinworth, 'it tends to make a man look old if he hasn't a halfpenny in his pocket.'[175] George had included his own version of this incident in his unfinished memoir, but added a telling detail: 'Well I said I think when a man has not a half penny in his pocket it makes him look old, and the duke made answer, so it do, so it do.' George concludes, as we might expect, with no hint of deference: 'I thought to myself, what do you know about it.'[176]

---

*In the grim classification of the period, this term was used for someone whose mental capacity was considered above that of an 'idiot' or 'imbecile'. Alice died in 1938 in Camberwell.

THE PRODIGAL SON

1. THE FATTED CALF,
2. THE ELDER BROTHER,
3. THE FATHER,
4. THE BOY BRINGING THE RING,
5. THE OLD SHOES,
6. NEW SHOES, 7 PRODIGAL SON, 8 THE BEST ROBE,
9. THE OLD COAT,

WHEN I WAS MODELING THIS PANEL, THE OLD DUKE OF BEDFORD COME INTO MY ROOM WITH A FRIEND AND THE FRIEND SAID, HE THOUGHT I HAD MADE THE PRODIGAL SON LOOKING TO OLD. WELL I SAID I THINK WHEN A MAN HAS NOT A HALF PENNY IN HIS POCKET IT MAKES HIM LOOK OLD, AND THE DUKE MADE ANSWER SO IT DO, SO IT DO; I THOUGHT TO MY SELF WHAT DO YOU KNOW ABOUT IT

THIS PANEL WAS REJECTED BY THE FIENDS OF THE R.A.

Unnumbered page from George Tinworth's autobiography, with a photograph of his terracotta relief *The Prodigal Son*, created in 1875. The text above lists the key figures within the scene and beneath, George recalls his encounter with the Duke of Bedford, alongside 'the fiends of the R.A.', so called for rejecting one of his panels.

In February 1921 Charlie Chaplin's first feature-length film, the silent comedy-drama *The Kid*, premiered in the United States to ecstatic reviews. Produced, directed, scored by and starring the thirty-one-year-old Englishman, the film portrayed his now famous alter ego, the Little Tramp, finding and then raising an abandoned infant with only his wits and innate fellow feeling to guide him. The pair's hand-to-mouth existence, told through scenes alternating between a run-down attic and the rough streets beyond, and between whimsical comedy and full-blown slapstick, is brought to a crisis when the authorities remove the distraught child from the tramp's care, with the prospect of a miserable life in a state-run institution. In contrast with the real world, Chaplin was in complete control of how this story would end: individual right triumphs over state might, with the child and tramp tearfully and joyously reunited.

At this remarkable moment in his career, Charlie Chaplin was compelled to return to his place of birth for the first time since 1912. Much had changed. The Great War, of course, had impacted every level of society, and Chaplin by turn hoped and feared how far the old familiar places and the people he had lived among as a youth had been transformed. The war had highlighted key areas relating to working men. Once again, the physical health of those needed to fight was revealed to be a national disgrace; this collective neglect drew attention to the appalling conditions in which swathes of the population were still living.

At the same time, electoral restrictions remained after the Third Reform Act of 1884, which excluded many veterans from voting in any forthcoming general election (eventually called, after the armistice, for 14 December 1918). The war-time coalition government under Liberal prime minister David Lloyd George scrambled to respond to this blatant injustice by passing the Representation of the People Act in February 1918, which expanded the vote to all men aged over twenty-one. As a result, by that year, five of the six demands of the Chartists in the 1830s and 1840s, championed by the Independent Labour Party from the 1890s, had been fulfilled.*

---

*Annual Parliaments, thankfully, would never become law.

The Act included women aged over thirty, but with a property qualification that would not be removed until 1928. Even so in 1918, at a stroke, the electorate expanded from around eight to twenty-one million: the question was, who would the new working-class voter support to form a government? Just three years after Charlie Chaplin's visit, the United Kingdom would be governed by James Ramsay MacDonald's Labour Party (Keir Hardie had died in 1915). The minority government lasted less than a year, but it established that this young party, created to represent 'all who labour', was ready and able to form a viable national government.

For Charlie Chaplin, resident in America but still a British citizen, this period had been a mixed blessing. His success and corresponding wealth were now truly extraordinary. Just two years since leaving England, in a letter to Syd from Los Angeles dated 9 August 1914, he declared: 'I stay at the best Club in the city where all the millionaires belong ... I have my own valet, some class to me, eh what?'[177] Here Charlie comes across as both delighted and incredulous. Even in September 1921, he seemed to finally recognise the dramatic change in his circumstances only after he was shown to his cabin on the RMS *Olympic* (the sister liner of the *Titanic*). In his autobiography, he recalled his less salubrious journey to New York with Karno's Company ten years before, mistakenly stating it was the same ship to stress what had changed over that decade.* During the earlier journey, Charlie and his fellow performers had been given a tour of the first-class luxury suites by a steward, their guide stressing to his audience the 'prohibitive price' of such accommodation. But in 1921 Charlie could easily afford these extravagances, observing, 'I had known London as a struggling young nondescript from Lambeth; now as a man celebrated and rich I would be seeing London as though for the first time.'[178] How he travelled and in what comfort he would spend his time while in London – he was staying at the Ritz on Piccadilly – was an important indicator that he had left the poverty years behind. But there was always the nagging fear, no matter the outward trappings of wealth, that poverty was never far away.

---

*It was in fact the SS *Oceanic*.

And, because he was celebrated and rich, journalists were seeking his opinion on the most pressing issues in national and international current affairs. As he later recalled, he was asked: what message he had for the people of England after the devastation of the war? What did he think of the 'Irish question'? And what of the Bolsheviks in Russia?

The headlines were overwhelmingly ecstatic, but this was tempered by less favourable commentary that had been circulating since the outbreak of war in July 1914 and amplified after America joined the Allies in April 1917. Chaplin was accused of being unpatriotic, a coward and even a traitor for not enlisting, and was subjected to a sustained media campaign driven by the proprietor of the *Daily Mail*, Lord Northcliffe. If Chaplin had survived his harrowing childhood in the vermin-infested streets of South London, only to die in the blood-stained mud of the Western Front, he would not have been unique. Chaplin, a self-proclaimed pacifist – in a 1914 letter to Syd, he says, 'I hope they don't make you fight over there this war is terrible'[179] – had attempted to enlist in the United States, only to be rejected for being underweight.

In September 1921 the assistant editor of *John Bull*, Charles Pilley,* under the subheading 'SOME REFLECTIONS UPON THE CORONATION OF KING CHARLES THE THIRD', meaning Chaplin, declared himself bewildered that a mere comedian should be heralded with such exaggerated adulation. In his opinion piece, Pilley summarised Charlie's meteoric rise:

> Not very long ago, after some years of unrewarded effort upon the English stage, Mr. Charles Chaplin sailed to America, where fame and fortune were to arrive upon the wings of opportunity ... Owing to that peculiarity of the kinema which enables a comedian to be in some thousands of

---

*Of D. H. Lawrence's *Women in Love*, published in 1920, Pilley thundered: 'I do not claim to be literary critic, but I know dirt when I smell it and here it is in heaps – festering, putrid heaps which smell to high Heaven' ('A Book The Police Should Ban', *John Bull*, 17 September 1921).

places at once, the rewards of success are enormous, and soon Charlie Chaplin became rich beyond the dreams of avarice.

Pilley rightly acknowledged that by the early 1920s moviemaking was big business 'and if Charlie was a millionaire before, he seems in a fair way to become the richest man alive'. He goes on to grudgingly concede that his subject 'has added considerably to the gaiety of nations, and I daresay the world would be the poorer for his loss. But I see no reason why he should receive the honour we pay to heroes.' In the good old days, Pilley continued, heroes had, one way or another, made sacrifices 'for the public good'. What did comedians or performers know of sacrifice? In those more balanced days, he continued, 'men who simply made us laugh did not divide the honours with those who kept the Empire safe from foreign enemies or guided the ship of State safely through troubled waters into the haven of security'. 'True,' he continued, 'we won the war, and the men who led our armies in the field' – some of whom, at the time and since, were considered donkeys leading lions – 'received their mead of recognition, but not one of them had a tithe of the public adulation we have paid to Charlie Chaplin.' He then rekindled the accusations of cowardice:

> I am not much interested to enquire why the home-sickness, which so touchingly affects him at this juncture, did not manifest itself during the black years when the homes of Great Britain were in danger through the menace of the Hun. It may be true, as had been argued, that Charlie Chaplin was better employed playing funny tricks in front of a camera than he would have been doing manly things behind a gun ... The point is that, in my humble judgement, we ought not to lose our heads over a man whose chief title to respect is that he can play the fool with inimitable cleverness. It is not of this tinsel stuff that life is made.[180]

The use of 'tinsel' to describe Chaplin's contribution to the world is telling – gaudy, superficial, commonplace. It recalls the man mocking Fred Karno's glittering houseboat: the visible rewards of working-class success. The trouble is that life as experienced by Chaplin and millions like him over the decades – and of which Charles Pilley had little or no comprehension – had informed the style and content of his films: whether *A Night in the Show* (based on Karno's sketch *Mumming Birds*), *The Vagabond*, *The Pawnshop*, *Easy Street*, *A Dog's Life*, which Chaplin stated had been inspired by Thomas Burke's novel *Limehouse Nights*, and even *Shoulder Arms*, thought to be the first film comedy about war, daringly set in the trenches and released just before Armistice Day. Far from mere 'tinsel', this was the very stuff of life, and Pilley's derision, whether by accident or design, was directed at an entire class rather than one individual. The great irony was that cinema, the democratic art form of which Chaplin was then king, had caused the terminal decline of music hall, the previous dominant working-class art form that had created him.

Although many agreed with Pilley, the very soldiers to whom Chaplin was unfavourably compared adored him: one Wilfred Owen wrote to his mother in November 1916, 'I have quite a veneration for Charles Chaplin by the way. Made me laugh almost as much as H. G. Wells.'[181] The *Illustrated London News* understood the value of laughter during a time of crisis, even if *John Bull* and Northcliffe did not. The front page of the 10 August 1918 issue reproduced an illustration of injured American and Canadian servicemen lying in a military hospital in France, watching the Little Tramp projected onto the ceiling above them. The caption reads, 'Wounded men who are unable to sit up or leave their beds ... are enabled to enjoy the antics of Charlie Chaplin and other heroes and heroines of the "movies", like their more fortunate comrades.'[182] But Chaplin's blend of tragi-comedy did much more than provide entertainment: to repurpose James Keir Hardie's phrase concerning the social settlements, his films encouraged his audiences 'to develop the human relationship'. Or, as E. M. Forster famously put it: to 'only connect'.*

Given the antipathy within sections of the press, however, the trepidation Chaplin felt on returning to England was

---

*From *Howards End*, published in 1910.

Chaplin photographed outside the Ritz, Piccadilly, September 1921. The taxi arrived at the hotel's side entrance in Arlington Street and was immediately surrounded by people eager to see the home-grown, self-made Hollywood star.

understandable. His ship docked at Southampton, where he was mobbed by well-wishers, after which he boarded a train to London. As he looked out of the carriage window, while the train entered the suburbs of South London, he exclaimed, 'London! There are familiar buildings ... I expected that England would be altered. It isn't. It's the same. The same as I left it, in spite of the War.' And then, as the train chugged through Lambeth, he cried, 'There's Doulton's Potteries! And look, there's the Queen's Head public-house that my cousin [presumably his uncle Spencer] used to own ... Now we are coming into the Cut.'[183] He was mobbed again while trying to leave Waterloo Station in a taxi, and once again outside the Ritz.

Within hours of his arrival at the hotel, Chaplin slipped out through the back door and hailed another taxi (in another version of this episode, recounted by Effie Wisdom, it is a chauffeur-driven Rolls-Royce). The Lambeth nobody, now the most famous man in the world, was going home. Yet, reflecting on his return in 1921 to the streets of his youth, Chaplin declared: 'As I wandered through Kennington, all that had happened to me there seemed like a dream, and what had happened to me in the States was the reality. Yet,' he confessed, 'I had a feeling of slight uneasiness that perhaps those gentle streets of poverty still had the power to trap me in the quick sands of their hopelessness.'[184] His elder son had stated that one, if not *the* reason for Charlie's return in 1921 was to see 'a boyhood sweetheart' – Hetty Kelly – only to be told that she had died during the great influenza epidemic of 1918–20: 'My father's idyllic dream of Hetty continued to haunt him through the years – perhaps it was partly because she had become inaccessible to him that his feelings of tenderness for her lasted so long.'[185]

The fear of poverty continued. But in addition to the famed traits of the working class, courage and humour, there were others that both Tinworth and Chaplin, the boys from Walworth and the men of Lambeth, exemplified: self-respect and pride in where they came from. In his memoirs of the Robert Browning Settlement, *Eighteen Years in the Central City Swarm*, published in 1912, Herbert Stead told a story about a group of Walworth folk who were touring St Paul's Cathedral and, while gazing upon the tomb of Lord Nelson, their guide, the Anglican Bishop of Stepney declared, rather grandly, 'This may be termed the very heart of London.' To which came the reply from one of the gathering, 'Of the city's square mile, maybe, yes,' and then continuing, without a pause, 'but of the Metropolis as a whole, no. The geographical centre of the County of London lies in Walworth,' he informed the bishop. 'Walworth is the heart of London. Walworth is the heart of the Heart of Empire.'[186]

Ernest Leslie and Nellie Elizabeth Robinson, photographed outside St George-the-Martyr, Battersea Park Road, Battersea on 2 July 1927 by Walter A. Lee of Clapham Junction.

EPILOGUE

'Pretty Good Metal'

William Henry Partridge was born in Rotherhithe, Kent – now in South-East London – on 30 October 1804.[1] He was baptised at St Mary Magdalene in Bermondsey and as an adult followed his father's trade as a corn miller. He married Elizabeth Leach at St Saviour's Church, Southwark in 1830.[2] Their daughter Elizabeth Sarah, baptised on 18 December 1836 at St John the Evangelist in Waterloo, married William Robinson, a gilder, at the same church on 12 March 1855.[3] Charlie Chaplin's grandmother, Mary Ann, had married her first husband at this church ten months earlier.

In the 1881 census, William Partridge, by now described as a widower, is a lodger at 39 Granby Place, a street in the Lower Marsh area of Lambeth.[4] The head of his household is named as John Mills, a general labourer, living with his wife Rachel, both in their late twenties. This street, as noted by George Duckworth in 1899, would be demolished as part of the extension of Waterloo Station. Curiously, on the same date, William Partridge's daughter, son-in-law and grandchildren are resident nearby, at 11 Gloucester Street: William Robinson (forty-four), a carver and gilder, Elizabeth (forty-three), William (twenty-five), an omnibus conductor, and Elizabeth (seventeen), Edward (fifteen), John (twelve) and Alfred (four), all listed as scholars: four children all engaged in formal learning.

Four years later, William Partridge left Granby Place to walk a long, lonely mile to the Lambeth Workhouse on Renfrew Road. On 22 February 1884 he was aged seventy-nine and immediately discharged to the infirmary. He returned to the workhouse proper in March, only to be sent to the infirmary three months later. There was a brief spell at his lodgings in Granby Place, but between 30

July and 18 November he was, once again, an inmate of Lambeth Workhouse. Another month in the infirmary was followed by readmittance (for the last time) to the workhouse. On 6 January 1885, he was transferred to the infirmary and died there on 15 January 1885, the cause given on his death certificate as 'Senectus [old age] – Bronchitis Longa'. He was eighty years old. The last year of his life – after decades working in a respected trade – was beset with serious illness, the ignominy of pauperism and nothing but local poor relief to fall back on: presumably his family could not afford to pay for his care and the Old Age Pensions Act, part of the Liberal government's social welfare reforms of 1908–1914, came too late.[5] Hannah Chaplin, having lived in the Waterloo area, like William, for several years – in lodgings on Oakley Street and York Road among others – would enter the same infirmary a decade later; within a few years, her two sons Charlie and Sydney would become inmates of the workhouse, to be sent to the Norwood Schools for paupers before returning to live with their father, his mistress and infant on nearby Kennington Road.

The Robinson family, in contrast to Elizabeth's father, enjoyed a settled home life. William Robinson's business was registered in the *Post Office London Directory* at 11 Gloucester Street for two decades, with William listed as variously a gilder, a wood carver and, combining the two, a 'Picture Frame Maker'.[6] By 1891 one of his sons, William junior, now aged thirty-five, had joined his father's trade. Elizabeth is a tailoress, as is her daughter, Elizabeth junior (twenty-seven); John (twenty-six) is a 'fitter of looking glasses', and Alfred Albert, born 21 March 1877, is still a scholar.[7] Around this date, according to family recollections, the Robinson carver-gilders were making picture frames for the National Gallery, just across the Thames at Trafalgar Square, and the new National Gallery of British Art at Millbank near Vauxhall Bridge (opened in 1897). The traditional, heavy, ornately carved and gilded wooden frames, used to embellish oil paintings, were pushed by William and his son around the dirty, busy streets of the metropolis on barrows covered in blankets. Some of these frames may still be hanging on the walls of the National Gallery or of what is now Tate Britain.

By 1897, Alfred Albert was helping his father and brother in the family business, and that year he married eighteen-year-old Eliza Letitia Davies at St John the Evangelist in Waterloo Road, the Robinsons' favoured church.[8] This is the same area and around the same time that the leader of the Forty Thieves gang, Polly Carr, had been living in nearby Stamford Street and when the 'Hooligan Gang' were marauding around Southwark.

By 1902, when their third son Ernest Leslie was born, Alfred and Eliza had moved to shared accommodation in Battersea, first at 6 Stewart's Road, then 81 Wadhurst Road (on census night in 1911, five individuals were sharing three rooms) and, by 1921, 9 Mundella Road, where eight family members (aged from forty-four to three and a half) occupied five rooms.[9] Ernest Leslie, called Ern, loved music and, although he could not read scores, taught himself to play the piano. He picked up songs 'by ear' and then improvised. In the 1921 census, then almost nineteen (he was just too young to have fought in 'The Great War'), Ern's most recent occupation is listed as an office porter for the Great Western Railway, but at this time he was 'out of work'. According to family anecdote, this period of unemployment affected him for the rest of his life, but not as you might think. On one occasion, when he was at his lowest ebb, with little money to his name, he was playing the piano in a local pub, but no one would stand him a drink. He swore he would never put himself in such a humiliating position ever again: this was the last time Ern touched alcohol.

It is likely through a mutual love of ragtime, jazz and popular American musicals like Sigmund Romberg's *The Desert Song* (1926) that Ern met Nellie Elizabeth Gould, who sang at local venues on amateur night, including the Grand 'Palace of Varieties' at Clapham Junction. They married in 1927 at St George-the-Martyr, Battersea – Ern's profession is now 'auto-collector' – and in the wedding album, under various photographs from the day, the bridegroom wrote cheeky captions like 'The Chief Mourners', 'Outside Old Bailey – Just After Sentence'.[10] By 1930, the Grand had been converted into a cinema, where the people of Clapham and Battersea could watch films starring their fellow South Londoner, now international star, Charlie Chaplin – his post-Depression critique on

The wedding party, photographed by Walter A. Lee of Clapham Junction, 1927. In the front row are (left) Alfred Albert and Eliza Robinson, their daughters Kathleen and Violet, Ern and Nellie, the bridesmaids Grace and Alice (Nellie's sisters), their mother Polly and (far right) their father Thomas, and brother Arthur Alfred.

Nellie's photograph of Ern and P.B. eating ice creams. On the reverse is written 'C 1935', so probably a summer holiday at Clacton-on-Sea, Essex, with P.B. (in her knitted swimsuit) aged five.

capitalism, *Modern Times* (1936), would have been particularly resonant to this audience – alongside another Karno success story, now one half of comedy duo Laurel and Hardy.

Prior to the birth of their only child, Patricia Betty, nicknamed 'P.B.', on 29 August 1930, Ern and Nellie were living in shared lodgings at 31 Ingrave Street: they are both listed on the electoral roll for Battersea in that year.[11] By 1938 they had moved several times, finally renting the second floor at 98 Queens Road, the same street where, as I have suggested above, Fred Karno's lover Marie Moore and her family had been living for several decades at the turn of the century.[12] P.B. followed in her parents' love of music, but rather than teaching herself the piano, she was given private lessons and eventually won a student scholarship: this follows the ambition of another working-class family, the Rowletts, fifty years before. No. 98 Queens Road – with separate households on each of the three main floors – would have rung with the strains of Beethoven and Irving Berlin, teased out from an old upright piano.

Members of the Gould and Robinson families were renters on the same street, while others still lodged on Mundella Road in Nine Elms, including Nellie's parents Pollie and Thomas Gould. Ern, who smoked all his adult life and suffered from asthma, dreamed of living in his own home in a more rural setting, with a garden to grow roses, lilies, sweet peas and violas, rather than renting a floor in someone else's house. And in 1939 he and Nellie put that dream into action, moving west to Hayes, Middlesex: their eight-year old daughter was so distressed to leave her beloved Battersea school that she ran home crying on her last day.

In the early hours of 10 September 1940, a German bombing raid destroyed most of Mundella Road. Some family members, now homeless, moved out to Hayes, including Nellie's younger sisters Alice and Grace, while some remained in South London. That same year, through his 'Great Dictator' character, Charlie Chaplin stirred the people of the world to unite and use their power for good, and three years later he delivered his BBC radio broadcast, celebrating the courage and humour of his fellow Londoners, among them the Robinsons and the Goulds, and his conviction that they had won 'by blood and tears' the right to a

P.B. aged five, photographed at the Ardington Studios,
Arding & Hobbs, Clapham Junction on 5 June 1936.

better future. And on 5 July 1945, thirty years after Keir Hardie's death, these working-class Londoners, men and women, used their hard-won power to vote for the radical change set out in one general election manifesto: 'The Labour Party makes no baseless promises. The future will not be easy. But this time the peace must be won. The Labour Party offers the nation a plan which will win the Peace for the People.' The plan to slay the five giants of want, disease, ignorance, squalor and idleness was presented under the simple headings: JOBS FOR ALL; INDUSTRY IN THE SERVICE OF THE NATION; HOUSES AND THE BUILDING PROGRAMME; EDUCATION AND RECREATION; HEALTH OF THE NATION AND ITS CHILDREN; SOCIAL INSURANCE AGAINST THE RAINY DAY. The post-war Labour government would establish universal social security for all Britons 'from cradle to grave', bringing to an end the infamous Poor Law system.

And eighty years after that, this book, telling individual working-class stories, a people's history, was written by P.B.'s daughter, a resident of Charlie Chaplin's London.

It is dedicated to my mother: who lived an ordinary, remarkable life.

Ern's photograph of Grace, Nellie and P.B. eating toffee apples on the beach at Thorpe Bay, Southend-on-Sea in 1936. Chaplin had visited this Essex seaside town as a child and then adult.

ACKNOWLEDGEMENTS

I wanted the lives of my own South London family to be part of the *Hard Streets* narrative but, initially, I was not sure how. What happened over the year leading to my mother's death in June 2024, as I was researching and writing the first draft, strengthened that resolve and indicated a solution. Thanks to my father, John for his blessing to reproduce family photographs. My mother's happy, big-hearted nature and her cheeky humour illuminate these old photographs, as does the love and bond between Nanny, Grandad and their beautiful, kind and delightful only child.

Given the personal circumstances over the creation of *Hard Streets*, I must first acknowledge the help, support and love of friends, colleagues, neighbours and family, in particular Auntie Beryl and Peter, Tabitha Barber, Christine Busher, Natasha Cade, Susanna Eastburn, Sarah Fraser, Jenny Gabrysch, Caro Howell, Tim Knapman, Roy Lidstone, Anne Lyles, Sarah McBryde, David McCulloch, Keith Miller, Franny Moyle, Romy Murray, Clare and Stephen Pardy, Matthew Plampin, Eileen Read, Christine Riding, James Robinson, Wendy Sheikh, Kathleen Soriano, Evelyn Taylor, David Teather, Peter Trippi and Will Tuckett.

Having caught the family history bug, I am delighted, after many decades, to be in communication with my cousin Lawrence in Australia. I hope other cousins – known and, currently, unknown – will contact me via my website *www.jacquelineriding.com*

My deep gratitude and thanks to the team at Profile Books: Cecily Gayford who championed the *Hard Streets* proposal back in 2023; and the staff and freelancers who steered it from early draft to glorious completion, Nick Humphrey, Emily Frisella, Robert Loyko-Greer, Georgina Difford, Nick de Somogyi, Sam Matthews, Aurora Engen, Steve Coventry-Panton and Jonathan Harley. A shout out to my previous editors, Michael Fishwick (Bloomsbury) and Richard Milbank (Head of Zeus) who kick-started and supported my first and second forays into trade non-fiction.

Many thanks to the brilliant Rosalind Crone who read and commented on the first full draft, and Arnold Lozano from the Chaplin Office for his help and advice. David Robinson's enormous Chaplin biography was my starting point and to hand throughout. Thanks to Kevin Brownlow, Caroline Brownlow and James Spinney for providing me with a transcript of Effie Wisdom's audio interview and for allowing me to quote from the text. My thanks and appreciation to the following individuals, archives and libraries: Alison Young of the British Music Hall Society; Croydon Archives; David Crump; Lambeth Archives; London Archives; Mandy Southern and the London Library staff; London School of Economics; Jonathan Oates at Southall Library (Ealing Borough); Jessa Brown, Patricia Dark, Chris Scales at Southwark Archives; Stoke-on-Trent City Archives; Mark Pomeroy, archivist of the Royal Academy of Arts; The National Archives; and Sarah Wise, whose seminar on Charles Booth at the London Archives was extremely helpful.

After a book proposal unexpectedly fizzled, my agent Bill Hamilton asked me, in his doughty onward-and-upward manner, what else have you got? I said I had a vague idea based on the intriguing presence of plaques declaring 'Charlie Chaplin Lived Here', which I had seen from the top deck of 59 buses while travelling up and down Kennington and Brixton Roads. OK, he replied, write it up, let's see how it goes. And here we are. Thank you!

Finally, in recent weeks I have had the pleasure of corresponding with the granddaughter of Emily Rivett, the girl who was Walworth's May Queen in 1898, later an apron-machinist and then, before the Great War, a teacher at the Robert Browning Settlement. Our exchanges are a reminder of how close the Victorians and Edwardians are to those living in the twenty-first century, alongside the pride that we, their descendants have in our working-class ancestors and our history.

Jacqueline Riding
Lambeth, South London
November 2025

PICTURE CREDITS

p. ii   Still from *The Kid*, 1921 © Alamy/Moviestore Collection Ltd.

p. viii   The cover of a four-page leaflet printed and published by the London Convention Council in 1941, including a full transcription of Chaplin's speech from *The Great Dictator*. Author's Collection.

p. 10   George Tinworth photographed decorating a vase in his studio at Doulton's Pottery, Lambeth, c.1904. Author's Collection.

p. 18   *A Physical Force Chartist Arming For The Fight*. Illustration by John Leech published in *Punch or The London Charivari*, vol. 15, 1848, p. 101. Author's Collection.

p. 20   Wet plate photograph of the Lambeth riverfront looking south towards Vauxhall by William Strudwick c.1867. This image was reproduced by kind permission of London Borough of Lambeth, Archives Department.

p. 22   Page 5 of George Tinworth's autobiography written c.1910–13. © The George Tinworth archive, London Borough of Southwark.

p. 39   Page 13 from George Tinworth's autobiography. © The George Tinworth archive, London Borough of Southwark.

p. 59   *William Cuffay*. Lithograph based on a drawing by William Dowling, 1848 © National Portrait Gallery, London.

p. 62   *Out-Door Relief*. Illustration by Phiz [Hablot Knight Browne] in James Grant, *Sketches in London: with twenty-four humorous illustrations by 'Phiz', and others* (London: T. Tegg, 1840), p. 244. Courtesy of the Wellcome Collection.

p. 65   *The Broker's Man*. Etching by George Cruikshank, from Charles Dickens's *Sketches by Boz*, 1836. Courtesy of the Wellcome Collection.

p. 75   *The Drunkard's Home*. Coloured etching by George Cruikshank, c.1842, after himself. Courtesy of the Wellcome Collection.

p. 77   George Cruikshank, *The Bottle: Plate VI*. Etching by George Cruikshank, 1847, after himself. Courtesy of the Wellcome Collection.

p. 94   *A Workhouse Dinner.* Illustration by Phiz [Hablot Knight Browne] in James Grant, *Sketches in London: with twenty-four humorous illustrations by 'Phiz', and others* (London: T. Tegg, 1840), p. 244. Courtesy of the Wellcome Collection.

p. 102   *Study from Life.* Terracotta relief by George Tinworth, 1870, illustrated in Edmund Gosse, *A Critical Essay on the Life and Works of George Tinworth* (London, 1883), illustration 1, catalogue p. 48. Used with permission courtesy of the London Library.

p. 120   Page 1 from George Tinworth's autobiography. © The George Tinworth archive, London Borough of Southwark.

p. 125   Page 47 from George Tinworth's autobiography, with a photograph of John Sparkes. © The George Tinworth archive, London Borough of Southwark.

p. 129   *An Associate of the Royal Academy Inspecting the Lambeth School of Art.* Illustration from *The Graphic*, 1 November 1884, p. 450 © Alamy/Penta Springs Limited.

p. 133   *The Crossing Sweeper.* Engraving by Charles William Sharpe, 1864, after William Powell Frith, 1858. Courtesy of the Wellcome Collection.

p. 138   *Portrait of a Man.* Terracotta bust by George Tinworth, late nineteenth century. Yale Center for British Art. Courtesy of the Yale Center for British Art, Friends of British Art Fund.

p. 141   Page 69 from George Tinworth's autobiography. © The George Tinworth archive, London Borough of Southwark.

p. 142   Photograph of Hannah Chaplin in stage costume. With permission from the The Chaplin Archives. Copyright © and/or Property of Roy Export Company Limited. All Rights Reserved

p. 145   *London Nomads.* Woodburytype photograph by John Thomson, c.1876 in J. Thomson and A. Smith Headingley, *Street Life in London* (London: Sampson Low, Marston, Searle and Rivington, 1877) © Alamy/SJArt.

p. 150   Photograph of George Tinworth wearing a medal. Author's Collection.

p. 152   Unnumbered page from George Tinworth's autobiography, with a photograph of *The Crucifixion*. © The George Tinworth archive, London Borough of Southwark.

p. 162   Sheet music cover for *Pals That Time Cannot Alter!*, written by Charles Chaplin and Will Godwin, sung by Charles Chaplin. Colour lithograph, published 1900. With permission from the The Chaplin Archives. Copyright © and/or Property of Roy Export Company Limited. All Rights Reserved

Picture Credits

p. 181 *Sunday Morning in the New Cut, Lambeth*. Wood engraving, published in the *Illustrated London News*, 27 January 1872. Author's Collection.

p. 183 Photograph of James Keir Hardie by an unknown photographer, c.1892 © Getty Images/London Stereoscopic Company/Stringer.

p. 194 Detail of *Caught in Time*. Photograph from the *Leisure Hour* article 'A Day in the Life of a Workhouse Boy', 1902. This image was reproduced by kind permission of London Borough of Lambeth, Archives Department.

p. 205 Photograph of infant pupils from the Hanwell Schools,1897. With permission from the The Chaplin Archives. Copyright © and/or Property of Roy Export Company Limited. All Rights Reserved

p. 214 *Caught in Time*. Photograph from the *Leisure Hour* article 'A Day in the Life of a Workhouse Boy', 1902. This image was reproduced by kind permission of London Borough of Lambeth, Archives Department.

p. 224 Photograph of R. Johnson greengrocer's shop, c.1897–8. This image was reproduced by kind permission of London Borough of Lambeth, Archives Department.

p. 227 Photograph of Kennington Cross, c.1903. Author's Collection.

p. 231 *Sufferers from the Floods*. Woodburytype photograph by John Thomson c.1876 in J. Thomson and A. Smith Headingley, *Street Life in London* (London: Sampson Low, Marston, Searle and Rivington, 1877) © Alamy/EMU history.

p. 234 *Playing Mother*. Pencil sketch by Dorothy Tennant, c.1890. © National Galleries of Scotland. Miss Helen Barlow Bequest 1976.

p. 268 Photograph of Emily Rivett as May Queen, 1898 © Robert Browning Settlement Papers from the collections of Southwark Archives, London Borough of Southwark.

p. 271 Page 517 from *Men who Reach the Masses*, c.1900 © Robert Browning Settlement Papers from the collections of Southwark Archives, London Borough of Southwark.

p. 282 Unnumbered page from George Tinworth's autobiography, with a photograph of his panel in memory of Lord Shaftesbury. © The George Tinworth archive, London Borough of Southwark.

p. 284 Photograph of Fred Karno in 'petticoats', c.1888 © Alamy/RGR Collection.

p. 290 *The Last Test Match at the Oval*. Photograph by R. W. Thomas, 1899. Author's Collection.

p. 334 Photograph of Wal Pink's stage play *Repairs* (possibly with Charlie

Chaplin's handwriting), 1906. With permission from the The Chaplin Archives. Copyright © and/or Property of Roy Export Company Limited. All Rights Reserved

p. 339 Photograph of Florence Henrietta 'Hetty' Kelly, possibly taken by Ernest Walter Histed in New York in 1911. With permission from the The Chaplin Archives. Copyright © and/or Property of Roy Export Company Limited. All Rights Reserved

p. 346 Unnumbered page from George Tinworth's autobiography, with a photograph of his terracotta relief The Prodigal Son, created in 1875. © The George Tinworth archive, London Borough of Southwark.

p. 352 Chaplin photographed outside the Ritz, Piccadilly, September 1921 © Topical Press Agency/Stringer.

p. 354 Photograph of Ernest Leslie and Nellie Elizabeth Robinson by Walter A. Lee of Clapham Junction, 1927. Author's Family Collection.

p. 358 Photograph of the Robinson and Gould wedding party by Walter A. Lee of Clapham Junction, 1927. Author's Family Collection.

p. 358 Nellie Robinson's photograph of Ern and PB eating ice-cream cones, 1935. Author's Family Collection.

p. 360 Photograph of PB aged five, taken at Arding & Hobbs, Clapham Junction, 5 June 1936. Author's Family Collection.

p. 361 Ern's photograph of Grace, Nellie and PB eating toffee apples on the beach at Thorpe Bay, Southend-on-Sea, 1936. Author's Family Collection.

NOTES

Prologue: 'The Dignity of a People'
1. *The Times*, 18 October 1938.
2. *Radio Times*, 5 March 1943: 'Transatlantic Call – People to People' ('No. 5 – "Lambeth Walk", by Marjorie Banks. Bob Trout, the well-known American broadcaster, visits South London, where, in a street made famous the world over by the popular song and dance, he meets the men and women of London at war'); schedule 'for the Forces' (5 p.m., 7 March 1943); Chaplin's words quoted in the *Daily News* (London), 8 March 1943.
3. *Cambridge Independent Press*, 8 November 1901.
4. Quoted in Carr (2017), p. 17.
5. Chaplin (1922), p. 59.
6. TNA, FO/395/663: 'Correspondence regarding Charles Chaplin's "The Dictator"', fol. 483–504; 'Report from the British Consulate, Los Angeles' (17 May 1939), fol. 489–91; see also Carr (2017), p. 2.
7. Ibid.: Letter from Rowland Kenney to Joseph Brooke-Wilkinson (16 June 1939), fol. 497–8; Letter from Joseph Brooke-Wilkinson to Rowland Kenney (21 June 1939), fol. 503–4; Rowland Kenney, file note (dated 24 June 1939), fol. 502.
8. TNA, KV/2/3700: No. 18, J. H. Marriott, file note (17 November 1952).
9. TNA, KV/2/3700: 'Charles Spencer Chaplin' (1952–8); 'Note for PF.710,549', signed by H. P. Goodwyn (24 February 1958).
10. Vincent (1982); Griffin (2014).
11. Vincent (1989); Mitch (1992).
12. Thomson and Smith (1877), pp. 24–7.
13. Introduction to Chaplin (2003) [*My Autobiography*] p. 4: henceforth *MA*.
14. George Tinworth, 'The Life of G. Tinworth: A London Boy that become Wheelwright and Sculptor', manuscript autobiography, SA, 920 TIN, p. 1: henceforth GTA.
15. Ibid., p. 4.
16. Ibid.
17. Ibid., p. 6.
18. Geduld (2019), p. 1.

1. Milk Street: 'The Necessaries of Life'

1   GTA, p. 16.
2   Ibid.
3   Chaplin (1979) [*My Early Years*], p. 1: henceforth *MEY*; *MA*, p. 9. All subsequent references give the pagination of both editions.
4   *Oxford English Dictionary* [henceforth *OED*], **cottage**, *n*., 1.a., citing Defoe, *Religious Courtship* (1722).
5   *Shoreditch Observer*, 28 March 1857.
6   See Roberts (1851).
7   Shelley (1832), p. 20.
8   GTA, p. 18.
9   Ibid., p. 37.
10 On communal childcare, see Ross (1993), pp. 133–7.
11 Mayhew (1850), p. 5.
12 GTA, p. 6.
13 Steinbach (2004), p. 11.
14 TLA, P85/MRY1, Item 395 (28 November 1804).
15 TNA, RG4/4202, Baptismal Register, York Street Chapel, Lock's Fields, Walworth, p. 13 (11 October 1812).
16 Ibid., pp. 2 and 4. Jabez was born 9 April 1807, and baptised 10 May 1807.
17 Christiana and Jabez were buried at St Laurence, Upminster, Essex, on 20 November and 28 November 1808 respectively (Essex Record Office, D/P 117/1/3: Burial Register, St Laurence, Upminster, p. 4).
18 TNA, RG4/1382, Baptismal Register, Upminster Hill Chapel (Independent), Essex, (11 October 1812); TNA, RG4/4202, p. 13.
19 Keziah, Caleb and Joshua are registered as born in Upminster, Essex and baptised at Upminster Hill Chapel (Independent), Essex (TNA, RG 4/1382, n.p.; digital image 21).
20 See Davenport (2020).
21 TNA, RG 4/4202, p. 13.
22 GTA, p. 7.
23 Gosse (1883), p. 7.
24 GTA, p. 1.
25 Ross (1993), p. 9.
26 For Tinworth's mention of Caleb, see GTA, p. 6.
27 Essex Record Office, D/P 177/1/10: Burials Register, St Laurence, Upminster (2 March 1815), p. 5 (no. 33).
28 'To an Infant Sister in Heaven', in Clare (2004), p. 5.
29 GTA, p. 14.
30 TLA, P92/TRI/018 (2 August 1841).
31 GTA, p. 12.
32 Ibid.
33 Ibid., p. 14.
34 Ibid., p. 13.

35 For the Surrey Chapel and 'The Ring', see Roberts and Godfrey (1950).
36 GTA, p. 14.
37 SA, 2022/25: York Street Chapel, Register of Members, 1790–1863. Jane is 'Ad[mission]. No. 1053' and her address is given as 'at Messrs. Jones, Lloyd & Lothbury'; there is a 'Mary Ann Daniel, Ad. No. 1815, who joined on 2 December 1855, and who was resident 'at Mr. Leftwich's Walworth Road'.
38 SA, RBSP Folder PC 360.76. White's document was read out at the inauguration of the Robert Browning Settlement on 14 June 1895.
39 Ibid.
40 GTA, pp. 12–14.
41 SA, RBSP 2022/25: York Street Chapel, Register of Members, 1790–1863.
42 Greenwood (1874), p. 288.
43 Lewis (1984), p. 8.
44 See Steinbach (2004), pp. 112–14.
45 See Lewis (1984), p. 10.
46 See Steinbach (2004), pp. 11 and 237; and Clark (1995), chapters 12 and 13.
47 Steinbach (2004), p. 13.
48 Quoted in Lewis (1984), p. 12.
49 Ross (1993), p. 5.
50 Mayhew (1850), p. 5.
51 Ibid.
52 See Shannon (2024).
53 Mayhew (1850), pp. 5–6.
54 GTA, p. 15.
55 See Ditchfield (1896), pp. 97–9.
56 GTA, p. 28.
57 Ibid.
58 A Vision of Britain through Time, www.visionofbritain.org.uk/unit/10128742/cube/TOT_POP
59 *Illustrated London News*, 20 August 1842.
60 GTA, pp. 16–18.
61 Ibid., p. 16.
62 *Illustrated London News*, 20 August 1842.
63 GTA, p. 29.
64 *Evening Star*, 18 August 1842.
65 *Illustrated London News*, 22 August 1846.
66 Lodge (2024), pp. 15–18.
67 Smith (1857), p. 257; see also Crone (2012), chapter 6 ('The Rise of Modern Crime Reporting'), pp. 209–56.
68 Clay (1861), pp. 509–10 and 533–4; see also Crone (2022), p. 87.
69 *MEY*, p. 94; *MA*, p. 94.
70 For the criminal justice system, the Bloody Code and its rationalisation, see Emsley (1996), pp. 251–3 and Devereaux (2023), pp. 284–320.
71 Bulwer-Lytton (1830), vol. 3, p. 278.

72 Bulwer-Lytton (1874), p. vii ('Preface to the Edition of 1840').
73 The author acknowledged this in his preface to its 1848 edition: see Bulwer-Lytton (1874), pp. ix–xii.
74 GTA, p. 16.
75 Ibid., p. 5.
76 Goodway (2002), p. 125.
77 GTA, p. 40.
78 Ibid., p. 18.
79 Ibid., p. 50.
80 St. John (1857), pp. 254–5.
81 GTA, p. 40.
82 St John (1857), p. 255.
83 *Illustrated London News*, 15 April 1848.
84 William Edward Kilburn, *The Chartist Meeting on Kennington Common* (daguerreotype, 10 April 1848): Royal Collection Trust, RCIN 2932484 (www.rct.uk/collection).
85 Chase (2007), p. 302.
86 *The Times*, 21 August 1848.
87 GTA, p. 88.

2. Victory Place: 'Our Only Crime Being Poverty'

1 GTA, p. 19.
2 Ibid., p. 18.
3 Ibid., p. 20. (Tinworth says he 'was about 8 years old then I think', but he must have been younger, given he was at Victory Place in 1851 when he was that age).
4 Dickens (1839), p. 30.
5 GTA, p. 20.
6 Ibid. (under insert).
7 TNA, HO 107/1566/508/14.
8 *Morning Herald*, 7 December 1848.
9 Ibid.
10 TNA, HO 107/1566/508/14.
11 GTA, p. 20 (under insert).
12 Ibid, p. 19.
13 Doyle (1893), pp. 167–8 and 177.
14 *London Evening Standard*, 20 October 1852.
15 *South London Journal*, 28 July 1857.
16 TNA, RG 9 341/75/33 (5 Hope Place [Street]).
17 I am indebted to Rosalind Crone for her summary of the complex situation regarding working-class formal education and learning prior to 1870.
18 GTA, p. 56.
19 Crone (2022), p. 250.
20 *South London Press*, 1 February 1873.

21 Parkinson (2008), p. 25.
22 GTA, p. 21.
23 Reeves (1913), p. 19.
24 Bosanquet (1896), pp. 60–1.
25 Quoted in Lewis (1984), p. 39.
26 GTA, p. 22.
27 Ibid.
28 See Higginbotham, 'The Workhouse', www.workhouses.org/uk.
29 *An Account* (1732), p. iii.
30 Ibid., pp. 75–7.
31 Ibid., pp. 76–7.
32 Ibid., p. 77.
33 Ibid., p. 78.
34 See Higginbotham, 'The Workhouse', www.workhouses.org/uk.
35 LSE, BOOTH/B/363, p. 77.
36 *Morning Advertiser*, 22 April 1840.
37 *Lloyd's Weekly Newspaper*, 31 March 1844.
38 TLA, SOBG/101/14.
39 Lewis (1984), p. 25.
40 TLA, SOBG/101/14 (pauper number 1558).
41 TLA, P92/GEO/233 (9 December 1842), p. 175 (no. 1396).
42 TLA, SOBG/035/001: Southwark Board of Guardians, St George-the-Martyr Board of Guardians: St George's Workhouse (Mint Street), Register of Deaths (November 1835–September 1854), p. 43. Here it states that Keziah was buried on 6 December.
43 TLA, P92/GEO/234 (1 April 1846).
44 *Morning Post*, 19 January 1846.
45 Ibid.
46 *The Globe*, 9 March 1847.
47 Ibid.
48 *South-London News*, 4 October 1856.
49 *Morning Herald*, 8 September 1840.
50 *Sun* (London), 24 September 1849.
51 *Shoreditch Observer*, 28 March 1857.
52 For an analysis of Greenwood's text see Koven (2004), pp. 25–87.
53 See King, Carter, et al. (2022).
54 *Weekly Dispatch*, 12 January 1862.
55 *South London Times*, 27 February 1858.
56 *Weekly Dispatch*, 12 January 1862.
57 *South London Times*, 27 February 1858.
58 *Old Bailey Proceedings Online*, trial of Alfred Feist (22 February 1858), www.oldbaileyonline.org/record/t18580222-354 (accessed 16 July 2025).

3. Hope Street: 'A New World'

1. GTA, p. 24.
2. TNA, RG 9 341/75/33.
3. LSE, BOOTH/B/365, p. 125.
4. GTA, p. 20 (insert).
5. TNA, RG 9 1449/95/42.
6. August (2014), p. 105.
7. GTA, p. 20 (insert).
8. Ibid., p. 23.
9. Ibid., p. 31.
10. Ibid., pp. 25–6.
11. See Clark (1995).
12. GTA, p. 27.
13. Ibid.
14. Ibid.
15. Ibid., pp. 33–4.
16. Ibid., p. 37.
17. Ibid., p. 24.
18. Ibid., p. 41.
19. Ibid.
20. Ibid., p. 30.
21. Ibid., p. 34.
22. Dickens (1859), pp. 519 and 516.
23. TNA, RG 9/341/75/33.
24. Scott (1946), pp. 54–5.
25. For the Rotunda, see Roberts and Godfrey (1950).
26. See Jackson (2019), pp. 32–94.
27. GTA, p. 34.
28. Ibid., p. 35.
29. Ibid., p. 34.
30. Ibid., p. 25.
31. Ibid.
32. *Morning Advertiser*, 18 July 1848.
33. *Morning Advertiser*, 18 May 1847.
34. *Sainsbury's Weekly Register and Advertising Journal*, 8 August 1863.
35. See Ross (1993), pp. 32–4.
36. See Butler (2024).
37. Burke (1924), p. 131; for Chaplin's admiration for Burke, see *New York Times*, 9 August 1925, quoted in Hayes (2005), p. 78.
38. Gosse (1883), p. 11; see also Salmon (1891), p. 444.
39. GTA, p. 1.
40. Ibid., p. 44.
41. Ibid., p. 14.

42 'A mug in Doulton ware contains a profile of Mr. Tinworth, which he facetiously describes as "G.T., his mug"' (Salmon (1891), p. 451).
43 GTA, p. 53.
44 Ibid., pp. 33 and 44.
45 Ibid., p. 33.
46 Ibid.
47 Ibid., p. 44.
48 Ibid., p. 45.
49 Sparkes (1874), p. 559; for Sparkes, see Werner (1989), pp. 9–18.
50 See *The Builder*, vol. 32, no. 1631 (9 May 1874), pp. 390–1 ('On Some Recent Inventions and Applications of Lambeth Stoneware').
51 Gosse (1970), p. 60.
52 GTA, p. 44.
53 Stoke-on-Trent City Archives, SD 1705/RD Box 160/20/01, p. 108. (This detail forms part of an extended reminiscence of the art school by George, which his wife Alice noted down over pp. 108–109.)
54 GTA, p. 44.
55 Ibid., p. 45.
56 Stoke-on-Trent City Archives, SD 1705/RD Box 160/20/01, p. 108.
57 GTA, p. 44.
58 Ibid., p. 47.
59 Ibid., p. 46.
60 Ibid., p. 47.
61 Ibid., pp. 47–8.
62 *South London Press*, 19 September 1913.
63 TNA, RG 9 339/35/8.
64 TNA, RG 10 670/32/23.
65 Robert Wallace Martin to Sydney Greenslade (Southall, 21 September 1913); Southall Library, Martin Brothers Archive, 55/16 and 55/17; see also P. Rose (1982), p. 16, n. 6.
66 GTA, p. 51.
67 Ibid., p. 52.
68 Ibid.
69 Ibid., p. 49.
70 Ibid.
71 Ibid., p. 62.
72 Ibid., p. 57.
73 RAA/TRE/3/13.
74 GTA, pp. 62–3.
75 RAA/TRE/3/13.
76 Siddal's recent biographer disputes this; see Marsh (2023), pp. 12–13.
77 GTA, p. 33.
78 Quoted in Postle and Vaughan (1999), p. 66. See also Bills (2004).
79 GTA, p. 60.

80 *The Exhibition of the Royal Academy of Arts. MDCCCLXVI: The Ninety-Eighth* (London: William Clowes and Sons, 1866), p. 49: see Turner and Hallett (2018).
81 Salmon (1891), p. 444.
82 Spielmann (1901), p. 23.
83 Gosse (1883), pp. 12–13.
84 According to the certificate, he died on 4 November 1866.
85 GTA, p. 42.
86 Ibid.
87 Ibid.
88 Gosse (1883), p. 16.
89 *South London Chronicle*, 22 December 1866.
90 *London Evening Standard*, 12 December 1866.
91 Gosse (1883), p. 16.
92 Salmon (1881), p. 444.
93 GTA, p. 48.
94 Obituary of John Sparkes, *The Times*, 19 December 1907; P. Rose (1982), p. 18.
95 GTA, p. 51.

4. East Street: 'Boiling Water'
1   TLA, P85/MRY1/432, p. 127 (no. 254).
2   See Frost (2008).
3   *MEY*, p. 8; *MA*, p. 16.
4   TNA, RG 10 619/79/49.
5   *MEY*, p. 8; *MA*, p. 16.
6   Charlie Chaplin Archive, ECC100019268, CH085; see also Sweet (2011).
7   Hancock (2023).
8   Hitchcock (2023).
9   *The Diary of Samuel Pepys* (Tuesday, 11 August 1668), www.pepysdiary.com (accessed 16 July 2025).
10 Henry Roberts after John Straeho, *Margaret Finch Queen of the Gypsies at Norwood*, etching and engraving, 1742: British Museum, 1851,0308.274 (www.britishmuseum.org/collection/).
11 Lysons (1796), p. 302, n. 49.
12 Capper (1808), p. 239.
13 'The Norwood Gipsies', Galer (1890), pp. 9–11 (p. 11).
14 *MEY*, p. 8; *MA*, p. 16.
15 TNA, RG 10 676/108/41; GTA, p. 51.
16 GTA, p. 59.
17 Ibid.
18 LA, TR630–TR634: Lambeth Electoral Registers, (Lambeth, St Mary Newington, Second Division, St Paul's Ward, 1875–1881).

19 LA, TR628 and TR629: Lambeth Electoral Registers (Lambeth, St Mary-at-Lambeth, Brixton Ward, Second Division, 1872 and 1873).
20 Ruskin (1875), p. 14.
21 GTA, p. 116.
22 TNA RG 11 540/61/40.
23 SA, L/SMS/B/6/39: Southwark Poor Rate Books, fol. 42 (p. 60), assessment no. 1848 (24 March 1880).
24 TLA, P85/PHI/24 (8 February 1881). The 1881 census gives her age as twenty-five (TNA, RG 11 540/61/40).
25 GTA, p. 56; Steinbach (2004), p. 17.
26 Stoke-on-Trent City Archives. SD 1705/RD Box 160/20/01, p. 32.
27 GTA, p. 64.
28 George Tinworth to Edmund Gosse (22 April 1882), Stoke-on-Trent City Archives, SD 1705/RD Box 160/11/2.
29 GTA, p. 112.
30 Ibid., p. 86.
31 Ibid.
32 Ibid.
33 Stoke-on-Trent City Archives, SD 1705/RDBox 160/20/01, p. 23.
34 Ibid., pp. 32–3.
35 TNA, RG 11 527/4/2.
36 *MEV*, p. 8; *MA*, p. 16.
37 Charlie Chaplin Archive, ECC100313962, CH146.
38 *MEY*, p. 5; *MA*, p. 13.
39 LSE, BOOTH/B/365, p. 131.
40 Stead (1912), pp. 9–10.
41 LSE, BOOTH/B/365, p. 143.
42 *MEY*, p. 5; *MA*, p. 13.
43 *MEY*, p. 5; *MA*, p. 14.
44 LSE, BOOTH/B/363, p. 25.
45 Ibid.
46 *MEY*, p. 9; *MA*, p. 17.
47 LSE, BOOTH/B/365, pp. 165–7.
48 TNA, RG 12 362/42/6.
49 Walkowitz (1980), pp. 14 and 9.
50 Booth, et al. (1902), p. 364.
51 *The Examiner* (May 1838), p. 347.
52 Walkowitz (1980), pp. 246–7.
53 Ibid., p. 247.
54 Gissing (1978), pp. 22–3.
55 LSE, BOOTH/B/365, p. 13.
56 *MEY*, p. 8; *MA*, p. 16.
57 Ibid.
58 Robinson (2001), p. 16.

59 Soverall (2021).
60 For a useful introduction, see Burtinshaw and Burt (2017).
61 TLA, SOBG/097/5 (entry 196: Mary Ann Hill).
62 Ibid.
63 Ibid. (entry 193).
64 Ibid.
65 Charlie Chaplin Archive, ECC100314755, CH021.
66 Charlie Chaplin Archive, ECC100314751, CH021.
67 *MEY*, p. 8; *MA*, p. 16.
68 Robinson (2001), pp. 16–17.
69 TLA, H22/BAN/B/1/013 (entry no. 5153, 1 March 1893); TLA, H22/BAN/B/03/11 (15 March 1895).
70 TLA, SOBG/111/35 (13 April 1896).
71 TLA, H22/BAN/B/3/12–14.
72 Robinson (2001), p. 16.
73 Ibid., p. 15.
74 *MEY*, p. 12; *MA*, p. 19.
75 Ibid.
76 LSE, BOOTH/A/47 ('F. B. Meyer, Christchurch': Sunday, 12 January 1902), MS, pp. 1–6 (digital pp. 130–5).
77 See O'Day (2020).
78 LSE, BOOTH/B/272, MS, p. 103 (digital p. 89).
79 Ibid.
80 Ibid., MS, p. 105 (digital p. 91).
81 Ibid., MS, pp. 55–7 (digital pp. 53–4).
82 Ibid., p. 72.
83 Ibid.
84 Ibid., p. 71.
85 *MEY*, pp. 14–15; *MA*, pp. 21–2.
86 Ibid.
87 *MEY*, pp. 12–13; MA, pp. 19–20.
88 Hardie, Henderson, et al. (1910), p. 53. For the Labour Church see J. Turner (2019).
89 Benn (1992), p. 538.
90 *South London Mail*, 22 July 1893.
91 *MEY*, p. 16; *MA*, p. 23.
92 *MEY*, pp. 16–17; *MA*, p. 23.
93 *MEY*, p. 18; *MA*, p. 25.
94 *MEY*, p. 13; *MA*, p. 20.
95 *MEY*, p. 19; *MA*, p. 25.
96 See Higginbotham, www.workhouses.org.uk/Lambeth/.
97 Rubenhold (2019), pp. 44–9.
98 Ibid., pp. 76–85.
99 Charlie Chaplin Archive, ECC100314185, CH15, p. 2.

100 LSE, BOOTH/B/363, p. 37.
101 Charlie Chaplin Archive, ECC100314185, CH15, p. 2.
102 LSE, BOOTH/B/363, p. 9.
103 Charlie Chaplin Archive, ECC100314185, CH15, p. 2.
104 *South London Press*, 27 April 1895.
105 TLA, SOBG/111/36.
106 TLA, LCC/EO/DIV08/ADD/AD/006, no. 1675 (2 September 1895).
107 See Robinson (2001), p. 721 ('Chronology').
108 *MEY*, p. 18; *MA*, p. 25.
109 TLA, SOBG/111/35, n.p. (30 May 1896), digital image 293.

5. Kennington Cross: 'This Dolorous Period'

1   Ross (1993), p. 5.
2   Robinson (2001), pp. 20–1.
3   Charlie Chaplin Archive, ECC100314749, CH021.
4   TLA, SOBG/111/35, n.p. (18 June 1896), digital image 331.
5   Ibid.
6   LSE, BOOTH/B/156, MS, p. 100 (digital p. 54).
7   Ibid.
8   Ibid.
9   Ibid., MS, p. 108 (digital p. 58). See also Booth (1896), p. 139.
10 Ibid., MS, pp. 100–2 (digital pp. 54–5).
11 Ibid., MS, p. 102 (digital p. 55).
12 Ibid.
13 Burke (1924), p. 151.
14 GTA, p. 102.
15 *MEY*, p. 1; *MA*, p. 9.
16 Anthony (2010), pp. 193–4.
17 P. Bailey (1998), p. 83; see also P. Bailey (1986).
18 LSE, BOOTH/B/156, MS, p. 102 (digital p. 55).
19 Ibid., MS, p. 104 (digital p. 56).
20 Ibid., MS, pp. 105–6 (digital p. 57).
21 Ibid., MS, p. 104 (digital p. 56).
22 Ibid., MS, p. 108 (digital p. 58). See also Booth (1896), p. 139.
23 *MEY*, p. 19; *MA*, p. 26.
24 Ibid.
25 *MEY*, p. 19; *MA*, pp. 26–7.
26 *MEY*, p. 19; *MA*, p. 26.
27 *Motion Picture Magazine* (March 1915), quoted in Hayes (2005), p. 5.
28 *New York Times* (9 August 1925), quoted in ibid., p. 78.
29 Witchard (2005).
30 *MEY*, p. 20; *MA* p. 27.
31 *MEY*, pp. 20–1; *MA*, p. 27.
32 *MEY*, p. 22; *MA*, p. 28.

33 Ibid.
34 *MEY*, p. 22; *MA*, p. 29.
35 Syd entered the ship's company on 17 November 1896, and was discharged on 20 January 1898 (TLA, MAB/2512/6138).
36 Ibid.
37 Ibid.
38 *MEY*, p. 23; *MA*, p. 30.
39 *MEY*, pp. 24–5; *MA*, p. 31.
40 *MEY*, pp. 25–6; *MA*, p. 32.
41 Chaplin junior (1960), pp. 8–9.
42 Charlie Chaplin Archive, ECC100314750, CH021.
43 *Croydon Chronicle and East Surrey Advertiser*, 1 January 1898.
44 *Croydon Express*, 1 January 1898.
45 *Croydon Times*, 5 January 1898.
46 *Croydon Chronicle and East Surrey Advertiser*, 1 January 1898.
47 *The Era*, 8 January 1898.
48 *South London Chronicle*, 15 January 1898.
49 TLA, P92/JN/004: Register of Baptisms, St John the Evangelist, Walworth, p. 201, no. 1606 (1 April 1885); TLA, LCC/EO/DIV08/KIN/AD/002: Admission and Discharge Register, King and Queen Street School, Walworth, no. 1254 (3 March 1890).
50 *South London Press*, 22 January 1898.
51 *South London Chronicle*, 22 January 1898.
52 *South London Mail*, 22 January 1898.
53 Gissing (1887), vol. 1, p. 91.
54 *MEY*, p. 26; *MA*, p. 32.
55 *MEY*, p. 26; *MA*, pp. 32–3.
56 TLA, LABG/149/001: Case Book of Settlement Officer, p. 44, entry 262, no. 1310 (21 July 1898); ibid., p. 49, entry 290, no. 1314 (13 August 1898); in the column for 'Result of Case' is written '2 children Norwood Schools 16 August 1898'.
57 *MEY*, p. 26; *MA*, p. 32.
58 TLA, LABG/149/001: Case Book of Settlement Officer, p. 49, entry 290, no. 1314; TLA, LABG/160/2: 'London County Asylum Cane Hill', pp. 215–30 (p. 225, as 'Hannah Chaplain'); Croydon Archives Service, CAN/2/1/1/6, no. 8348 (15 September 1898).
59 Robinson (2001), pp. 26–7.
60 Anthony (2010), p. 193.
61 The claim was made by Louise Brooks in 'Charlie Chaplin Remembered', *Film Culture*, 40 (Spring 1966), quoted in Weissman (2008), p. 17.
62 *MEY*, p. 9; *MA*, pp. 16–17.
63 Weissman (2008), p. 14.
64 Robinson (2001), pp. 26 and 3; Stein (2010), pp. 9–10.

65 TLA, LABG/149/001, p. 44, no. 262 (21 July 1898) and p. 49, no. 290 (13 August 1898).
66 *MEY*, p. 27; *MA*, pp. 33–40.
67 LSE, BOOTH B/272, MS, pp. 77–9 (digital pp. 74–6).
68 Gissing (1887), vol. 1, p. 64.
69 LSE, BOOTH/B/363, pp. 231–3.
70 Ibid., p. 233.
71 Ibid., p. 241.
72 Ibid., pp. 241–5.
73 GTA, p. 70.
74 Charlie Chaplin Archive, ECC100019271, CH085.
75 LSE, BOOTH B/272, p. 71.
76 *MEY*, pp. 27–8; *MA*, pp. 33–4.
77 Ibid.
78 *MEY*, p. 28; *MA*, p. 34.
79 Ibid.
80 *MEY*, pp. 28–9; *MA*, pp. 34–5.
81 *MEY*, p. 28; *MA*, p. 35.
82 Ibid.
83 LSE, BOOTH/B/272, MS, p. 81 (digital p. 77).
84 *MEY*, p. 30; *MA*, p. 36.
85 *MEY*, pp. 30–1; *MA*, p. 36.
86 *MEY*, p. 31; *MA*, p. 37.
87 Gissing (1887), vol. 1, p. 63.
88 *MEY*, p. 31; *MA*, p. 37.
89 LSE, BOOTH/B/363, pp. 81–5.
90 Gissing (1887), vol. 1, pp. 63–4.
91 Ibid, p. 64.
92 *MEY*, p. 31; *MA*, p. 35.
93 *MEY*, pp. 31–2; *MA*, p. 35.
94 *MEY*, p. 32; *MA*, p. 37.
95 Chaplin (1922), p. 92.
96 *MEY*, pp. 29–30; *MA*, p. 35.
97 The song was composed by Charles Osborne in 1898 for Millie Lindon (1869–1940). See Anthony (2012), p. 90.
98 *MEY*, p. 30; *MA*, p. 36.
99 LSE, BOOTH/363, p. 217.
100 LSE, BOOTH/B/363, pp. 217–19.
101 See P. Bailey (1998), pp. 110–11.
102 Chaplin (1922), p. 104.
103 Ibid., p. 105.
104 *Globe and Commercial Advertiser* [New York] (19 February 1916), quoted in Hayes (2005), p. 15; see also Robinson (2001), pp. 119–20.
105 Thomson and Smith (1877), p. 27.

106 *MEY*, pp. 33–4; *MA*, p. 39.
107 *MEY*, p. 34; *MA*, p. 39.
108 Ibid.
109 Croydon Archives Service, CAN/2/1/1/6, no. 8348 (12 November 1898); TLA, LABG/160/2, p. 225 (12 November 1898).
110 *MEY*, p. 34; *MA*, p. 39.

6. New Cut: 'The Human Relationship'
1 'Directory of Settlements', in Reason (1898), pp. 179–90 (p. 183).
2 Ross (1993), p. 11.
3 Quoted in Ross (1993), p. 17.
4 Galton (1883), p. 307.
5 See Crone (2022), pp. 292–3; also Wiener (1990), pp. 236–44 and V. Bailey (2019), pp. 20 and 40.
6 See Searle (2013), pp. 194–5.
7 *New York Times*, 9 August 1925, in Hayes (2005), pp. 75–9 (p. 78).
8 Burke (1924), p. 27.
9 Ibid., p. 145.
10 *The Echo*, 8 February 1888.
11 Ibid.
12 *The Gentlewoman*, 2 May 1891.
13 LSE, BOOTH/B/363, p. 111.
14 Ibid., pp. 109–11.
15 Ibid., p. 109.
16 Ibid., p. 101.
17 Ibid., p. 91.
18 Ibid., p. 99.
19 *Reynolds's Newspaper*, 29 April 1894.
20 *South London Press*, 20 August 1898.
21 Ibid.
22 *South London Press*, 30 September 1899.
23 See Rubenhold (2019), pp. 35–42.
24 LSE, BOOTH B/272, MS, pp. 75–7 (digital pp. 73–4).
25 LSE, BOOTH/B/363, p. 81.
26 *Weekly Dispatch*, 29 March 1896.
27 Ross (1993), pp. 133–7.
28 See *Morning Leader*, 26 March 1896; and *Old Bailey Proceedings Online*, trial of Mary [Polly] Carr (23 March 1896), www.oldbaileyonline.org/record/t18960323-330 (accessed 16 July 2025).
29 Ibid.
30 Ibid.
31 RAA/TRE/3/21, entries for 24 April, 25 April and 3 June 1896; for details on individual artist's models, see also victorianweb.org/painting/models/index.html.

32 GTA, p. 89; the former marine's stories fill a page of Tinworth's memoir: see GTA, p. 92.
33 *Weekly Dispatch*, 29 March 1896.
34 *Sunday Express*, 22 October 1933; see also Postle and Vaughan (1999), p. 92.
35 *Old Bailey Proceedings Online*, trial of Mary [Polly] Carr (23 March 1896), www.oldbaileyonline.org/record/t18960323-330 (accessed 16 July 2025).
36 *Weekly Dispatch*, 26 March 1896.
37 *Old Bailey Proceedings Online*, trial of Mary [Polly] Carr (23 March 1896), www.oldbaileyonline.org/record/t18960323-330 (accessed 16 July 2025).
38 See Shoemaker (2023).
39 *The Digital Panopticon*, Mary Carr b.1871 (https://www.digitalpanopticon.org/life?id=obpdef1-330-18960323, accessed 16 July 2025).
40 LSE, BOOTH/B/363, p. 181.
41 Ibid., p. 183.
42 Ibid., p. 189.
43 Ibid., p. 211.
44 Ibid., p. 213.
45 Ibid., pp. 213–15.
46 Ibid., p. 221.
47 SA, RBSP 2022/25: Minutes of the Meeting of the 'Mission' Committee (10 September 1894). It was proposed and carried that the name of the hall be altered to Robert Browning Hall, and that £300 be forthcoming as the Warden's stipend for the first year; Herbert Stead further proposed 'to engage the services of Mr T. Bryan M.A. as assistant & also some lady helpers'. On 8 November 1894 the property intended as the settlement house on York Street had fallen through, and an approach was being made to the Fishmongers' Company, 'who own a good deal of property near the Hall to see if they could help in the matter'.
48 Reason (1898), pp. 179–90 ('Directory of Settlements'), p. 183.
49 GTA, p. 52.
50 'Browning Hall, Walworth', *The Christian*, 15 June 1899, p. 17; inserted at LSE, BOOTH/B/277, MS, p. 142 (digital p. 199).
51 See Walkowitz (1980), pp. 246–56.
52 SA, 2022/25: 'Robert Browning Settlement Annual Report for 1902' (1903), p. 20 (citing *Reviews of Reviews Annual*, 1903).
53 Ibid.
54 Flower (1903), pp. 622–3.
55 LSE, BOOTH/B/277, MS, p. 143 (digital p. 199).
56 Ibid., MS, p. 147 (digital p. 203).
57 'Robert Browning Settlement Annual Report for 1898' (1899), pp. 1–48 (digital pp. 211–37), inserted at LSE BOOTH/B/277, MS, p. 163 (digital p. 211): henceforth RBS Annual Report 1898.
58 Ibid., p. 3 (digital p. 213).
59 Ibid., p. 24 (digital p. 224).

60 Ibid., p. 23 (digital p. 223).
61 Ibid., p. 13 (digital p. 218).
62 Ibid., p. 11 (digital p. 217).
63 Ibid.
64 Ibid., pp. 15–17 (digital pp. 219–20).
65 Stead (1912), p. 79.
66 RBS Annual Report 1898, p. 14 (digital p. 219).
67 Ibid.
68 Ibid., p. 33 (digital p. 228).
69 Stead (1912), pp. 132–3.
70 Ibid., p. 113.
71 SA, RBSP 2022/25: 'Robert Browning Settlement Annual Report for 1897' (1898), p. 16.
72 SA, RBSP 2022/25, Box 3: Winifred Price to R. M. Dunnico (1898).
73 Flower (1903), p. 617.
74 *Daily News Weekly*, 10 March 1900.
75 RBS Annual Report 1898, p. 10 (digital p. 217).
76 SA, 2022/25 RBSP, PAM 360.76 BRO Fletcher (1899).
77 Ibid., p. 249.
78 RBS Annual Report 1898, p. 6 (digital p. 216).
79 *South London Press*, 18 June 1898.
80 GTA, p. 93.
81 Ibid.
82 Stead (1912), p. 8.
83 LSE, BOOTH B/272, p. 71.
84 TNA, RG 12 622/73/27.
85 GTA, p. 1.
86 Stead (1912), pp. 132–3.
87 Ibid.
88 GTA, p. 76.
89 Vincent van Gogh to Theo van Gogh (30 April 1874), in Jansen, Luijten and Bakker (2024), Letter 022.
90 Burke (1924), pp. 145–6.
91 *MEY*, p. 6; *MA*, p. 14.
92 RBS Annual Report 1898, p. 24 (digital p. 224).
93 Stead (1912), p. 28.
94 RBS Annual Report 1898, p. 4 (digital p. 214).
95 Ibid., p. 19 (digital p. 221).
96 Ibid.
97 Ibid., pp. 20–1 (digital p. 222).
98 W. Besant (1912), pp. 324–5.
99 Ibid., p. 326.
100 RBS Annual Report 1898, pp. 5–6 (digital pp. 214–15).
101 W. Besant (1912), pp. 327–8.

102 LSE, BOOTH/B/277, MS, p. 149 (digital p. 204).
103 *Daily News Weekly*, 10 March 1900.
104 LSE, BOOTH/B/277, MS, pp. 151–3 (digital pp. 205–6).
105 Ibid.
106 'Dulcima' (1901), pp. 418 and 420.
107 *Cambridge Independent Press*, 8 November 1901.

7. Lambeth Walk: 'Girls and their Lovers'

1 TNA, J77/824/5040: Papers associated with Westcott vs Westcott (1904–5), including a copy (dated 24 June 1904) of the marriage certificate (original dated 15 January 1889).
2 TNA, RG 12 78/169/34, no. 263 (listed as 'Karno').
3 Daggett (1942), p. 26; Anthony (2012), p. 196.
4 LA, IV 183/7/3a [1899], n.p.
5 *MEY*, pp. 38–40; *MA*, pp. 44–5.
6 Quoted in Robinson (2001), p. 31.
7 Chaplin junior (1960), p. 9.
8 Chaplin (1922), pp. 84–5.
9 Robinson (2001), p. 36.
10 Ibid., p. 37.
11 *MEY*, p. 50; *MA*, p. 54.
12 *MEY*, p. 46; *MA*, p. 50.
13 *MEY*, pp. 1–2; *MA*, pp. 9–10.
14 Brownlow, interview with Effie Wisdom (1983), timestamp 00:08:30–00:13:57.
15 Ibid., timestamp 00:19:52–00:26:20.
16 Ibid., timestamp 00:13:57–00:19:52.
17 *MEY*, p. 46; *MA*, p. 50.
18 Ross (1993), pp. 27 and 37–9.
19 *MEY*, pp. 46–7; *MA*, pp. 50–1.
20 LA, IV 183/7/3a [1899], n.p.
21 *MEY*, pp. 17–18; *MA*, p. 24.
22 LA, IV 183/7/3a [1899], n.p.
23 Ibid.
24 Maugham (1951), p. vii.
25 Ibid.
26 Ibid., pp. vii–viii.
27 LA, IV183/7/3a [1899] n.p.; see also Barraclough (2011).
28 'St Mary, Prince's Road, Lambeth Parish Newsletter', pp. 1–4, p. 1 (digital pp. 96–8, p. 96), inserted at LSE BOOTH/B/272, MS, p. 115 (digital p. 96).
29 LA, IV183/7/3a [1899], n.p.
30 'St Mary, Prince's Road, Lambeth Parish Newsletter', pp. 1–4, p. 4; (digital pp. 96–8, p. 98), inserted at LSE, BOOTH/B/272, MS, p. 115 (digital p. 96).
31 LA, IV183/7/3a [1899], n.p.

32 LSE, BOOTH/B/272, MS, p. 69 (digital p. 70).
33 Ibid., MS, p. 73 (digital p. 72).
34 Ibid., pp. 73–5 (digital pp. 72–3).
35 Purser (1995), p. 95.
36 LSE, BOOTH B/272: 'Hercules Club', insert facing MS, p. 77 (digital p. 75); see also Russell and Rigby (1908).
37 Ibid., 'Daisy Club', insert facing MS, p. 75; (digital p. 73).
38 Ibid., MS, pp. 79–81 (digital pp. 76–7), and ibid., 'Daisy Club' insert facing MS, p. 75 (digital p. 73).
39 *MEY*, pp. 54–5; *MA*, p. 58.
40 *MEY*, p. 55; *MA*, p. 59.
41 LA, IV 183/7/3a [1899], n. p.
42 *MEY*, p. 55; *MA*, p. 56.
43 LA, IV 183/7/3a [1899], n. p.
44 *MEY*, p. 57; *MA*, p. 60.
45 *MEY*, pp. 57–8; *MA*, pp. 61–2.
46 *MEY* p. 61; *MA*, p. 64.
47 Ibid.
48 *MEY*, p. 65; *MA*, pp. 67–8.
49 Chaplin junior (1960), p. 10.
50 *MEY*, p. 68; *MA*, pp. 68–9.
51 TLA, LABG/176/3, n.p. (1 May 1903), digital image 876.
52 *MEY*, p. 69; *MA*, p. 69.
53 Brownlow, interview with Effie Wisdom (1983), timestamp 00:08:30–00:13:57.
54 Ibid., timestamp 00:43:16–00:45:40.
55 Ibid., timestamp 00:17:40–00:26:58.
56 *MEY*, p. 72; *MA*, p. 64.
57 *MEY*, p. 74; *MA*, p. 75.
58 *The Era*, 30 April 1904.
59 Anthony (2012), p. 48.
60 TNA, J77/824/5040: Papers associated with Westcott vs Westcott, 1904–5.
61 Anthony (2012), pp. 199–200.
62 Gallagher (1971), p. 67.
63 Ibid.
64 Quoted in Ibid.
65 *MEV*, p. 32; *MA*, pp. 37–8.
66 *MEV*, p. 33; *MA*, p. 39.
67 *MEY*, p. 9; *MA*, p. 17.
68 Stead (1912), p. 79.
69 Gissing (1887), vol. 1, pp. 81–2.
70 *Old Bailey Proceedings Online*, trial of Frederick James (10 April 1899), www.oldbaileyonline.org/record/t18990410-325?text=Andrews (accessed 16 July 2025).

71 LSE, BOOTH/B/365, p. 23.
72 *Lloyd's Weekly Newspaper*, 19 March 1899.
73 Ibid.
74 See Frost (2008), pp. 32–51.
75 *St James's Gazette*, 18 March 1899.
76 See Frost (2008), pp. 32–51.
77 *London Daily Chronicle*, 3 May 1899.
78 LSE, BOOTH/B/272, MS, p. 107 (digital p. 92).
79 See Lodge (2024), pp. 141–203.
80 LSE, BOOTH B/272, pp. 107–9; (digital pp. 92–3).
81 'St Mary, Prince's Road, Lambeth Parish Newsletter', p. 1 (digital p. 96), inserted at ibid., MS, p. 115 (digital p. 96).
82 LSE, BOOTH B/272, MS, p. 109 (digital p. 93).
83 Stead (1912), p. 8.
84 TNA, J77/824/5040: 'The Petition of Edith Westcott' (24 June 1904).
85 TNA, RG 12 423/92/15/105.
86 TNA, RG 13 446/100/3/16.
87 *The Era*, 21 February 1903.
88 *The Stage* 6 April 1905.
89 *The Era*, 12 August 1905.
90 TNA, J 77/824/5040, 'Answer of Respondent', 20 July 1904.
91 Ibid., 'Petition of Frederick John Westcott', 23 July 1904.
92 Quoted in Anthony (2012), p. 196.
93 *MEY*, p. 121; *MA*, p. 116.
94 Crump (2021), pp. 111–25; Gallagher (1971), pp. 59–65.
95 Crump (2021), pp. 111, 117–25.
96 TNA, RG 14 195/02/04/91.
97 TNA, J77/824/5040: 'Answer [by Edith Westcott] to the Petition [by Frederick Westcott]' (10 August 1904).
98 Ibid., 'Decree of Judicial Separation' (25 May 1905).
99 TNA, RG 14 195/02/04/91.
100 Crump (2021), p. 155.
101 *Daily News*, 26 May 1905.
102 *Morning Leader*, 26 May 1905.
103 TNA, RG 14 26/01/33/07.
104 Crump (2021), p. 438.
105 Ibid., pp. 441 and 522.
106 *MEY*, pp. 76–7; *MA*, p. 78.
107 *MEY*, pp. 52–3; *MA*, pp. 56–7.
108 *Weekly Dispatch*, 7 June 1885.
109 *London and Provincial Entr'acte*, 24 July 1886.
110 *Evening News*, 14 November 1894.
111 *South London Press*, 13 November 1897.
112 Ibid.

113 *MEY*, p. 53; *MA*, p. 57.
114 *MEY*, p. 47; *MA*, p. 51.
115 Ibid.
116 TNA, RG 13 416/32/4/29.
117 LSE, BOOTH/B/365, p. 145.
118 *MEY*, pp. 87–8; *MA*, p. 87; Croydon Archives Service, CAN/2/1/1/6, no. 10400 'recovered' (2 January 1904); TLA, LABG/156/01, n.p., digital image 31.
119 *MEY*, p. 88; *MA*, p. 87.
120 *MEY*, p. 88; *MA*, pp. 87–8; Croydon Archives Service CAN/2/1/1/7, no. 1112 (18 March 1905); TLA, LABG/156/01, where it is recorded that Hannah 'went from the [Lambeth] Infirmary' to Banstead Asylum (18 March 1905).
121 *MEY*, p. 88; *MA*, p. 88.
122 Charlie Chaplin Archives, ECC100008363, CH080.
123 Charlie Chaplin Archives, ECC100008366, CH080.
124 Stead (1912), p. 116.
125 See Riding (2018), chapter 11.
126 See Steinbach (2004), pp. 236–40.
127 'White Slavery in London', *The Link*, 23 June 1888.
128 Stead (1912), p. 116.
129 *The Times*, 7 November 1905.
130 Stead (1912), pp. 115–18.
131 *Daily News*, 15 November 1905 and 14 December 1905.
132 *Daily News*, 15 November 1905.
133 Ibid., p. 118.
134 Ibid, p. 119.
135 *The Era*, 20 October 1906.
136 *Morning Leader*, 27 November 1906.
137 *The Stage*, 29 November 1906.
138 Ibid.
139 *The Era*, 12 August 1905.
140 *The Era*, 20 October 1906.
141 *The Era*, 12 August 1905.
142 *MEY*, p. 94; *MA*, p. 94.
143 *MEY*, p. 93; *MA*, p. 92.
144 *The Stage*, 9 February 1961.
145 Quoted in Robinson (2001), p. 80.
146 Chaplin junior (1960), p. 9.
147 Ibid.
148 *MEY*, p. 100; *MA*, p. 98.
149 Chaplin junior (1960), p. 23.
150 *MEY*, p. 104; *MA*, pp. 101–2.
151 *MEY*, p. 104; *MA*, p. 102.

152 Ibid.
153 Brownlow, interview with Effie Wisdom (1983), timestamp 00:13:57–00:17:40.
154 Robinson (2001), pp. 83–3.
155 *MEY*, pp. 105–8; *MA*, pp. 102–3.
156 Quoted in Robinson (2001), p. 85.
157 Chaplin junior (1960), p. 27.
158 Ibid., p. 33. See also Robinson (2001), pp. 364–5, pp. 367–71, pp. 394–402.
159 L. Chaplin (1966), p. 4. This passage is quoted in full in Robinson (2001), pp. 368–9.
160 *MEY*, p. 118; *MA*, p. 113.
161 *MEY*, p. 123; *MA*, p. 118.
162 Ibid.
163 *MEY*, p. 139; *MA*, p. 132.
164 TLA, LABG/156/2, n.p., digital image 311; Croydon Archives Service CAN/2/1/1/7, no. 1112.
165 'Fred Karno's Houseboat', *Pall Mall Gazette*, 22 January 1913.
166 *MEY*, p. 140; *MA*, p. 133.
167 Ibid.
168 Ibid.
169 *MEY*, p. 141; *MA*, p. 134.
170 *Southwark and Bermondsey Recorder*, 19 September 1913.
171 Bedford (2011).
172 *South London Press*, 12 September 1913.
173 TNA, RG 14 41/01/24/219.
174 Robert Wallace Martin to Sydney Greenslade (Southall, 21 September 1913); Southall Library, Martin Brothers Archive, 55/16 and 55/17.
175 *Southwark and Bermondsey Recorder*, 19 September 1913.
176 GTA, p. 112.
177 Charlie Chaplin Archive, ECC100313993, CH148.
178 *MA*, pp. 260–1.
179 Charlie Chaplin Archive, ECC100313993, CH148.
180 Pilley (1921).
181 Owen (2023), pp. 232–3 (p. 233).
182 *Illustrated London News*, 10 August 1918.
183 Chaplin (1922), p. 71.
184 *MA*, p. 266.
185 Chaplin junior (1960), p. 29.
186 Stead (1912), p. 6.

Epilogue: 'Pretty Good Metal'
1 TLA, P71/MMG/011: Register of Baptisms, St Mary Magdalene, Bermondsey (25 November 1804). My thanks to Linda Riding Johnson for charting the early history of the Partridge/Robinson families.

2   TLA, P29/SAV/3050/001: Register of Marriages, St Saviour, Southwark, p. 181, no. 739 (24 May 1830).
3   TLA, P85/JNA3/051: Register of Marriages, St John the Evangelist, Waterloo, p. 235, no. 470.
4   TNA, RG 11 586/80/43/1341134.
5   TLA, LABG/167/011: Renfrew Road Workhouse, Creed Register, M–R (1884–1886): William Partridge, 79, admitted 22 February 1884 from 39 Granby Place and discharged 22 February 1884 'To Infirmary', n.p. (digital images 842–3); admitted 7 March 1884 from 'Infirmary' and discharged 7 June 1884 'To Infirmary', n.p. (digital images 844–5); admitted 30 July 1884 from 39 Granby Place and discharged 18 November 1884 'To Infirmary', n.p. (digital images 852–3); admitted 16 December 1884 from 'Infirmary' and discharged 6 January 1885 'To Infirmary', n.p. (digital images 862–3). This register was searched to the last entry, dated 26 March 1886, and no further references to William Partridge were found.
6   *Post Office London Directory* for 1885 (p. 339); 1890 (p. 350); 1895 (p. 377); 1900 (p. 414); and 1905 (p. 430).
7   TNA, RG 12 390/88/28/6095500.
8   TLA, P85/JNA3/081, p. 157, no. 313 (1 August 1897).
9   TLA, P70/GEO/011, p. 6, no. 42; TNA, RG 13 443/174, p. 33, schedule 226; and TNA, RG 15 2213/29/231/02213.
10 TLA, P70/GEO/025, p. 121, no. 242 (2 July 1927), where Ernest's residence is still given as 9 Mundella Road.
11 TLA, LCC/PER/B: Electoral Register, 1930, Battersea, Wandsworth, Polling District M, No. VI, Winstanley Ward, nos 974 and 975.
12 TLA, LCC/PER/B: Electoral Register, 1938, Battersea, Wandsworth, Polling District C, No. 1, Nine Elms Ward, nos 3439 and 3440.

BIBLIOGRAPHY

Archive and Manuscript Collections

Charlie Chaplin Archive (www.charliechaplinarchive.org)
ECC100008363, CH080: Letter from Hannah Chaplin to Sydney and Charles Chaplin, London, 3 July 1905.
ECC100008366, CH080: Letter from Hannah Chaplin to Sydney and Charles Chaplin, London, 20 August 1905.
ECC100019268, CH085: Letter from Jack Hill to Charles Chaplin [1950–1977].
ECC100019271, CH085: Letter from Charles Horatio Shepherd to Charles Chaplin, New York, 10 July 1915.
ECC100313962, CH146: Certified Copy [dated 17 April 1919] of an Entry of Marriage at St John's Walworth, 22 June 1885.
ECC100313993, CH148: Letter from Charles Chaplin to Sydney Chaplin, Los Angeles Athletic Club, 9 August 1914.
ECC100314185, CH15: Register for Admission to the Lambeth Infirmary (copy), 27 July 1895.
ECC100314749, CH021: Extracts from the minutes of the St Saviour's Board of Guardians meeting, 9 June 1896.
ECC100314750, CH021: Letter to Spencer Chaplin (copy), 16 November 1897.
ECC100314751, CH021: St Saviour's Union, Surrey: Order of Reception for a Pauper Lunatic (copy), 23 February 1893.
ECC100314755, CH021: Certificate of Medical Practitioner: Form 8 (copy), 23 February 1893.

Croydon Archives Service
CAN/2/1/1/6–7 Cane Hill Hospital (Asylum) Female Registers, 1883–1905, 1905–1936.
CAN/2/3/2 Medical Register, Females, 1907–1914.

Essex Record Office
D/P 117/1/3 Burial Register, St Laurence, Upminster, Essex.

LA (Lambeth Archives)
TR628–TR634: Lambeth Electoral Registers, 1872–1881.

IV183/1/3/1–5: Records of the Lady Margaret Hall Settlement: Memoranda and Articles of Association, Minutes, Agendas [&c.] (1879–1989).
IV183/7/3a: Reminiscences (manuscript and typed transcript) by Katherine E. M. Thicknesse, resident from 1899–1902 [compiled in the 1940s].

LSE (London School of Economics)
5WUS: Records of the Women's University Settlement (later known as the Blackfriars Settlement), 1887–1973:
    5WUS/1/A: Council Minute Books, Box FL600 Vols I and II (1887).
    5WUS/1/C :AGM SUBS, Box FL605 (1888).
    5WUS/1/G: General and Constitutional Box, FL606 (1890).
    5WUS/3: Add. Records (publications), Box FL617.
Charles Booth Notebooks (https://booth.lse.ac.uk):
BOOTH/A/47: George H. Duckworth's Notebook: Religious Influences, West Southwark and North Lambeth, Newington and Walworth, Bermondsey, Rotherhithe District 31 [Lambeth and St Saviour's Southwark], District 32 [Trinity Newington and St Mary Bermondsey] ... District 34 [Lambeth and Kennington], District 41 [St Peter Walworth and St Mary Newington] (1899–1902).
BOOTH/B/156: George H. Duckworth's Notebook: Art and Amusement (1896).
BOOTH/B/272: George H. Duckworth and Ernest Aves's Notebook: Church of England District 34 [Lambeth and Kennington] (1899).
BOOTH/B/277: George H. Duckworth's Notebook: Nonconformist District 41 [St Peter Walworth and St Mary Newington], 1899–1900; including a copy of the Robert Browning Settlement Annual Report (RBS Annual Report) for 1898, pasted onto MS p. 163 (digital p. 211).
BOOTH/B/363: George H. Duckworth's Notebook: Police District 31 [Lambeth and St Saviour's Southwark], District 34 [Lambeth and Kennington] (1899–1902).
BOOTH/B/365: George H. Duckworth's Notebook: Police District 32 [Trinity Newington and St Mary Bermondsey], District 33 [St James Bermondsey and Rotherhithe], District 34 [Lambeth and Kennington], District 35 [Kennington (2nd) and Brixton], District 41 [St Peter Walworth and St Mary Newington], District 42 [St George Camberwell], District 45 [Deptford] (1899).

RAA (Royal Academy of Arts Library and Archive)
RAA/TRE/3/13: Cashbook, 1857–1881.
RAA/TRE/3/21: Cashbook, 1893–1896.

SA (Southwark Archives)
920 TIN: George Tinworth, manuscript autobiography [GTA], with miscellaneous letters.

L/SMS/B/6/39 Poor Rate Books, Surrey, Newington, St Mary Newington, 1880.
RBSP 2022/25: Robert Browning Settlement Papers, including (currently uncatalogued):
    Annual Reports (RBS Annual Report) for the years 1897 and 1902.
    Box 3: Letter from Mrs Winifred Price, 41 Hart Road, Takapuna, Auckland 9, New Zealand to Mrs R. M. Dunnico of the Robert Browning Settlement, with enclosures, including a copy of the original studio photograph of Emily Rivett (the writer's mother) dated 1898.
    Folder PC 360.76: Typescript memoir by the Reverend Edward White (1 June 1895) and manuscript covering letter by Francis Herbert Stead (24 June 1895).
    Minutes of the Meeting of the 'Mission' Committee, 10 September–8 November 1894.
    PAM 360.76 BRO *Men Who Reach the Masses: Mr Herbert* Stead, [1900–1905]
    PAM 360.76. BRO Fletcher, A. E. 'Robert Browning Anniversary', *The New Age* (11 May 1899), 249–50.
    Sunday School Register, 1840–1855.
    York Street Chapel, Register of Members, 1790–1863.

Southall Library
Martin Brothers Archive, 55/16 and 55/17: Letter from Robert Wallace Martin to Sydney Greenslade, Southall, 21 September 1913.

Stoke-on-Trent City Archives
G272/2/7/3/1/14: The Minton Archive/Royal Doulton Company Records. Workforce Records (Lambeth Factory): Records of Individuals: George Tinworth.
SD 1705/RD Box 160/11/1–6: Correspondence between George Tinworth and Edmund Gosse 1880–1892.
SD 1705/RD Box 160/20/01: Diary for 1888 kept by Mrs George Tinworth (Alice Tinworth).

TLA (The London Archives; formerly London Metropolitan Archives)
H22 BAN/B/1/13: London County Asylum Banstead (later Banstead Hospital), Register of Admissions, 1893.
H22 BAN/B/3/11: London County Asylum Banstead (later Banstead Hospital), Discharge Order Book: M[ale] + F[emale], 1895.
H22 BAN/B/3/12–14: Discharge Order Books: M[ale] + F[emale], 1896–1900.
LABG/140/045 Lambeth Board of Guardians, Settlement Examinations, Rough, 13 September 1897–29 November 1898.
LABG/149/001: Lambeth Board of Guardians, Case Book of Settlement Officer, 11 February 1898–10 October 1899.

LABG/156/1-2: Lambeth Board of Guardians, Admission and Discharge Books and Summary, Lunatics, Patients and Children in Asylums, Hospitals, and Schools (1903–1912).

LABG/160/1-2: Lambeth Board of Guardians, Registers of Lunatics in Miscellaneous Asylums but Chargeable to Lambeth (1867–1903).

LABG/162/021: Lambeth Board of Guardians, Workhouse, Princes Road, Admission and Discharge Register, April 1895–December 1895.

LABG/167/9: Lambeth Board of Guardians, Workhouse, Renfrew Road, Creed Register A–E (1884).

LABG/176/3: Lambeth Board of Guardians, Workhouse, Brook Drive: Infirmary Registers, Discharges, Daily Return of Patients (1903).

LCC/EO/DIV08/ADD/AD/002: Addington Street School, Lambeth: Admission and Discharge Register for Boys, 1891–1920.

LCC/EO/DIV08/KIN/AD/002: King and Queen Street School, Walworth: Admission and Discharge Register for Infants, 1887–1891.

LCC/PER/B: Electoral Register 1930, Battersea, Wandsworth, Polling District M, No. VI, Winstanley Ward.

LCC/PER/B: Electoral Register 1938, Battersea, Wandsworth, Polling District C, No. 1, Nine Elms Ward.

MAB/2512/06001–06250: Metropolitan Asylums Board, Training Ship *Exmouth* Boys' Record Book (15 July 1896–19 February 1897).

P29/SAV/3050: Register of Marriages, St Saviour, Southwark (1 January 1822–30 December 1834).

P70/GEO/011: Register of Baptisms, St George-the-Martyr, Battersea (10 August 1902–29 August 1906).

P70/GEO/025: Register of Marriages, St George-the-Martyr, Battersea (31 March 1923–2 January 1932).

P71/MMG/011: Register of Baptisms, St Mary Magdalene, Bermondsey (2 January 1803–30 December 1804).

P85/JNA3/051: Register of Marriages, St John the Evangelist, Waterloo (13 July 1854–1 April 1857).

P85/JNA3/081: Register of Marriages, St John the Evangelist, Waterloo (2 November 1889–4 December 1904).

P85/MRY1/395: Register of Marriages, St Mary at Lambeth (27 April 1803–6 October 1806).

P85/MRY1/432: Register of Marriages, St Mary at Lambeth (23 December–28 July 1861).

P85/PHI/24: Register of Marriages, St Philip, Lambeth, Kennington Road (1 January 1880–31 October 1882).

P92/GEO/233: Register of Burials, St George-the-Martyr, Borough High Street, Southwark (1 November 1839–31 January 1845).

P92/GEO/234: Register of Burials, St George-the-Martyr, Borough High Street, Southwark (1 January 1845–31 July 1849).

P92/JN/004: Register of Baptisms, St John the Evangelist, Walworth (18 March 1883–14 May 1892).

P92/TRI/18: Register of Marriages, Holy Trinity, Newington (1 July–31 March 1841).

SOBG/035/001: Southwark Board of Guardians, St George-the-Martyr Board of Guardians: St George's Workhouse (Mint Street) Register of Deaths (November 1835–September 1854).

SOBG/97/5: Southwark Board of Guardians, St Mary Newington and St Saviour's Union Board of Governors: Orders, Examinations, Report Books etc. relating to Lunatics (1 November 1891–30 June 1893).

SOBG/101/14: Southwark Board of Guardians, St Mary Newington and St Saviour's Union Board of Governors: Workhouse, Infirmary [&c.], Christ Church Workhouse: Admission and Discharge Registers (1 May 1842–31 August 1843).

SOBG/101/17: Southwark Board of Guardians, St Mary Newington and St Saviour's Union Board of Governors: Workhouse, Infirmary [&c.]: Admission and Discharge Registers (1 August 1843–31 January 1845).

SOBG/111/30: Southwark Board of Guardians, St Mary Newington and St Saviour's Union Board of Governors: Workhouse, Infirmary [&c.]: Newington Workhouse, Westmoreland Road: Admission and Discharge Registers (1 June 1892–31 March 1893).

SOBG/111/35: Southwark Board of Guardians, St Mary Newington and St Saviour's Union Board of Governors: Workhouse, Infirmary [&c.]: Admission and Discharge Registers (1 December 1895–30 September 1896).

SOBG/111/36: Southwark Board of Guardians, St Mary Newington and St Saviour's Union Board of Governors: Workhouse, Infirmary [&c.]: Newington Workhouse, Westmoreland Road: Admission and Discharge Registers (1 September 1896–30 June 1897).

TNA (The National Archives)

FO 395/663: Foreign Office: News Department, General Correspondence from 1906.

HO 107: 1841 and 1851 censuses of England and Wales.

J77/824/5040: Court for Divorce and Matrimonial Causes: Files 1899–1909 (Appellant: Frederick John Westcott; Respondent: Edith Westcott, 1904); papers include a copy (dated 24 June 1904) of the marriage certificate (original dated 15 January 1889).

KV 2/3700: The Security Service: Personal (PF Series) Files: 'Communists and Suspected Communists, including Russian and Communist Sympathisers', Charles Spencer CHAPLIN, alias Charlie CHAPLIN (22 September 1952–18 November 1958).

RG 4/1382: Register of Births, Marriages and Deaths surrendered to the Non-Parochial Registers Commissions of 1837 and 1857: Upminster, Upminster Hill Chapel (Independent), Essex (1801–1837).

RG 4/4202: Register of Births, Marriages and Deaths surrendered to the Non-Parochial Registers Commissions of 1837 and 1857: Walworth, York Street, Lock's Fields (Independent). London: Births and Baptisms (1804–1837).
RG 9: 1861 census of England and Wales.
RG 10: 1871 census of England and Wales.
RG 11: 1881 census of England and Wales.
RG 12: 1891 census of England and Wales.
RG 13: 1901 census of England and Wales.
RG 14: 1911 census of England and Wales.
RG 15: 1921 census of England and Wales.

Printed Sources and Websites
An Account of Several Work-houses for Employing and Maintaining the Poor, second edition (London: Joseph Downing, 1732).
Anthony, Barry, *The King's Jester: The Life of Dan Leno, Victorian Comic Genius* (London: I. B. Tauris, 2010).
——, *Chaplin's Music Hall: The Chaplins and Their Circle in the Limelight* (London: I. B. Tauris, 2012).
August, Andrew, *The British Working Class, 1832–1940* (London and New York: Routledge, 2014)
Bailey, Peter, ed., *Music Hall: The Business of Pleasure* (Milton Keynes: Open University Press, 1986).
——, *Popular Culture and Performance in the Victorian City* (Cambridge: Cambridge University Press, 1998).
Bailey, Victor, *The Rise and Fall of the Rehabilitative Ideal, 1895–1970* (Abingdon: Routledge, 2019).
Barraclough, Joan, 'Anne Emily Cummins (1869–1936)', *Oxford Dictionary of National Biography* (2011).
Baxter, G. R. Wythen, *The Book of the Bastiles; or, The History of the Working of the New Poor-Law* (London: John Stephens, 1841).
Bedford, R. P., 'George Tinworth (1843–1913)', revised by Peter Rose, *Oxford Dictionary of National Biography* (2011).
Benn, Caroline, *Keir Hardie* (London: Hutchinson, 1992).
Besant, Annie, *The Law of Population: Its Consequences* (London: Freethought Publishing Co. [c.1877]).
Besant, Walter, *South London* (London: Chatto and Windus, 1912).
Bills, Mark, 'William Frith's "The Crossing Sweeper": An Archetypal Image of Mid-Nineteenth-Century London', *The Burlington Magazine*, vol. 146, no. 1214, May 2004, pp. 300–7.
Blacker, John F., *The ABC of English Salt-Glaze Stoneware from Dwight to Doulton* (London: Stanley Paul & Co., 1922).
Booth, Charles, ed., *Life and Labour of the People in London, Volume VIII: Population Classified by Trades (continued)* (London: Macmillan and Co., 1896).

———, et al., *Life and Labour of the People in London: 3rd Series: Religious Influences, Vol. 7* (London: Macmillan and Co., 1902).
Bosanquet, Helen, *Rich and Poor* (London: Macmillan and Co., 1896).
Brownlow, Kevin, *The Search for Charlie Chaplin* (London: UKA Press, 2010).
Bulwer-Lytton, Edward, *Paul Clifford*, 3 vols (London: Henry Colburn and Richard Bentley, 1830).
———, *Paul Clifford* (London: George Routledge and Sons, 1874).
Burke, Thomas, *The Wind and the Rain: A Book of Confessions* (London: Thornton Butterworth, 1924).
Burtinshaw, Kathryn, and John Burt, *Lunatics, Imbeciles and Idiots: A History of Insanity in Nineteenth-Century Britain and Ireland* (Barnsley: Pen & Sword, 2017).
Butler, Kris, *Drink Maps in Victorian Britain* (Oxford: Bodleian Library Publishing, 2024).
Capper, Benjamin Pitts, *A Topographical Dictionary of the United Kingdom* (London: Richard Phillips, 1808).
Carlile, Richard, *Every Woman's Book; or, What Is Love? Containing Most Important Instructions for the Prudent Regulation of the Principle of Love* (London: R. Carlile, 1826).
Carr, Richard, *Charlie Chaplin: A Political Biography from Victorian Britain to Modern America* (London and New York: Routledge, 2017).
Chadwick, Edwin, *Report on the Sanitary Conditions of the Labouring Population of Great Britain* (London: Her Majesty's Stationery Office, 1842).
Chase, Malcolm, *Chartism: A New History* (Manchester: Manchester University Press, 2007).
Chaplin, Charlie, *My Wonderful Visit* (London: Hurst & Blackett, 1922).
———, *My Early Years*, partial reissue of *My Autobiography* (London: Bodley Head, 1979) [*MEY*].
———, *My Autobiography* (1964), with an introduction by David Robinson (London: Penguin Modern Classics, 2003) [*MA*].
Chaplin junior, Charles, *My Father, Charlie Chaplin* (New York: Random House, 1960).
Chaplin, Lita Grey, with Morton Cooper, *My Life with Chaplin: An Intimate Memoir* (New York: B. Geis Associates, 1966).
Clare, John, *Selected Poems*, ed. Jonathan Bate (London: Faber, 2004).
Clark, Anna, *The Struggle for the Breeches: Gender and the Making of the British Working Class* (London: Rivers Oram Press, 1995).
Clay, William Lowe, *The Prison Chaplain: A Memoir of the Rev. John Clay* (Cambridge and London: Macmillan and Co., 1861).
Crone, Rosalind, *Violent Victorians: Popular Entertainment in Nineteenth-Century London* (Manchester: Manchester University Press, 2012).
———, *Illiterate Inmates: Educating Criminals in Nineteenth-Century England* (Oxford: Oxford University Press, 2022).

———, with Lesley Hoskins, and Rebecca Preston, *Guide to the Criminal Prisons of Nineteenth-Century England* (Centre for the History of Crime, Policing and Justice, The Open University, 2018), www.prisonhistory.org.

Crump, David, *Fred Karno: The Legend Behind the Laughter* (Redditch: Brewin Books, 2021).

Daggett, Charles, 'Chaplin Salutes Karno', *Variety* (7 January 1942), p. 26.

Daunton, M. J., *House and Home in the Victorian City: Working-Class Housing 1850–1914* (London: Edward Arnold, 1983).

Davenport, Romola J., 'Urbanisation and Mortality in Britain, c.1800–50', *Economic History Review*, vol. 73, no. 2 (May 2020), pp. 455–85.

Devereaux, Simon, *Execution, State and Society in England, 1660–1900* (Cambridge: Cambridge University Press, 2023).

Dickens, Charles, *Oliver Twist; or, The Parish Boy's Progress*, 3 vols (London: Richard Bentley, 1838).

———, *Sketches by Boz: Illustrative of Every-day Life and Every-day People*, new edition (London: Chapman and Hall, 1839).

———, *The Life and Adventures of Martin Chuzzlewit* (London: Chapman and Hall, 1859).

Digby, Anne, *Pauper Palaces* (London: Routledge & Kegan Paul, 1978).

Ditchfield, P. H., *Old English Customs Extant at the Present Time: An Account of Local Observances, Festival Customs, and Ancient Ceremonies yet Surviving in Great Britain* (London: George Redway, 1896).

Doyle, Arthur Conan, 'The Adventure of The Blue Carbuncle', in *The Adventures of Sherlock Holmes*, second edition (London: George Newnes, 1893), pp. 156–80.

'Dulcima', 'Darker Surrey', *The Surrey Magazine*, vol. 2 (1901), pp. 417–20.

Emsley, Clive, *Crime and Society in England 1750–1900*, second edition (Harlow: Longman, 1996).

Eyles, Desmond, *The Doulton Lambeth Wares*, revised by Louise Irvine (Shepton Beauchamp: Richard Dennis Publications, 2002).

Flower, B. O., 'The Story of a Victorious Social Experiment', *The Arena*, vol. 29 (January–June 1903), pp. 616–24.

Frost, Ginger S., *Living in Sin: Cohabiting as Husband and Wife in Nineteenth-Century England* (Manchester: Manchester University Press, 2008).

Galer, Allan M., *Norwood and Dulwich Past and Present, with Historical and Descriptive Notes* (London: Truslove and Shirley, 1890).

Gallagher, J. P., *Fred Karno: Master of Mirth and Tears* (London: Robert Hale, 1971).

Galton, F., *Inquiries into Human Faculty and Its Development* (London: Macmillan and Co., 1883).

Geduld, H. M., ed., *Charlie Chaplin's Own Story* [1916], (1985; Bloomington: Indiana University Press, 2019).

Gissing, George, *Thyrza: A Tale*, 3 vols (London: Smith, Elder & Co., 1887).

———, *London and the Life of Literature in Late Victorian England: The Diary of George Gissing, Novelist*, ed. Pierre Coustillas (Hassocks, Sussex: Harvester Press, 1978).

Goldhill, Simon, and Ruth Jackson Ravenscroft, ed., *Victorian Engagements with the Bible and Antiquity: The Shock of the Old* (Cambridge: Cambridge University Press, 2023).

Goodway, David, *London Chartism 1838–1848* (Cambridge: Cambridge University Press, 2002).

Gosse, Edmund W., *A Critical Essay on the Life and Works of George Tinworth ... with a Descriptive Catalogue Annexed* (London: Fine Art Society Ltd, 1883).

———, *Sir Henry Doulton: The Man of Business as a Man of Imagination* (1899), ed. Desmond Eyles (London: Hutchinson, 1970).

Greenwood, James, 'At a Penny Wedding', in *The Wilds of London* (London: Chatto and Windus, 1874), pp. 288–94.

Griffin, Emma, *Liberty's Dawn: A People's History of the Industrial Revolution* (New Haven and London: Yale University Press, 2014).

Hancock, Ian, 'Charlie Chaplin's Romani Roots', *Travellers Times* (15 August 2023), https://www.travellerstimes.org.uk/features/charlie-chaplins-romani-roots-ian-hancock (accessed 24 February 2024).

Hardie, J. Keir, Arthur Henderson, et al., *Labour and Religion: By Ten Labour Members of Parliament and of Other Bodies ... Speakers at Browning Hall During Labour Week* (St Albans: Gibbs and Bamforth, 1910).

Haven, Lisa Stein, *The Early Years of Charlie Chaplin: Final Shorts and First Features* (Barnsley: White Owl, 2023).

Hayes, Kevin J., ed., *Charlie Chaplin: Interviews* (Jackson: University Press of Mississippi, 2005).

Higginbotham, Peter, *Workhouses of London and the South East* (The History Press: Stroud, 2019).

———, 'The Workhouse', www.workhouses.org.uk.

Hitchcock, Tim, et al., 'The Romani and Travellers', www.oldbaileyonline.org/about/gypsy-traveller (2023).

Jackson, Lee, *Palaces of Pleasures: From Music Halls to the Seaside and Football, How the Victorians Invented Mass Entertainment* (New Haven: Yale University Press, 2019).

Jansen Leo, Hans Luijten and Nienke Bakker, ed., *Vincent van Gogh: The Letters* (Amsterdam and The Hague: Van Gogh Museum and Huygens ING, 2009), https://vangoghletters.org (version: December 2024).

Jensen, Oskar, *Vagabonds: Life on the Streets of Nineteenth-Century London* (Richmond: Duckworth, 2022).

Kelley, Victoria, *Soap and Water: Cleanliness, Dirt and the Working Classes in Victorian and Edwardian Britain* (London: I. B. Tauris, 2010).

King, Stephen, Paul Carter, et al., *In Their Own Write: Contesting the New Poor Law 1834–1900* (Montreal and Kingston: McGill-Queen's University Press, 2022).

Knowlton, Charles, *Fruits of Philosophy: A Treatise on the Population Question* (1832), ed. Charles Bradlaugh and Annie Besant (London: Freethought Publishing Company, 1877).

Koven, Seth, *Slumming: Sexual and Social Politics in Victorian London* (Princeton: Princeton University Press, 2004).

Lewis, Jane, *Women in England, 1870–1950: Sexual Divisions and Social Change* (Brighton: Wheatsheaf Books, 1984).

——, *Women and Social Action in Victorian and Edwardian England* (Aldershot: Edward Elgar, 1991).

Lodge, Sarah, *The Mysterious Case of the Victorian Female Detective* (London and New Haven: Yale University Press, 2024).

London Convention Council of the Communist Party of Great Britain, *You – The People Have the Power* (London: London Convention Council, 1941).

Louvish, Simon, *Chaplin: The Tramp's Odyssey* (London: Faber and Faber, 2009).

Lynn, Kenneth S., *Charlie Chaplin and His Times* (New York: Simon & Schuster, 1997).

Lysons, Daniel, *The Environs of London: Being an Historical Account of the Towns, Villages, and Hamlets, Within Twelve Miles of that Capital ... Volume the Fourth. Counties of Herts, Essex and Kent* (London: T. Cadell junior and W. Davies, 1796).

Marsh, Jan, *Elizabeth Siddal: Her Story* (London: Pallas Athene, 2023).

Maugham, W. Somerset, *Liza of Lambeth* (1897), Collected Edition (London: William Heinemann Ltd, 1951).

Mayhew, Henry, 'Labour and the Poor. Metropolitan Districts [From our Special Correspondent] Letter LII', in the *Morning Chronicle*, 16 May 1850, pp. 5–6.

Mitch, David F., *The Rise of Popular Literacy in Victorian England: The Influence of Private Choice and Public Policy* (Philadelphia: University of Pennsylvania Press, 1992).

Morton, William H. and Henry Chance Newton, *Sixty Years' Stage Service, being a record of the life of Charles Morton* (London: Gale and Polden Ltd, 1905)

O'Day, Rosemary, 'Ernest Harry Aves (1857–1917)', *Oxford Dictionary of National Biography* (8 October 2020).

Owen, Wilfred, *Selected Letters*, ed. Jane Potter (Oxford: Oxford University Press, 2023).

Parkinson, Alan F., *Charlie Chaplin's South London* (London: Quality School Brochures, 2008).

Pilley, W. Charles, 'Chaplin and the "Kid": Reflections upon the Coronation of King Charles the Third', *John Bull* (24 September 1921).

Postle, Martin, and William Vaughan, *The Artist's Model: From Etty to Spencer* (London: Merrell Holberton, 1999).

Purser, John, 'Voices of the Past: Jack Yeats and Thomas MacGreevy in Conversation', *Yeats Annual*, issue 11 (1995), pp. 87–104.

Reason, Will, ed., *University and Social Settlements* (London: Methuen & Co., 1898).

Reeves, Maud Pember, *Round About a Pound a Week* (London: G. Bell and Sons, 1913).

Riding, Jacqueline, *Peterloo: The Story of the Manchester Massacre* (London: Head of Zeus, 2018).

Roberts, Henry, *Model Houses for Families: Built in Connexion with the Great Exhibition of 1851* (London: Society of for Improving the Condition of the Labouring Classes, 1851).

Roberts, Howard, and Walter H. Godfrey, ed., *Survey of London: Bankside. Parishes of St Saviour and Christchurch, Southwark* (London: London County Council, 1950); www.british-history.ac.uk/survey-london/vol22.

Robinson, David, *Chaplin: His Life and Art* (London: Penguin, 2001).

Rose, Jonathan, *The Intellectual Life of the British Working Classes* (New Haven and London: Yale University Press, 2001).

Rose, Peter, *George Tinworth* (Los Angeles: CDN Corporation, 1982).

Ross, Ellen, *Love and Toil: Motherhood in Outcast London, 1870–1918* (Oxford: Oxford University Press, 1993).

Rowntree, B. Seebohm, *Poverty: A Study of Town Life* (London: Macmillan and Co., 1901)

Rubenhold, Hallie, *The Five: The Untold Lives of the Women Killed by Jack the Ripper* (London: Doubleday, 2019).

Ruskin, John, *Notes on Some of the Principal Pictures Exhibited in the Rooms of the Royal Academy: 1875* (London: Ellis and White, 1875).

Russell, Charles E. B., and L. M. Rigby, *Working Lads' Clubs* (London: Macmillan, 1908).

St John, James Augustus, *Louis Napoleon, Emperor of the French: A Biography* (London: Chapman and Hall, 1857).

Salmon, Edward, 'George Tinworth and his Work', *Strand Magazine*, vol. 2, issue 11 (1891), pp. 443–52.

Scotland, Nigel, *Squires in the Slums: Settlements and Missions in Late Victorian London* (London: I. B. Tauris, 2007).

Scott, Harold, *The Early Doors: Origins of the Music Hall* (London: Nicholson & Watson, 1946).

Searle, Geoffrey R., *A New England? Peace and War, 1886–1918* (Oxford: Oxford University Press, 2013).

Shannon, Mary L., *Billy Waters Is Dancing: or, How a Black Sailor Found Fame in Regency Britain* (New Haven and London: Yale University Press, 2024).

Shelley, Percy Bysshe, *The Masque of Anarchy: A Poem*, with a preface by Leigh Hunt (London: Edward Moxon, 1832).

Shoemaker, Robert, et al., 'Crimes Tried at the Old Bailey: Explanations of Types and Categories of Indictable Offences', www.oldbaileyonline.org/about/crimes (2023).

Smiles, Samuel, *Self-Help; with Illustrations of Character and Conduct* (London: John Murray, 1859).

Smith, Charles Manby, *Curiosities of London Life; or, Phases, Physiological and Social, of the Great Metropolis* (London: W. and F. G. Cash, 1857).
Southwark Heritage Blog, southwarkheritage.wordpress.com.
Soverall, Lisa, 'Newington Lodge: Remembering an Institution' (28 May 2021), Southwark Heritage Blog, https://southwarkheritage.wordpress.com.
Sparkes, John, 'On Some Recent Inventions and Applications of Lambeth Stoneware, Terra Cotta, and Other Pottery for Internal and External Decorations', *Journal of the Society of Arts* (1 May 1874), pp. 557–66.
Spielmann, M. H., *British Sculpture and Sculptors of To-Day* (London: Cassell and Co., 1901).
Stead, F[rancis] Herbert, *Eighteen Years in the Central City Swarm: An Account of the Robert Browning Settlement at Walworth* (London: W. A. Hammond, 1912).
Stein, Lisa K., *Syd Chaplin: A Biography* (Jefferson: McFarland & Co., 2010).
Steinbach, Susie, *Women in England 1760–1914: A Social History* (London: Weidenfeld & Nicolson, 2004).
Strange, Julie-Marie, *Fatherhood and the British Working Class, 1865–1914* (Cambridge: Cambridge University Press, 2015).
Summerscale, Kate, *The Suspicions of Mr. Whicher: The Murder at Road Hill House* (London: Bloomsbury, 2008).
Sweet, Matthew, 'Was Charlie Chaplin a Gypsy?', *Guardian* (17 February 2011).
Thomson, J., and Adolphe Smith, *Street Life in London* (London: Sampson Low, Marston, Searle and Rivington, 1877).
Turner, Alwyn, *Little Englanders: Britain in the Edwardian Era* (London: Profile, 2024).
Turner, Jacqueline, *The Labour Church: Religion and Politics in Britain, 1890–1924* (London: I. B. Tauris, 2018).
Turner, Sarah Victoria, and Mark Hallett, ed., *The Royal Academy of Arts Summer Exhibition: A Chronicle, 1769–2018* (Paul Mellon Centre for Studies in British Art, 2018): www.paul-mellon-centre.ac.uk/publications/browse/ra-chronicle.
Vincent, David, *Bread, Knowledge and Freedom: A Study of Nineteenth-Century Working Class Autobiography* (London and New York: Methuen, 1982).
———, *Literacy and Popular Culture: England 1750–1914* (Cambridge: Cambridge University Press, 1989).
Walkowitz, Judith R., *Prostitution and Victorian Society: Women, Class, and the State* (Cambridge: Cambridge University Press, 1980).
———, *City of Dreadful Delight: Narratives of Sexual Danger in Late-Victorian London* (Chicago: University of Chicago Press, 1992).
Ward, Michael, *Unceasing War on Poverty: Beatrice & Sidney Webb and their World* (Canterbury: The Conrad Press, 2024).
Werner, Alex, 'John Charles Lewis Sparkes 1833–1907', *The Journal of the Decorative Arts Society 1850–the Present*, no. 13 (1989), pp. 9–18.
Weissman, Stephen, M., *Chaplin: A Life* (New York: Arcade Publishing, 2008).
Wiener, Martin J., *Reconstructing the Criminal: Culture, Law and Policy in England, 1820–1914* (Cambridge: Cambridge University Press, 1990).

Willes, Margaret, *The Gardens of the British Working Class* (New Haven and London: Yale University Press, 2015).
Wise, Sarah, *The Blackest Streets: The Life and Death of a Victorian Slum* (London: Vintage, 2009).
Witchard, Anne, 'Thomas Burke, the "Laureate of Limehouse": A New Biographical Outline', *English Literature in Transition, 1880–1920*, vol. 48, no. 2 (2005), pp. 164–87.
——, 'Thomas Burke, *Limehouse Nights: Tales of Chinatown* (1916)' in *London Fictions*, ed. Andrew Whitehead and Jerry White (Nottingham: Five Leaves Publications, 2013), pp. 67–76.

Media Interviews
Brownlow, Kevin, audio interview (transcript) with Effie Wisdom (recorded 28 February 1983): quoted with kind permission by Kevin Brownlow and James Spinney.
The Real Charlie Chaplin (directed by Peter Middleton and James Spinney, 2021).

INDEX

The 10.30 Down Express 315
An Account of Several Work-houses 79–80
Adult School 277
Ainsworth, William Harrison 48
Albert, Prince 25–6, 57
Alexandra, Queen 155, 326, 327–8
Allen, George 82
Anatomy Act 1832 99
Andrews, Frederick James 310–12
Anstruther, G. E. 263
Anthony, Barry 215
The Arena 261, 269
Argyle, Jesse 236[n]
Armstrong, Eliza 260
Ashley-Cooper, Anthony *see* Shaftesbury, Earl of, Anthony Ashley-Cooper
Asquith MP, Herbert Henry 258
Astley, Philip 45, 46[n]
Attlee MP, Clement 2, 360-1
August, Andrew 105
Aves, Ernest 16, 177, 179, 217, 222, 236, 247, 298–300, 312–13

Bailey, George 158
Bailey, Peter 200–1, 229
Bale, Edwin 124
Balfour MP, Arthur James 328[n]
Bamford, Samuel 51
Banstead Asylum 174, 187
Barlow, Frances 149

Barlow, Hannah 149
Barlow Street, Southwark 74, 161, 163–4, 168–9, 176
Barnett, Henrietta 236–7
Barnett, Reverend Samuel 236, 237
Barry, Sir Charles 127
Baxter, George Robert Wythen 84
Bazalgette, Sir Joseph 122, 300
BBC radio broadcast 1, 2
Bean Street, Southwark 243
Bedford, Duke of 345, 346
begging 212
Bell, Charlie 307
Bell, Clara 307
Bell, Vanessa (née Stephen) 158–9
Bennett, Mrs 299–300
Bentham, Jeremy 105
Berry, Mary 114
Berry, Mary Ann 114
Besant, Annie 105, 220, 326–7
Besant, Sir Walter 279–80
Beveridge Report 2
Bills, Richard 211
Binks, Rummy 230
birth control 105, 220
Blake, James 268
Blake, William 19–20
Bleak House 47
Blewitt, John 114
Bligh, Captain William 29
Bloody Code 49
Boer War 289–90
Bonser, Anne 88, 89–90, 91

Bonser, William 88, 89–90, 91
The Book of the Bastiles 84
Booth, Charles 15–16, 32, 81, 119, 158, 163, 164–5, 177, 196, 236, 238, 257, 262, 278–9
Bosanquet, Helen 74, 176
The Bottle 77
Boulton, Matthew 20
Bowers, Robert W. 127
Bradlaugh MP, Charles 105
Brammall, Winifred 319
The Branded Woman 315
Brewer, Daniel 114
Briant, Lawrence 264
Briant, Mrs 264, *271*
Broad Street, Lambeth 141, 143, 148, 208, 217-8, 225, 230, 231, 274, 300
Broadfoote, Marguerite 317
Brogden, Detective Sergeant 250
broker's man 64–6, *65*
Bromfield, Reverend George 177–8, 312–13
Brooke-Wilkinson, Joseph 6
Browne, Hablot Knight 'Phiz' 62, *94*
Browning Garden 265–6, 268–70, 272, 274
Browning Hall *39*, 258, 261–6, 268, 270, 278, 326
Browning, Robert 31, 38–9, 258, 259, 270, 272
Brownlow, Kevin 291[n], 305
Bryan, Frances 262, 266, 272
Bryan, Thomas Albert 260–1, 262–3, 268–9, 272, 280–1
Bryant & May Factory, Bow 326–7
Bull, William 98
Bulwer-Lytton, Edward 49–50
Burgess, Anthony 245
Burk, Ann 85
Burk, Catherine 85
Burk, Charles 85

Burke, Thomas 4, 118, 198, 200, 205–6, 238–9, 268, 276, 351
Burke, William 99
Burnand, Lily 331
Burne-Jones, Edward 251, 253
Burns MP, John 184
Burns, Robert 262
Bush, Esther 212
Bush, James 212
Butcher's Row, Southwark 243
Butler, Frank A. 149
Butt, Mrs 123–4

Caine, Michael 203
Camberwell Fair 44–7, 48, 50, 148
Cambridge Independent Press 281
Cane Hill Asylum 214–15, 216, 233, 304, 325, 338, 342
Canterbury Music Hall 115, 188, 201, 208, 219, 322, 330, 335
Capper, Benjamin Pitts 147
Carlile, Richard 51, 105, 114
Carr, Mary 'Polly' 246, 248–52, 253–5, 286, 287
Carr, Richard 7
Carson, Kittie 329
Casey's Circus 49, 334, 335
Chadwick, Edwin 72
Chamberlain, Minnie 255
Chamberlain, Neville 5
'Champagne Charlie' 229
Chaplin, Albert (uncle) 302
Chaplin, Charles (son) 208, 304, 335, 336, 340–1
Chaplin, Charles Spencer (father) 188, 191–2, 195–6, 202, 208, 216–17
   Charles Horatio Shepherd's visit 219
   court appearance 210–11, 213

Index

death 301–2
last meeting 300–1
marriage 157–8
performances *162*, 186–7, 202, 209–10
separation 161
sons living with 216, 219–23, 232–3
violence 308–9
Chaplin, Charlie
Barlow Street 74, 161, 163–4, 176
birth 4
Casey's Circus 334, 335
and Charles Horatio Shepherd 219
cowardice accusations 349, 350
Dick Turpin turn 49, 334
Easy Street 158, 351
education 74, 191–2, 206
Eight Lancashire Lads 288–9
first love 338–40
The Football Match 336
Glenshaw Mansions 336–8
The Great Dictator 2, 5–6, 359
hair 204
Hanwell School 195, 205–8, *205*, 287
Jim, the Romance of a Cockney 320
joins 'Fun Factory' 334–5
Kennington Road 24, 37, 160, 176, 187, 200, 216, 219–25, 232–3
The Kid 180, 291, 340, 347
'Life itself is a comedy...' 17
living with father 216, 219–23, 232–3
Mumming Birds 229, 334, 338
My Autobiography 9, 13, 239
My Wonderful Visit 229–30, 289
New Cut market, Lambeth 223, 225–6
Norwood Schools 214
pawn shops 63
Rummy Binks 230

seaside 186
Sherlock Holmes 320, 324, 334
workhouse 82, 192–3, 195, 202–4, 213–14
Chaplin, Ellen Elizabeth (née Smith - Chaplin's grandmother) 146, 158
Chaplin, Geraldine (daughter) 216
Chaplin, Hannah (née Hill – mother) 11, 74, *142*, 143–4, 163–4, 169, 186, 290, 303–4, 309, 320–1, 340
Cane Hill Asylum 214–15, 216, 233, 304, 325, 338, 342
Charles' death 301, 302
church 38, 177, 179–82
end of theatre career 176
Lambeth Infirmary 187–9
and Leo Dryden 175–6
marriage 157–8
separation 161
syphilis 215–16
West Square 160, 175, 176
workhouse/infirmary 79, 191–6, 202–3, 206, 213–14
Chaplin, Lita (née Grey – wife) 340–1
Chaplin, Mildred Harris (wife) 340
Chaplin, Minnie (Syd's wife) 342
Chaplin, Norman Spencer (son) 340
Chaplin, Oona (wife) 146
Chaplin, Spencer (grandfather) 146, 158, 217, 219
Chaplin, Spencer William Tunstill (uncle) 208, 217, 219
Chaplin, Syd (Chaplin's half-brother) 74, 158, 160, 161, 163, 175, 180, 186, 210–11, 213, 290–2, 305
father 215–16
Glenshaw Mansions 336–8
Hanwell School 195, 206–8, 287
HMS *Exmouth* 207, 221, 287
hop-picking 324

joins 'Fun Factory' 334–5
living with Charles 216, 219–23, 233
marriage 342
Norwood Schools 192, 214
travels 301, 303
workhouse 187, 189, 191–2, 195, 203–4
Chappell, Constable 244
Charity Organisation Society (COS) 241, 287
Chartism *18*, 33, 41, 53–60, 61, 64, 159, 326
Chaucer, Geoffrey 21
Chevalier, Albert 197
chimney sweeps 108–9
Chisley, Eliza 117
Chisley, Ellen S. 117
Chisley, George 117
cholera 72, 92, 111, 122
Christ Church-St Saviour's workhouse 79, 81–91, 170–1, 173, 180
Churchill MP, Sir Winston 2, 5
Clandon Street Wheelwright Shop 103, 107, 117, 119–20, *120*, 137, 140
Clare, Bessey 34–5
Clare, John 34–5, 170
Clark, Phoebe 99, 100
Clarke, Charles 244
Clay, Reverend John 48
Claybury Asylum, Essex 191
Clayton, Reverend George 30, 38
Clifford, Paul 49–50
Clive, F. Wybert 315
A Clockwork Orange 245
Clothing Club 265, *271*
Clough, Mary 86
Coal Club 265, *271*
Cobbett, William 53
Cole, Augustus N. 114
Cole, Sir Henry 123
Collins, Wilkie 170

Communist Party of Great Britain *x*
Conan Doyle, Sir Arthur 71
Cooper's Arms, Southwark 116
Corby, William 114
corpses 95, 97–100
Corsi, Antonio 251
Cotham, Reverend G. T. 158
Council on Education 73
Courtney, Kathleen 299
Coutt, Bert 338
Coutts & Co 328
Cowper, William 262
Criminal Law Amendment Act 1885 165–6, 312
Crippen, Dr Hawley Harvey 329[n]
A Critical Essay on the Life and Works of George Tinworth 155
Crowder, Charles 201
Croydon Chronicle and East Surrey Advertiser 209
Croydon Express 209
Croydon Times 209
Cruikshank, George *65*, *75*, *77*
Crump, David 317
Cuffay, William 57–60, *59*
Cummins, Anne Emily 296
Curiosities of London Life 47–8

Daily Mail 349
Daily News 319, 328
Daily News Weekly 269–70, 280
Daisy Club for Working and Factory Girls 299–300
Daniel, Frances (Tinworth's grandmother) 36, 37–8
Daniel, George junior (Tinworth's uncle) 36
Daniel, George senior (Tinworth's grandfather) 36, 37–8
Darby, Fred 210

Darnley, Herbert 332, 334
Darwinism 185–6
Davies, Ann 114
Deane, Sir Henry Bargrave 307
Debussy, Claude 341
Defoe, Daniel 24
Dene, Dorothy (née Pullen) 253
Denman, Mr 210, 322
Dickens, Charles 4, 14, 47, 64, *65*, 78–9, 113, 264
Digby, Anne 170
Digweed, Ellen 273, 344
Digweed, William 153
Dimmock, Ebenezer 113–14
Dimmock, Sarah 113–14
dissection, bodies for 97–9, 100
Donnelly, Edmund 157
Doulton, Sir Henry 122–3, 137, 140, *141*, 149, 153, 155, 156, 270, 272–3
Doulton, Henry Lewis 138[n], 272
Doulton, John 187
Doulton pottery *10*, 11, 20, 32, 119, 122–3, 137, 140, *141*, 148–9, 151, 217–19, 272–4, 300
Dowling, William Paul *59*
The Drunkard's Home 75
Dryden, Leo 175–6
Dryden, Wheeler (Chaplin's half-brother) 175–6
Duchy of Cornwall 23, 185
Duckworth, George 16, 103, 158–61, 163, 168, 177–8, 188–9, 196, 198, 201–2, 217–18, 223, 228, 237–8, 242–3, 247–8, 255–6, 261, 280, 293, 310, 355

Early Birds 315, 335
East India Company 36
East London Orphan Asylum, Clapton 205–6

East Street, Southwark 28, 143-4, 158-60, 161, 168, 171, 173
Eastlake PRA, Sir Charles 130
Easy Street 158
The Echo 240, 241
education 8–9, 72–4, 153, 191–2, 206
  Adult School 277
  Hanwell School 195, 206–8, 287, 324–5
  workhouses 80, 82, 95
Education Act 1870 73, 76, 206
Education Act 1880 73
Edward the Black Prince 23
Edward VII, King 123, 155, 179[n], 290, 326
Edwards, Catherine Adeline *125*
Edwards, Reverend Allen 178
Eight Lancashire Lads 288–9
Eleanor of Castile 23[n]
Elementary Education Act 1870 73
Elephant House, Southwark 67, 68[n]
Eliot, George 151, 152
Elmore, Belle 329
The Era 306, 315, 325, 329, 330, 332, 333
eugenics 238, 290
Evening News 322
Evening Star 45–6
Exmouth, HMS 205, 207, 208, 221, 287

Fabian Society 74, 184[n]
Factory Act 1833 72–3
Farmers Road, Southwark 213
Fawcett, Millicent 286
Feist, Alfred 97, 98–100
Fielding, Henry 48
Fildes, Mary 326
Finch, Margaret 146–7
First World War 3, 292, 339, 347–8, 349-51

Fishmongers' Company 22–3, 76
Fletcher, A. E. 272
'Flower Mission' 266
Foley, John Henry 131[n]
Folies-Bergère, Paris 341
The Football Match 336
'For Old Times' Sake' 228
Forster, E. M. 351
Forty Thieves 246, 248–51, 252, 254–5, 286
Fox, Charles 114
Freeman, Winnie 268[n]
Frith, William Powell 132, *133*, 134, 250
Frost, John 53–4
'The Fun Factory' 285–6, 317, 332–4
Furnival's Inn, Holborn 113

Gagging laws 51
Gainsborough, Thomas 134
Galer, Allan 147
Gallagher, Joseph 317–18
Galton, Francis 238
gardens 24–5, 275–6, 294
  Browning 265–6, 268–70, 272, 274
Garibaldi, Giuseppe 60, 252
Gatti's Palace of Varieties 321
General Lying-In Hospital 295[n]
The Gentlewoman 241
George III, King 30
Gibbons, Walter 305–6
Gillette, William Hooker 320
Gills, Ann 114
Gills, Mark 114
Gipsy Hill, Lambeth and Southwark 146
Gissing, George 4, 14, 166–8, 212–13, 217, 223, 225–6, 310
Gissing, Marianne Helen 166–8
Gladstone, Catherine 155

Gladstone, Helen 240
Gladstone MP, William Ewart 155, 258
Glenshaw Mansions, Lambeth 336–8, 342
The Globe 88
The Gold Rush 205, 341
Goldsmith, Oliver 262
Goldstein, Wolf 321
Goodhugh, Amelia 153–4
Goodway, David 54
Goodwyn, H. P. 7
Goose Club 265, *271*, 293
Gosse, Edmund 33, 119, 123, 135, 137, 140, 155, 156
Gould, Alice *358*, 359
Gould, Grace *358*, 359, *361*
Gould, Pollie 359
Gould, Thomas 359
Gow, Miss 255–6
Grace Sisters 209
Graham, Mary 70
Grain, Sergeant 254
Grand Palace of Varieties 357
Grant PRA, Sir Francis 130
Grant, James *62*, *94*
Gray, Detective Sergeant 250
Gray Street, Southwark 256
Gray, Thomas 262, 263
Grays, Essex 205
Great Chartist Meeting (1848) 7, 55–60, 216
The Great Dictator 2, 5–6, 359
Great Irish Famine 54, 144
Green, Inspector 160–1
Green, Mary 88–9, 173
Greenland, Charles 99–100
Greenland, Emma 99–100
Greenland, John 99–100
Greenwood, James 40, 95
Gregory, Canon Robert 122, 137

Index

Grey, Anna de 329, 331
Grey, Charles, 2nd Earl 51
Griffin, Emma 8
Grimwood, Eliza 165, 166, 247
Gun Street, Southwark 243, 256
Guy's Hospital, Southwark 97–8, 99, 100, 111–12
Gwynn, Olive 324

Hall, Frank 196–8, 201–2, 301
Hancock, Ian 146
Handel, George Frideric 123, 124
Hanwell School 195, 204–8, 287, 324–5
Hardy, Thomas 13, 17, 48[n], 52
Hare, William 99
Harley, Lily *see* Chaplin, Hannah (née Hill - mother)
Harman, Sarah 250–1
Harris, James 35
Harris, Martha 100–1, 169–70
Harris, Mary 35
Hawkes, Sidney 215–16
Hawkins, Emma 163
Hawkins, John 163
Hay, Colonel John 269, 270, 272
Hay, Miss 272
Hercules Club, Lambeth 298–9
Hill, Charles Frederick (Chaplin's grandfather) 11, 101, 143–4, 146, 147–8, 158, 168, 171, 173, 289, 342
Hill, Henry Hodges 143
Hill, Jack 146, 158
Hill, Kate (Chaplin's aunt) 144, 157
Hill, Mary Ann (née Terry – Chaplin's grandmother) 11, 101, 143–4, 146, 147–8, 158, 164, 168–75, 187, 355
Hill, Octavia 25, 240, 257–8
Hill, Roland 38

Hill, Sydney John *see* Chaplin, Syd
Hindrum, Captain 207
His First Offence 252
Hodges, Henry Lamphee 143
Hodges, John George 191
Hogarth, William 17, 48, 122, 134
Hogg, Robert 97–8, 100
Holden, Cyril 208
Holden, Fred 335
Holland, William 201
Holman Hunt, William 253
Holmstock, Louis 322, 324
Holst, Gustav 323[n]
Holt, Edward 244
homosexuality 166
Hone, Charlotte 85
Hoole, Elijah 258
Hooligan Boys/Gang 244–5
Hoover, J. Edgar 6, 341
Hope Street, Southwark 103–42, 160
Horace, Professor 209
Horner, Alan Edgar 339
hot pressers 112–13
Howard, Walter junior 209
Hubbard, Elizabeth 69
Hubbard, John 69
Hubbard, William 165
Hugman, Maria 114
Hugman, William 114
Hulme, Alex 245
Hunt MP, Henry 'Orator' 51, 326

Illustrated London News 44–5, 46, 47, 56, 57, *181*, 234, *234*, 351
Inquiry into Life and Labour in London 15
Invalid Children's Aid 294
Isaacs, Annie Maud 171, 215

'Jack the Ripper' 166
Jack-in-the-Green parade 43–4, 266
Jackson, Alfred 288, 292
Jackson, William 288–9
Jacob, Naomi 307, 317
Jail Birds 306, 335
Jameson, Frederick 245
Jarvis, Henry 92
Jim, the Romance of a Cockney 320
Jones, Emily *224*
Jones RA, George 131[n]
'Juleen's Wonder of the World' 209

Karno, Edith *see* Westcott, Edith Blanche (née Cuthbert)
Karno, Fred (Frederick John Wescott) 229, *284*, 285–7, 305–8, 313–20, 332–6, 338, 341–4, 348
Kauffman RA, Angelica 253
Kay, James Phillips 73
Keats, John 97, 262
Keir, David 182
Keir Hardie MP, James 3, 7–8, 182–6, *183*, 258, 281, 283, 328, 348, 351
Keir, Mary 182
Kelly, Arthur 339
Kelly, Hetty 338–40, *339*, 353
Kemp, Harry 211–12
Kenney, Rowland 6
Kennington Common 7, 53, 55, 56–8, 61, 262
Kennington Cross 178, 216, 226–7, *227*, 308
'Kennington Murder' 310-12
Kennington Park 25–6, 148, 212, 213, 216, 336
Kennington Road 23–4, 37, 60, 127, 153, 200, 216–23, 226–30, *227*, 232–3, 285–8, 291–5, 303, 308, 310, 356

Kerby, Miss 255
The Kid 180, 291, 340–1, 347
Kilburn, William Edward 57
King, Elizabeth Kate 172
King, Sarah Ann 172, 215
Knowlton, Charles 105

Labouchere MP, Henry 166
Labour Party 3, 182–4, 348, 360–1
Ladies Music Hall Guild (LMHG) 329–31, 332
Lady Margaret Hall Settlement (LMHS) 16, 286, 287–8, 293–9, 301–2
Lambeth Infirmary 187–8, 189-90, 191, 193, 214, 289, 304, 325, 355-6
Lambeth School of Art (LSA) 11, 73, 121–9, *129*, 137, 139–40, 149
"The Lambeth Walk" 1
Lambeth Walk, Lambeth 143, 198, 217, *224*, 225, 247, 285–354
Landseer RA, Charles 131[n]
Landseer RA, Sir Edwin 134
Langridge, Edith 287
Lansdowne, Lord 73
Laurel, Stan 286, 338
Lawrence, D. H. 349[n]
Leech, John *18*
legal advice, Robert Browning Settlement 264
Leighton PRA, Frederic, Lord 11, 134, 253
The Leisure Hour 194
Lelant, Ann 70
Lelant, George 70
Lelant, Henry 70
Leno, Dan 114, 197–200, *199*, 215, 332, 342
Lester, 'Dashing' Eva 321–4
Lewes, George Henry 152

Lewis, Jane 40
Lewis, John Frederick 134
Leybourne, George 229
Liberal Party 2[n], 4, 138[n], 184, 241, 258, 328[n], 347, 356
'The Life of G Tinworth: A London Boy that become Wheelwright and Sculptor' 12–14
Lindon, Millie 228
Little Dorrit 79
Little Tramp 5, 200, 230, 336, 347, 351
Liverpool, Lord 51
Livingstone, David 182, 270
Liza of Lambeth 295
Lloyd George, David 347
Lloyd, Marie 142[n], 244, 307, 329, 331, 334
Lloyd, Mary 253–4
Lloyd's Weekly Newspaper 84–5, 310, 328
Lock's Fields, Walworth, Southwark 66–7, 70, 77–8, 79, 87, 146, 161
London Evening Standard 71, 139
London Labour and the London Poor 27
London Street Arabs 234, 252
Louis Philippe, King 54, 55
Louise (Charles' partner) 219–22, 232–3, 302, 308–9, 324–5
Louise's son (Chaplin's half-brother) 220–1, 325
Love and Toil 33–4
Lubbock, Gertrude 241
Lubbock, Sir John 241
Luddites 30, 51
Lunacy Act 1890 172
lunatic asylums 160, 170–1, 191, 200, 214–15
Lysons, Daniel 147

McCarthy, Walter 303
McCarthyism 5, 7
MacDonald, James Ramsay 258, 348
McLennan Citrine, Walter 8
Magee, Michael 250–1, 254
Malthus, Thomas Robert 105[n]
Manby Smith, Charles 47–8
Marochetti, Baron Carlo 131[n]
Marriage Act 1753 30
Marriage Act 1895 306–7
Marriott, J. H. 7
Martin, Anna 76
Martin Chuzzlewit 113
Martin, Edwin 127, 149
Martin, Margaret 127, 128
Martin, Robert Thomas 127, 128
Martin, Robert Wallace 127–9, 137, 149, 345
Martin, Walter 127, 149
Match Girls' Strike 326–7
Matrimonial Causes Act 1857 312
Maugham, William Somerset 295
Maurice, [John] Frederick Denison 124
May Day celebrations 43–4, 266–8, 267
Mayhew, Henry 15, 27, 35, 42, 67, 83
Mayne, Sir Richard 58
Me and My Girl 1
medical care 111–12, 263–4
Men who Reach the Masses 271
Metropolitan Gardens Association 265–6
Meyer, Reverend Frederick Brotherton 176–7, 182
Milk Street, Southwark 19–61, 71, 87
  wheelwright shop 22, 26
Mill, John Stuart 126
Millais PRA, Sir John Everett 11, 131, 134, 253
Millis, Maria 41

Mills, John 355
Mills, Rachel 355
Mitch, David 8
Mite, Major 209
Mixer, Louisa 98
Moore, Elizabeth Winifred 314–15
Moore, Marie 314–15, 317, 318–20, 359
Moore, Thomas William 314–15
moral statistics movement 118
Morgan, Mrs 264
Morning Advertiser 82, 84, 116–17
Morning Herald 68
Morning Leader 254, 319, 330
Morning Post 87–8, 97–8
Morris, William 11
Morton, Charles 115, 201[n]
Moser, Mary 253
Mumming Birds 229, 334, 335, 338
Mundella Road, Battersea 357, 359
Music Hall Artists' Railway Association 331–2
Music Hall Benevolent Fund 196, 301
Mutiny Act 1797 32
My Autobiography 9, 13, 239
My Father, Charlie Chaplin 208, 340
My Life with Chaplin 341
My Wonderful Visit 229–30, 289

Napoleon Bonaparte 30, 50, 67
Napoleon III, Emperor (Louis-Napoleon) 54, 55, 56, 67, 201
National Trust 25, 240
Nelson, Lord Horatio 67, 353
Nelson Square, Southwark 237, 239–42, 246, 256, 286
New Cut market, Lambeth *181*, 223, 225–6
The New Woman's Club 286–7
Newgate novels 48–9
Newgate prison 83

Newington Butts, Southwark 57, 188, 303, 311, 337
Newington Workhouse 79, 91–8, 100–1, 151, 169–73, 175, 191, 192–3, 204, 206, 325
Newport Rising 53–4
Nichols, Mary Ann 'Polly' 187, 192, 247
Northcliffe, Lord 349
Northern Star 53
Norwood Schools 82, 92, 192, 214, 216, 221

Oakley Street, Lambeth 60, 180–1, 189, 356
O'Connor, Feargus 53, 54, 55, 57, 58
O'Dell, Sergeant F. J. 242, 243, 256
Old Vic 180
Oldman, E. S. 210
Oliver Twist 78
Orwell, George 2, 5
Osborne, Charles 228
Ottway, Detective Sergeant 245, 246
the Oval 21, 143, 276, *290*
Owen, Wilfred 351

Packham, Miss 247–8, 251
Pall Mall Gazette 95, 327
Pall Mall Magazine 343
Palmer, Beatrix Maud, Countess of Selborne, 257
Palmer, William 86
Pankhurst, Emmeline 286, 327
Partridge, Elizabeth (née Leach) 355
Partridge, William Henry 355–6
Paul Clifford 49–50, 60
pawn shops and brokers 41, 63, 70, 89, 106, 107, 110, 126, 134, 166–7, 176, 290

Payne, Millie 331
Peabody Buildings 247
Peabody, George 247
Peace and Wrath in Low Life 134–6, 139–40, 140[n], 252
Pearce, William 114
Peckham House, Camberwell 342
Pember Reeves, Maud 74, 278
Pember Reeves, Hon. William 278
'penny dreadfuls' 47, 243, 316
pension scheme 263, 278–9, 356
Pepys, Samuel 146
Percy, Fred 209
Peterloo Massacre 51
Petty, Ellen 90, 170, 173
Philip, John Birnie 127
Pickett, Edith 324
Picturegoer Weekly 316
Pilley, Charles 349–50, 351
Pink, Walter Augustus 334–5, *334*
Pitt the Younger, William 50, 51
Pleasant Sunday Afternoon club 264, 274–5
Pleasant Tuesday Afternoon club 264–5, *271*, 326
Poole, Mrs 244
Poor Law Commission 81
Poor Laws 27, 79, 81, 82, 361
Poverty: A Study in Town Life 15
Powell, Thomas 58
Pownall, Frederick Hyde 174
Pownall Terrace, Lambeth 291, 303–5, 320, 323
Prendered, William 30[n]
Pritchard, Rosa *see* Lester, 'Dashing' Eva
The Prodigal Son 346
prostitution 164–6, 168–9, 188–9
Pudney, George 196
Pugin, Augusts Welby Northmore 127

Punch 18

Queen of the Night 315
Queen's Fund for the Unemployed 328

Reed, Jessie 210
Reeve, Reverend John 179, 217, 219, 222, 248, 273, 298, 300
Reform Act 1832 50, 52, 53, 86
Relief of the Poor Act 1723 80
Renfrew Road workhouse, Lambeth 187–93, 214, 355–6
Repairs 334, *334*
Representation of the People Act 1918 347–8
Reynolds PRA, Sir Joshua 134
Reynolds's Newspaper 244
Richard II, King 23
Richards, Dr G. W. 263–4
Rivett, Emily 266–8, *267*
Robert Browning Settlement (RBS) 7, 16, 258–72, 274–81, 313, 326
Robinson, Alfred Albert 356–7, *358*
Robinson, David 9, 146, 169, 175, 192, 215, 216, 289
Robinson, Eliza Letitia (née Davies) 357, *358*
Robinson, Elizabeth Sarah (née Partridge) 355, 356
Robinson, Ernest Leslie *354*, 357, *358*, 359, *361*
Robinson, Nellie Elizabeth (née Gould) *354*, 357, *358*, 359, *361*
Robinson, Patricia Betty 'P. B.' *358*, 359, *360*, *361*
Robinson, William 355, 356
Rogers, Ann 69
Rogers, John 69

Romani families 144–7, *145*
Rosenbaum, William 211–12
Ross Combination 210
Ross, Ellen 33–4, 35[n], 42, 195, 237, 293
Rothschild, Baron, Nathaniel Meyer 278
the Rotunda 51, 114–16
Rowlett, Mrs 8–9, *231*
Rowntree, Benjamin Seebohm 15
Royal Academy of Arts 70, 251–2
  'Summer' Exhibition 134–6, 137, 151, 154–5, 251
Royal Academy Schools 11, 129–32, 134, 137, 251
Royal College of Art 137
Royal Commission on the Housing of the Working Class 25
Rubenhold, Hallie 187
Ruskin, John 11, 12, 43[n], 124, 151, 239
Russell, Lord John 58

Sainsbury's Weekly Register and Advertising Journal 117
St George-the-Martyr workhouse 78–9, 80–1
St John, James Augustus 55
St Saviour's Poor Law Union 81–2
Salamanca, Lambeth 296–8
Salmon, Edward 135, 140
Saltmarshe, Sergeant 188
Sanitary Aid Committee 300
Sargent, John Singer 251, 253
Sawyer, Mary Ann 311–12
Scott, Harold 114
Second World War 1-2, 359–61
Self-Help; with Illustrations of Character and Conduct 32
settlement movement 16, 236–7, 239–42, 255–72, 274–81, 286–7

see also Lady Margaret Hall Settlement (LMHS); Robert Browning Settlement; Women's University Settlement (WUS)
Sewell, Margaret 228–9, 232, 241–2, 243, 255, 257, 287
Shaddock, Mark 97
Shaftesbury, Earl of, Anthony Ashley-Cooper 41, 72, 233, *282*, 333
Sharpe, Charles William *133*
Shaw, Daniel 86
Shaw, Elizabeth 86
Shaw, George Bernard 184, 248[n]
Shaw, Lawrence 86
Shaw, Lil 331
Sheepshanks, Miss 255, 257
Shelley, Percy Bysshe 25–6
Shepherd, Charles Horatio 219
Sheppard, Jack 48–9, 50
Sheppard, James 246
Sherlock Holmes 320, 324, 334
Sherlock, Mrs 167
Shirley, Reverend A. 297
Shoreditch Observer 24–5, 92–5
Short, Elizabeth Frances 310–12
Siddal, Elizabeth 131
Sidmouth, Lord, Henry Addington 51
Singer sewing machines 157
Sketches by Boz 64, *65*
Sketches in London 62, *94*
Small, Arthur 251
smallpox 170
Smiles, Samuel 32–3
Smith, Abraham 245
Smith, Edward 244
Smith, Jack 230–2, *231*
Society for Improving the Condition of the Labouring Classes 25
Society for the Prevention of Cruelty to Children (SPCC) 233

South London Chronicle 210–11
South London Mail 184
South London Palace 142, 244, 305
South London Press 74, 244–5, 269, 270, 272, 322
South London Times and Lambeth Observer 100
South Wales Daily News 321
Southend-on-sea, Essex 186, 294, *361*
Spafford, Horatio Gates 212
Sparkes, John 122–4, *125*, 131, 132, 137, *138*, 140, 148, 156
special constables 56
Spielmann, Marion Harry 135
Spurgeon, Reverend Charles 78[n]
The Stage 330–1
Stamford Street, Lambeth 246–51
Stamp, Terence 203
Stanley, Henry Morton 234, 237, 252
Stansfield, Mary 30[n]
Stead, Bessie 262, 264
Stead, [Francis] Herbert 159, 250[n], 259–61, 263, 264, 273, 280, 309, 313, 326–9, 353
  Adult School 277
  ditties 161[n]
  May Day celebrations 266
  pension scheme 278
  PSA 274–5
  settlement garden 266, 270
Stead, William Thomas 166, 260, 262, 327, 340, 342
Stein, Lisa 216
Steinbach, Susie 29, 41, 326
Straker's Printers and Stationers 303
Street Life in London, 1877 8–9, *231*
Strudwick, William 20
Study from Life 102
suffrage 7, 50, 53, 56, 86, 149, 151, 159, 286, 347–8
suffragettes 286, 327

Summerscale, Kate 47
Summerscales, Miss 297
Sumner, Archbishop John Bird 123
Sun Beer House, Southwark 116–17
Sunday Express 253–4
The Surrey Magazine 281
Surrey Row, Southwark 256–7
'survival of the fittest' 185–6
The Suspicions of Mr Whicher 47
Swabey, Stephen 30
syphilis 67, 215–16, 254

Tate, Sir Henry 252[n]
taxation 50
Taylor, Tom 139, 156
temperance movement 33, 118–19, 184–5
Temple, Archbishop Frederick 179
Tennant, Dorothy *234*, 252–3
Theatrical Ladies Guild 329
Thicknesse, Katherine 287, 293–5, 296–8, 301–2
Thomas, Charles 189–91
Thompson, Mary 100
Thomson, John 8–9, *145*, 230, *231*
Thrift Club 265, *271*
Thyrza: A Tale 212–13, 217, 310
Tilley, Vesta 331[n]
The Times 1, 58, 139, 327
Tinworth, Alice (née Digweed – wife) 13, *22*, 153–4, 156–7, 218, 273, 345
Tinworth, Caleb (uncle) 31, 34, 35, 67
Tinworth, Charles (brother) 69, 72, 126–7, 137, 148, 345
Tinworth, Christiana (aunt) 30
Tinworth, Elizabeth Ann (née Stansfield – grandmother) 29–32, 35, 39, 41

Tinworth, George 9–14, *10*, 16–17, 76–9, *150*, 259, 270, 272, 274
  breakdown 273
  Brighton 156
  broken arm 111–12
  burial 136
  death 344–5
  Doulton pottery *10*, 11, 119, 137, 140–1, 148–9, 151, 218, 272–4
  education 72–3
  exhibition 155
  fireworks factory 110–11
  flowers 276
  Garibaldi's visit 60
  Hope Street 103–42
  hot pressers 112–13
  Lambeth School of Art 11, 73, 121–9, 139–40, 149
  local pride 219
  Lord Shaftesbury panel *282*
  marriage 153
  May Day celebrations 266
  Milk Street 19–61, 71
  models 132, 252
  pawn shops 63
  Peace and Wrath in Low Life 134–6, 139–40, 140[n], 252
  The Prodigal Son 346
  Rome trip 273
  the Rotunda 114–16
  Royal Academy Schools 11, 129–32, 134, 137, 251
  special constable 56
  Study from Life 102
  terracotta reliefs *10*, *102*, 119–21, *120*, 126–7, 134–6, 137, 151, 154–5
  Tinworth Street 218
  workhouse 78
  York Minster panel *152*
Tinworth, Jabez (uncle) 30
Tinworth, James (grandfather) 28–32, 35
Tinworth, James (uncle) 34, 35, 36, 104–6, 136
Tinworth, Jane (née Daniel – mother) 22, 23, 33, 35, 36, 37, 38–41, 52, 73, 74, 76–7, 103–4, 106, 118, 119–21, 126, 130, 137, 148, 153–4
  burial 136
  death 154
  Victory Place 67, 68, 69
Tinworth, Jemima (aunt) 31
Tinworth, Joshua (father) 26–7, 30–4, 35–6, 38, 39–40, 50, 52–3, 55, 58, 74, 76–7, 90, 103–4, 106, 126, 129
  attitude to women 107–8
  death 136–7
  debt 63–6
  fake gun 109
  sweeps 108–9
  tools theft 107
  Victory Place 67, 69
Tinworth, Keren (aunt) 31
Tinworth, Keziah (aunt) 30–1, 67, 86–7, 91
Tinworth, Sarah (née Shepherd) 36, 104–5
Tinworth Street, Lambeth 12, 218
Tinworth, Thomas (brother) 69, 72, 137, 148, 345
Tolpuddle Martyrs 32
Toynbee Hall 236, 264
trade unions 32
Turner RA, J. M. W. 12, 67, 135
Turpin, Dick 48–9, 50
typhoid 72, 111

United Artists 339
'urban penalty' 31

Vagrancy Act 1824 212
van Gogh, Vincent 276
Vaughan Williams, Ralph 323[n]
Vernon, Daisy 210
Victoria, Queen 58, 209, 290
Victory Place, Southwark 66–74, 112
Vincent, David 8, 73

Walett, Edward 114
Walett, Elizabeth 114
Walkowitz, Judith 164, 166
Walton, Frederick 337
Walworth Common, Southwark 19, 71, 79, 100, 110
Warner, Richard 'Dick' 197
Waters, Billy 42
Waters, Sergeant 223, 225, 247, 251
Webb, Beatrice 237
Weekes RA, Henry 130, 131[n]
Weekly Dispatch 95, 97, 248–51, 252, 253–4
Weissman, Stephen 216
Wellington, Duke of, Arthur Wellesley 51, 56, 67
West, Bell 86, 87
West Square, Southwark 160, 175, 176
Westcott, Edith Blanche (née Cuthbert) 285, 305, 306–8, 313–20, 329–30, 332
Westcott, Frederick Arthur 305, 317, 318
Westcott, Frederick John *see* Karno, Fred
Westcott, Leslie Karno 314, 315–16, 317, 318
Whicher, Jonathan 'Jack' 47
Whistler, James Abbott McNeill 253
White, Reverend Edward 38–9, 259
White, George 70
Whitechapel Murders 164, 187, 243

Whitehead, Mary 98, 99
Whiteley, William 332
Whitham, James 172
Williams, Dr John Frederick 172
Wilson MP, Havelock 184
The Wind and the Rain 118, 198, 205, 238–9
Wisdom, Effie 291–2, 305, 338, 352
Witchard, Anne 205–6
Wolfe, Edward 114
Women's University Settlement (WUS) 16, 240–2, 255–7, 286
Wood, Robert 71
Wooler, Thomas Jonathan 53
Woolf, Virginia (née Stephen) 158–9
Wordsworth, Reverend Christopher 298[n]
workhouses 28, 42, 78–101, 169–70, 187–92, 202–4, 213–14
see also Christ Church-St Saviour's workhouse; Newington Workhouse; Renfrew Road workhouse; St George-the-Martyr workhouse
Working Men's College, Camden 11, 124
Wragg, Professor 209
Wright, Rosina 189–91
Wyatt, Sergeant E. 159
Wynn, Elizabeth 35

Yankee Doodle Girls 338
Yeats, Jack Butler 299
York Minster panel *152*
York Road, Lambeth 188, 191, 196, 246, 301
York Street Chapel, Walworth 30, 31, 38, 40, 67, 87, 258–9
Young Women's Bible Class 266